BOLLINGEN SERIES

THE
LIMITS OF ART

3 · From Goethe to Joyce

POETRY AND PROSE CHOSEN BY
ANCIENT AND MODERN CRITICS

COLLECTED AND EDITED BY
HUNTINGTON CAIRNS

BOLLINGEN SERIES

PRINCETON UNIVERSITY PRESS

73-16625

TO THE MEMORY
OF
MARY MELLON
1904–1946

Εἰ καὶ ἄπιστα κλύουσι, λέγω τάδε· φημὶ γὰρ ἤδη
τέχνης εὑρῆσθαι τέρματα τῆσδε σαφῆ
χειρὸς ὑφ' ὑμετέρης· ἀνυπέρβλητος δὲ πέπηγεν
οὖρος. ἀμώμητον δ' οὐδὲν ἔγεντο βροτοῖς.

This I say, even though they that hear believe not: I declare
that the clear limits of this art have been found under my
hand, and the goal is set that may not be overpassed, though
there is no human work with which fault may not be found.

PARRHASIUS

PREFACE

THIS WORK presents selections of poetry and prose that have been held by competent critics to touch, in one way or another, the limits of art. That is to say, the selections have been pronounced perfect or the greatest of their kind. With each selection there is printed the judgment of the critic. I have thus, in the compilation of the work, employed a method the opposite of that used in the conventional anthology. My starting point was neither the poet nor the poem, but the critic; the volume therefore differs from the customary anthology of selections from standard authors. The work of a recognized writer is not included here unless in the considered judgment of a responsible critic it is, in some sense, superlative.

It should also be remarked that this volume brings criticism itself to the bar of judgment. Here is what criticism has held, at various times and places since its beginnings in ancient Greece, to be supreme in poetry or prose. I venture to think that on the whole its estimates have been sound. I have asked only that the critic's appreciation of his selection be in terms of its value as poetry or prose, and that there be a basis for believing he is competent to make the estimate. Where a critic has a long-established reputation I have attempted no careful weighing of his position, although, in the course of editing, I may have rejected many of his judgments. Coleridge, of course, I have admitted without hesitation, although there are those who now deny that he is a critic at all; however, I have included none of his appreciations which rest upon the circumstances that the poems promote a virtuous life or a sound view of religion. I should add that American and German critics are so hesitant to cite examples of excellence that their literatures are perhaps not as widely represented here as they deserve. This characteristic may possibly be the product of local conditions, as it is in Germany, where the taught tradition of the university seminars forbids the use of superlatives; but it is also individual, as we can see in the frugality with which such well qualified critics as W. P. Ker and Oliver Elton engage in the practice.

It will be seen from the book's epigraph that I have borrowed the phrase the "limits of art" from the Greek Anthology; it suggests both the idea of perfection and the idea of greatness, a distinction recognized long ago by Longinus, when he remarked on the difference between the flawless and the sublime. Criticism unfortunately has not arrived at any generally accepted understanding of either idea. Nevertheless,

xi

it has been the practice of nearly every important critic, from ancient to modern times, to apply these ideas to concrete examples. Perhaps the most satisfactory approaches are still Aristotle's conception that a poem is perfect when it cannot be added to or subtracted from, and Longinus' view that a poem is great when it transports or overwhelms the reader. There is, of course, the further limit, the requirement discussed by Aristotle, that art must discover the universal, that which is enduring and essential. It is the essence of the critical function to judge literature; when the critic is in the presence of poetry or prose that is wholly excellent, it would seem that he violates no sound canon when he pronounces it so. Art is wayward and baffling, it tends always to escape the rigid formula; it is however possible to contrast, to search for, the specific qualities that give literature its character. When the critic who does this has also knowledge and a sense of form we find, as we can see from Saintsbury's *History of Criticism,* that we have described the practice and equipment of all great critics in the history of the craft. If the critic goes further and states why the arrangement of a handful of words in a certain order possesses excellence, he is also discharging a legitimate function of criticism. "To like and dislike rightly," Bosanquet once wrote, "is the goal of all culture worth the name." Why are the first four words of the *Republic* pleasing to the ear, if placed in one order, as Plato discovered, and displeasing if placed in another? In the present work, when the critic has attempted to answer this difficult question, I have allowed him the additional space for his exposition; but that task, unluckily, is one that the critic too often sidesteps.

In all cases save two—Walpole's letter to the Rev. William Cole and Cowper's to the Rev. John Newton—every extract has been specified by the critic; for that reason many of them are of a fragmentary nature. If the critic gave his approbation to a single verse and not to the whole poem, I have not attempted to enlarge the area of his selection. Similarly, if he has designated Homer or Shakespeare or Dante as the first poet of the world and has not exhibited a passage to enforce his estimate, I have not printed his views nor attempted to make his opinion more particular by extracting an example of quotable length. Dryden thought that the English language reached its highest perfection in Beaumont and Fletcher; Shelley believed that the truth and splendor of Plato's imagery and the melody of his language were the most intense that it was possible to conceive; but they were not specific and their judgments are thus omitted from this volume. The reader should not assume, therefore, that because a passage is not specified in the context of the criticism quoted in its support that it is not specified by the critic at all. In the few cases where the criticism has not been definite I have turned to other sources, as, for example, to the authorized life of Tennyson for his favorite Virgilian lines to associate with the general tribute

> Wielder of the stateliest measure
> ever moulded by the lips of man.

Considerations of space have sometimes compelled me to make a choice where the critic has given more than one example of perfection or greatness. In one instance I have ventured to shorten a passage: the *De Corona* extract from Demosthenes, which is supported by Lord Brougham's famous judgment. Some poems, of course, because of their length, I have not been able to present. Gautier, for example, insisted that Alfred de Vigny's *Eloa* was the most beautiful and the most perfect poem in the French language; while present-day taste undoubtedly would not accept this estimate, it is with regret that I have been forced to omit the poem.

I have not hesitated to print extracts that are no more than a sentence or even a phrase. However, it may well be that some emotional association is involved in the critic's choice of the single word or two. Henry James' selection, for example, of "summer afternoon", as the most beautiful phrase in the English language probably carries a personal connotation. It is significant that in *The Portrait of a Lady*, when Isabel Archer and Gilbert Osmond are engaged, the most that Osmond can promise is that life for them will be "one long summer afternoon". In any event, the element of the personal is here too plainly present and I have therefore excluded such examples.

Although the volume to a degree exhibits some of the vagaries in the history of taste, that aspect is largely fortuitous. My intention has been to include only such passages as informed criticism would be inclined to rank at the highest level, whatever the period of the critic—such passages, that is, as have come to my notice, for an anthology of this nature can of course lay no claim to completeness. I must add that my inclusion of a passage does not necessarily imply an endorsement of the degree of the critic's enthusiasm, although it does imply a recognition of the merits of his selection and of his own authority to speak in the particular case; I doubt, for example, that any critic of standing today would concur in Johnson's estimate of the Congreve passage; nevertheless, that it is a great passage I think scarcely anyone would deny.

For the most part I have avoided the appraisal of the biographer, on the ground that his enthusiasm for his subject is likely to prompt him to excessive judgment. Nevertheless, on several occasions I have admitted criticism written by the author in praise of his own work; but in all instances the opinions are not incompatible with the estimates of other good critics. Many of the passages could have been supported by additional critical statements, but a mere repetition of authority seemed to serve no purpose. I have attempted everywhere to exclude the rhetorical superlative as exemplified by the otherwise excellent criticism of Hazlitt.

The passages have been uniformly printed in the language that evoked the critic's praise; to do otherwise would amount to a misrepresentation. However, translations have been provided in all cases save that of La Harpe. As a substitute for a translation of La Harpe's *La Prophétie de Cazotte* I have appended Saintsbury's witty condensation, with its supplementary information. The translations which have been made especially for this work are intended as no more than literal versions of the original. Occasionally, as in the Balzac passage, the criticism stresses not the original language but the general character of the piece; in those instances the extracts are printed only in translation. Where translations themselves have been the object of the critic's praise, as in the case of Chapman's rendering of Homer, the selected passage is included under the translator's name, and is followed by the original text for the convenience of the reader.

HUNTINGTON CAIRNS

National Gallery of Art
Washington, D. C.

NOTE TO THE PAPERBACK EDITION

The Limits of Art has been trisected into more or less equal parts for the paperback edition. The texts and critiques are unchanged; the indexes have been adapted for each of the three parts, but the acknowledgments and glossary are given in full.

ACKNOWLEDGMENTS

THE EDITOR wishes to express his appreciation for special assistance on editorial problems from many sources. He is particularly indebted to the following: the late Dr. Joseph Quincy Adams, Mabel A. Barry, René Batigne, Ruth E. Carlson, Mary Elizabeth Charlton, Frances Cheney, Marie Compton, A. D. Emmart, Dr. Elio Gianturco, Edith Hamilton, Dr. George N. Henning, Burnley Hodgson, Macgill James, Dean Martin McGuire, Dr. James G. McManaway, David Mearns, Elizabeth Mongan, Christopher Saintsbury, John H. Scarff, Fern Rusk Shapley, Katherine Shepard, Everett E. Smith, E. Millicent Sowerby, Charles C. Stotler, L. O. Teach and John Walker. The editor wishes to thank Miss Kay Becker, of the Catholic University of America, Washington, D. C., and Professor John B. McDiarmid, of the Johns Hopkins University, Baltimore, Md., for undertaking the task of reading the proofs of the Greek passages, and Professor Leonard Dean, of Tulane University, New Orleans, La., for reading the proofs of the Chaucer selections. The epigraph from Parrhasius was translated by the late Professor J. W. Mackail.

The following libraries have been of assistance in making source material available: Boston Public Library, Boston, Mass.; Bryn Mawr College Library, Bryn Mawr, Pa.; Catholic University Library, Washington, D. C.; University of Chicago Library, Chicago, Ill.; Columbia University Library, New York, N. Y.; District of Columbia Library, Washington, D. C.; George Washington University Library, Washington, D. C.; Grosvenor Library, Buffalo, N. Y.; Harvard College Library, Cambridge, Mass.; Lehigh University Library, Bethlehem, Pa.; Library of Congress, Washington, D. C.; National Gallery of Art Library, Washington, D. C.; Peabody Institute Library, Baltimore, Md.; University of Pennsylvania Library, Philadelphia, Pa.; Princeton University Library, Princeton, N. J.; University of Rochester Library, Rochester, N. Y.; Smithsonian Institution Library, Washington, D. C.; U. S. Department of Justice Library, Washington, D. C.; University of Virginia Library, Charlottesville, Va.; Yale University Library, New Haven, Conn.

For permission to use the copyrighted material included in this work acknowledgment is made to the following publishers and others: from Henry Adams Bellows' translation of the *Poetic Edda*, by permission of the American-Scandinavian Foundation, New York; Aldous Huxley's translation of Mallarmé's "L'Après-midi d'un faune", by permission of

New York, publisher in the United States; from E. J. Trechmann's translation of C.-A. Sainte-Beuve's *Causeries du lundi*, by permission of E. P. Dutton & Co., Inc., New York, publisher in the United States; from Hilaire Belloc, *Avril* (1904), by permission of E. P. Dutton & Co., Inc., New York, publisher in the United States; from Sir Frank Marzial's translation of Geoffroi de Villehardouin's *La Conquête de Constantinople* (Everyman's Library) by permission of E. P. Dutton & Co., Inc., New York, publisher in the United States; from E. B. Pusey's translation of the *Confessions of St. Augustine* (Everyman's Library) by permission of E. P. Dutton & Co., Inc., New York, publisher in the United States; extracts taken from the *Nibelungenlied*, translated by Margaret Armour (Everyman's Library), published by E. P. Dutton & Co., Inc., New York; extracts taken from *Anglo-Saxon Poetry*, by R. K. Gordon, published by E. P. Dutton & Co., Inc., New York; from *The Collected Essays and Papers of George Saintsbury*, by permission of E. P. Dutton & Co., Inc., New York, publisher in the United States; Horace's "Celebration for Neptune", translated by Roselle Mercier Montgomery; reprinted from *Forum* by permission of the Events Publishing Company, Inc.; from George Frederic Lees' translation of Rimbaud's "A Season in Hell" by permission of The Fortune Press, London; from A. R. Waller's translation of Molière's *Tartuffe*, reprinted by permission from *Molière—Complete Works in French and English* (8 Vols. Cr. 8vo, cloth) published by John Grant, Edinburgh; from Henry Thomas' translation of Lope de Vega's *The Star of Seville*, by permission of The Gregynog Press, Newtown, Montgomeryshire, England; from Joan Redfern's translation of *History of Italian Literature* by Francesco De Sanctis, by permission of Harcourt, Brace and Company, Inc., New York; from T. S. Eliot's "The Love Song of J. Alfred Prufrock", from *Collected Poems*, by permission of Harcourt, Brace and Company, Inc.; Louis Untermeyer's translation of Heine's "Ein Fichtenbaum Steht Einsam" from *Heinrich Heine: Paradox and Poet*, Volume 2, by Louis Untermeyer, copyright 1937, by Harcourt, Brace and Company, Inc.; from Aldous Huxley, *Texts & Pretexts* (1933), by permission of Harper & Brothers, New York; poems and prose extracts from Algernon Charles Swinburne, *Collected Poetical Works*, by permission of Harper & Brothers, New York; Sir William Watson's "Hymn to the Sea", from *The Poems of Sir William Watson, 1878–19*, by permission of George G. Harrap & Company Limited, London; texts and translations reprinted by permission of the publishers from the Loeb Classical Library: from Aeschylus, *The Persians*, translated by Herbert Weir-Smyth; from Aristotle, *Metaphysics*, translated by Hugh Tredennick; from Aristotle, *Art of Rhetoric*, translated by J. H. Freese; from Cicero, *Pro Archia Poeta*, translated by N. H. Watts; from Demosthenes, *De Corona*, translated by C. A. and J. H. Vince; from Euripides, *Daughters of Troy*, translated by Arthur S. Way;

from Herodotus, translated by A. D. Godley; from Hesiod, translated by H. G. Evelyn-White; from Homer, the *Iliad,* translated by A. T. Murray; from Homer, the *Odyssey,* translated by A. T. Murray; from Horace, *Odes,* translated by C. E. Bennett; from Isocrates, *Areopagiticus,* translated by George Norlin; from Longinus, translated by W. Hamilton Fyfe; from Lucian, translated by A. M. Harmon; from Lucretius, translated by W. H. D. Rouse; from Pindar, translated by Sir John Sandys; from Plato, the *Apology* and *Crito,* translated by H. N. Fowler; from Seneca, *Medea,* translated by Frank Justus Miller; from Sextus Propertius, translated by H. E. Butler; from Sophocles, *Ajax, Electra* and *Oedipus at Colonus,* translated by F. Storr; from Tacitus, *Agricola,* translated by Maurice Hutton; from Tacitus, *Annals,* translated by John Jackson; from Theocritus, *Idylls,* translated by J. M. Edmonds; from Virgil, *Aeneid* and *Georgics,* translated by H. R. Fairclough; Cambridge, Mass.; Harvard University Press; extracts reprinted by permission of the publishers from Gilbert Murray—*The Classical Tradition in Poetry,* Cambridge, Mass.; Harvard University Press, 1927; J. B. Leishman's translation of "Der Blinde Sänger" from *The Select Poems of Friedrich Hölderlin,* by permission of The Hogarth Press, London; from Norman Macleod's *German Lyric Poetry* (1930) by permission of The Hogarth Press, London; Norman Cameron's translation of Rimbaud's "Bateau Ivre", by permission of The Hogarth Press, London; from Helen Waddell, *The Wandering Scholars* (1927) and *Mediaeval Latin Lyrics* (1929), by permission of Constable and Company, Ltd., London, and published in the United States by Henry Holt and Company; from Henry Adams, *Mont-Saint-Michel and Chartres,* by permission of Houghton Mifflin Company, Boston; from Amy Lowell, *Six French Poets* (1915), by permission of Houghton Mifflin Company, Boston; from Charles Eliot Norton's translation of Dante's *Divine Comedy,* by permission of Houghton Mifflin Company, Boston; from *The Trophies* (translation of *Les Trophées* of José-Maria de Heredia) by John Hervey, The John Day Company, New York, 1929; from C. K. Scott Moncrieff's *The Letters of Abelard and Heloise,* by permission of Alfred A. Knopf, Inc., New York; from Maurice Baring, *Have You Anything to Declare?* by permission of Alfred A. Knopf, Inc., New York; Emily Dickinson, "The Chariot", from *The Poems of Emily Dickinson,* edited by Martha Dickinson Bianchi and Alfred Leete Hampson, reprinted by permission of Little, Brown & Company, Boston; translations from *The Poems of Victor Hugo* (1909), by permission of Little, Brown & Company, Boston; from Jacques Chevalier, *Pascal,* translated by Lilian A. Clare, by permission of Longmans, Green & Co., Inc., New York; from J. W. Mackail, *Lectures on Greek Poetry* (1910) by permission of Longmans, Green & Co., Inc., New York; from J. W. Mackail, *Studies in Humanism* (1938) by permission of Longmans, Green & Co., Inc., New York; translations by

Andrew Lang from *The Poetical Works of Andrew Lang*, by permission of Longmans, Green & Co., Inc., New York and London, and the representatives of the late Andrew Lang; from J. S. Phillimore's translation of Sophocles' *Antigone*, by permission of Longmans, Green & Co., Inc., New York; from W. Rhys Roberts' translation of Dionysius of Halicarnassus, *De Compositione Verborum*, by permission of Macmillan & Co., Ltd., London; from John Morley, *Voltaire* (1903), by permission of Macmillan & Co., Ltd., London; from F. W. H. Myers, *Essays Classical and Modern*, by permission of Macmillan & Co., Ltd., London; from J. A. K. Thomson, *The Greek Tradition* (1915), by permission of The Macmillan Company, New York; from W. B. Yeats, *Essays* (1924), by permission of The Macmillan Company, New York, and The Macmillan Company of Canada, Ltd.; from *Theocritus, Bion and Moschus*, translated by Andrew Lang (1889), by permission of The Macmillan Company, publishers; from Edith Sitwell, *A Poet's Notebook*, by permission of Miss Sitwell and Macmillan & Co., Ltd., London; from W. B. Yeats, *Autobiography* (1938), by permission of The Macmillan Company, publishers; from A. E. Housman's *The Name and Nature of Poetry* (1933), by permission of The Macmillan Company, publishers; from *Pierre de Ronsard: Sonnets pour Hélène* (1934), by Humbert Wolfe, by permission of The Macmillan Company, publishers; from W. B. Yeats, *Collected Poems* (1933), by permission of The Macmillan Company, publishers; from the Globe Edition of the *Works of Geoffrey Chaucer*, edited by A. W. Pollard and others (1898), by permission of The Macmillan Company, publishers; Wallace Fowlie's translation of Rimbaud's "Mémoire", by permission of J. Laughlin, New Directions, New York; from Edith Sitwell, *The Pleasures of Poetry*, by permission of W. W. Norton & Company, Inc.; from T. E. Shaw's translation of Homer's *Odyssey*, by permission of Oxford University Press, New York; from Lytton Strachey, *Landmarks in French Literature* (1923), by permission of Oxford University Press, London; "The Leaden Echo and the Golden Echo", from *The Poems of Gerard Manley Hopkins*, by permission of Oxford University Press, London, and the poet's family; from Bonamy Dobrée, *Variety of Ways* (1932), by permission of Oxford University Press; from James Rhoades' translation of Virgil's *Aeneid*, by permission of Oxford University Press; from Sir William Marris' translations of the *Iliad* and *Catullus*, by permission of Sir William Marris and the Oxford University Press; from Anna Maria Armi's translation of Petrarch, by permission of Pantheon Books Inc., New York; from translations by J. A. Carlyle, Thomas Okey and P. H. Wicksteed of Dante's *The Divine Comedy*, by permission of Random House, Inc., (The Modern Library) New York; from Charles M. Doughty, *Travels in Arabia Deserta* (1888) by permission of Random House, Inc., New York; song from W. S. Gilbert's *Pinafore*, by permission of Random House, Inc., New York; from W. D. Ross's

CONTENTS

xxiv

THE LIMITS OF ART

THE PROPHECY OF CAZOTTE

Il me semble que c'était hier, et c'était cependant au commencement de 1788. Nous étions à table chez un de nos confrères à l'académie, grand seigneur et homme d'esprit. La compagnie était nombreuse et de tout état, gens de cour, gens de robe, gens de lettres, académiciens, etc. on avait fait grande chère comme de coutume. Au dessert, les vins de Malvoisie et de Constance ajoutaient à la gaieté de bonne compagnie cette sorte de liberté qui n'en gardait pas toujours le ton: on en était alors venu dans le monde au point où tout est permis pour faire rire. Chamfort nous avait lu de ses contes impies et libertins, et les grandes dames avaient écouté, sans avoir même recours à l'éventail. Delà un déluge de plaisanteries sur la religion: l'un citait une tirade de la Pucelle; l'autre rappelait ces vers *philosophiques* de Diderot,

> Et des boyaux du dernier prêtre,
> Serrez le cou du dernier roi.

et d'applaudir. Un troisième se lève, et tenant son verre plein: *oui, messieurs* (s'écrie-il), *je suis aussi sûr qu'il n'y a pas de Dieu, que je suis sûr qu'Homère est un sot;* et en effet, il était sûr de l'un comme de l'autre; et l'on avait parlé d'Homère et de Dieu; et il y avait là des convives qui avaient dit du bien de l'un et de l'autre. La conversation devient plus sérieuse; on se répand en admiration sur *la révolution* qu'avait faite Voltaire, et l'on convient que c'est là le premier titre de sa gloire. "Il a donné le ton à son siècle, et s'est fait lire dans l'anti-chambre comme dans le sallon." Un des convives nous raconta, en pouffant de rire, que son coëffeur lui avait dit, tout en le poudrant, *voyez-vous, monsieur, quoique je ne sois qu'un misérable carabin, je n'ai pas plus de religion qu'un autre.* On conclut que *la révolution* ne tardera pas à se consommer; qu'il faut absolument *que la superstition et le fanatisme fassent place à la philosophie,* et l'on en est à calculer la probabilité de l'époque, et quels seront ceux de la société qui verront *le règne de la raison.* Les plus vieux se plaignaient de ne pouvoir s'en flatter; les jeunes se réjouissaient d'en avoir une espérance très-vraisemblable; et l'on félicitait sur-tout l'académie d'avoir *préparé le grand-œuvre,* et d'avoir été le chef-lieu, le centre, le mobile de *la liberté de penser.*

Un seul des convives n'avait point pris de part à toute la joie de cette conversation, et avait même laissé tomber tout doucement quelques plaisanteries sur notre bel enthousiasme. C'était Cazotte, homme aimable et original, mais malheureusement infatué des rêveries des illuminés. Il prend la parole et du ton le plus sérieux: "Messieurs (dit-il), soyez satisfaits, vous verrez tous cette *grande et sublime révolution* que vous desirez tant. Vous savez que je suis un peu prophète; je vous le répète, vous la verrez." On lui répond par le refrein connu, *faut pas être grand sorcier pour ça.*—"Soit, mais peut-être faut-il l'être un peu plus pour ce qui me reste à vous dire. Savez-vous ce qui arrivera de cette *révolution,* ce qui en arrivera pour vous, tout tant que vous êtes ici, et ce qui en sera la suite immédiate, l'effet bien prouvé, la conséquence bien reconnue?—" "Ah! voyons, (dit Condorcet avec son air et son rire sournois et niais), *un philosophe* n'est pas fâché de rencontrer un prophète:—vous, M. de Condorcet, vous expirerez étendu sur le pavé d'un cachot, vous mourrez du poison que vous aurez pris, pour vous dérober au bourreau, du poison que *le bonheur* de ce temps-là vous forcera de porter toujours sur vous."

Grand étonnement d'abord; mais on se rappelle que le bon Cazotte est sujet à rêver tout éveillé, et l'on rit de plus belle.—"M. Cazotte, le conte que vous nous faites ici n'est pas si plaisant que votre *Diable amoureux.* Mais quel diable vous a mis dans la tête ce *cachot* et ce *poison* et ces *bourreaux?* Qu'est-ce que tout cela peut avoir de commun avec la *philosophie* et le *règne de la raison?*—C'est précisément ce que je vous dis: c'est au nom de la philosophie, de l'humanité, de la liberté, c'est sous le règne de la raison qu'il vous arrivera de finir ainsi, et ce sera bien le *règne de la raison;* car alors elle aura des *temples,* et même il n'y aura plus dans toute la France, en ce temps-là, que des *temples de la raison.*"—"Par ma foi (dit Chamfort avec le rire du sarcasme), vous ne serez pas un des prêtres de ces temples-là.—Je l'espère; mais vous, M. de Chamfort, qui en serez un et très-digne de l'être, vous vous couperez les veines de vingt-deux coups de rasoir, et pourtant vous n'en mourrez que quelques mois après." On se regarde et on rit encore. "Vous, M. Vicq-d'Azyr, vous ne vous ouvrirez pas les veines vous-même, mais après vous les ferez ouvrir six fois dans un jour au milieu d'un accès de goutte, pour être plus sûr de votre fait, et vous mourrez dans la nuit. Vous, M. de Nicolaï, vous mourrez sur l'échafaud; vous, M. Bailly, sur l'échafaud; vous, M. de Malesherbes, sur l'échafaud . . .—Ah! Dieu soit béni (dit Roucher) il paraît que monsieur n'en veut qu'à l'académie; il vient d'en faire une terrible exécution; et moi, grâces au ciel. . . .—Vous! vous mourrez aussi sur l'échafaud."—Oh! c'est une gageure (s'écrie-t-on de toute part), il a juré de tout exterminer.—"Non, ce n'est pas moi qui l'ai juré.—Mais nous serons donc subjugués par les Turcs et les Tartares? Encore. . .—Point du tout; je vous l'ai dit: vous serez alors gouvernés par la seule *philosophie,* par la seule *raison.* Ceux qui vous traiteront ainsi seront tous des *philosophes,* auront à tout moment dans la bouche toutes les mêmes phrases que vous débitez depuis une heure, répéteront toutes vos maximes, citeront tout comme vous les vers de Diderot et de la Pucelle . . ."—On se disait à l'oreille, vous voyez bien qu'il est fou; car il gardait toujours le plus grand sérieux.—"Est-ce que vous ne voyez pas qu'il plaisante; et vous savez qu'il entre toujours du merveilleux dans ses plaisanteries.—Oui (répondit Chamfort), mais son merveilleux n'est pas gai; il est trop patibulaire; et quand tout cela arrivera-t-il?—Six ans ne se passeront pas que tout ce que je vous dis ne soit accompli."

—Voilà bien des miracles; (et cette fois c'était moi-même qui parlais), et vous ne m'y mettez pour rien.—Vous y serez pour un miracle tout au moins aussi extraordinaire: vous serez alors chrétien.

Grandes exclamations.—Ah! (reprit Chamfort) je suis rassuré; si nous ne devons périr que quand la Harpe sera chrétien, nous sommes immortels.

—Pour çà (dit alors Mme la duchesse de Grammont), nous sommes bien heureuses, nous autres femmes, de n'être pour rien dans les *révolutions*. Quand je dis pour rien, ce n'est pas que nous ne nous en mêlions toujours un peu; mais il est reçu qu'on ne s'en prend pas à nous, et notre sexe . . .—Votre sexe, mesdames, ne vous en défendra pas cette fois; et vous aurez beau ne vous mêler de rien, vous serez traitées tout comme les hommes, sans aucune différence quelconque.—Mais qu'est-ce que vous dites donc là, M. Cazotte? c'est la fin du monde que vous nous prêchez.—Je n'en sais rien; mais ce que je sais, c'est que vous, madame la duchesse, vous serez conduite à l'échafaud, vous et beaucoup d'autres dames avec vous, dans la charrette du bourreau, et les mains liées derrière le dos.—Ah! j'espère que dans ce cas-là j'aurai du moins un carrosse drapé de noir.—Non, madame; de plus grandes dames que vous iront comme vous en charrette, et les mains liées comme vous.—De plus grandes dames! quoi! les Princesses du sang?—De plus grandes dames encore . . . Ici un mouvement très-sensible dans toute la compagnie, et la figure du maître se rembrunit: on commençait à trouver que la plaisanterie était forte. Mme de Grammont, pour dissiper le nuage, n'insista pas sur cette dernière réponse, et se contenta de dire du ton le plus léger: *vous verrez qu'il ne me laissera seulement pas un confesseur.*—Non, madame, vous n'en aurez pas, ni vous, ni personne. Le dernier supplicié qui en aura un par grace, sera. . . .

Il s'arrêta un moment.—Eh! bien! quel est donc l'heureux mortel qui aura cette prérogative?—C'est la seule qui lui restera; et ce sera le roi de France.

Le maître de la maison se leva brusquement, et tout le monde avec lui. Il alla vers M. Cazotte, et lui dit avec un ton pénétré: mon cher M. Cazotte, c'est assez faire durer cette facétie lugubre. Vous la poussez trop loin, et jusqu'à compromettre la société où vous êtes et vous-même. Cazotte ne répondit rien, et se disposait à se retirer, quand Mme de Grammont, qui voulait toujours éviter le sérieux et ramener la gaîté, s'avança vers lui: "Monsieur le prophète, qui nous dites à tous notre bonne aventure, vous ne nous dites rien de la vôtre." Il fut quelque temps en silence et les yeux baissés.—"Madame, avez-vous lu le siège de Jérusalem, dans Josèphe?—Oh! sans doute. Qu'est-ce qui n'a pas lu çà? Mais faites comme si je ne l'avais pas lu.—Eh! bien, madame, pendant ce siège, un homme fit sept jours de suite le tour des remparts, à la vue des assiégeans et des assiégés, criant incessamment d'une voix sinistre et tonnante: *malheur à Jérusalem;* et le septième jour, il cria: *malheur à Jérusalem, malheur à moi-même!* et dans le moment une pierre énorme lancée par les machines ennemies, l'atteignit et le mit en pièces."

Et après cette réponse, M. Cazotte fit sa révérence, et sortit.

According to La Harpe—testimony, it should be remembered, given many years after the event—a brilliant company were collected, some time in the year 1788, at the house of some unnamed academician, who was also a man of high rank. Among them were assembled Chamfort, La Harpe himself, Condorcet, Bailly, Cazotte, the learned Vicq d'Azyr, Roucher, chief poet of the deplorable descriptive school which Saint-Lambert and Delille had introduced, and many others, with a plentiful admixture of merely fashionable company, and numerous ladies, with Madame de Grammont at their head. The company, if we may trust La Harpe, who had, it must be remembered, become at the time of writing violently orthodox (so that Marie Joseph Chénier contrasted his *feu céleste* with Naigeon's *feu d'enfer*), had been indulging in free feasting and free drinking of the kind recorded in fable of the Holbachians. Chamfort had read "impious and libertine tales," for which the reader of his works will not search in vain. A guest had informed the audience that he did not believe in the existence of God, and that he did believe that Homer was a fool. Another had cited with gusto the remark of his barber, "I am not a gentleman, sir; but I assure you I am not a bit more religious than if I were." Encouraged by these cheering instances, the company begin to forecast the good time coming. Suddenly Cazotte, who was known as an oddity and an *illuminé,* as well as from his admirable tale, the *Diable Amoureux,* breaks in. The good time *will* come, and he can tell them what its fruits will be. Condorcet will die self-poisoned on a prison floor; Chamfort will give himself a score of gashes in the vain hope of escaping from the Golden Age. As each guest, treating the matter at first as a joke, ironically asks for his own fate, the revelations grow more precise. Vicq d'Azyr, Bailly, Roucher have their evil fortunes told. At last the crowning moment of incredulity is reached when the prophet announces the fate of La Harpe. "La Harpe sera chrétien." The company are almost consoled when they think that their own misfortunes depend necessarily upon such an impossible contingency as this. But there is still an unpleasant impression from the gravity and the mystical reputation of the speaker. To dissipate it Madame de

Grammont makes some light remark about the hardship which, by the conventions of society, prevents women from reaping the fruits of the Revolution. Cazotte replies to her promptly. There is no exemption for women in the Golden Age. She herself, her friends, and even her betters will share the fate of Bailly and Roucher. "At least," she cries, "you will give me the consolation of a confessor?" "No," is the answer. "The last victim who will be so attended will die before you, and he will be the King of France." This is too much even for such an assembly, and the host interferes. But the valiant duchess is irrepressible. She asks Cazotte whether he alone is exempted from all these evils, and receives for answer only a gloomy quotation from Josephus, relating to the fate of the madman who at the siege of Jerusalem ended his forebodings by crying, "Woe to myself!" Then Cazotte makes his bow and leaves the room. Before six years had passed every word of his prophecy was fulfilled. Vicq d'Azyr had succeeded, and Chamfort had failed, in their attempts to copy the high Roman fashion. Roucher and Bailly and Madame de Grammont and the rest had looked through the dismal window, and Cazotte himself had been the hero of perhaps the most famous and most pitiful of the revolutionary legends. As for the Christianity of La Harpe, that perhaps is a question of definition.

George Saintsbury

With his PROPHÉTIE DE CAZOTTE *in his hand, he may present himself even to a stubborn generation to whom his* COURS DE LITTÉRATURE *is no longer a living law: they will be satisfied with this single memorable page, and after reading it will salute him.*

C.-A. SAINTE-BEUVE
Causeries du lundi (1851)

JOHANN WOLFGANG VON GOETHE

1 7 4 9 — 1 8 3 2

DAS GÖTTLICHE

Edel sei der Mensch,
Hilfreich und gut!
Denn das allein
Unterscheidet ihn
Von allen Wesen,
Die wir kennen.

Heil den unbekannten
Höhern Wesen,
Die wir ahnen!
Ihnen gleiche der Mensch;
Sein Beispiel lehr' uns
Jene glauben.

Denn unfühlend
Ist die Natur:
Es leuchtet die Sonne
Über Bös' und Gute,
Und dem Verbrecher
Glänzen, wie dem Besten,
Der Mond und die Sterne.

Wind und Ströme,
Donner und Hagel
Rauschen ihren Weg
Und ergreifen,
Vorüber eilend,
Einen um den andern.

Auch so das Glück
Tappt unter die Menge,
Fasst bald des Knaben
Lockige Unschuld,
Bald auch den kahlen
Schuldigen Scheitel.

Nach ewigen, ehrnen,
Grossen Gesetzen
Müssen wir alle
Unseres Daseins
Kreise vollenden.

Nur allein der Mensch
Vermag das Unmögliche:
Er unterscheidet,
Wählet und richtet;
Er kann dem Augenblick
Dauer verleihen.

Er allein darf
Den Guten lohnen,
Den Bösen strafen,
Heilen und retten,
Alles Irrende, Schweifende
Nützlich verbinden.

Und wir verehren
Die Unsterblichen,
Als wären sie Menschen,
Täten im grossen,
Was der Beste im kleinen
Tut oder möchte.

Der edle Mensch
Sei hilfreich und gut!
Unermüdet schaff' er
Das Nützliche, Rechte,
Sei uns ein Vorbild
Jener geahneten Wesen!

THE GODLIKE

Noble be man,
Helpful and good!
For that alone
Distinguisheth him
From all the beings
Unto us known.

Hail to the beings,
Unknown and glorious,
Whom we forebode!
From *his* example
Learn we to know them!

For unfeeling
Nature is ever:
On bad and on good
The sun alike shineth;
And on the wicked,
As on the best,
The moon and stars gleam.

Tempest and torrent,
Thunder and hail,
Roar on their path,
Seizing the while,
As they haste onward,
One after another.

Even so, fortune
Gropes 'mid the throng—
Innocent boyhood's
Curly head seizing,—
Seizing the hoary
Head of the sinner.

After laws mighty,
Brazen, eternal,
Must all we mortals
Finish the circuit
Of our existence.

Man, and man only
Can do the impossible;
He 'tis distinguisheth,
Chooseth and judgeth;
He to the moment
Endurance can lend.

He and he only
The good can reward,
The bad can he punish,
Can heal and can save;
All that wanders and strays
Can usefully blend.

And we pay homage
To the immortals
As though they were men,
And did in the great,
What the best, in the small,
Does or might do.

Be the man that is noble,
Both helpful and good,
Unweariedly forming
The right and the useful,
A type of those beings
Our mind hath foreshadow'd!

(1782)
Translated by Edgar A. Bowring

One of the noblest of all poems.

ALFRED LORD TENNYSON
Alfred Lord Tennyson: A Memoir by Hallam Tennyson (1897)

JOHANN WOLFGANG VON GOETHE

1 7 4 9 — 1 8 3 2

THE BATTLE OF VALMY

Von hier und heute geht eine neue Epoche der Weltgeschichte aus, und ihr könnt sagen, ihr seid dabei gewesen.

Here and now begins a new epoch of world history, and you, gentlemen, can say that you "were there".

(1792)

No general, no diplomat, let alone the philosophers, ever so directly felt history "becoming". It is the deepest judgment that any man ever uttered about a great historical act in the moment of its accomplishment.

OSWALD SPENGLER
Der Untergang des Abendlandes (1918)
Translated by Charles Francis Atkinson

JOHANN WOLFGANG VON GOETHE

1 7 4 9 — 1 8 3 2

FAUST AND MARGARET

FAUST

Süss Liebchen!

MARGARETE

Lasst einmal!
(*Sie pflückt eine Sternblume und zupft die Blätter ab, eins nach dem andern.*)

FAUST

Was soll das? Einen Strauss?

MARGARETE

Nein, es soll nur ein Spiel.

FAUST

Wie?

MARGARETE

Geht! Ihr lacht mich aus.

(*Sie rupft und murmelt.*)

961

FAUST

Was murmelst du?

MARGARETE (*halblaut*)

Er liebt mich—Liebt mich nicht.

FAUST

Du holdes Himmelsangesicht!

MARGARETE (*fährt fort*)

Liebt mich—Nicht—Liebt mich—Nicht—
(*Das letzte Blatt ausrupfend, mit holder Freude*)
Er liebt mich!

FAUST

Sweet darling!

MARGARET

Wait a moment!
(*She picks a star-flower and plucks the petals one by one*).

FAUST

What is that? A bouquet?

MARGARET

No, it is only a game.

FAUST

What?

MARGARET

Go away! You will laugh at me!
(*She plucks the petals and murmurs.*)

FAUST

What are you murmuring?

MARGARET (*Under her breath*) He loves me—loves me not—

FAUST

Lovely, heavenly vision!

MARGARET (*Continues*)

Loves me—not—loves me—not
(*Plucks the last petal with joy*)
He loves me!

Faust (1808)

The height of lyric eloquence. . . . It was quite out of the question to portray anything more simple or familiar than the young girl who plucks the petals from the daisy and says: He loves me; He loves me not! But no one had availed himself of that theme previous to the days of Goethe. It was the egg of Columbus; and its effect was incalculable. By this addition the field of art was extended.

GEORG BRANDES
Wolfgang Goethe (1924)

JOHANN WOLFGANG VON GOETHE

1 7 4 9 — 1 8 3 2

PRAYER

(*In der Mauerhöhle ein Andachtsbild der Mater dolorosa,
Blumenkrüge davor.*)

GRETCHEN (*steckt frische Blumen in die Krüge*)
Ach neige,
Du Schmerzenreiche,
Dein Antlitz gnädig meiner Not!

Das Schwert im Herzen,
Mit tausend Schmerzen
Blickst auf zu deines Sohnes Tod.

Zum Vater blickst du,
Und Seufzer schickst du
Hinauf um sein' und deine Not.

Wer fühlet,
Wie wühlet
Der Schmerz mir im Gebein?
Was mein armes Herz hier banget,
Was es zittert, was verlanget,
Weisst nur du, nur du allein!

Wohin ich immer gehe,
Wie weh, wie weh, wie wehe
Wird mir im Busen hier!
Ich bin, ach! kaum alleine,
Ich wein', ich wein', ich weine,
Das Herz zerbricht in mir.

(*In a niche of the wall a shrine, with an image of the Mater
Dolorosa. Pots of flowers before it.*)

MARGARET (*putting fresh flowers in the pots*).
Incline, O Maiden,
Thou sorrow-laden,
Thy gracious countenance upon my pain!

The sword Thy heart in,
With anguish smarting,
Thou lookest up to where Thy Son is slain!

Thou seest the Father;
Thy sad sighs gather,
And bear aloft Thy sorrow and His pain!

Ah, past guessing,
Beyond expressing,
The pangs that wring my flesh and bone!
Why this anxious heart so burneth,
Why it trembleth, why it yearneth,
Knowest Thou, and Thou alone!

Where'er I go, what sorrow,
What woe, what woe and sorrow
Within my bosom aches!
Alone, and ah! unsleeping,
I'm weeping, weeping, weeping,
The heart within me breaks.

Faust (1808)
Translated by Bayard Taylor

Goethe reached the highest height of poetry in Gretchen's appeal to the Madonna.

FRANK HARRIS
My Life and Loves (1922–27)

JOHANN WOLFGANG VON GOETHE

1 7 4 9 — 1 8 3 2

WANDRERS NACHTLIED

Über allen Gipfeln
Ist Ruh,
In allen Wipfeln
Spürest du
Kaum einen Hauch;
Die Vögelein schweigen im Walde.
Warte nur, balde
Ruhest du auch.

WANDERER'S NIGHT SONG

O'er all the hill-tops
Is quiet now,
In all the tree-tops
Hearest thou
Hardly a breath;
The birds are asleep in the trees:
Wait; soon like these
Thou too shalt rest.

Translated by Henry Wadsworth Longfellow

Most flawless of all lyrics.

J O H N   L I V I N G S T O N   L O W E S
Convention and Revolt in Poetry (1919)

JOHANN WOLFGANG VON GOETHE

1 7 4 9 — 1 8 3 2

MIGNON

Kennst du das Land, wo die Zitronen blühn,
Im dunkeln Laub die Gold-Orangen glühn,
Ein sanfter Wind vom blauen Himmel weht,
Die Myrte still und hoch der Lorbeer steht?
Kennst du es wohl?—Dahin! Dahin
Möcht' ich mit dir, o mein Geliebter, ziehn.

Kennst du das Haus? Auf Säulen ruht sein Dach,
Es glänzt der Saal, es schimmert das Gemach,
Und Marmorbilder stehn und sehn mich an:
Was hat man dir, du armes Kind, getan?
Kennst du es wohl?—Dahin! Dahin
Möcht' ich mit dir, o mein Beschützer, ziehn.

Kennst du den Berg und seinen Wolkensteg?
Das Maultier sucht im Nebel seinen Weg;
In Höhlen wohnt der Drachen alte Brut;
Es stürzt der Fels und über ihn die Flut.
Kennst du ihn wohl?—Dahin! Dahin
Geht unser Weg! o Vater, lass uns ziehn!

Know'st thou the land where the fair citron blows,
Where the bright orange midst the foliage glows,
Where soft winds greet us from the azure skies,
Where silent myrtles, stately laurels rise,
Know'st thou it well?
                         'Tis there, 'tis there,
That I with thee, beloved one, would repair!

Know'st thou the house? On columns rests its pile,
Its halls are gleaming, and its chambers smile,
And marble statues stand and gaze on me:
"Poor child! what sorrow hath befallen thee?"
Know'st thou it well?
                         'Tis there, 'tis there,
That I with thee, protector, would repair!

Know'st thou the mountain, and its cloudy bridge?
The mule can scarcely find the misty ridge;
In caverns dwells the dragon's olden brood,
The frowning crag obstructs the raging flood.
Know'st thou it well?
                         'Tis there, 'tis there,
Our path lies—Father—thither, oh repair!
                    Translated by Edgar A. Bowring

Goethe's 'Kennst du das Land' is a perfect poem.
                              ALFRED LORD TENNYSON
Alfred Lord Tennyon: A Memoir by Hallam Tennyson (1897)

JOHANN WOLFGANG VON GOETHE

1 7 4 9 — 1 8 3 2

HAMLET

You all know Shakespeare's incomparable 'Hamlet:' our public reading of it at the castle yielded every one of us the greatest satisfaction.
On that occasion we proposed to act the play; and I, not knowing what
I undertook, engaged to play the prince's part. This I conceived that I
was studying, while I began to get by heart the strongest passages, the
soliloquies, and those scenes in which force of soul, vehemence and elevation of feeling, have the freest scope; where the agitated heart is
allowed to display itself with touching expressiveness.

I further conceived that I was penetrating quite into the spirit of the character, while I endeavored, as it were to take upon myself the load of deep melancholy under which my prototype was laboring, and in this humor to pursue him through the strange labyrinths of his caprices and his singularities. Thus learning, thus practising, I doubted not but I should by and by become one person with my hero.

But, the farther I advanced, the more difficult did it become for me to form any image of the whole, in its general bearings; till at last it seemed as if impossible. I next went through the entire piece, without interruption; but here, too, I found much that I could not away with. At one time the characters, at another time the manner of displaying them, seemed inconsistent; and I almost despaired of finding any general tint, in which I might present my whole part with all its shadings and variations. In such devious paths I toiled, and wandered long in vain; till at length a hope arose that I might reach my aim in quite a new way.

I set about investigating every trace of Hamlet's character, as it had shown itself before his father's death: I endeavored to distinguish what in it was independent of this mournful event, independent of the terrible events that followed; and what most probably the young man would have been, had no such thing occurred.

Soft, and from a noble stem, this royal flower had sprung up under the immediate influences of majesty: the idea of moral rectitude with that of princely elevation, the feeling of the good and dignified with the consciousness of high birth, had in him been unfolded simultaneously. He was a prince, by birth a prince; and he wished to reign, only that good men might be good without obstruction. Pleasing in form, polished by nature, courteous from the heart, he was meant to be the pattern of youth and the joy of the world.

Without any prominent passion, his love for Ophelia was a still presentiment of sweet wants. His zeal in knightly accomplishments was not entirely his own: it needed to be quickened and inflamed by praise bestowed on others for excelling in them. Pure in sentiment, he knew the honorable-minded, and could prize the rest which an upright spirit tastes on the bosom of a friend. To a certain degree, he had learned to discern and value the good and the beautiful in arts and sciences; the mean, the vulgar, was offensive to him; and, if hatred could take root in his tender soul, it was only so far as to make him properly despise the false and changeful insects of a court, and play with them in easy scorn. He was calm in his temper, artless in his conduct, neither pleased with idleness, nor too violently eager for employment. The routine of a university he seemed to continue when at court. He possessed more mirth of humor than of heart: he was a good companion, pliant, courteous, discreet, and able to forget and forgive an injury, yet never able to unite himself with those who overstepped the limits of the right, the good, and the becoming.

When we read the piece again, you shall judge whether I am yet on the proper track.

Wilhelm Meisters Lehrjahre (1796)
Translated by Thomas Carlyle

We come suddenly upon what we do not hesitate to pronounce the most able, eloquent, and profound exposition of the character of Hamlet, as conceived by our great dramatist, that has ever been given to the world. . . . There is nothing so good as this in any of our own commentators— nothing at once so poetical, so feeling, and so just.

FRANCIS LORD JEFFREY
Literary Criticism (1825)

THOMAS CHATTERTON

1 7 5 2 — 1 7 7 0

SONG FROM ÆLLA

O sing unto my roundelay,
O drop the briny tear with me;
Dance no more at holyday,
Like a running river be:
    My love is dead,
    Gone to his death-bed
All under the willow-tree.

Black his cryne as the winter night,
White his rode as the summer snow,
Red his face as the morning light,
Cold he lies in the grave below:
    My love is dead,
    Gone to his death-bed
All under the willow-tree.

Sweet his tongue as the throstle's note,
Quick in dance as thought can be,
Deft his tabor, cudgel stout;
O he lies by the willow-tree!
    My love is dead,
    Gone to his death-bed
All under the willow-tree.

Hark! the raven flaps his wing
In the brier'd dell below;
Hark! the death-owl loud doth sing
To the nightmares, as they go:
    My love is dead,
      Gone to his death-bed
All under the willow-tree.

See! the white moon shines on high;
Whiter is my true-love's shroud:
Whiter than the morning sky,
Whiter than the evening cloud:
    My love is dead,
      Gone to his death-bed
All under the willow-tree.

Here upon my true-love's grave
Shall the barren flowers be laid;
Not one holy saint to save
All the coldness of a maid:
    My love is dead,
      Gone to his death-bed
All under the willow-tree.

With my hands I'll dent the briers
Round his holy corse to gre:
Ouph and fairy, light your fires,
Here my body still shall be:
    My love is dead,
      Gone to his death-bed
All under the willow-tree.

Come, with acorn-cup and thorn,
Drain my heartès blood away;
Life and all its good I scorn,
Dance by night, or feast by day:
    My love is dead,
      Gone to his death-bed
All under the willow-tree.

(1769)

Few more exquisite specimens of this kind can be found in our language than the Minstrel's song in Ælla.

HENRY CARY
Lives of English Poets (1845)

1 7 5 4 — 1 8 2 4

THE LAW OF POETRY

Rien de ce qui ne transporte pas n'est poésie. La lyre est, en quelque manière, un instrument ailé.

Nothing that does not transport us is poetry. The lyre is, in some respects, a winged instrument.

Pensées (1842)

The famous, the immortal, ninth "Pensée" of the Poetry section . . . is positively startling. It is, of course, only Longinus, dashed a little with Plato, and transferred from the abstract Sublime to the sublimest part of literature, Poetry. But generations had read and quoted Longinus without making the transfer; and when made it is EN QUELQUE MANIÈRE *(to use the author's judicious limitation, which some people dislike so much), final. Like other winged things, and more than any of them, poetry is itself hard to catch; it is difficult to avoid crushing and maiming it when you think to catch it. But this is as nearly perfect a definition by resultant, by form, as can be got at.*

GEORGE SAINTSBURY
A History of Criticism (1904)

WILLIAM BLAKE

1 7 5 7 — 1 8 2 7

SONG

Thou the golden fruit dost bear,
I am clad in flowers fair;
Thy sweet boughs perfume the air,
And the turtle buildeth there.

There she sits and feeds her young,
Sweet I hear her mournful song;
And thy lovely leaves among,
There is love: I hear his tongue.

Poetical Sketches (1783)

As perfect as well can be.

ALGERNON CHARLES SWINBURNE
William Blake (1866)

WILLIAM BLAKE

1 7 5 7 — 1 8 2 7

SILENT, SILENT NIGHT

Silent, Silent Night
Quench the holy light
Of thy torches bright.

For possess'd of Day
Thousand spirits stray
That sweet joys betray

Why should joys be sweet
Used with deceit
Nor with sorrows meet?

But an honest joy
Does itself destroy
For a harlot coy.

Poems from the Rossetti Ms. (c. 1793)

Verse more nearly faultless and of a more difficult perfection was never accomplished.

ALGERNON CHARLES SWINBURNE
William Blake (1866)

WILLIAM BLAKE

1 7 5 7 — 1 8 2 7

SUN-FLOWER

Ah, Sun-flower! weary of time.

Songs of Experience (1794)

The most moving and most complete single line in English poetry.

CECIL DAY LEWIS
A Hope for Poetry (1934)

THE ANCIENT TREES

Hear the voice of the Bard!
Who Present, Past, & Future, sees;
Whose ears have heard
The Holy Word
That walk'd among the ancient trees,

Calling the lapsed Soul,
And weeping in the evening dew;
That might controll
The starry pole,
And fallen, fallen light renew!

"O Earth, O Earth, return!
"Arise from out the dewy grass;
"Night is worn,
"And the morn
"Rises from the slumberous mass.

"Turn away no more;
"Why wilt thou turn away?
"The starry floor,
"The wat'ry shore,
"Is giv'n thee till the break of day."

Songs of Experience (1794)

SONG

Memory, hither come,
    And tune your merry notes;
And, while upon the wind
    Your music floats,
I'll pore upon the stream,
Where sighing lovers dream,
And fish for fancies as they pass
Within the watery glass.

I'll drink of the clear stream,
    And hear the linnet's song;
And there I'll lie and dream
    The day along:

And, when night comes, I'll go
   To places fit for woe,
Walking along the darken'd valley
   With silent Melancholy.

Poetical Sketches (1783)

SEVEN OF MY SWEET LOVES

My Spectre around me night & day
Like a Wild beast guards my way.
My Emanation far within
Weeps incessantly for my Sin.

A Fathomless & boundless deep,
There we wander, there we weep;
On the hungry craving wind
My Spectre follows thee behind.

He scents thy footsteps in the snow,
Wheresoever thou dost go
Thro' the wintry hail & rain.
When wilt thou return again?

Dost thou not in Pride & scorn
Fill with tempests all my morn,
And with jealousies & fears
Fill my pleasant nights with tears?

Seven of my sweet loves thy knife
Has bereaved of their life.
Their marble tombs I built with tears
And with cold & shuddering fears.

Seven more loves weep night & day
Round the tombs where my loves lay,
And seven more loves attend each night
Around my couch with torches bright.

And seven more Loves in my bed
Crown with wine my mournful head,
Pitying & forgiving all
Thy transgressions, great & small.

When wilt thou return & view
My loves, & them to life renew?
When wilt thou return & live?
When wilt thou pity as I forgive?

Poems from the Rossetti Ms. (1800–03)

IN WEARY NIGHT

Tho' thou art Worship'd by the Names Divine
Of Jesus & Jehovah, thou art still
The Son of Morn in weary Night's decline,
The lost Traveller's Dream under the Hill.

The Gates of Paradise (1793)

*For me the most poetical of all poets is Blake. I find his lyrical note as
beautiful as Shakespeare's and more beautiful than anyone else's; and
I call him more poetical than Shakespeare, even though Shakespeare
has so much more poetry, because poetry in him preponderates more
than in Shakespeare over everything else, and instead of being confounded in a great river can be drunk pure from a slender channel of
its own. Shakespeare is rich in thought, and his meaning has power of
itself to move us, even if the poetry were not there: Blake's meaning is
often unimportant or virtually non-existent, so that we can listen with
all our hearing to his celestial tune.*

A. E. HOUSMAN
The Name and Nature of Poetry (1933)

ROBERT BURNS

1 7 5 9 — 1 7 9 6

HOLY WILLIE'S PRAYER

O Thou, wha in the Heavens dost dwell,
Wha, as it pleases best thysel',
Sends ane to heaven and ten to hell,
    A' for thy glory,
And no for ony guid or ill
        They've done afore thee!

I bless and praise thy matchless might,
Whan thousands thou hast left in night,
That I am here afore thy sight,
        For gifts an' grace
A burnin' an' a shinin' light,
        To a' this place.

What was I, or my generation,
That I should get sic exaltation?
I, wha deserve most just damnation,
　　　　For broken laws,
Sax thousand years 'fore my creation,
　　　　Thro' Adam's cause.

When frae my mither's womb I fell,
Thou might hae plungèd me in hell,
To gnash my gums, to weep and wail,
　　　　In burnin' lakes,
Where damnèd devils roar and yell,
　　　　Chain'd to their stakes;

Yet I am here a chosen sample,
To show thy grace is great and ample;
I'm here a pillar in thy temple,
　　　　Strong as a rock,
A guide, a buckler, an example
　　　　To a' thy flock.

O Lord, thou kens what zeal I bear.
When drinkers drink, and swearers swear,
And singin' there and dancin' here,
　　　　Wi' great an' sma':
For I am keepit by thy fear
　　　　Free frae them a'.

But yet, O Lord! confess I must
At times I'm fash'd wi' fleshy lust;
An' sometimes too, in warldly trust,
　　　　Vile self gets in;
But thou remembers we are dust,
　　　　Defil'd in sin.

O Lord! yestreen, thou kens, wi' Meg—
Thy pardon I sincerely beg;
O! may't ne'er be a livin' plague
　　　　To my dishonour,
An' I'll ne'er lift a lawless leg
　　　　Again upon her.

Besides I farther maun allow,
Wi' Lizzie's lass, three times I trow—
But, Lord, that Friday I was fou,
　　　　When I cam near her,
Or else thou kens thy servant true
　　　　Wad never steer her.

May be thou lets this fleshly thorn
Beset thy servant e'en and morn
Lest he owre high and proud should turn,
    That he's sae gifted;
If sae, thy hand maun e'en be borne,
    Until thou lift it.

Lord, bless thy chosen in this place,
For here thou hast a chosen race;
But God confound their stubborn face,
    And blast their name,
Wha bring thy elders to disgrace
    An' public shame.

Lord, mind Gawn Hamilton's deserts,
He drinks, an' swears, an' plays at cartes,
Yet has sae mony takin' arts
    Wi' grit an' sma',
Frae God's ain priest the people's hearts
    He steals awa'.

An' when we chasten'd him therefor,
Thou kens how he bred sic a splore
As set the warld in a roar
    O' laughin' at us;
Curse thou his basket and his store,
    Kail and potatoes.

Lord, hear my earnest cry an' pray'r,
Against that presbyt'ry o' Ayr;
Thy strong right hand, Lord, make it bare
    Upo' their heads;
Lord, weigh it down, and dinna spare,
    For their misdeeds.

O Lord my God, that glib-tongu'd Aiken,
My very heart and soul are quakin',
To think how we stood sweatin', shakin',
    An' piss'd wi' dread,
While he, wi' hingin' lips and snakin',
    Held up his head.

Lord, in the day of vengeance try him;
Lord, visit them wha did employ him,
And pass not in thy mercy by them,
    Nor hear their pray'r:
But, for thy people's sake, destroy them,
    And dinna spare.

But, Lord, remember me and mine
Wi' mercies temp'ral and divine,
That I for gear and grace may shine
      Excell'd by nane,
And a' the glory shall be thine,
      Amen, Amen!

          (1785)

The most perfect bit of satire in English poetry.

HERBERT J. C. GRIERSON and J. C. SMITH
A Critical History of English Poetry (1944)

ROBERT BURNS

1 7 5 9 — 1 7 9 6

TO A MOUNTAIN DAISY

On turning one down with the Plough, in April 1786.

Wee, modest, crimson-tippèd flow'r,
Thou's met me in an evil hour;
For I maun crush amang the stour
      Thy slender stem:
To spare thee now is past my pow'r,
      Thou bonie gem.

Alas! it's no thy neibor sweet,
The bonie lark, companion meet,
Bending thee 'mang the dewy weet,
      Wi' spreckl'd breast!
When upward-springing, blythe, to greet
      The purpling east.

Cauld blew the bitter-biting north
Upon thy early, humble birth;
Yet cheerfully thou glinted forth
      Amid the storm,
Scarce rear'd above the parent-earth
      Thy tender form.

The flaunting flow'rs our gardens yield,
High shelt'ring woods and wa's maun shield;
But thou, beneath the random bield
                        O' clod or stane,
Adorns the histie stibble field,
                        Unseen, alane.

There, in thy scanty mantle clad,
Thy snawie bosom sun-ward spread,
Thou lifts thy unassuming head
                        In humble guise;
But now the share uptears thy bed,
                        And low thou lies!

Such is the fate of artless maid,
Sweet flow'ret of the rural shade!
By love's simplicity betray'd,
                        And guileless trust;
Till she, like thee, all soil'd, is laid
                        Low i' the dust.

Such is the fate of simple bard,
On life's rough ocean luckless starr'd!
Unskilful he to note the card
                        Of prudent lore,
Till billows rage, and gales blow hard,
                        And whelm him o'er!

Such fate to suffering worth is giv'n,
Who long with wants and woes has striv'n,
By human pride or cunning driv'n,
                        To mis'ry's brink;
Till wrench'd of ev'ry stay but Heav'n,
                        He, ruin'd, sink!

Ev'n thou who mourn'st the Daisy's fate,
That fate is thine—no distant date;
Stern Ruin's plough-share drives elate,
                        Full on thy bloom,
Till crush'd beneath the furrow's weight,
                        Shall be thy doom!

There is nothing in all poetry which touches it.

THEODORE WATTS-DUNTON
Poetry and the Renascence of Wonder (1914)

TIME IS SETTING

The wan Moon is setting behind the white wave,
And Time is setting with me, oh.

Open the Door to Me, Oh (1793)

*There are no lines with more melancholy beauty than these by Burns
. . . . and these lines are perfectly symbolical. Take from them the whiteness of the moon and of the wave, whose relation to the setting of Time
is too subtle for the intellect, and you take from them their beauty.
But, when all are together, moon and wave and whiteness and setting
Time and the last melancholy cry, they evoke an emotion which cannot be evoked by any other arrangement of colours and sounds and
forms. We may call this metaphorical writing, but it is better to call it
symbolical writing, because metaphors are not profound enough to be
moving, when they are not symbols, and when they are symbols they
are the most perfect of all, because the most subtle, outside of pure
sound, and through them one can the best find out what symbols are.
If one begins the reverie with any beautiful lines that one can remember, one finds they are like those by Burns.*

W. B. YEATS
Ideas of Good and Evil (1900)

ROBERT BURNS

1 7 5 9 — 1 7 9 6

THE FAREWELL

It was a' for our rightfu' King
We left fair Scotland's strand;
It was a' for our rightfu' King
We e'er saw Irish land,
My dear—
We e'er saw Irish land.

Now a' is done that men can do,
And a' is done in vain;
My love and native land fareweel,
For I maun cross the main,
My dear—
For I maun cross the main.

He turn'd him right and round about
Upon the Irish shore,
And gae his bridle-reins a shake,
With adieu for evermore,
My dear—
With adieu for evermore!

The sodger frae the wars returns,
The sailor frae the main;
But I hae parted frae my love
Never to meet again,
My dear—
Never to meet again.

When day is gane, and night is come,
And a' folk bound to sleep,
I think on him that's far awa
The lee-lang night, and weep,
My dear—
The lee-lang night, and weep.

(1794)

The noblest of Burns's, perhaps of all, Jacobite ditties, 'It was a' for our rightfu' king,' one of the great achievements of romantic patriot song in any form of English.

OLIVER ELTON
A Survey of English Literature (1920)

FRIEDRICH VON SCHILLER

1 7 5 9 — 1 8 0 5

AN DIE FREUDE

Freude, schöner Götterfunken,
Tochter aus Elysium,
Wir betreten feuertrunken,
Himmlische, dein Heiligtum.

980

Deine Zauber binden wieder,
Was die Mode streng geteilt,
Alle Menschen werden Brüder,
Wo dein sanfter Flügel weilt.
Seid umschlungen, Millionen!
Diesen Kuss der ganzen Welt!
Brüder—überm Sternenzelt
Muss ein lieber Vater wohnen.

Wem der grosse Wurf gelungen,
Eines Freundes Freund zu sein,
Wer ein holdes Weib errungen,
Mische seinen Jubel ein!
Ja—wer auch nur *eine* Seele
Sein nennt auf dem Erdenrund!
Und wer's nie gekonnt, der stehle
Weinend sich aus diesem Bund.
Was den grossen Ring bewohnet,
Huldige der Sympathie!
Zu den Sternen leitet sie,
Wo der Unbekannte thronet.

Freude trinken alle Wesen
An den Brüsten der Natur,
Alle Guten, alle Bösen
Folgen ihrer Rosenspur.
Küsse gab sie uns und Reben,
Einen Freund, geprüft im Tod,
Wollust ward dem Wurm gegeben,
Und der Cherub steht vor Gott.
Ihr stürzt nieder, Millionen?
Ahnest du den Schöpfer, Welt?
Such ihn überm Sternenzelt!
Über Sternen muss er wohnen.

Freude heisst die starke Feder
In der ewigen Natur.
Freude, Freude treibt die Räder
In der grossen Weltenuhr.
Blumen lockt sie aus den Keimen,
Sonnen aus dem Firmament,
Sphären rollt sie in den Räumen,
Die des Sehers Rohr nicht kennt.
Froh, wie seine Sonnen fliegen
Durch des Himmels prächt'gen Plan,
Wandelt, Brüder, eure Bahn,
Freudig wie ein Held zum Siegen.

Aus der Wahrheit Feuerspiegel
Lächelt sie den Forscher an.
Zu der Tugend steilem Hügel
Leitet sie des Dulders Bahn.
Auf des Glaubens Sonnenberge
Sieht man ihre Fahnen wehn,
Durch den Riss gesprengter Särge
Sie im Chor der Engel stehn.
Duldet mutig, Millionen!
Duldet für die bessre Welt!
Droben überm Sternenzelt
Wird ein grosser Gott belohnen.

ODE TO JOY

Joy, of flame celestial fashioned,
Daughter of Elysium,
By that holy fire impassioned
To thy sanctuary we come.
Thine the spells that reunited
Those estranged by Custom dread,
Every man a brother plighted
Where thy gentle wings are spread.
Millions in our arms we gather,
To the world our kiss be sent!
Past the starry firmament,
Brothers, dwells a loving Father.

Who that height of bliss has provèd
Once a friend of friends to be,
Who has won a maid belovèd
Join us in our jubilee.
Whoso holds a heart in keeping,
One—in all the world—his own—
Who has failed, let him with weeping
From our fellowship begone!
All the mighty globe containeth
Homage to Compassion pay!
To the stars she leads the way
Where, unknown, the Godhead reigneth.

All drink joy from Mother Nature,
All she suckled at her breast,
Good or evil, every creature,
Follows where her foot has pressed.

Love she gave us, passing measure,
   One Who true in death abode,
E'en the worm was granted pleasure,
   Angels see the face of God.
     Fall ye millions, fall before Him,
       Is thy Maker, World, unknown?
     Far above the stars His throne
     Yonder seek Him and adore Him.

Joy, the spring of all contriving,
   In eternal Nature's plan,
Joy set wheels on wheels a-driving
   Since earth's horologe began;
From the bud the blossom winning
   Suns from out the sky she drew,
Spheres through boundless ether spinning
   Worlds no gazer's science knew.
     Gladsome as her suns and glorious
       Through the spacious heavens career,
       Brothers, so your courses steer
     Heroes joyful and victorious.

She from Truth's own mirror shining
   Casts on sages glances gay,
Guides the sufferer unrepining
   Far up Virtue's steepest way;
On the hills of Faith all-glorious
   Mark her sunlit banners fly,
She, in death's despite, victorious,
   Stands with angels in the sky.
     Millions, bravely sorrows bearing,
       Suffer for a better time!
     See, above the starry clime
     God a great reward preparing.

Translated by Norman Macleod

His poetry was the fruit of reflection—not a simple reaction to experience; and the struggle to obtain an inner harmony and a wide outlook on Nature and Man was accompanied by a struggle for expression, for only with pain and effort did Schiller beat his music out. When he was at last master of his instrument, he attained a rush and sweep of rhythm never before felt in German poetry—not even in Goethe. Schiller was a poet of ideas and ideals, and the philosophies of his time find an expression in his verse. In his "Ode to Joy," we have the noblest rendering of that enthusiasm for Humanity which heralded, if it did not survive, the French Revolution.

NORMAN MACLEOD
German Lyric Poetry (1930)

FRIEDRICH VON SCHILLER

1 7 5 9 — 1 8 0 5

WHERE MORTALS DWELL

Durch die Strassen der Städte,
Vom Jammer gefolget,
Schreitet das Unglück—
Lauernd umschleicht es
Die Häuser der Menschen,
Heute an dieser
Pforte pocht es,
Morgen an jener,
Aber noch keinen hat es verschont.
Die unerwünschte
Schmerzliche Botschaft
Früher oder später
Bestellt es an jeder
Schwelle, wo ein Lebendiger wohnt.

Through the streets of the city,
By misery followed,
Misfortune strides,
And lurking she creeps
Round the houses of men.
To-day upon this
Portal she knocks,
To-morrow on that.
But none spares she wholly.
Sooner or later,
The dreaded, unwelcome
Message of pain,
She prints upon every
Threshold where mortals dwell.

Die Braut von Messina (1803)
Act iv, Scene iv
Translated by Benjamin W. Wells

In stateliness and dignity of diction, the "Bride of Messina" is perhaps unsurpassed in German, and the true classical irony, "that mixture of jest and earnest which for many is more mysterious and darker than all mysteries," as Schlegel has said, the irony of fate, radically different from that "irony" that was then suffering such abuse at the hands of the romanticists, was represented here with greater strength than ever before or since in Germany.

BENJAMIN W. WELLS
Modern German Literature (1901)

FRIEDRICH VON SCHILLER

1 7 5 9 — 1 8 0 5

DAS LIED VON DER GLOCKE

Vivos voco.   Mortuos plango.   Fulgura frango.

Fest gemauert in der Erden
Steht die Form, aus Lehm gebrannt.
Heute muss die Glocke werden!
Frisch, Gesellen, seid zur Hand!
  Von der Stirne heiss
  Rinnen muss der Schweiss,
Soll das Werk den Meister loben;
Doch der Segen kommt von oben.
Zum Werke, das wir ernst bereiten,
Geziemt sich wohl ein ernstes Wort;
Wenn gute Reden sie begleiten,
Dann fliesst die Arbeit munter fort.
So lasst uns jetzt mit Fleiss betrachten,
Was durch die schwache Kraft entspringt;
Den schlechten Mann muss man verachten,
Der nie bedacht, was er vollbringt.
Das ist's ja, was den Menschen zieret,
Und dazu ward ihm der Verstand,
Dass er im innern Herzen spüret,
Was er erschafft mit seiner Hand.

Nehmet Holz vom Fichtenstamme,
Doch recht trocken lasst es sein,
Dass die eingepresste Flamme

985

Schlage zu dem Schwalch hinein!
  Kocht des Kupfers Brei,
  Schnell das Zinn herbei,
Dass die zähe Glockenspeise
Fliesse nach der rechten Weise!

Was in des Dammes tiefer Grube
Die Hand mit Feuers Hilfe baut,
Hoch auf des Turmes Glockenstube,
Da wird es von uns zeugen laut.
Noch dauern wird's in späten Tagen
Und rühren vieler Menschen Ohr
Und wird mit dem Betrübten klagen
Und stimmen zu der Andacht Chor.
Was unten tief dem Erdensohne
Das wechselnde Verhängnis bringt,
Das schlägt an die metallne Krone,
Die es erbaulich weiter klingt.

  Weisse Blasen seh' ich springen;
  Wohl! die Massen sind im Fluss.
Lasst's mit Aschensalz durchdringen,
Das befördert schnell den Guss.
    Auch von Schaume rein
    Muss die Mischung sein,
Dass vom reinlichen Metalle
Rein und voll die Stimme schalle.

Denn mit der Freude Feierklange
Begrüsst sie das geliebte Kind
Auf seines Lebens erstem Gange,
Den es in Schlafes Arm beginnt.
Ihm ruhen noch im Zeitenschosse
Die schwarzen und die heitern Lose;
Der Mutterliebe zarte Sorgen
Bewachen seinen goldenen Morgen.—
Die Jahre fliehen pfeilgeschwind.
Vom Mädchen reisst sich stolz der Knabe,
Er stürmt ins Leben wild hinaus,
Durchmisst die Welt am Wanderstabe,
Fremd kehrt er heim ins Vaterhaus.
Und herrlich, in der Jugend Prangen,
Wie ein Gebild aus Himmelshöhn,
Mit züchtigen, verschämten Wangen
Sieht er die Jungfrau vor sich stehn.

Da fasst ein namenloses Sehnen
Des Jünglings Herz, er irrt allein,
Aus seinen Augen brechen Tränen,
Er flieht der Brüder wilden Reihn.
Errötend folgt er ihren Spuren
Und ist von ihrem Gruss beglückt,
Das Schönste sucht er auf den Fluren,
Womit er seine Liebe schmückt.
O zarte Sehnsucht, süsses Hoffen,
Der ersten Liebe goldne Zeit!
Das Auge sieht den Himmel offen,
Es schwelgt das Herz in Seligkeit;
O, dass sie ewig grünen bliebe,
Die schöne Zeit der jungen Liebe!

   Wie sich schon die Pfeifen bräunen!
   Dieses Stäbchen tauch' ich ein,
   Sehn wir's überglast erscheinen,
   Wird's zum Gusse zeitig sein.
      Jetzt, Gesellen, frisch!
      Prüft mir das Gemisch,
    Ob das Spröde mit dem Weichen
    Sich vereint zum guten Zeichen.

Denn wo das Strenge mit dem Zarten,
Wo Starkes sich und Mildes paarten,
Da gibt es einen guten Klang.
Drum prüfe, wer sich ewig bindet,
Ob sich das Herz zum Herzen findet!
Der Wahn ist kurz, die Reu' ist lang.—
Lieblich in der Bräute Locken
Spielt der jungfräuliche Kranz,
Wenn die hellen Kirchenglocken
Laden zu des Festes Glanz.
Ach! des Lebens schönste Feier
Endigt auch den Lebensmai,
Mit dem Gürtel, mit dem Schleier
Reisst der schöne Wahn entzwei.
Die Leidenschaft flieht,
Die Liebe muss bleiben;
Die Blume verblüht,
Die Frucht muss treiben.
Der Mann muss hinaus
Ins feindliche Leben,
Muss wirken und streben

Und pflanzen und schaffen,
Erlisten, erraffen,
Muss wetten und wagen,
Das Glück zu erjagen.
Da strömet herbei die unendliche Gabe,
Es füllt sich der Speicher mit köstlicher Habe,
Die Räume wachsen, es dehnt sich das Haus.
Und drinnen waltet
Die züchtige Hausfrau,
Die Mutter der Kinder,
Und herrschet weise
Im häuslichen Kreise,
Und lehret die Mädchen
Und wehret den Knaben,
Und reget ohn' Ende
Die fleissigen Hände,
Und mehrt den Gewinn
Mit ordnendem Sinn,
Und füllet mit Schätzen die duftenden Laden,
Und dreht um die schnurrende Spindel den Faden,
Und sammelt im reinlich geglätteten Schrein
Die schimmernde Wolle, den schneeichten Lein,
Und füget zum Guten den Glanz und den Schimmer,
Und ruhet nimmer.

Und der Vater mit frohem Blick
Von des Hauses weitschauendem Giebel
Überzählet sein blühend Glück,
Siehet der Pfosten ragende Bäume
Und der Scheunen gefüllte Räume
Und die Speicher, vom Segen gebogen,
Und des Kornes bewegte Wogen,
Rühmt sich mit stolzem Mund:
Fest, wie der Erde Grund,
Gegen des Unglücks Macht
Steht mir des Hauses Pracht!—
Doch mit des Geschickes Mächten
Ist kein ew'ger Bund zu flechten,
Und das Unglück schreitet schnell.

Wohl! nun kann der Guss beginnen,
Schön gezacket ist der Bruch.
Doch bevor wir's lassen rinnen,
Betet einen frommen Spruch!
Stosst den Zapfen aus!
Gott bewahr' das Haus!

Rauchend in des Henkels Bogen
Schiesst's mit feuerbraunen Wogen.

Wohltätig ist des Feuers Macht,
Wenn sie der Mensch bezähmt, bewacht;
Und was er bildet, was er schafft,
Das dankt er dieser Himmelskraft.
Doch furchtbar wird die Himmelskraft,
Wenn sie der Fessel sich entrafft,
Einhertritt auf der eignen Spur,
Die freie Tochter der Natur.
Wehe, wenn sie losgelassen,
Wachsend ohne Widerstand,
Durch die volkbelebten Gassen
Wälzt den ungeheuren Brand!
Denn die Elemente hassen
Das Gebild der Menschenhand.
Aus der Wolke
Quillt der Segen,
Strömt der Regen;
Aus der Wolke, ohne Wahl,
Zuckt der Strahl.
Hört ihr's wimmern hoch vom Turm?
Das ist Sturm!
Rot wie Blut
Ist der Himmel,
Das ist nicht des Tages Glut!
Welch Getümmel
Strassen auf!
Dampf wallt auf!
Flackernd steigt die Feuersäule,
Durch der Strasse lange Zeile
Wächst es fort mit Windeseile;
Kochend wie aus Ofens Rachen
Glühn die Lüfte, Balken krachen,
Pfosten stürzen, Fenster klirren,
Kinder jammern, Mütter irren,
Tiere wimmern
Unter Trümmern;
Alles rennet, rettet, flüchtet,
Taghell ist die Nacht gelichtet.
Durch der Hände lange Kette
Um die Wette
Fliegt der Eimer, hoch im Bogen
Spritzen Quellen Wasserwogen.

Heulend kommt der Sturm geflogen,
Der die Flamme brausend sucht.
Prasselnd in die dürre Frucht
Fällt sie, in des Speichers Räume,
In der Sparren dürre Bäume;
Und als wollte sie im Wehen
Mit sich fort der Erde Wucht
Reissen in gewalt'ger Flucht,
Wächst sie in des Himmels Höhen
Riesengross!
Hoffnungslos
Weicht der Mensch der Götterstärke,
Müssig sieht er seine Werke
Und bewundernd untergehn.

Leergebrannt
Ist die Stätte,
Wilder Stürme rauhes Bette.
In den öden Fensterhöhlen
Wohnt das Grauen,
Und des Himmels Wolken schauen
Hoch hinein.

Einen Blick
Nach dem Grabe
Seiner Habe
Sendet noch der Mensch zurück—
Greift fröhlich dann zum Wanderstabe.
Was Feuers Wut ihm auch geraubt,
Ein süsser Trost ist ihm geblieben:
Er zählt die Häupter seiner Lieben,
Und sieh! ihm fehlt kein teures Haupt.

In die Erd' ist's aufgenommen,
Glücklich ist die Form gefüllt;
Wird's auch schön zu Tage kommen,
Dass es Fleiss und Kunst vergilt?
Wenn der Guss misslang?
Wenn die Form zersprang?
Ach, vielleicht, indem wir hoffen,
Hat uns Unheil schon getroffen.

Dem dunkeln Schoss der heil'gen Erde
Vertrauen wir der Hände Tat,
Vertraut der Sämann seine Saat
Und hofft, dass sie entkeimen werde
Zum Segen nach des Himmels Rat.

Noch köstlicheren Samen bergen
Wir trauernd in der Erde Schoss
Und hoffen, dass er aus den Särgen
Erblühen soll zu schönerm Los.

Von dem Dome,
Schwer und bang,
Tönt die Glocke
Grabgesang.
Ernst begleiten ihre Trauerschläge
Einen Wandrer auf dem letzten Wege.

Ach! die Gattin ist's, die teure,
Ach! es ist die treue Mutter,
Die der schwarze Fürst der Schatten
Wegführt aus dem Arm des Gatten,
Aus der zarten Kinder Schar,
Die sie blühend ihm gebar,
Die sie an der treuen Brust
Wachsen sah mit Mutterlust—
Ach! des Hauses zarte Bande
Sind gelöst auf immerdar;
Denn sie wohnt im Schattenlande,
Die des Hauses Mutter war;
Denn es fehlt ihr treues Walten,
Ihre Sorge wacht nicht mehr;
An verwaister Stätte schalten
Wird die Fremde, liebeleer.

Bis die Glocke sich verkühlet,
Laszt die strenge Arbeit ruhn;
Wie im Laub der Vogel spielet,
Mag sich jeder gütlich tun.
Winkt der Sterne Licht,
Ledig aller Pflicht
Hört der Bursch die Vesper schlagen,
Meister muss sich immer plagen.

Munter fördert seine Schritte
Fern im wilden Forst der Wandrer
Nach der lieben Heimathütte.
Blökend ziehen heim die Schafe,
Und der Rinder
Breitgestirnte, glatte Scharen
Kommen brüllend,
Die gewohnten Ställe füllend.

Schwer herein
Schwankt der Wagen,
Kornbeladen;
Bunt von Farben
Auf den Garben
Liegt der Kranz,
Und das junge Volk der Schnitter
Fliegt zum Tanz.
Markt und Strasse werden stiller;
Um des Lichts gesell'ge Flamme
Sammeln sich die Hausbewohner,
Und das Stadttor schliesst sich knarrend.
Schwarz bedecket
Sich die Erde;
Doch den sichern Bürger schrecket
Nicht die Nacht,
Die den Bösen grässlich wecket;
Denn das Auge des Gesetzes wacht.

Heil'ge Ordnung, segenreiche
Himmelstochter, die das Gleiche
Frei und leicht und freudig bindet,
Die der Städte Bau gegründet,
Die herein von den Gefilden
Rief den ungesell'gen Wilden,
Eintrat in der Menschen Hütten,
Sie gewöhnt zu sanften Sitten
Und das teuerste der Bande
Wob, den Trieb zum Vaterlande!

Tausend fleiss'ge Hände regen,
Helfen sich in munterm Bund,
Und in feurigem Bewegen
Werden alle Kräfte kund.
Meister rührt sich und Geselle
In der Freiheit heil'gem Schutz;
Jeder freut sich seiner Stelle,
Bietet dem Verächter Trutz.
Arbeit ist des Bürgers Zierde,
Segen ist der Mühe Preis;
Ehrt den König seine Würde,
Ehret uns der Hände Fleiss.
Holder Friede,
Süsse Eintracht,
Weilet, weilet
Freundlich über dieser Stadt!

Möge nie der Tag erscheinen,
Wo des rauhen Krieges Horden
Dieses stille Tal durchtoben,
Wo der Himmel,
Den des Abends sanfte Röte
Lieblich malt,
Von der Dörfer, von der Städte
Wildem Brande schrecklich strahlt!

Nun zerbrecht mir das Gebäude,
Seine Absicht hat's erfüllt,
Dass sich Herz und Auge weide
An dem wohlgelungnen Bild.
Schwingt den Hammer, schwingt,
Bis der Mantel springt!
Wenn die Glock' soll auferstehen,
Muss die Form in Stücken gehen.

Der Meister kann die Form zerbrechen
Mit weiser Hand, zur rechten Zeit;
Doch wehe, wenn in Flammenbächen
Das glühnde Erz sich selbst befreit!
Blindwütend, mit des Donners Krachen,
Zersprengt es das geborstne Haus,
Und wie aus offnem Höllenrachen
Speit es Verderben zündend aus.
Wo rohe Kräfte sinnlos walten,
Da kann sich kein Gebild gestalten;
Wenn sich die Völker selbst befrein,
Da kann die Wohlfahrt nicht gedeihn.
Weh, wenn sich in dem Schoss der Städte
Der Feuerzunder still gehäuft,
Das Volk, zerreissend seine Kette,
Zur Eigenhilfe schrecklich greift!
Da zerret an der Glocke Strängen
Der Aufruhr, dass sie heulend schallt
Und, nur geweiht zu Friedensklängen,
Die Losung anstimmt zur Gewalt.

Freiheit und Gleichheit! hört man schallen;
Der ruh'ge Bürger greift zur Wehr,
Die Strassen füllen sich, die Hallen,
Und Würgerbanden ziehn umher.
Da werden Weiber zu Hyänen
Und treiben mit Entsetzen Scherz;
Noch zuckend, mit des Panthers Zähnen,
Zerreissen sie des Feindes Herz.

Nichts Heiliges ist mehr, es lösen
Sich alle Bande frommer Scheu;
Der Gute räumt den Platz dem Bösen,
Und alle Laster walten frei.
Gefährlich ist's, den Leu zu wecken,
Verderblich ist des Tigers Zahn;
Jedoch der schrecklichste der Schrecken,
Das ist der Mensch in seinem Wahn.
Weh denen, die dem Ewigblinden
Des Lichtes Himmelsfackel leihn!
Sie strahlt ihm nicht, sie kann nur zünden
Und äschert Städt' und Länder ein.

Freude hat mir Gott gegeben!
Sehet! wie ein goldner Stern
Aus der Hülse, blank und eben,
Schält sich der metallne Kern.
Von dem Helm zum Kranz
Spielt's wie Sonnenglanz,
Auch des Wappens nette Schilder
Loben den erfahrnen Bilder.

Herein! herein!
Gesellen alle, schliesst den Reihen,
Dass wir die Glocke taufend weihen!
Concordia soll ihr Name sein.
Zur Eintracht, zu herzinnigem Vereine
Versammle sie die liebende Gemeine.

Und dies sei fortan ihr Beruf,
Wozu der Meister sie erschuf:
Hoch überm niedern Erdenleben
Soll sie im blauen Himmelszelt
Die Nachbarin des Donners schweben
Und grenzen an die Sternenwelt,
Soll eine Stimme sein von oben,
Wie der Gestirne helle Schar,
Die ihren Schöpfer wandelnd loben
Und führen das bekränzte Jahr.
Nur ewigen und ernsten Dingen
Sei ihr metallner Mund geweiht,
Und stündlich mit den schnellen Schwingen
Berühr' im Fluge sie die Zeit.
Dem Schicksal leihe sie die Zunge;
Selbst herzlos, ohne Mitgefühl,
Begleite sie mit ihrem Schwunge
Des Lebens wechselvolles Spiel.

Und wie der Klang im Ohr vergehet,
Der mächtig tönend ihr entschallt,
So lehre sie, dass nichts bestehet,
Dass alles Irdische verhallt.

Jetzo mit der Kraft des Stranges
Wiegt die Glock' mir aus der Gruft,
Dass sie in das Reich des Klanges
Steige, in die Himmelsluft!
Ziehet, ziehet, hebt!
Sie bewegt sich, schwebt!
Freude dieser Stadt bedeute,
Friede sei ihr erst Geläute.

SONG OF THE BELL

Fastened deep in firmest earth,
Stands the mould of well burnt clay.
Now we'll give the bell its birth;
Quick, my friends, no more delay!
From the heated brow
Sweat must freely flow,
If to your master praise be given:
But the blessing comes from Heaven.

To the work we now prepare
A serious thought is surely due;
And cheerfully the toil we'll share,
If cheerful words be mingled too.
Then let us still with care observe
What from our strength, yet weakness, springs:
For he respect can ne'er deserve
Who hands alone to labor brings.
'Tis only this which honors man;
His mind with heavenly fire was warmed,
That he with deepest thought might scan
The work which his own hand has formed.

With splinters of the driest pine
Now feed the fire below;
Then the rising flame shall shine,
And the melting ore shall flow.
Boils the brass within,
Quickly add the tin;

That the thick metallic mass
Rightly to the mould may pass.

What with the aid of fire's dread power
    We in the dark, deep pit now hide,
Shall, on some lofty, sacred tower,
    Tell of our skill and form our pride.
And it shall last to days remote,
    Shall thrill the ear of many a race;
Shall sound with sorrow's mournful note,
    And call to pure devotion's grace.
Whatever to the sons of earth
    Their changing destiny brings down,
To the deep, solemn clang gives birth,
    That rings from out this metal crown.

See, the boiling surface, whitening,
    Shows the whole is mixing well;
Add the salts, the metal brightening,
    Ere flows out the liquid bell.
        Clear from foam or scum
        Must the mixture come,
That with a rich metallic note
The sound aloft in air may float.

Now with joy and festive mirth
    Salute that loved and lovely child,
Whose earliest moments on the earth
    Are passed in sleep's dominion mild.
While on Time's lap he rests his head,
The fatal sisters spin their thread;
    A mother's love, with softest rays,
    Gilds o'er the morning of his days.—
But years with arrowy haste are fled.
His nursery bonds he proudly spurns;
    He rushes to the world without;
After long wandering, home he turns,
    Arrives a stranger and in doubt.
There, lovely in her beauty's youth,
    A form of heavenly mould he meets,
Of modest air and simple truth;
    The blushing maid he bashful greets.
A nameless feeling seizes strong
    On his young heart. He walks alone;
To his moist eyes emotions throng;

His joy in ruder sports has flown.
He follows, blushing, where she goes;
    And should her smile but welcome him,
The fairest flower, the dewy rose,
    To deck her beauty seems too dim.
O tenderest passion! Sweetest hope!
    The golden hours of earliest love!
Heaven's self to him appears to ope;
    He feels a bliss this earth above.
O, that it could eternal last!
That youthful love were never past!

See how brown the liquid turns!
    Now this rod I thrust within;
If it's glazed before it burns,
    Then the casting may begin.
        Quick, my lads, and steady,
        If the mixture's ready!
When the strong and weaker blend,
Then we hope a happy end:
Whenever strength with softness joins,
When with the rough the mild combines,
    Then all is union sweet and strong.
Consider, ye who join your hands,
If hearts are twined in mutual bands;
    For passion's brief, repentance long.
How lovely in the maiden's hair
The bridal garland plays!
And merry bells invite us there,
Where mingle festive lays.
Alas! that all life's brightest hours
    Are ended with its earliest May!
That from those sacred nuptial bowers
    The dear deceit should pass away!
        Though passion may fly,
            Yet love will endure;
        The flower must die,
            The fruit to insure.
        The man must without,
            Into struggling life;
            With toiling and strife,
            He must plan and contrive;
            Must be prudent to thrive;
            With boldness must dare,
            Good fortune to share.

'Tis by means such as these, that abundance is poured
In a full, endless stream, to increase all his hoard,
   While his house to a palace spreads out.

         Within doors governs
         The modest, careful wife,
         The children's kind mother;
         And wise is the rule
         Of her household school.
         She teaches the girls,
         And she warns the boys;
         She directs all the bands
         Of diligent hands,
         And increases their gain
         By her orderly reign.
And she fills with her treasures her sweet-scented chests;
From the toil of her spinning-wheel scarcely she rests;
And she gathers in order, so cleanly and bright,
The softest of wool, and the linen snow-white:
The useful and pleasant she mingles ever,
         And is slothful never.
   The father, cheerful, from the door,
      His wide-extended homestead eyes;
   Tells all his smiling fortunes o'er;
   The future columns in his trees,
   His barn's well furnished stock he sees,
   His granaries e'en now o'erflowing,
   While yet the waving corn is growing.
         He boasts with swelling pride,
         "Firm as the mountain's side
         Against the shock of fate
         Is now my happy state."
   Who can discern futurity?
   Who can insure prosperity?
         Quick misfortune's arrow flies.

   Now we may begin to cast;
      All is right and well prepared:
   Yet, ere the anxious moment's past,
      A pious hope by all be shared.
         Strike the stopper clear!
         God preserve us here!
   Sparkling, to the rounded mould
   It rushes hot, like liquid gold.

How useful is the power of flame,
If human skill control and tame!
And much of all that man can boast,
Without this child of Heaven, were lost.
But frightful is her changing mien,
When, bursting from her bonds, she's seen
To quit the safe and quiet hearth,
And wander lawless o'er the earth.
Woe to those whom then she meets!
  Against her fury who can stand?
Along the thickly peopled streets
  She madly hurls her fearful brand.
Then the elements, with joy,
Man's best handiwork destroy.
   From the clouds
   Falls amain
   The blessed rain:
   From the clouds alike
   Lightnings strike.
Ringing loud the fearful knell,
  Sounds the bell.
  Dark blood-red
   Are all the skies;
But no dawning light is spread.
   What wild cries
   From the streets arise!
   Smoke dims the eyes.
Flickering mounts the fiery glow
Along the street's extended row,
Fast as fiercest winds can blow.
Bright, as with a furnace flare,
And scorching, is the heated air;
Beams are falling, children crying,
Windows breaking, mothers flying,
Creatures moaning, crushed and dying,—
All is uproar, hurry, flight,
And light as day the dreadful night.
Along the eager living lane,
   Though all in vain,
Speeds the bucket. The engine's power
Sends the artificial shower.
But see, the heavens still threatening lower!
The winds rush roaring to the flame.
Cinders on the store-house frame,

And its drier stores, fall thick;
While kindling, blazing, mounting quick,
As though it would, at one fell sweep,
    All that on the earth is found
    Scatter wide in ruin round,
Swells the flame to heaven's blue deep,
        With giant size.
        Hope now dies.
    Man must yield to Heaven's decrees.
    Submissive, yet appalled, he sees
His fairest works in ashes sleep.

        All burnt over
        Is the place,
The storm's wild home. How changed its face!
    In the empty, ruined wall
        Dwells dark horror;
    While heaven's clouds in shadow fall
        Deep within.

        One look,
        In memory sad,
        Of all he had,
    The unhappy sufferer took,—
Then found his heart might yet be glad.
    However hard his lot to bear,
His choicest treasures still remain:
He calls for each with anxious pain,
    And every loved one's with him there.
To the earth it's now committed.
    With success the mould is filled.
To skill and care alone's permitted
    A perfect work with toil to build.
        Is the casting right?
        Is the mould yet tight?
Ah! while now with hope we wait,
Mischance, perhaps, attends its fate.
To the dark lap of mother earth
    We now confide what we have made;
    As in earth too the seed is laid,
In hope the seasons will give birth
    To fruits that soon may be displayed.
And yet more precious seed we sow
    With sorrow in the world's wide field;
And hope, though in the grave laid low,

A flower of heavenly hue 't will yield.
           Slow and heavy
              Hear it swell!
           'Tis the solemn
              Passing bell!
Sad we follow, with these sounds of woe,
Those who on this last, long journey go.
   Alas! the wife,—it is the dear one,—
   Ah! it is the faithful mother,
   Whom the shadowy king of fear
   Tears from all that life holds dear;—
   From the husband,—from the young,
   The tender blossoms, that have sprung
   From their mutual, faithful love,
   'Twas hers to nourish, guide, improve.
   Ah! the chain which bound them all
      Is for ever broken now;
   She cannot hear their tender call,
      Nor see them in affliction bow.
   Her true affection guards no more;
      Her watchful care wakes not again:
   O'er all the once loved orphan's store
      The indifferent stranger now must reign.
   Till the bell is safely cold,
      May our heavy labor rest;
   Free as the bird, by none controlled,
      Each may do what pleases best.
         With approaching night,
            Twinkling stars are bright.
   Vespers call the boys to play;
   The master's toils end not with day.

Cheerful in the forest gloom,
   The wanderer turns his weary steps
To his loved, though lowly home.
   Bleating flocks draw near the fold;
         And the herds,
Wide-horned, and smooth, slow-pacing come
      Lowing from the hill,
      The accustomed stall to fill.
            Heavy rolls
            Along the wagon,
            Richly loaded.
            On the sheaves,
            With gayest leaves

They form the wreath;
And the youthful reapers dance
Upon the heath.
Street and market all are quiet,
And round each domestic light
Gathers now a circle fond,
While shuts the creaking city-gate.
Darkness hovers
O'er the earth.
Safety still each sleeper covers
As with light,
That the deeds of crime discovers;
For wakes the law's protecting might.

Holy Order! rich with all
The gifts of Heaven, that best we call,—
Freedom, peace, and equal laws,—
Of common good the happy cause!
She the savage man has taught
What the arts of life have wrought;
Changed the rude hut to comfort, splendor,
And filled fierce hearts with feelings tender
And yet a dearer bond she wove,—
Our home, our country, taught to love.

A thousand active hands, combined
For mutual aid, with zealous heart,
In well apportioned labor find
Their power increasing with their art.
Master and workmen all agree,
Under sweet Freedom's holy care,
And each, content in his degree,
Warns every scorner to beware.
Labor is the poor man's pride,—
Success by toil alone is won.
Kings glory in possessions wide,—
We glory in our work well done.

Gentle peace!
Sweet union!
Linger, linger,
Kindly over this our home!
Never may the day appear,
When the hordes of cruel war
Through this quiet vale shall rush;
When the sky,

With the evening's softened air,
  Blushing red,
Shall reflect the frightful glare
  Of burning towns in ruin dread.

Now break up the useless mould:
  Its only purpose is fulfilled.
May our eyes, well pleased, behold
  A work to prove us not unskilled.
    Wield the hammer, wield,
    Till the frame shall yield!
That the bell to light may rise,
The form in thousand fragments flies.

The master may destroy the mould
  With careful hand, and judgment wise.
But, woe!—in streams of fire, if rolled,
  The glowing metal seek the skies!
Loud bursting with the crash of thunder,
  It throws aloft the broken ground;
Like a volcano rends asunder,
  And spreads in burning ruin round.
When reckless power by force prevails,
  The reign of peace and art is o'er;
And when a mob e'en wrong assails,
  The public welfare is no more.
Alas! when in the peaceful state
  Conspiracies are darkly forming;
The oppressed no longer patient wait;
  With fury every breast is storming.
Then whirls the bell with frequent clang;
  And Uproar, with her howling voice,
Has changed the note, that peaceful rang,
  To wild confusion's dreadful noise.

Freedom and equal rights they call,—
  And peace gives way to sudden war;
The street is crowded, and the hall,—
  And crime is unrestrained by law:
E'en woman, to a fury turning,
  But mocks at every dreadful deed;
Against the hated madly burning,
  With horrid joy she sees them bleed.
Now naught is sacred;—broken lies
  Each holy law of honest worth;
The bad man rules, the good man flies,
  And every vice walks boldly forth.

There's danger in the lion's wrath,
   Destruction in the tiger's jaw;
But worse than death to cross the path
   Of man, when passion is his law.
Woe, woe to those who strive to light
   The torch of truth by passion's fire!
It guides not;—it but glares through night
   To kindle freedom's funeral pyre.

God has given us joy to-night!
   See how, like the golden grain
From the husk, all smooth and bright,
   The shining metal now is ta'en!
     From top to well formed rim,
     Not a spot is dim;
E'en the motto, neatly raised,
Shows a skill may well be praised.

     Around, around,
Companions all, take your ground,
And name the bell with joy profound!
Concordia is the word we've found
Most meet to express the harmonious sound,
That calls to those in friendship bound.

Be this henceforth the destined end
To which the finished work we send
High over every meaner thing,
   In the blue canopy of heaven,
Near to the thunder let it swing,
   A neighbour to the stars be given.
Let its clear voice above proclaim,
   With brightest troops of distant suns,
The praise of our Creator's name,
   While round each circling season runs.
To solemn thoughts of heart-felt power
   Let its deep note full oft invite,
And tell, with every passing hour,
   Of hastening time's unceasing flight.
Still let it mark the course of fate;
   Its cold, unsympathizing voice
Attend on every changing state
   Of human passions, griefs, and joys.
And as the mighty sound it gives
   Dies gently on the listening ear,
We feel how quickly all that lives
   Must change, and fade, and disappear.

Now, lads, join your strength around!
　　Lift the bell to upper air!
And in the kingdom wide of sound
　　Once placed, we'll leave it there.
　　　　All together! heave!
　　　　Its birth-place see it leave!—
Joy to all within its bound!
Peace its first, its latest sound!

Translated by Henry Wadsworth Longfellow

The "Song of the Bell" is the most wonderful testimony of what constitutes perfect poetic genius. Here, in alternating meters and with pictorial vividness of the highest order, by means of few briefly sketched strokes the total picture is conveyed, embracing all events of human and social life that spring from every emotion. And all of this is always symbolically connected with the tolling of the bell, the poem closely following the purposes the bell serves at various occasions. I do not know of a poem in any language which, in such condensed form, reveals such a wide poetic orbit, covering the gamut of all of the deepest human emotions, and which, entirely in lyric style, depicts life and its most important phases and events as one epoch surrounded by natural borders. The poetic clearness is still further intensified by the fact that the visions conjured up in the distance by the imagination, simultaneously correspond to the actual description of an object, and that the two thus formed thought columns run parallel side by side toward the same goal.

WILHELM VON HUMBOLDT
Briefwechsel zwischen Schiller und Wilhelm v. Humboldt (1830)

RICHARD PORSON

1 7 5 9 — 1 8 0 8

NATURAL PHILOSOPHY

He was in his customary state one night. Wishing to blow out his candle, and seeing, as is said to be the way of the inebriated, two flames side by side where there was only one, he three times directed his swaying steps to the wrong image, and three times blew, with no effect, for the non-existent cannot be extinguished. Whereupon he drew back, balanced himself, and gave verdict: "Damn the nature of things!"

Anecdote

To the drunkenness of Porson we owe, it must be granted, the pro-
foundest utterance of pessimism that has ever fallen from mortal lips.

PAUL ELMER MORE
Selected Shelburne Essays (1935)

ANDRÉ CHÉNIER

1 7 6 2 — 1 7 9 4

NÉÈRE

Mais telle qu'à sa mort, pour la dernière fois,
Un beau cygne soupire, et de sa douce voix,
De sa voix qui bientôt lui doit être ravie,
Chante, avant de partir, ses adieux à la vie:
Ainsi, les yeux remplis de langueur et de mort,
Pâle, elle ouvrit sa bouche en un dernier effort:

"O vous, du Sébethus naïades vagabondes,
Coupez sur mon tombeau vos chevelures blondes.
Adieu, mon Clinias! moi, celle qui te plus,
Moi, celle qui t'aimai, que tu ne verras plus.
O cieux, ô terre, ô mer, prés, montagnes, rivages,
Fleurs, bois mélodieux, vallons, grottes sauvages,
Rappelez-lui souvent, rappelez-lui toujours
Néère tout son bien, Néère ses amours;
Cette Néère, hélas! qu'il nommait sa Néère,
Qui, pour lui criminelle, abandonna sa mère;
Qui, pour lui fugitive, errant de lieux en lieux,
Aux regards des humains n'osa lever les yeux.
Oh! soit que l'astre pur des deux frères d'Hélène
Calme sous ton vaisseau la vague ionienne;
Soit qu'aux bords de Pœstum, sous ta soigneuse main,
. Les roses deux fois l'an couronnent ton jardin,
Au coucher du soleil, si ton âme attendrie
Tombe en une muette et molle rêverie,
Alors, mon Clinias, appelle, appelle-moi.
Je viendrai, Clinias; je volerai vers toi.
Mon âme vagabonde, à travers le feuillage,
Frémira; sur les vents ou sur quelque nuage
Tu la verras descendre, ou du sein de la mer,
S'élevant comme un songe, étinceler dans l'air,

1006

Et ma voix, toujours tendre et doucement plaintive,
Caresser, en fuyant, ton oreille attentive."

Ev'n as a lovely swan before he dies,
For the last time, with tender accent sighs,
With a sweet voice, that soon shall cease to be,
Sings, ere he goes, his parting melody:
So, her eyes full of languor and of death,
All pale, she spoke, striving for her last breath:

"Ye wandering naïads of a stream so dear,
Sever your golden locks upon my bier.
Farewell, my Clinias! Thy love was true;
We part for ever; ah! I loved thee too.
O Heaven, Earth, Sea, O mountains, fields and dales,
Flowers, murmuring woods, and savage grots, and vales,
Oft to his mind recall, and still recall
His own Néère, his love, his life, his all;
Néère, alas! whom he called his Néère,
Who, sinful, left her home his lot to share;
Who for him fugitive from place to place,
No more might raise her eyes to human face.
O when the star of Hellen's twins for thee
Beneath thy vessel calm the Ionian sea,
Or when on Pœstum's banks, taught by thy care,
The garden twice a year shall roses bear,
At sunset, if thy heart should gently beat,
Wrapt in a silent reverie and sweet,
Then call, my Clinias, then call on me.
I will come, Clinias; I'll fly to thee.
My errant sprite will sigh the leaves among;
Upon the clouds or breezes borne along,
Descending will appear, or she will seem,
Arising from the ocean, like a dream,
And my voice, ever tender, fleeting near,
Shall, sweetly plaintive, soothe thy listening ear."

Bucoliques, xiii
Translated by Charles Richard Cammell

The simplest and most touching, and one of the most perfectly beautiful poems of the French language.

JOSÉ-MARIA DE HEREDIA
Le Manuscrit des *Bucoliques* (Revue des Deux Mondes, 1905)

LES BELLES FONT AIMER

Jeune fille ton cœur avec nous veut se taire.
Tu fuis, tu ne ris plus; rien ne saurait te plaire.
La soie à tes travaux offre en vain des couleurs;
L'aiguille sous tes doigts n'anime plus des fleurs.
Tu n'aimes qu'à rêver, muette, seule, errante,
Et la rose pâlit sur ta bouche expirante.
Ah! mon œil est savant et depuis plus d'un jour,
Et ce n'est pas à moi qu'on peut cacher l'amour.

Les belles font aimer; elles aiment. Les belles
Nous charment tous. Heureux qui peut être aimé d'elles!
Sois tendre, même faible (on doit l'être un moment),
Fidèle, si tu peux. Mais conte-moi comment,
Quel jeune homme aux yeux bleus, empressé sans audace,
Aux cheveux noirs, au front plein de charme et de grâce . . .
Tu rougis? On dirait que je t'ai dit son nom.
Je le connais pourtant. Autour de ta maison
C'est lui qui va, qui vient; et, laissant ton ouvrage,
Tu vas, sans te montrer, épier son passage.
Il fuit vite; et ton œil, sur sa trace accouru,
Le suit encor longtemps quand il a disparu.
Nul, en ce bois voisin où trois fêtes brillantes
Font voler au printemps nos nymphes triomphantes,
Nul n'a sa noble aisance et son habile main
A soumettre un coursier aux volontés du frein.

BEAUTIES AROUSE LOVE

Young girl, your heart prefers silence with us; you dash away and
laugh no longer; nothing pleases you. Silk vainly offers its colors to your
industrious hands; no longer does the needle bring flowers to life under
your fingers. Your only passion is dreaming, silent, alone, wandering,
and the rose pales on your languishing lips. Ah! my eye is too keen and
too experienced to conceal from me that you are in love. Beauties arouse
love; and they themselves love. Beauties charm us. Happy is he who
can be loved by them! Be tender, even yielding (one should be for a
moment); faithful, if you can. But tell me how, and who, is the young
man with blue eyes, eager but not bold, with black hair, with forehead

full of charm and grace? Are you blushing? One would think I almost named him. I know him, however. It is he who goes and comes around your house, and, abandoning your work, you run without showing yourself to watch for his passing. He goes quickly; and your eye following after his footsteps seeks him long after he has vanished. Doubtless no one in this nearby wood, where three brilliant festivals make our triumphant nymphs carol aloft in springtime, possesses his noble ease and ability of hand to subject a race horse to the will of the bit.

Œuvres posthumes (1819)

It is impossible to portray better and to leave more understood in fewer words. This short fragment comprises a sketch of an entire gracious romance whose continuation is easy to anticipate, a marvellous portrait worthy of a great Greek artist and of his imitator. André Chénier here attains perfection.

ÉMILE FAGUET
Histoire de la poésie française (1936)

ANDRÉ CHÉNIER

1 7 6 2 — 1 7 9 4

LA JEUNE TARENTINE

Pleurez, doux alcyons! ô vous oiseaux sacrés!
Oiseaux chers à Téthys! doux alcyons, pleurez!

Elle a vécu, Myrto, la jeune Tarentine!
Un vaisseau la portait aux bords de Camarine:
Là, l'hymen, les chansons, les flûtes, lentement
Devaient la reconduire au seuil de son amant.
Une clef vigilante a, pour cette journée,
Dans le cèdre enfermé sa robe d'hyménée,
Et l'or dont au festin ses bras seraient parés,
Et pour ses blonds cheveux les parfums préparés.
Mais, seule sur la proue, invoquant les étoiles,
Le vent impétueux qui soufflait dans les voiles
L'enveloppe: étonnée et loin des matelots,
Elle crie, elle tombe, elle est au sein des flots.

Elle est au sein des flots, la jeune Tarentine!
Son beau corps a roulé sous la vague marine.

Téthys, les yeux en pleurs, dans le creux d'un rocher
Aux monstres dévorants eut soin de le cacher.
Par ses ordres bientôt les belles Néréides
L'élèvent au-dessus des demeures humides,
Le portent au rivage, et dans ce monument
L'ont au cap du Zéphyr déposé mollement;
Puis de loin, à grands cris appelant leurs compagnes,
Et les nymphes des bois, des sources, des montagnes,
Toutes, frappant leur sein et traînant un long deuil,
Répétèrent, hélas! autour de son cercueil:
Hélas! chez ton amant tu n'es point ramenée,
Tu n'as point revêtu ta robe d'hyménée,
L'or autour de tes bras n'a point serré de nœuds,
Les doux parfums n'ont point coulé sur tes cheveux.

THE YOUNG TARENTINE

Weep, gentle halcyons, by the moaning deep,
Loved birds of Tethys, sacred halcyons, weep!
   The young Tarentine, Myrto, is no more!
Myrto who sailed for Camarina's shore,
Where Hymen for her coming, all day long,
Sat waiting, myrtle-crowned, with flute and song
To lift her past the threshold as a bride.
Her wedding-robe lay shining, Tyrian-dyed,
In cedarn chest, and golden bands lay there,
And odorous nard to sprinkle on her hair.
   Charmed by the stars, all heedless of the gale
That rose afar and puffed the bellying sail,
She seaward leans—no sailor at her side—
She shrieks, she falls, she sinks below the tide.
The young Tarentine in the sea is lost,
Her lovely body by the salt waves tossed.
   White Tethys, grieving, in a hollow rock
From dragon jaws and the mad ocean's shock
Hides her away, and ever-weeping bids
The band attendant of her Nereids
Lift her, thus sepulchred, from out the deep
To where a promontory rises steep,
Sacred to Zephyr. Here the golden-tressed
Tarentine virgin lies in lonely rest.
Here all the sister nymphs flock from their fountains,
Fair Dryades and Oreads from the mountains.

In slow procession round her tomb they move,
Mourning her early death and hapless love,
Beating their breasts and crying loud, "Alas!
Alas, that thy brief day so soon should pass!
Thou hast not rested in thy lover's arms,
No hymeneal robe has graced thy charms,
Thy slender wrists no golden circlets wear,
No bridal wreath perfumes thy floating hair."

Œuvres posthumes (1819)
Translated by William Frederic Giese

Son of a Greek mother, he was born at Constantinople, traveled in Italy, and stayed three years in London. He read the English and Italian poets in the original. But above everything his contact with Greek poetry is probably the most intimate known to modern man. He is, even more than Ronsard, our great poet-philologer.

ALBERT THIBAUDET
Histoire de la littérature française (1936)

ANDRÉ CHÉNIER

1 7 6 2 — 1 7 9 4

TESTAMENT

Il est las de partager la honte de cette foule immense qui en secret abhorre autant que lui, mais qui approuve et encourage, au moins par son silence, des hommes atroces et des actions abominables. La vie ne vaut pas tant d'opprobre. Quand les tréteaux, les tavernes et les lieux de débauche vomissent par milliers des législateurs, des magistrats et des généraux d'armée qui sortent de la boue pour le bien de la patrie, il a, lui, une autre ambition, et il ne croit pas démériter de sa patrie en faisant dire un jour: Ce pays, qui produisit alors tant de prodiges d'imbécillité et de bassesse, produisit aussi un petit nombre d'hommes qui ne renoncèrent ni à leur raison ni à leur conscience; témoins des triomphes du vice, ils restèrent amis de la vertu et ne rougirent point d'être gens de bien. Dans ces temps de violence, ils osèrent parler de justice; dans ces temps de démence, ils osèrent examiner; dans ces temps de la plus abjecte hypocrisie, ils ne feignirent point d'être des scélérats pour acheter leur repos aux dépens de l'innocence opprimée; ils ne cachèrent point leur haine à des bourreaux qui, pour payer leurs amis et punir leurs ennemis, n'épargnaient rien, car il ne leur en coûtait que des crimes;

et un nommé. **A. C.** (*André Chénier*) fut un des cinq ou six que ni la frénésie générale, ni l'avidité, ni la crainte, ne purent engager à ployer le genou devant des assassins couronnés, à toucher des mains souillées de meurtres, et à s'asseoir à la table où l'on boit le sang des hommes.

He is weary of sharing the shame of this immense crowd who secretly abhor as much as he does, but who approve and encourage, at least by their silence, atrocious men and abominable actions. Life is not worth so much opprobrium. When the booths, the taverns and houses of debauchery vomit by the thousand legislators, magistrates and army generals who rise out of the mire for the good of their country, *he* has another ambition, and he does not think himself undeserving of his country, if some day he makes her say: This country, which at that time produced so many prodigies of imbecility and baseness, also produced a small number of men who renounced neither their reason nor their conscience; witnessing the triumphs of vice, they remained friends of virtue and did not blush to be honourable men. In these times of violence they dared to speak of justice; in these times of dementia, they dared to question; in these times of the most abject hypocrisy, they did not feign to be wicked in order to buy their repose at the price of oppressed innocence; they did not conceal their hatred from villains who, to reward their friends and punish their enemies, spared nothing, for it cost them nothing but crimes; and a certain A. C. (*André Chénier*) was among those five or six whom neither the general frenzy, nor avidity, nor fear, could induce to bend the knee before crowned assassins, to touch hands stained by murders, and to sit down to a table where they drink human blood.

Whatever political line a man may follow (and I do not pretend that that followed by André Chénier was strictly speaking the only and the true one), this manner of being and feeling in a time of revolution, especially when it is finally confirmed and consecrated by death, will be ever reputed MORALLY *the most heroic and the most beautiful, the most worthy of all to be proposed to the respect of man.*

C.-A. SAINTE-BEUVE
Causeries du lundi (1851)
Translated by E. J. Trechmann

HONOR, GLORY AND WEALTH

Soldats, vous êtes nus, mal nourris; le gouvernement vous doit beaucoup, il ne peut rien vous donner. Votre patience, le courage que vous montrez au milieu de ces rochers, sont admirables; mais ils ne vous procurent aucune gloire; aucun éclat ne rejaillit sur vous. Je veux vous conduire dans les plus fertiles plaines du monde. De riches provinces, de grandes villes seront en votre pouvoir; vous y trouverez, honneur, gloire et richesses. Soldats d'Italie, manquerez-vous de courage ou de constance?

Soldiers, you are naked, poorly fed; the government owes you much, it can give you nothing. Your patience, the courage that you show in the midst of these rocks, are admirable, but they bring you no glory; no renown reflects on you. I want to lead you to the most fertile plains of the world. Rich provinces, large cities will be in your power; you will find there honor, glory, and wealth. Soldiers of Italy, will you lack courage or constancy?

Proclamation du général en chef, à l'ouverture de la campagne, au quartier général à Nice, 28 mars 1796.

He instinctively discovered the military eloquence of which he is the model; he invented the form of address suited to French valour and made to electrify. Henri IV had his flashes of eloquence, happy sallies of wit which were repeated by Crillon and the nobles; but, here was wanted an eloquence on the new level of the great operations, adapted to the measure of those armies risen from the people, the brief, grave, familiar, monumental address. From the first day, among his means for waging great war, Napoleon discovered that one.

C.-A. SAINTE-BEUVE
Causeries du lundi (1849)
Translated by E. J. Trechmann

WILLIAM WORDSWORTH

1 7 7 0 — 1 8 5 0

A SENSE SUBLIME

Whose dwelling is the light of setting suns.

Tintern Abbey (1798)

The line is almost the grandest in the English language.

ALFRED LORD TENNYSON

Alfred Lord Tennyson: A Memoir by Hallam Tennyson (1897)

WILLIAM WORDSWORTH

1 7 7 0 — 1 8 5 0

NATURE'S GIFTS TO LUCY

"The stars of midnight shall be dear
To her; and she shall lean her ear
In many a secret place
Where rivulets dance their wayward round,
And beauty born of murmuring sound
Shall pass into her face."

Three Years She Grew in
Sun and Shower (1800)

Take those two last lines, and realize how impossible it would have been for them to have been written by Shakespeare, or Spenser, or Milton, or whomever one may happen to think the greatest of his predecessors; and it will help one to measure the authentic greatness of Wordsworth.

For that great advance of sympathy with nature, the quiet, unadorned purity of style which Wordsworth reached in his happiest moments of inspiration was surely the best. It is so singularly free from mannerism, from that accent of individual self-importance which at other times fell on his work; so pure and unmannered and natural.

At its best his form is so pure that it rises to a style which seems to embrace the highest common factor of other styles.

LAURENCE HOUSMAN

A Wordsworth Anthology (1946)

WILLIAM WORDSWORTH

1 7 7 0 — 1 8 5 0

SLEEPLESS SOUL

The sleepless Soul that perished in his pride.
>   Resolution and Independence (1802)

*I will back that against any of Mr. Arnold's three representative quota-
tions from Homer, from Dante, and from Shakespeare.* It is like nothing from any other hand: the unspeakable greatness of its quality is
Wordsworth's alone: and I doubt if it would really be as rash as it might
seem to maintain that there is not and never will be a greater verse in
all the world of song.*
>   ALGERNON CHARLES SWINBURNE
>   Miscellanies (1886)

WILLIAM WORDSWORTH

1 7 7 0 — 1 8 5 0

THE SOLITARY REAPER

> Behold her, single in the field,
> Yon solitary Highland Lass!
> Reaping and singing by herself;
> Stop here, or gently pass!
> Alone she cuts and binds the grain,
> And sings a melancholy strain;
> O listen! for the Vale profound
> Is overflowing with the sound.
>
> No Nightingale did ever chaunt
> More welcome notes to weary bands
> Of travellers in some shady haunt,
> Among Arabian sands:
> A voice so thrilling ne'er was heard
> In spring-time from the Cuckoo-bird,
> Breaking the silence of the seas
> Among the farthest Hebrides.

---

* For the Matthew Arnold quotations see Appendix.

Will no one tell me what she sings?—
Perhaps the plaintive numbers flow
For old, unhappy, far-off things,
And battles long ago:
Or is it some more humble lay,
Familiar matter of to-day?
Some natural sorrow, loss, or pain,
That has been, and may be again?

Whate'er the theme, the Maiden sang
As if her song could have no ending;
I saw her singing at her work,
And o'er the sickle bending;—
I listened, motionless and still;
And, as I mounted up the hill
The music in my heart I bore,
Long after it was heard no more.

(1803)

*I will give it as my opinion now, that if we were to grant the indepen-
dence of poetic music or magic, then no poet is so rich in these qualities
as Wordsworth. He had the capacity of endowing words of the most
commonplace associations with the light or radiant emanation of ideal
glory. The most perfect example of this supernal strain is, in my own
opinion, the poem called* THE SOLITARY REAPER, *which poem I would
always send out into the world of letters to represent the quintessence
of English poetry.*

HERBERT READ
Phases of English Poetry (1929)

WILLIAM WORDSWORTH

1 7 7 0 — 1 8 5 0

THE BOY'S FEAR AFTER STEALING
A TRAPPED BIRD FROM A SNARE

Low breathings coming after me, and sounds
Of undistinguishable motion, steps
Almost as silent as the turf they trod.

The Prelude (1799–1805), i

1016

HE REMEMBERS THE VISTA
OF A TOWERING PEAK

After I had seen
That spectacle, for many days, my brain
Worked with a dim and undetermined sense
Of unknown modes of being; o'er my thoughts
There hung a darkness, call it solitude
Or blank desertion. No familiar shapes
Remained, no pleasant images of trees,
Of sea or sky, no colours of green fields;
But huge and mighty forms, that do not live
Like living men, moved slowly through the mind
By day, and were a trouble to my dreams.

The Prelude (1799–1805), i

The second passage is an enlargement of the first, and they are both great poetry. The poetic mind is aware of 'low breathings', 'sounds of undistinguishable motion', 'unknown modes of being', 'huge and mighty forms'. It is the pressure of the genius on the outer consciousness.

CHARLES WILLIAMS
The English Poetic Mind (1932)

WILLIAM WORDSWORTH

1 7 7 0 — 1 8 5 0

SOLITUDE

The antechapel where the statue stood
Of Newton with his prism and silent face,
The marble index of a mind for ever
Voyaging through strange seas of Thought, alone.

The Prelude (1799–1805), iii

No finer lines on solitude are found in English.

IRVING BABBITT
Rousseau and Romanticism (1919)

WILLIAM WORDSWORTH

1 7 7 0 — 1 8 5 0

TO H. C.

SIX YEARS OLD

O thou! whose fancies from afar are brought;
Who of thy words dost make a mock apparel,
And fittest to unutterable thought
The breeze-like motion and the self-born carol;
Thou faery voyager! that dost float
In such clear water, that thy boat
May rather seem
To brood on air than on an earthly stream;
Suspended in a stream as clear as sky,
  Where earth and heaven do make one imagery;
O blessed vision! happy child!
Thou art so exquisitely wild,
I think of thee with many fears
For what may be thy lot in future years.

  I thought of times when Pain might be thy guest,
Lord of thy house and hospitality;
And Grief, uneasy lover! never rest
But when she sate within the touch of thee.
O too industrious folly!
O vain and causeless melancholy!
Nature will either end thee quite;
Or, lengthening out thy season of delight,
Preserve for thee, by individual right,
A young lamb's heart among the full-grown flocks.
What hast thou to do with sorrow,
Or the injuries of to-morrow?
Thou art a dew-drop, which the morn brings forth,
Ill fitted to sustain unkindly shocks,
Or to be trailed along the soiling earth;
A gem that glitters while it lives,
And no forewarning gives;
But, at the touch of wrong, without a strife
Slips in a moment out of life.

(1807)

When Hartley [Coleridge] was six years old, he addressed to him these
verses, perhaps the best ever written on a real and visible child.

WALTER BAGEHOT
Literary Studies (1878)

WILLIAM WORDSWORTH

1 7 7 0 — 1 8 5 0

THE WORLD

Great God! I'd rather be
A Pagan suckled in a creed outworn;
So might I, standing on this pleasant lea,
Have glimpses that would make me less forlorn;
Have sight of Proteus rising from the sea;
Or hear old Triton blow his wreathèd horn.

The World is too Much with Us (1806)

*The most famous expression in English of that longing for the perished
glory of Greek myth which appears in much Romantic poetry.*

A. C. BRADLEY
Oxford Lectures on Poetry (1923)

WILLIAM WORDSWORTH

1 7 7 0 — 1 8 5 0

TO TOUSSAINT L'OUVERTURE

Thou hast left behind
Powers that will work for thee; air, earth, and skies;
There's not a breathing of the common wind
That will forget thee; thou hast great allies;
Thy friends are exultations, agonies,
And love, and man's unconquerable mind.

(1807)

The finest sextet to be found anywhere.

FRANK HARRIS
My Life and Loves (1922–27)

ODE

INTIMATIONS OF IMMORTALITY
FROM RECOLLECTIONS
OF EARLY CHILDHOOD

I

There was a time when meadow, grove, and stream,
The earth, and every common sight,
   To me did seem
  Apparelled in celestial light,
The glory and the freshness of a dream.
It is not now as it hath been of yore;—
   Turn wheresoe'er I may,
    By night or day,
The things which I have seen I now can see no more.

II

  The Rainbow comes and goes,
  And lovely is the Rose,
  The Moon doth with delight
Look round her when the heavens are bare,
  Waters on a starry night
  Are beautiful and fair;
 The sunshine is a glorious birth;
 But yet I know, where'er I go,
That there hath past away a glory from the earth.

III

Now, while the birds thus sing a joyous song,
 And while the young lambs bound
  As to the tabor's sound,
To me alone there came a thought of grief:
A timely utterance gave that thought relief,
  And I again am strong:
The cataracts blow their trumpets from the steep;
No more shall grief of mine the season wrong;
I hear the Echoes through the mountains throng,

The Winds come to me from the fields of sleep,
    And all the earth is gay;
      Land and sea
   Give themselves up to jollity,
     And with the heart of May
  Doth every Beast keep holiday;—
     Thou Child of Joy,
Shout round me, let me hear thy shouts, thou happy
     Shepherd-boy!

IV

Ye blessèd Creatures, I have heard the call
  Ye to each other make; I see
The heavens laugh with you in your jubilee;
    My heart is at your festival,
    My head hath its coronal,
The fulness of your bliss, I feel—I feel it all.
   Oh evil day! if I were sullen
   While Earth herself is adorning,
     This sweet May-morning,
   And the Children are culling
     On every side,
  In a thousand valleys far and wide,
  Fresh flowers; while the sun shines warm,
And the Babe leaps up on his Mother's arm:—
   I hear, I hear, with joy I hear!
  —But there's a Tree, of many, one,
A single Field which I have looked upon,
Both of them speak of something that is gone:
   The Pansy at my feet
   Doth the same tale repeat:
Whither is fled the visionary gleam?
Where is it now, the glory and the dream?

V

Our birth is but a sleep and a forgetting:
The Soul that rises with us, our life's Star,
   Hath had elsewhere its setting,
     And cometh from afar:
   Not in entire forgetfulness,
   And not in utter nakedness,
But trailing clouds of glory do we come
   From God, who is our home:

Heaven lies about us in our infancy!
Shades of the prison-house begin to close
    Upon the growing Boy,
But He beholds the light, and whence it flows,
    He sees it in his joy;
The youth, who daily farther from the east
    Must travel, still is Nature's Priest,
    And by the vision splendid
    Is on his way attended;
At length the Man perceives it die away,
And fade into the light of common day.

VI

Earth fills her lap with pleasures of her own;
Yearnings she hath in her own natural kind,
And, even with something of a Mother's mind,
    And no unworthy aim,
    The homely Nurse doth all she can
To make her Foster-child, her Inmate Man,
    Forget the glories he hath known,
And that imperial palace whence he came.

VII

Behold the Child among his new-born blisses,
A six years' Darling of a pigmy size!
See, where 'mid work of his own hand he lies,
Fretted by sallies of his mother's kisses,
With light upon him from his father's eyes!
See, at his feet, some little plan or chart,
Some fragment from his dream of human life,
Shaped by himself with newly-learned art;
    A wedding or a festival,
    A mourning or a funeral;
        And this hath now his heart,
    And unto this he frames his song:
        Then will he fit his tongue
To dialogues of business, love, or strife;
    But it will not be long
    Ere this be thrown aside,
    And with new joy and pride
The little Actor cons another part;
Filling from time to time his "humorous stage"
With all the Persons, down to palsied Age,
That Life brings with her in her equipage;

As if his whole vocation
Were endless imitation.

VIII

Thou, whose exterior semblance doth belie
   Thy Soul's immensity;
Thou best Philosopher, who yet dost keep
Thy heritage, thou Eye among the blind,
That, deaf and silent, read'st the eternal deep,
Haunted for ever by the eternal mind,—
   Mighty Prophet! Seer blest!
   On whom those truths do rest,
Which we are toiling all our lives to find,
In darkness lost, the darkness of the grave;
Thou, over whom thy Immortality
Broods like the Day, a Master o'er a Slave,
A Presence which is not to be put by;
Thou little Child, yet glorious in the might
Of heaven-born freedom on thy being's height,
Why with such earnest pains dost thou provoke
The years to bring the inevitable yoke,
Thus blindly with thy blessedness at strife?
Full soon thy Soul shall have her earthly freight,
And custom lie upon thee with a weight,
Heavy as frost, and deep almost as life!

IX

   O joy! that in our embers
   Is something that doth live,
   That nature yet remembers
   What was so fugitive!
The thought of our past years in me doth breed
Perpetual benediction: not indeed
For that which is most worthy to be blest—
Delight and liberty, the simple creed
Of Childhood, whether busy or at rest,
With new-fledged hope still fluttering in his breast:—
   Not for these I raise
   The song of thanks and praise;
  But for those obstinate questionings
  Of sense and outward things,
  Fallings from us, vanishings;
  Blank misgivings of a Creature

Moving about in worlds not realised,
High instincts before which our mortal Nature
Did tremble like a guilty Thing surprised:
    But for those first affections,
    Those shadowy recollections,
  Which, be they what they may,
Are yet the fountain light of all our day,
Are yet a master light of all our seeing;
   Uphold us, cherish, and have power to make
Our noisy years seem moments in the being
Of the eternal Silence: truths that wake,
    To perish never;
Which neither listlessness, nor mad endeavour,
    Nor Man nor Boy,
Nor all that is at enmity with joy,
Can utterly abolish or destroy!
    Hence in a season of calm weather
    Though inland far we be,
Our Souls have sight of that immortal sea
    Which brought us hither,
    Can in a moment travel thither,
And see the Children sport upon the shore,
And hear the mighty waters rolling evermore.

X

Then sing, ye Birds, sing, sing a joyous song!
    And let the young Lambs bound
    As to the tabor's sound!
We in thought will join your throng,
    Ye that pipe and ye that play,
    Ye that through your hearts to-day
    Feel the gladness of the May!
What though the radiance which was once so bright
Be now for ever taken from my sight,
    Though nothing can bring back the hour
Of splendour in the grass, of glory in the flower;
    We will grieve not, rather find
    Strength in what remains behind;
    In the primal sympathy
    Which having been must ever be;
    In the soothing thoughts that spring
    Out of human suffering;
    In the faith that looks through death,
In years that bring the philosophic mind.

And O, ye Fountains, Meadows, Hills, and Groves,
Forebode not any severing of our loves!
Yet in my heart of hearts I feel your might;
I only have relinquished one delight
To live beneath your more habitual sway.
I love the Brooks which down their channels fret,
Even more than when I tripped lightly as they;
The innocent brightness of a new-born Day
    Is lovely yet;
The Clouds that gather round the setting sun
Do take a sober colouring from an eye
That hath kept watch o'er man's mortality;
Another race hath been, and other palms are won.
Thanks to the human heart by which we live,
Thanks to its tenderness, its joys, and fears,
To me the meanest flower that blows can give
Thoughts that do often lie too deep for tears.

          (1807)

*The Ode remains not merely the greatest, but the one really, dazzlingly,
supremely great thing he ever did. Its theory has been scorned or im-
pugned by some; parts of it have even been called nonsense by critics
of weight. But, sound or unsound, sense or nonsense, it is poetry, and
magnificent poetry, from the first line to the last—poetry than which
there is none better in any language, poetry such as there is not perhaps
more than a small volume-full in all languages.*

GEORGE SAINTSBURY
A History of Nineteenth Century Literature (1896)

FRIEDRICH HÖLDERLIN

1 7 7 0 — 1 8 4 3

DER BLINDE SÄNGER

Ἔλυσεν αἰνὸν ἄχος ἀπ᾽ ὀμμάτων Ἄρης

SOPHOCLES

Wo bist du, Jugendliches! das immer mich
Zur Stunde weckt des Morgens, wo bist du, Licht?
    Das Herz ist wach, doch bannt und hält in
    Heiligem Zauber die Nacht mich immer.

Sonst lauscht' ich um die Dämmerung gern, sonst harrt'
Ich gerne dein am Hügel, und nie umsonst!
    Nie täuschten mich, du Holdes, deine
      Boten, die Lüfte, denn immer kamst du,

Kamst allbeseligend den gewohnten Pfad
Herein in deiner Schöne, wo bist du, Licht!
    Das Herz ist wieder wach, doch bannt und
      Hemmt die unendliche Nacht mich immer.

Mir grünten sonst die Lauben; es leuchteten
Die Blumen, wie die eigenen Augen, mir;
    Nicht ferne war das Angesicht der
      Meinen und leuchtete mir und droben

Und um die Wälder sah ich die Fittige
Des Himmels wandern, da ich ein Jüngling war;
    Nun sitz ich still allein, von einer
      Stunde zur anderen und Gestalten

Aus Lieb und Leid der helleren Tage schafft
Zur eignen Freude nun mein Gedanke sich,
    Und ferne lausch' ich hin, ob nicht ein
      Freundlicher Retter vieleicht mir komme.

Dann hör' ich oft die Stimme des Donnerers
Am Mittag, wenn der eherne nahe kommt,
    Wenn ihm das Haus bebt und der Boden
      Unter ihm dröhnt und der Berg es nachhallt.

Den Retter hör' ich dann in der Nacht, ich hör'
Ihn tödtend, den Befreier, belebend ihn,
    Den Donnerer vom Untergang zum
      Orient eilen, und ihm nach tönt ihr,

Ihm nach, ihr meine Saiten! es lebt mit ihm
Mein Lied, und wie die Quelle dem Strome folgt,
    Wohin er denkt, so muss ich fort und
      Folge dem Sicheren auf der Irrbahn.

Wohin? wohin? ich höre dich da und dort
Du Herrlicher! und rings um die Erde tönts
    Wo endest du? und was, was ist es
      Über den Wolken und o wie wird mir?

Tag! Tag! Du über stürzenden Wolken! sei
Willkommen mir! es blühet mein Auge dir.
    O jugendlicht! o Glück! das alte
      Wieder! doch geistiger rinnst du nieder

Du goldner Quell aus heiligem Kelch! und du,
Du grüner Boden, friedliche Wieg'! und du,
  Haus meiner Väter! und ihr Lieben,
  Die mir begegneten einst, o nahet,

O kommt, dass euer, euer die Freude sei,
Ihr alle, dass euch segne der Sehende!
  O nimmt, dass ichs ertrage, mir das
  Leben, das Göttliche mir vom Herzen.

THE BLIND SINGER

Where are you, ever-youthful, that day by day
Awakened me at morning, where are you, Light?
  My heart's indeed awake, but still in
  Sacred enchantment the Night enchains me.

How gladly once I'd hearken at dawn, or wait,
And never vainly, out on the hill for you:
  Your messengers, dear Light, the breezes,
  Never deceived, for you always came then,

Came all-enkindling down the accustomed path
In all your wonted beauty. Where are you, Light?
  My heart's awake once more, and yet this
  Night that is infinite bans and binds me.

For me the leaves once glittered in green, for me,
Like my own eyes, the flowers were luminous;
  The countenance of those I loved still
  Lightened upon me, and high above me

And round the woods, in days of my youth, I saw
The winged things of heaven go wandering;
  But now I sit alone in silence,
  Hour after hour, with thought still weaving

From love and sorrow gathered in brighter days
The shapes that only serve for its own delight,
  And hearken lest far off some kindly
  Rescuer be not perchance approaching.

And often then the voice of the Thunderer,
Whose brazen car draws nearer at noon, I hear,
  When all the house will quake, and Earth will
  Rumble below and the hills re-echo:

The Rescuer then I hear in the night, I hear
The Slayer, Liberator, Reviver then,
    The Thund'rer, who from Occident to
    Orient hastens, and you re-echo,

Whom you, my strings, re-echo! With whom my song
Revives, and, ev'n as springs after rivers speed,
    I needs must go where he shall choose, and
    Follow his certainty through the mazes.

But where? But where? I hear you on ev'ry hand,
Whose glory all the earth is resounding with:
    Where will you end? And what, what is it
    Over the clouds there, and, oh, where am I?

Day! Day! arising over the ruining
Of clouds! My eyes, they blossom to welcome you!
    O Light of Youth! O Joy restored, but
    Now a more spiritual essence, pouring

From consecrated chalice your golden stream!
And you, my peaceful cradle, green Earth! And you,
    My fathers' house! and you, my dear ones,
    You that would throng to me once, come hither,

Oh, come, that his delight may be your delight,
And that to-day the Seer may bless you all,
    Oh, come and take, that I may bear it,
    Take from my heart this divine existence!

Translated by J. B. Leishman

Perhaps greater mastery of technique than in any other German poem.

AGNES STANSFIELD
Hölderlin (1944)

FRIEDRICH HÖLDERLIN

1 7 7 0 — 1 8 4 3

THE DEATH OF EMPEDOCLES

Ihr dürft leben,
solange ihr Odem habt; ich nicht. Es muss
beizeiten weg, durch wen der Geist geredet.
Es offenbart die göttliche Natur
sich göttlich oft durch Menschen, so erkennt
das vielversuchende Geschlecht sie wieder,

doch hat der Sterbliche, dem sie das Herz
mit ihrer Wonne füllten, sie verkündet,
o lasst sie dann zerbrechen das Gefäss,
damit es nicht zu anderm Brauche dien'
und Göttliches zum Menschenwerke werde.
Lasst diese Glücklichen doch sterben, lasst,
eh sie in Eigenmacht und Tand und Schmach
vergehn, die Freien sich bei guter Zeit
den Göttern liebend opfern. Mein ist dies
und wohlbewusst ist mir mein Los und längst
am jugendlichen Tage hab' ich mirs
geweissagt; ehret mirs! Und wenn ihr morgen
mich nimmer findet, sprecht: veralten sollt'
er nicht und Tage zählen, dienen nicht
der Sorge, Krankheit, ungesehen ging
er weg und keines Menschen Hand begrub ihn,
und keines Auge weiss von seiner Asche;
denn anders ziemt es nicht für ihn, vor dem
in todesfroher Stund' am heilgen Tage
das Göttliche den Schleier abgeworfen.

You are permitted to live so long as you have breath; not I. He
through whom the spirit has spoken must depart early. Often the divine
Nature reveals itself divinely through man, and it is, as a consequence,
again recognized by a much-endeavoring generation. However as soon
as Nature has been proclaimed by a mortal, whose heart she filled with
her rapture, let Nature break the vessel, so that it may not serve other
uses and so that the divine may not become the work of man. Let such
happy ones die—let the free offer themselves in good time, lovingly as
a sacrifice for the Gods, before they perish by their arbitrary power and
trifling and shame. This is my lot, and well aware am I of it. Long ago
in the early days of my youth I foretold it myself. Honor me for it! And
if tomorrow you no longer find me, say: to grow old and count the days
was not for him, nor to serve sorrow's illness. He departed unseen, and
no human hand buried him, and no eye knows of his ashes. For anything else would not have been fitting for him before whom on the holy
day, in the joyful hour of death, divinity cast off its veil.

Der Tod des Empedokles (1798–99)

*Never surely did any poet speak so out of his heart, yet in language so
perfect and so glorious.*

MARSHALL MONTGOMERY
Studies in the Age of Goethe (1931)

FLODDEN FIELD

But as they left the darkening heath
More desperate grew the strife of death.
The English shafts in volleys hailed,
In headlong charge their horse assailed;
Front, flank, and rear, the squadrons sweep
To break the Scottish circle deep
　That fought around their king.
But yet, though thick the shafts as snow,
Though charging knights like whirlwinds go,
Though billmen ply the ghastly blow,
　Unbroken was the ring;
The stubborn spearmen still made good
Their dark impenetrable wood,
Each stepping where his comrade stood
　The instant that he fell.
No thought was there of dastard flight;
Linked in the serried phalanx tight,
Groom fought like noble, squire like knight,
　As fearlessly and well.
　　　　　　Marmion, a Tale of Flodden Field (1808), vi

Here, at least, Scott rose to epic heights.
　　　　HERBERT J. C. GRIERSON and J. C. SMITH
　　　　A Critical History of English Poetry (1944)

———

SIR WALTER SCOTT

1 7 7 1 — 1 8 3 2

MEG MERRILIES

'Ride your ways,' said the gipsy, 'ride your ways, Laird of Ellan-gowan—ride your ways, Godfrey Bertram! This day have ye quenched seven smoking hearths—see if the fire in your ain parlour burn the blither for that. Ye have riven the thack off seven cottar houses—look if your ain roof-tree stand the faster. Ye may stable your stirks in the shealings at Derncleugh—see that the hare does not couch on the hearthstane at

Ellangowan. Ride your ways, Godfrey Bertram—what do ye glower after our folk for? There's thirty hearts there that wad hae wanted bread ere ye had wanted sunkets, and spent their life-blood ere ye had scratched your finger. Yes—there's thirty yonder, from the auld wife of an hundred to the babe that was born last week, that ye have turned out o' their bits o' bields, to sleep with the tod and the blackcock in the muirs! Ride your ways, Ellangowan! Our bairns are hinging at our weary backs—look that your braw cradle at hame be the fairer spread up; not that I am wishing ill to little Harry, or to the babe that's yet to be born—God forbid—and make them kind to the poor, and better folk than their father!—And now, ride e'en your ways; for these are the last words ye'll ever hear Meg Merrilies speak, and this is the last reise that I'll ever cut in the bonny woods of Ellangowan.'

So saying, she broke the sapling she held in her hand and flung it into the road.

Guy Mannering (1815)

What wonder if the world sat up to listen! To praise such a composition would be superfluous indeed, and I cite it for no such purpose. A man who could miss or mistake the impression, would be beyond instruction by words. . . . "RIDE YOUR WAYS," said the gipsy; and in what other tongue could she have condensed her point—luxury, pride, domination, defied and bidden go to their own end—into three such sounds as these?

Equally remarkable, perhaps even more so, if judged by the prevalent laxity of English rhetoric, is the faultless structure of the speech, the perfect attainment of that symmetry without stiffness which makes a frame organic. . . . Here Scott's craft is supreme, good enough for Racine, Euripides, or the Homer of the Ninth ILIAD.

A. W. VERRALL

Collected Literary Essays, Classical and Modern (1913)

SAMUEL TAYLOR COLERIDGE

1 7 7 2 — 1 8 3 4

YOUTH AND AGE

Verse, a breeze mid blossoms straying,
Where Hope clung feeding, like a bee—
Both were mine! Life went a-maying
    With Nature, Hope, and Poesy,
        When I was young!

1031

When I was young? —Ah, woful When!
Ah! for the change 'twixt Now and Then!
This breathing house not built with hands,
This body that does me grievous wrong,
O'er aery cliffs and glittering sands,
How lightly then it flashed along:—
Like those trim skiffs, unknown of yore,
On winding lakes and rivers wide,
That ask no aid of sail or oar,
That fear no spite of wind or tide!
Nought cared this body for wind or weather
When Youth and I lived in't together.

Flowers are lovely; Love is flower-like;
Friendship is a sheltering tree;
O! the joys, that came down shower-like,
Of Friendship, Love, and Liberty,
                    Ere I was old!

Ere I was old? Ah woful Ere,
Which tells me, Youth's no longer here!
O Youth! for years so many and sweet,
'Tis known, that Thou and I were one,
I'll think it but a fond conceit—
It cannot be that Thou art gone!
Thy vesper-bell hath not yet tolled:—
And thou wert aye a masker bold!

What strange disguise hast now put on,
To make believe, that thou art gone?
I see these locks in silvery slips,
This drooping gait, this altered size:
But Spring-tide blossoms on thy lips,
And tears take sunshine from thine eyes!
Life is but thought: so think I will
That Youth and I are house-mates still.

Dew-drops are the gems of morning,
But the tears of mournful eve!
Where no hope is, life's a warning
That only serves to make us grieve,
                    When we are old:

That only serves to make us grieve
With oft and tedious taking-leave,
Like some poor nigh-related guest,
That may not rudely be dismist;

Yet hath outstayed his welcome while,
And tells the jest without the smile.

(1823–32)

*This is one of the most perfect poems, for style, feeling, and everything,
that ever were written.*

JAMES HENRY LEIGH HUNT
Imagination and Fancy (1844)

SAMUEL TAYLOR COLERIDGE

1 7 7 2 — 1 8 3 4

FRANCE, AN ODE

I

Ye clouds! that far above me float and pause,
   Whose pathless march no mortal may control!
   Ye ocean-waves! that, wheresoe'er ye roll,
Yield homage only to eternal laws!
Ye woods! that listen to the night-birds' singing,
   Midway the smooth and perilous slope reclined,
Save when your own imperious branches swinging,
   Have made a solemn music of the wind!
Where, like a man beloved of God,
Through glooms, which never woodman trod,
   How oft, pursuing fancies holy,
My moonlight way o'er flowering weeds I wound,
   Inspired, beyond the guess of folly,
By each rude shape and wild unconquerable sound!
O ye loud waves! and O ye forests high!
   And O ye clouds that far above me soared!
Thou rising sun! thou blue rejoicing sky!
   Yea, every thing that is and will be free!
Bear witness for me, wheresoe'er ye be,
   With what deep worship I have still adored
   The spirit of divinest Liberty.

II

When France in wrath her giant-limbs upreared,
   And with that oath, which smote air, earth and sea,
   Stamped her strong foot and said she would be free,
Bear witness for me, how I hoped and feared!

1033

With what a joy my lofty gratulation
  Unawed I sang, amid a slavish band:
And when to whelm the disenchanted nation,
  Like fiends embattled by a wizard's wand,
    The monarchs marched in evil day,
    And Britain join'd the dire array;
  Though dear her shores and circling ocean,
Though many friendships, many youthful loves
  Had swoln the patriot emotion
And flung a magic light o'er all her hills and groves;
Yet still my voice, unaltered, sang defeat
  To all that braved the tyrant-quelling lance,
And shame too long delay'd and vain retreat!
For ne'er, O Liberty! with partial aim
I dimmed thy light or damped thy holy flame;
  But blessed the paeans of delivered France,
And hung my head and wept at Britain's name.

III

'And what,' I said, 'though blasphemy's loud scream
  With that sweet music of deliverance strove!
  Though all the fierce and drunken passions wove
A dance more wild than e'er was maniac's dream!
  Ye storms, that round the dawning east assembled,
The sun was rising, though he hid his light!'
  And when, to soothe my soul, that hoped and trembled
The dissonance ceased, and all seemed calm and bright;
  When France her front deep-scarr'd and gory
  Concealed with clustering wreaths of glory;
    When, insupportably advancing,
  Her arm made mockery of the warrior's tramp;
    While timid looks of fury glancing,
  Domestic treason, crushed beneath her fatal stamp,
Writhed like a wounded dragon in his gore;
  Then I reproached my fears that would not flee;
'And soon,' I said, 'shall Wisdom teach her lore
In the low huts of them that toil and groan!
And, conquering by her happiness alone,
  Shall France compel the nations to be free,
Till love and joy look round, and call the earth their own.'

IV

Forgive me, Freedom! O forgive those dreams!
  I hear thy voice, I hear thy loud lament,
  From bleak Helvetia's icy caverns sent—

1034

I hear thy groans upon her blood-stained streams!
  Heroes, that for your peaceful country perished,
And ye that, fleeing, spot your mountain-snows
  With bleeding wounds; forgive me, that I cherished
One thought that ever blessed your cruel foes!
    To scatter rage, and traitorous guilt,
    Where Peace her jealous home had built;
      A patriot-race to disinherit
Of all that made their stormy wilds so dear;
      And with inexpiable spirit
To taint the bloodless freedom of the mountaineer—
O France, that mockest Heaven, adulterous, blind,
    And patriot only in pernicious toils!
Are these thy boasts, champion of human kind?
  To mix with kings in the low lust of sway,
Yell in the hunt, and share the murderous prey;
To insult the shrine of Liberty with spoils
  From freemen torn; to tempt and to betray?

                      V

    The sensual and the dark rebel in vain,
Slaves by their own compulsion! In mad game
They burst their manacles and wear the name
    Of Freedom, graven on a heavier chain!
    O Liberty! with profitless endeavour
Have I pursued thee, many a weary hour;
    But thou nor swell'st the victor's strain, nor ever
Didst breathe thy soul in forms of human power.
    Alike from all, howe'er they praise thee,
    (Not prayer, nor boastful name delays thee)
      Alike from priestcraft's harpy minions,
And factious blasphemy's obscener slaves,
      Thou speedest on thy subtle pinions,
The guide of homeless winds, and playmate of the waves!
And there I felt thee!—on that sea-cliff's verge,
  Whose pines, scarce travelled by the breeze above,
Had made one murmur with the distant surge!
Yes, while I stood and gazed, my temples bare,
And shot my being through earth, sea and air,
  Possessing all things with intensest love,
    O Liberty! my spirit felt thee there.

                                            (1798)

The conversation turned after dinner on the lyrical poetry of the day,
and a question arose as to which was the most perfect ode that had been

*produced. Shelley contended for Coleridge's on Switzerland, beginning,
"Ye clouds."*

PERCY BYSSHE SHELLEY
in Thomas Medwin's Conversations of Lord Byron (1824)

SAMUEL TAYLOR COLERIDGE

1 7 7 2 — 1 8 3 4

KUBLA KHAN

In Xanadu did Kubla Khan
  A stately pleasure-dome decree:
Where Alph, the sacred river, ran
Through caverns measureless to man
  Down to a sunless sea.
So twice five miles of fertile ground
  With walls and towers were girdled round:
And there were gardens bright with sinuous rills
Where blossom'd many an incense-bearing tree;
And here were forests ancient as the hills,
Enfolding sunny spots of greenery.

But O, that deep romantic chasm which slanted
Down the green hill athwart a cedarn cover!
A savage place! as holy and enchanted
As e'er beneath a waning moon was haunted
By woman wailing for her demon-lover!
And from this chasm, with ceaseless turmoil seething,
As if this earth in fast thick pants were breathing,
A mighty fountain momently was forced;
Amid whose swift half-intermitted burst
Huge fragments vaulted like rebounding hail,
Or chaffy grain beneath the thresher's flail:
And 'mid these dancing rocks at once and ever
It flung up momently the sacred river.
Five miles meandering with a mazy motion
Through wood and dale the sacred river ran,
Then reach'd the caverns measureless to man,
And sank in tumult to a lifeless ocean:
And 'mid this tumult Kubla heard from far
Ancestral voices prophesying war!

The shadow of the dome of pleasure
    Floated midway on the waves;
Where was heard the mingled measure
    From the fountain and the caves.
It was a miracle of rare device,
A sunny pleasure-dome with caves of ice!

A damsel with a dulcimer
    In a vision once I saw:
It was an Abyssinian maid,
    And on her dulcimer she play'd,
Singing of Mount Abora.
Could I revive within me,
    Her symphony and song,
To such a deep delight 'twould win me,
That with music loud and long,
I would build that dome in air,
That sunny dome! those caves of ice!
And all who heard should see them there,
And all should cry, Beware! Beware!
His flashing eyes, his floating hair!
Weave a circle round him thrice,
    And close your eyes with holy dread,
    For he on honey-dew hath fed,
And drunk the milk of Paradise.

(1798)

It is not easy to think of a greater piece of poetry than KUBLA KHAN.
*. . . This statement is wont to upset some people terribly. A friend of
mine, most right honourable in the literary sense, has said plaintively,
"Really, after all, the* ODYSSEY *is a greater poem than* K. K." *Certainly it
is—in the sense that the hogshead is a greater health than the nipperkin;
but in no other. I once read a very clever paper in which the writer,
taking the same side, asked passionately and repeatedly at the end,
"*WHY *are we to call* K. K. *'pure poetry'?" Unluckily he had answered
himself a dozen lines before, in the words, "The interest of* K. K. *is to
find out how it produces a poetical effect—for it does—* OUT OF SO LITTLE."
WE *have found out—by adding to the little, to the almost nothing, of
the opium dreams, the pure poetry of verse and diction and atmosphere
generally.*

GEORGE SAINTSBURY
A History of English Prosody (1910)

CHRISTABEL

PART THE FIRST

'Tis the middle of night by the castle clock,
And the owls have awakened the crowing cock;
Tu—whit!—Tu—whoo!
And hark, again! the crowing cock
How drowsily it crew.

Sir Leoline, the Baron rich,
Hath a toothless mastiff bitch
From her kennel beneath the rock
Maketh answer to the clock,
Four for the quarters, and twelve for the hour;
Ever and aye, by shine and shower,
Sixteen short howls, not over loud;
Some say, she sees my lady's shroud.

Is the night chilly and dark?
The night is chilly, but not dark.
The thin grey cloud is spread on high,
It covers but not hides the sky.
The moon is behind, and at the full;
And yet she looks both small and dull.
The night is chill, the cloud is grey:
'Tis a month before the month of May,
And the Spring comes slowly up this way.

The lovely lady, Christabel,
Whom her father loves so well,
What makes her in the wood so late,
A furlong from the castle gate?
She had dreams all yesternight
Of her own betrothed knight;
And she in the midnight wood will pray
For the weal of her lover that's far away.

She stole along, she nothing spoke,
The sighs she heaved were soft and low,
And naught was green upon the oak,
But moss and rarest mistletoe:
She kneels beneath the huge oak tree,
And in silence prayeth she.

The lady sprang up suddenly,
The lovely lady, Christabel!
It moaned as near, as near can be,
But what it is, she cannot tell.—
On the other side it seems to be,
Of the huge, broad-breasted, old oak tree.

The night is chill; the forest bare;
Is it the wind that moaneth bleak?
There is not wind enough in the air
To move away the ringlet curl
From the lovely lady's cheek—
There is not wind enough to twirl
The one red leaf, the last of its clan,
That dances as often as dance it can,
Hanging so light, and hanging so high,
On the topmost twig that looks up at the sky.

Hush, beating heart of Christabel!
Jesu, Maria, shield her well!
She folded her arms beneath her cloak,
And stole to the other side of the oak.
What sees she there?

There she sees a damsel bright,
Drest in a silken robe of white,
That shadowy in the moonlight shone:
The neck that made that white robe wan,
Her stately neck, and arms were bare;
Her blue-veined feet unsandal'd were
And wildly glittered here and there
The gems entangled in her hair.
I guess, 'twas frightful there to see
A lady so richly clad as she—
Beautiful exceedingly!
'Mary mother, save me now!'
(Said Christabel) 'And who art thou?'

The lady strange made answer meet,
And her voice was faint and sweet:—
'Have pity on my sore distress,
I scarce can speak for weariness:
Stretch forth thy hand, and have no fear!'
Said Christabel, 'How camest thou here?'
And the lady, whose voice was faint and sweet,
Did thus pursue her answer meet:—

'My sire is of a noble line,
And my name is Geraldine:
Five warriors seized me yestermorn,
Me, even me, a maid forlorn:
They choked my cries with force and fright,
And tied me on a palfrey white.
The palfrey was as fleet as wind,
And they rode furiously behind.
They spurred amain, their steeds were white;
And once we crossed the shade of night.
As sure as Heaven shall rescue me,
I have no thought what men they be;
Nor do I know how long it is
(For I have lain entranced I wis)
Since one, the tallest of the five,
Took me from the palfrey's back,
A weary woman, scarce alive.
Some muttered words his comrades spoke:
He placed me underneath this oak,
He swore they would return with haste;
Whither they went I cannot tell—
I thought I heard, some minutes past,
Sounds as of a castle-bell.
Stretch forth thy hand' (thus ended she),
'And help a wretched maid to flee.'

Then Christabel stretched forth her hand
And comforted fair Geraldine:
'O well, bright dame! may you command
The service of Sir Leoline;
And gladly our stout chivalry
Will he send forth and friends withal
To guide and guard you safe and free
Home to your noble father's hall.'

She rose: and forth with steps they passed
That strove to be, and were not, fast.
Her gracious stars the lady blest,
And thus spake on sweet Christabel:
'All our household are at rest,
The hall as silent as the cell;
Sir Leoline is weak in health
And may not well awakened be,
But we will move as if in stealth
And I beseech your courtesy,
This night to share your couch with me.'

They crossed the moat, and Christabel
Took the key that fitted well;
A little door she opened straight,
All in the middle of the gate;
The gate that was ironed within and without,
Where an army in battle array had marched out.
The lady sank, belike through pain,
And Christabel with might and main
Lifted her up, a weary weight,
Over the threshold of the gate:
Then the lady rose again,
And moved, as she were not in pain.

So free from danger, free from fear,
They crossed the court: right glad they were.
And Christabel devoutly cried
To the lady by her side,
'Praise we the Virgin all divine
Who hath rescued thee from thy distress!'
'Alas, alas!' said Geraldine,
'I cannot speak for weariness.'
So free from danger, free from fear,
They crossed the court: right glad they were.

Outside her kennel, the mastiff old
Lay fast asleep, in moonshine cold.
The mastiff old did not awake
Yet she an angry moan did make!
And what can ail the mastiff bitch?
Never till now she uttered yell
Beneath the eye of Christabel.
Perhaps it is the owlet's scritch:
For what can ail the mastiff bitch?

They passed the hall, that echoes still,
Pass as lightly as you will!
The brands were flat, the brands were dying,
Amid their own white ashes lying;
But when the lady passed, there came
A tongue of light, a fit of flame;
And Christabel saw the lady's eye,
And nothing else saw she thereby,
Save the boss of the shield of Sir Leoline tall,
Which hung in a murky old niche in the wall.
'O softly tread,' said Christabel,
'My father seldom sleepeth well.'

Sweet Christabel her feet doth bare,
And jealous of the listening air
They steal their way from stair to stair,
Now in glimmer, and now in gloom,
And now they pass the Baron's room,
As still as death, with stifled breath!
And now have reached her chamber door;
And now doth Geraldine press down
The rushes of the chamber floor.

The moon shines dim in the open air,
And not a moonbeam enters here.
But they without its light can see
The chamber carved so curiously,
Carved with figures strange and sweet,
All made out of the carver's brain,
For a lady's chamber meet:
The lamp with twofold silver chain
Is fastened to an angel's feet.
The silver lamp burns dead and dim;
But Christabel the lamp will trim.
She trimmed the lamp, and made it bright,
And left it swinging to and fro,
While Geraldine, in wretched plight,
Sank down upon the floor below.

'O weary lady, Geraldine,
I pray you, drink this cordial wine!
It is a wine of virtuous powers;
My mother made it of wild flowers.'

'And will your mother pity me,
Who am a maiden most forlorn?'
Christabel answered—'Woe is me!
She died the hour that I was born.
I have heard the grey-haired friar tell,
How on her deathbed she did say,
That she should hear the castle-bell
Strike twelve upon my wedding-day.
O mother dear! that thou wert here!"
'I would,' said Geraldine, 'she were!'

But soon with altered voice, said she—
'Off, wandering mother! Peak and pine,
I have power to bid thee flee.'
Alas, what ails poor Geraldine?

Why stares she with unsettled eye?
Can she the bodiless dead espy?
And why with hollow voice cries she,
'Off, woman, off! this hour is mine—
Though thou her guardian spirit be,
Off, woman, off! 'tis given to me.'

Then Christabel knelt by the lady's side,
And raised to heaven her eyes so blue—
'Alas!' said she, 'this ghastly ride—
Dear lady! it hath wildered you!'
The lady wiped her moist cold brow,
And faintly said, ' 'Tis over now!'

Again the wild-flower wine she drank:
Her fair large eyes 'gan glitter bright,
And from the floor whereon she sank,
The lofty lady stood upright;
She was most beautiful to see,
Like a lady of a far countrée.

And thus the lofty lady spake—
'All they who live in the upper sky,
Do love you, holy Christabel!
And you love them, and for their sake
And for the good which me befell,
Even I in my degree will try,
Fair maiden, to requite you well.
But now unrobe yourself; for I
Must pray, ere yet in bed I lie.'

Quoth Christabel, 'So let it be!'
And as the lady bade, did she.
Her gentle limbs did she undress,
And lay down in her loveliness.

But through her brain of weal and woe
So many thoughts moved to and fro,
That vain it were her lids to close;
So half-way from the bed she rose,
And on her elbow did recline
To look at the lady Geraldine.

Beneath the lamp the lady bowed,
And slowly rolled her eyes around;
Then drawing in her breath aloud,
Like one that shuddered, she unbound

The cincture from beneath her breast:
Her silken robe, and inner vest,
Dropt to her feet, and full in view,
Behold! her bosom and half her side—
A sight to dream of, not to tell!
O shield her! shield sweet Christabel!

Yet Geraldine nor speaks nor stirs;
Ah! what a stricken look was hers!
Deep from within she seems half-way
To lift some weight with sick assay,
And eyes the maid and seeks delay;
Then suddenly as one defied
Collects herself in scorn and pride,
And lay down by the Maiden's side!—
And in her arms the maid she took,
      Ah wel-a-day!
And with low voice and doleful look
These words did say:
'In the touch of this bosom there worketh a spell,
Which is lord of thy utterance, Christabel!
Thou knowest to-night, and wilt know to-morrow,
This mark of my shame, this seal of my sorrow;
     But vainly thou warrest,
       For this is alone in
      Thy power to declare,
       That in the dim forest
      Thou heard'st a low moaning,
And found'st a bright lady, surpassingly fair:
And didst bring her home with thee in love and in charity,
To shield her and shelter her from the damp air.'

THE CONCLUSION TO PART THE FIRST

It was a lovely sight to see
The lady Christabel, when she
Was praying at the old oak tree.
      Amid the jagged shadows
      Of mossy leafless boughs,
      Kneeling in the moonlight,
      To make her gentle vows;
Her slender palms together prest,
Heaving sometimes on her breast;
Her face resigned to bliss or bale—
Her face, oh call it fair not pale,

And both blue eyes more bright than clear,
Each about to have a tear.

With open eyes (ah woe is me!)
Asleep, and dreaming fearfully,
Fearfully dreaming, yet I wis,
Dreaming that alone, which is—
O sorrow and shame! Can this be she,
The lady, who knelt at the old oak tree?
And lo! the worker of these harms,
That holds the maiden in her arms,
Seems to slumber still and mild,
As a mother with her child.

A star hath set, a star hath risen,
O Geraldine! since arms of thine
Have been the lovely lady's prison.
O Geraldine! one hour was thine—
Thou'st had thy will! By tairn and rill,
The night-birds all that hour were still.
But now they are jubilant anew,
From cliff and tower, tu—whoo! tu—whoo!
Tu—whoo! tu—whoo! from wood and fell!

And see! the lady Christabel
Gathers herself from out her trance;
Her limbs relax, her countenance
Grows sad and soft; the smooth thin lids
Close o'er her eyes; and tears she sheds—
Large tears that leave the lashes bright!
And oft the while she seems to smile
As infants at a sudden light!

Yea, she doth smile, and she doth weep,
Like a youthful hermitess,
Beauteous in a wilderness,
Who, praying always, prays in sleep.
And, if she move unquietly,
Perchance, 'tis but the blood so free,
Comes back and tingles in her feet.
No doubt, she hath a vision sweet.
What if her guardian spirit 'twere,
What if she knew her mother near?
But this she knows, in joys and woes,
That saints will aid if men will call:
For the blue sky bends over all!

'Each matin bell,' the Baron saith,
'Knells us back to a world of death.'
These words Sir Leoline first said,
When he rose and found his lady dead:
These words Sir Leoline will say,
Many a morn to his dying day!

And hence the custom and law began,
That still at dawn the sacristan,
Who duly pulls the heavy bell,
Five and forty beads must tell
Between each stroke—a warning knell,
Which not a soul can choose but hear
From Bratha Head to Wyndermere.

Saith Bracy the bard, 'So let it knell!
And let the drowsy sacristan
Still count as slowly as he can!
There is no lack of such, I ween
As well fill up the space between.
In Langdale Pike and Witch's Lair,
And Dungeon-ghyll so foully rent,
With ropes of rock and bells of air
Three sinful sextons' ghosts are pent,
Who all give back, one after t'other,
The death-note to their living brother;
And oft too, by the knell offended,
Just as their one! two! three! is ended,
The devil mocks the doleful tale
With a merry peal from Borrowdale.'

The air is still! through mist and cloud
That merry peal comes ringing loud;
And Geraldine shakes off her dread,
And rises lightly from the bed;
Puts on her silken vestments white,
And tricks her hair in lovely plight,
And nothing doubting of her spell
Awakens the lady Christabel.
'Sleep you, sweet lady Christabel?
I trust that you have rested well.'

And Christabel awoke and spied
The same who lay down by her side—

O rather say, the same whom she
Raised up beneath the old oak tree!
Nay, fairer yet! and yet more fair!
For she belike hath drunken deep
Of all the blessedness of sleep!
And while she spake, her looks, her air
Such gentle thankfulness declare,
That (so it seemed) her girded vests
Grew tight beneath her heaving breasts.
'Sure I have sinned!' said Christabel,
'Now heaven be praised if all be well!'
And in low faltering tones, yet sweet,
Did she the lofty lady greet
With such perplexity of mind
As dreams too lively leave behind.

So quickly she rose, and quickly arrayed
Her maiden limbs, and having prayed
That He, who on the cross did groan,
Might wash away her sins unknown,
She forthwith led fair Geraldine
To meet her sire, Sir Leoline.

The lovely maid and the lady tall
Are pacing both into the hall,
And pacing on through page and groom
Enter the Baron's presence-room.

The Baron rose, and while he prest
His gentle daughter to his breast,
With cheerful wonder in his eyes
The lady Geraldine espies,
And gave such welcome to the same,
As might beseem so bright a dame!

But when he heard the lady's tale,
And when she told her father's name,
Why waxed Sir Leoline so pale,
Murmuring o'er the name again,
'Lord Roland de Vaux of Tryermaine?'

Alas! they had been friends in youth;
But whispering tongues can poison truth;
And constancy lives in realms above;
And life is thorny; and youth is vain:
And to be wroth with one we love,
Doth work like madness in the brain.

And thus it chanced, as I divine,
With Roland and Sir Leoline.
Each spake words of high disdain.
And insult to his heart's best brother:
They parted—ne'er to meet again!
But never either found another
To free the hollow heart from paining—
They stood aloof, the scars remaining,
Like cliffs which had been rent asunder;
A dreary sea now flows between.
But neither heat, nor frost, nor thunder,
Shall wholly do away, I ween,
The marks of that which once hath been.

Sir Leoline, a moment's space,
Stood gazing on the damsel's face:
And the youthful Lord of Tryermaine
Came back upon his heart again.

O then the Baron forgot his age,
His noble heart swelled high with rage;
He swore by the wounds in Jesu's side,
He would proclaim it far and wide
With trump and solemn heraldry,
That they, who thus had wronged the dame,
Were base as spotted infamy!
'And if they dare deny the same,
My herald shall appoint a week
And let the recreant traitors seek
My tourney court—that there and then
I may dislodge their reptile souls
From the bodies and forms of men!'
He spake: his eye in lightning rolls!
For the lady was ruthlessly seized; and he kenned
In the beautiful lady the child of his friend!

And now the tears were on his face,
And fondly in his arms he took
Fair Geraldine, who met the embrace,
Prolonging it with joyous look.
Which when she viewed, a vision fell
Upon the soul of Christabel,
The vision of fear, the touch and pain!
She shrunk and shuddered, and saw again—
(Ah, woe is me! Was it for thee,
Thou gentle maid! such sights to see?)

Again she saw that bosom old,
Again she felt that bosom cold,
And drew in her breath with a hissing sound:
Whereat the Knight turned wildly round,
And nothing saw, but his own sweet maid
With eyes upraised, as one that prayed.

The touch, the sight, had passed away,
And in its stead that vision blest,
Which comforted her after-rest,
While in the lady's arms she lay,
Had put a rapture in her breast,
And on her lips and o'er her eyes
Spread smiles like light!
                      With new surprise,
'What ails then my beloved child?'
The Baron said—His daughter mild
Made answer, 'All will yet be well!'
I ween, she had no power to tell
Aught else: so mighty was the spell.

Yet he, who saw this Geraldine,
Had deemed her such a thing divine.
Such sorrow with such grace she blended,
As if she feared she had offended
Sweet Christabel, that gentle maid!
And with such lowly tones she prayed,
She might be sent without delay
Home to her father's mansion.

                           'Nay!
Nay, by my soul!' said Leoline.
'Ho! Bracy the bard, the charge be thine!
Go thou, with music sweet and loud,
And take two steeds with trappings proud,
And take the youth whom thou lov'st best
To bear thy harp, and learn thy song,
And clothe you both in solemn vest,
And over the mountains haste along,
Lest wandering folk, that are abroad,
Detain you on the valley road.
'And when he has crossed the Irthing flood,
My merry bard! he hastes, he hastes
Up Knorren Moor, through Halegarth Wood,
And reaches soon that castle good
Which stands and threatens Scotland's wastes.

'Bard Bracy! bard Bracy! your horses are fleet,
Ye must ride up the hall, your music so sweet,
More loud than your horses' echoing feet!
And loud and loud to Lord Roland call,
"Thy daughter is safe in Langdale hall!
Thy beautiful daughter is safe and free—
Sir Leoline greets thee thus through me.
He bids thee come without delay
With all thy numerous array;
And take thy lovely daughter home:
And he will meet thee on the way
With all his numerous array
White with their panting palfreys' foam":
And by mine honour! I will say,
That I repent me of the day
When I spake words of fierce disdain
To Roland de Vaux of Tryermaine!—
—For since that evil hour hath flown,
Many a summer's sun hath shone;
Yet ne'er found I a friend again
Like Roland de Vaux of Tryermaine.'

The lady fell, and clasped his knees,
Her face upraised, her eyes o'erflowing;
And Bracy replied, with faltering voice,
His gracious hail on all bestowing;—
'Thy words, thou sire of Christabel,
Are sweeter than my harp can tell;
Yet might I gain a boon of thee,
This day my journey should not be,
So strange a dream hath come to me;
That I had vowed with music loud
To clear yon wood from thing unblest,
Warned by a vision in my rest!
For in my sleep I saw that dove,
That gentle bird, whom thou dost love,
And call'st by thy own daughter's name—
Sir Leoline! I saw the same,
Fluttering, and uttering fearful moan,
Among the green herbs in the forest alone.
Which when I saw and when I heard,
I wonder'd what might ail the bird:
For nothing near it could I see,
Saw the grass and green herbs underneath the old tree.

'And in my dream, methought, I went
To search out what might there be found;
And what the sweet bird's trouble meant,
That thus lay fluttering on the ground.
I went and peered, and could descry
No cause for her distressful cry;
But yet for her dear lady's sake
I stooped, methought, the dove to take,
When lo! I saw a bright green snake
Coiled around its wings and neck.
Green as the herbs on which it couched,
Close by the dove's its head it crouched;
And with the dove it heaves and stirs,
Swelling its neck as she swelled hers!
I woke; it was the midnight hour,
The clock was echoing in the tower;
But though my slumber was gone by,
This dream it would not pass away—
It seems to live upon the eye!
And thence I vowed this selfsame day,
With music strong and saintly song
To wander through the forest bare,
Lest aught unholy loiter there.'

Thus Bracy said: the Baron, the while,
Half-listening heard him with a smile;
Then turned to Lady Geraldine,
His eyes made up of wonder and love;
And said in courtly accents fine,
'Sweet maid, Lord Roland's beauteous dove,
With arms more strong than harp or song,
Thy sire and I will crush the snake!'
He kissed her forehead as he spake,
And Geraldine in maiden wise,
Casting down her large bright eyes,
With blushing cheek and courtesy fine
She turned her from Sir Leoline;
Softly gathering up her train,
That o'er her right arm fell again;
And folded her arms across her chest,
And couched her head upon her breast,
And looked askance at Christabel——
Jesu, Maria, shield her well!

A snake's small eye blinks dull and shy,
And the lady's eyes they shrunk in her head,
Each shrunk up to a serpent's eye,
And with somewhat of malice, and more of dread,
At Christabel she looked askance!—
One moment—and the sight was fled!
But Christabel in dizzy trance
Stumbling on the unsteady ground
Shuddered aloud, with a hissing sound;
And Geraldine again turned round,
And like a thing, that sought relief,
Full of wonder and full of grief,
She rolled her large bright eyes divine
Wildly on Sir Leoline.

The maid, alas! her thoughts are gone,
She nothing sees—no sight but one!
The maid, devoid of guile and sin,
I know not how, in fearful wise
So deeply had she drunken in
That look, those shrunken serpent eyes,
That all her features were resigned
To this sole image in her mind:
And passively did imitate
That look of dull and treacherous hate!
And thus she stood, in dizzy trance,
Still picturing that look askance
With forced unconscious sympathy
Full before her father's view—
As far as such a look could be,
In eyes so innocent and blue!

And when the trance was o'er, the maid
Paused awhile, and inly prayed:
Then falling at the Baron's feet,
'By my mother's soul do I entreat
That thou this woman send away!'
She said: and more she could not say:
For what she knew she could not tell,
O'er-mastered by the mighty spell.

Why is thy cheek so wan and wild,
Sir Leoline? Thy only child
Lies at thy feet, thy joy, thy pride,
So fair, so innocent, so mild;
The same, for whom thy lady died!

O by the pangs of her dear mother
Think thou no evil of thy child!
For her, and thee, and for no other,
She prayed the moment ere she died:
Prayed that the babe, for whom she died,
Might prove her dear lord's joy and pride!
    That prayer her deadly pangs beguiled,
        Sir Leoline!
    And wouldst thou wrong thy only child,
        Her child and thine?

Within the Baron's heart and brain
If thoughts like these had any share,
They only swelled his rage and pain,
And did but work confusion there.
His heart was cleft with pain and rage,
His cheeks they quivered, his eyes were wild,
Dishonour'd thus in his old age;
Dishonour'd by his only child,
And all his hospitality
To the insulted daughter of his friend
By more than woman's jealousy
Brought thus to a disgraceful end—
He rolled his eye with stern regard
Upon the gentle minstrel bard,
And said in tones abrupt, austere—
'Why, Bracy! dost thou loiter here?
I bade thee hence!' The bard obeyed;
And turning from his own sweet maid,
The aged knight, Sir Leoline,
Led forth the lady Geraldine!

THE CONCLUSION TO PART THE SECOND

A little child, a limber elf,
Singing, dancing to itself,
A fairy thing with red round cheeks
That always finds, and never seeks,
Makes such a vision to the sight
As fills a father's eyes with light;
And pleasures flow in so thick and fast
Upon his heart, that he at last
Must needs express his love's excess
With words of unmeant bitterness.
Perhaps 'tis pretty to force together
Thoughts so all unlike each other;

To mutter and mock a broken charm,
To dally with wrong that does no harm.
Perhaps 'tis tender too and pretty
At each wild word to feel within
A sweet recoil of love and pity.
And what, if in a world of sin
(O sorrow and shame should this be true!)
Such giddiness of heart and brain
Comes seldom save from rage and pain,
So talks as it's most used to do.

(1797–1801)

In the Edinburgh Review it was assailed with a malignity and a spirit of personal hatred that ought to have injured only the work in which such a tirade appeared: and this review was generally attributed (whether rightly or no I know not) to a man (William Hazlitt), who both in my presence and in my absence has repeatedly pronounced it the finest poem in the language.

WILLIAM HAZLITT
S. T. Coleridge's Biographia Literaria (1817)

SAMUEL TAYLOR COLERIDGE

1 7 7 2 — 1 8 3 4

SYMPTOMS OF POETIC POWER

In the application of these principles to purposes of practical criticism as employed in the appraisal of works more or less imperfect, I have endeavoured to discover what the qualities in a poem are, which may be deemed promises and specific sypmtoms of poetic power, as distinguished from general talent determined to poetic composition by accidental motives, by an act of the will, rather than by the inspiration of a genial and productive nature. In this investigation, I could not, I thought, do better, than keep before me the earliest work of the greatest genius, that perhaps human nature has yet produced, our *myriadminded* Shakspere. I mean the "Venus and Adonis," and the "Lucrece"; works which give at once strong promises of the strength, and yet obvious proofs of the immaturity, of his genius. From these I abstracted the following marks, as characteristics of original poetic genius in general.

1054

1. In the "Venus and Adonis," the first and most obvious excellence is the perfect sweetness of the versification; its adaptation to the subject; and the power displayed in varying the march of the words without passing into a loftier and more majestic rhythm than was demanded by the thoughts, or permitted by the propriety of preserving a sense of melody predominant. The delight in richness and sweetness of sound, even to a faulty excess, if it be evidently original, and not the result of an easily imitable mechanism, I regard as a highly favourable promise in the compositions of a young man. "The man that hath not music in his soul" can indeed never be a genuine poet. Imagery (even taken from nature, much more when transplanted from books, as travels, voyages, and works of natural history); affecting incidents; just thoughts; interesting personal or domestic feelings; and with these the art of their combination or intertexture in the form of a poem; may all by incessant effort be acquired as a trade, by a man of talents and much reading, who, as I once before observed, has mistaken an intense desire of poetic reputation for a natural poetic genius; the love of the arbitrary end for a possession of the peculiar means. But the sense of musical delight, with the power of producing it, is a gift of imagination; and this together with the power of reducing multitude into unity of effect, and modifying a series of thoughts by some one predominant thought or feeling, may be cultivated and improved, but can never be learned. It is in these that *poeta nascitur non fit*.

2. A second promise of genius is the choice of subjects very remote from the private interests and circumstances of the writer himself. At least I have found, that where the subject is taken immediately from the author's personal sensations and experiences, the excellence of a particular poem is but an equivocal mark, and often a fallacious pledge, of genuine poetic power. We may perhaps remember the tale of the statuary, who had acquired considerable reputation for the legs of his goddesses, though the rest of the statue accorded but indifferently with ideal beauty; till his wife, elated by her husband's praises, modestly acknowledged that she herself had been his constant model. In the "Venus and Adonis" this proof of poetic power exists even to excess. It is throughout as if a superior spirit more intuitive, more intimately conscious, even than the characters themselves, not only of every outward look and act, but of the flux and reflux of the mind in all its subtlest thoughts and feelings, were placing the whole before our view; himself meanwhile unparticipating in the passions, and actuated only by that pleasureable excitement, which had resulted from the energetic fervor of his own spirit in so vividly exhibiting, what it had so accurately and profoundly contemplated. I think, I should have conjectured from these poems, that even then the great instinct, which impelled the poet to the drama, was secretly working in him, prompting him by a series and never broken chain of imagery, always vivid and, because un-

broken, often minute; by the highest effort of the picturesque in words, of which words are capable, higher perhaps than was ever realized by any other poet, even Dante not excepted; to provide a substitute for that visual language, that constant intervention and running comment by tone, look and gesture, which in his dramatic works he was entitled to expect from the players. His Venus and Adonis seem at once the characters themselves, and the whole representation of those characters by the most consummate actors. You seem to be told nothing, but to see and hear everything. Hence it is, that from the perpetual activity of attention required on the part of the reader; from the rapid flow, the quick change, and the playful nature of the thoughts and images; and above all from the alienation, and, if I may hazard such an expression, the utter *aloofness* of the poet's own feelings, from those of which he is at once the painter and the analyst; that though the very subject cannot but detract from the pleasure of a delicate mind, yet never was poem less dangerous on a moral account. Instead of doing as Ariosto, and as, still more offensively, Wieland has done, instead of degrading and deforming passion into appetite, the trials of love into the struggles of concupiscence; Shakspere has here represented the animal impulse itself, so as to preclude all sympathy with it, by dissipating the reader's notice among the thousand outward images, and now beautiful, now fanciful circumstances, which form its dresses and its scenery; or by diverting our attention from the main subject by those frequent witty or profound reflections, which the poet's ever active mind has deduced from, or connected with, the imagery and the incidents. The reader is forced into too much action to sympathize with the merely passive of our nature. As little can a mind thus roused and awakened be brooded on by mean and indistinct emotion, as the low, lazy mist can creep upon the surface of a lake, while a strong gale is driving it onward in waves and billows.

3. It has been before observed that images, however beautiful, though faithfully copied from nature, and as accurately represented in words, do not of themselves characterize the poet. They become proofs of original genius only as far as they are modified by a predominate passion; or by associated thoughts or images awakened by that passion; or when they have the effect of reducing multitude to unity, or succession to an instant; or lastly, when a human and intellectual life is transferred to them from the poet's own spirit,

> Which shoots its being through earth, sea, and air.

In the two following lines for instance, there is nothing objectionable, nothing which would preclude them from forming, in their proper place, part of a descriptive poem:

> Behold yon row of pines, that shorn and bowed
> Bend from the sea-blast, seen at twilight eve.

But with a small alteration of rhythm, the same words would be equally in their place in a book of topography, or in a descriptive tour. The same image will rise into semblance of poetry if thus conveyed:

> Yon row of bleak and visionary pines,
> By twilight glimpse discerned, mark! how they flee
> From the fierce sea-blast, all their tresses wild
> Streaming before them.

I have given this as an illustration, by no means as an instance, of that particular excellence which I had in view, and in which Shakspere even in his earliest, as in his latest, works surpasses all other poets. It is by this, that he still gives a dignity and a passion to the objects which he presents. Unaided by any previous excitement, they burst upon us at once in life and in power.

> Full many a glorious morning have I seen
> *Flatter* the mountain tops with sovereign eye.
> SHAKSPERE, Sonnet 33rd

> Not mine own fears, nor the prophetic soul
> Of the wide world dreaming on things to come—

❂   ❂   ❂   ❂

> The mortal moon hath her eclipse endured,
> And the sad augurs mock their own presage;
> Incertainties now crown themselves assured,
> And Peace proclaims olives of endless age.
> Now with the drops of this most balmy time
> My Love looks fresh, and DEATH to me subscribes!
> Since spite of him, I'll live in this poor rhyme,
> While he insults o'er dull and speechless tribes.
> And thou in this shalt find thy monument,
> When tyrants' crests, and tombs of brass are spent.
> Sonnet 107

As of higher worth, so doubtless still more characteristic of poetic genius does the imagery become, when it moulds and colors itself to the circumstances, passion, or character, present and foremost in the mind. For unrivalled instances of this excellence, the reader's own memory will refer him to the LEAR, OTHELLO, in short to which not of the "*great, ever living, dead man's*" dramatic works? *Inopem me copia fecit.* How true it is to nature, he has himself finely expressed in the instance of love in Sonnet 98.

From you have I been absent in the spring,
When proud pied April drest in all its trim
Hath put a spirit of youth in every thing,
That heavy Saturn laughed and leaped with him.
Yet nor the lays of birds, nor the sweet smell
Of different flowers in odour and in hue,
Could make me any summer's story tell,
Or from their proud lap pluck them, where they grew:
Nor did I wonder at the lilies white,
Nor praise the deep vermilion in the rose;
They were, though sweet, but figures of delight,
Drawn after you, you pattern of all those.
Yet seemed it winter still, and, you away,
As with your shadow I with these did play!

Scarcely less sure, or if a less valuable, not less indispensable mark

Γονίμου μὲν ποιητοῦ —
— ὅστις ῥῆμα γενναῖον λάχοι,

will the imagery supply, when, with more than the power of the painter, the poet gives us the liveliest image of succession with the feeling of simultaneousness!

With this, he breaketh from the sweet embrace
Of those fair arms, that held him to her heart,
And homeward through the dark lawns runs apace:
Look! how a bright star shooteth from the sky,
So glides he in the night from Venus' eye.

4. The last character I shall mention, which would prove indeed but little, except as taken conjointly with the former; yet without which the former could scarce exist in a high degree, and (even if this were possible) would give promises only of transitory flashes and a meteoric power; is DEPTH, and ENERGY of THOUGHT. No man was ever yet a great poet, without being at the same time a profound philosopher. For poetry is the blossom and the fragrancy of all human knowledge, human thoughts, human passions, emotions, language. In Shakspere's *poems* the creative power and the intellectual energy wrestle as in a war embrace. Each in its excess of strength seems to threaten the extinction of the other. At length in the DRAMA they were reconciled, and fought each with its shield before the breast of the other. Or like two rapid streams, that, at their first meeting within narrow and rocky banks, mutually strive to repel each other and intermix reluctantly and in tumult; but soon finding a wider channel and more yielding shores blend, and dilate, and flow on in one current and with one voice. The "Venus and Adonis" did not perhaps allow the display of the deeper passions. But the story of Lucretia seems to favor and even demand their

intensest workings. And yet we find in *Shakspere's* management of the tale neither pathos, nor any other *dramatic* quality. There is the same minute and faithful imagery as in the former poem, in the same vivid colors, inspirited by the same impetuous vigor of thought, and diverging and contracting with the same activity of the assimilative and of the modifying faculties; and with a yet larger display, a yet wider range of knowledge and reflection; and lastly, with the same perfect dominion, often *domination,* over the whole world of language. What then shall we say? even this; that Shakspere, no mere child of nature; no automaton of genius; no passive vehicle of inspiration possessed by the spirit, not possessing it; first studied patiently, meditated deeply, understood minutely, till knowledge, become habitual and intuitive, wedded itself to his habitual feelings, and at length gave birth to that stupendous power, by which he stands alone, with no equal or second in his own class; to that power which seated him on one of the two glory-smitten summits of the poetic mountain, with Milton as his compeer, not rival. While the former darts himself forth, and passes into all the forms of human character and passion, the one Proteus of the fire and the flood; the other attracts all forms and things to himself, into the unity of his own IDEAL. All things and modes of action shape themselves anew in the being of MILTON; while SHAKSPERE becomes all things, yet for ever remaining himself. O what great men hast thou not produced, England! my country! truly indeed—

> Must *we* be free or die, who speak the tongue,
> Which SHAKSPERE spake; the faith and morals hold,
> Which MILTON held. In every thing we are sprung
> Of earth's first blood, have titles manifold!
>
> WORDSWORTH

Biographia Literaria (1817), xv

The whole of Chapter XV., for instance, in which the specific elements of "poetic power" are "distinguished from general talent determined to poetic composition by accidental motives," requires a close and sustained effort of the attention, but those who bestow it will find it amply repaid. I know of no dissertation conceived and carried out in terms of the abstract which in the result so triumphantly justifies itself upon application to concrete cases. As regards the question of poetic EXPRESSION, and the laws by which its true form is determined, Coleridge's analysis is, it seems to me, final. I cannot, at least, after the most careful reflection upon it, conceive it as being other than the absolutely last word on the subject.

H. D. TRAILL
Samuel Taylor Coleridge (1902)

1059

ROBERT SOUTHEY

1774 — 1843

ODE

WRITTEN DURING THE NEGOCIATIONS
WITH BUONAPARTE, IN JANUARY, 1814

1

Who counsels peace at this momentous hour,
When God hath given deliverance to the oppress'd,
    And to the injured power?
Who counsels peace, when Vengeance like a flood
    Rolls on, no longer now to be repress'd;
      When innocent blood
From the four corners of the world cries out
    For justice upon one accursed head;
When Freedom hath her holy banner spread
    Over all nations, now in one just cause
    United; when with one sublime accord
      Europe throws off the yoke abhorr'd,
And Loyalty and Faith and Ancient Laws
    Follow the avenging sword!

2

Woe, woe to England! woe and endless shame,
    If this heroic land,
    False to her feelings and unspotted fame,
    Hold out the olive to the Tyrant's hand!
    Woe to the world, if Buonaparte's throne
      Be suffer'd still to stand!
For by what names shall Right and Wrong be known, . .
    What new and courtly phrases must we feign
    For Falsehood, Murder, and all monstrous crimes,
    If that perfidious Corsican maintain
      Still his detested reign,
And France, who yearns even now to break her chain,
    Beneath his iron rule be left to groan?
      No! by the innumerable dead
    Whose blood hath for his lust of power been shed,
    Death only can for his foul deeds atone;
That peace which Death and Judgment can bestow,
    That peace be Buonaparte's . . that alone!

3

For sooner shall the Ethiop change his skin,
Or from the Leopard shall her spots depart,
Than this man change his old flagitious heart.
Have ye not seen him in the balance weighed,
And there found wanting?—On the stage of blood
Foremost the resolute adventurer stood;
And when, by many a battle won,
He placed upon his brow the crown,
Curbing delirious France beneath his sway,
Then, like Octavius in old time,
Fair name might he have handed down,
Effacing many a stain of former crime.
Fool! should he cast away that bright renown!
Fool! the redemption proffer'd should he lose!
When Heaven such grace vouchsafed him that the way
To Good and Evil lay
Before him, which to choose.

4

But Evil was his Good,
For all too long in blood had he been nurst,
And ne'er was earth with verier tyrant curst.
Bold men and bad,
Remorseless, godless, full of fraud and lies,
And black with murders and with perjuries,
Himself in Hell's whole panoply he clad;
No law but his own headstrong will he knew,
No counsellor but his own wicked heart.
From evil thus portentous strength he drew,
And trampled under foot all human ties,
All holy laws, all natural charities.

5

O France! beneath this fierce Barbarian's sway
Disgraced thou art to all succeeding times;
Rapine, and blood, and fire have mark'd thy way,
All loathsome, all unutterable crimes.
A curse is on thee, France! from far and wide
It hath gone up to Heaven; all lands have cried
For vengeance upon thy detested head;
All nations curse thee, France! for wheresoe'er
In peace or war thy banner hath been spread,

All forms of human woe have follow'd there:
The Living and the Dead
Cry out alike against thee! They who bear,
Crouching beneath its weight, thine iron yoke,
Join in the bitterness of secret prayer
The voice of that innumerable throng
Whose slaughtered spirits day and night invoke
The everlasting Judge of right and wrong,
How long, O Lord! Holy and Just, how long!

6

A merciless oppressor hast thou been,
Thyself remorselessly oppress'd meantime;
Greedy of war, when all that thou couldst gain
Was but to dye thy soul with deeper crime,
And rivet faster round thyself the chain.
O blind to honour, and to interest blind,
When thus in abject servitude resign'd
To this barbarian upstart, thou couldst brave
God's justice, and the heart of humankind!
Madly thou thoughtest to enslave the world,
Thyself the while a miserable slave;
Behold the flag of vengeance is unfurl'd!
The dreadful armies of the North advance;
While England, Portugal, and Spain combined
Give their triumphant banners to the wind,
And stand victorious in the fields of France.

7

One man hath been for ten long wretched years
The cause of all this blood and all these tears;
One man in this most awful point of time
Draws on thy danger, as he caused thy crime.
Wait not too long the event,
For now whole Europe comes against thee bent;
His wiles and their own strength the nations know;
Wise from past wrongs, on future peace intent,
The People and the Princes, with one mind,
From all parts move against the general foe:
One act of justice, one atoning blow,
One execrable head laid low,
Even yet, O France! averts thy punishment:
Open thine eyes! too long hast thou been blind;
Take vengeance for thyself, and for mankind!

8

France! if thou lov'st thine ancient fame,
Revenge thy sufferings and thy shame!
By the bones that bleach on Jaffa's beach;
By the blood which on Domingo's shore
Hath clogg'd the carrion-birds with gore;
By the flesh that gorged the wolves of Spain,
Or stiffen'd on the snowy plain
Of frozen Muscovy;
By the bodies that lie all open to the sky,
Tracking from Elbe to Rhine the Tyrant's flight;
By the widow's and the orphan's cry,
By the childless parent's misery,
By the lives which he hath shed,
By the ruin he hath spread,
By the prayers that rise for curses on his head,
Redeem, O France! thine ancient fame,
Revenge thy sufferings and thy shame;
Open thine eyes! . . too long hast thou been blind;
Take vengeance for thyself, and for mankind!

9

By those horrors which the night
Witness'd, when the torches' light
To the assembled murderers show'd
Where the blood of Condé flow'd;
By thy murder'd Pichegru's fame;
By murder'd Wright, . . an English name;
By murder'd Palm's atrocious doom;
By murder'd Hofer's martyrdom;
Oh! by the virtuous blood thus vilely spilt,
The Villain's own peculiar private guilt,
Open thine eyes! too long hast thou been blind!
Take vengeance for thyself and for mankind!

Since Milton's immortal imprecation,—

'Avenge, oh Lord, thy slaughtered Saints whose bones
Lie scattered on the Alpine mountains cold' . . . .

there has been no occasional poem equal to it in grandeur and power.
Nor any indeed equal to it in art.

HENRY TAYLOR
in Ward's The English Poets (1880)

LOCULUS AUREOLUS

I would seriously recommend to the employer of our critics, young and old, that he oblige them to pursue a course of study such as this: that under the superintendence of some respectable student from the university, they first read and examine the contents of the book; a thing greatly more useful in criticism than is generally thought; secondly, that they carefully write them down, number them, and range them under their several heads; thirdly, that they mark every beautiful, every faulty, every ambiguous, every uncommon expression. Which being completed, that they inquire what author, ancient or modern, has treated the same subject; that they compare them, first in smaller, afterward in larger portions, noting every defect in precision and its causes, every excellence and its nature; that they graduate these, fixing *plus* and *minus,* and designating them more accurately and discriminately by means of colours, stronger or paler. For instance, purple might express grandeur and majesty of thought; scarlet, vigour of expression; pink, liveliness; green, elegant and equable composition: these however and others, as might best attract their notice and serve their memory. The same process may be used where authors have not written on the same subject, when those who have are wanting, or have touched it but incidentally. Thus Addison and Fontenelle, not very like, may be compared in the graces of style, in the number and degree of just thoughts and lively fancies: thus the dialogues of Cicero with those of Plato, his ethics with those of Aristoteles, his orations with those of Demosthenes. It matters not if one be found superior to the other in this thing, and inferior in that; the exercise is taken; the qualities of two authors are explored and understood, and their distances laid down, as geographers speak, from accurate survey. The *plus* and *minus* of good and bad and ordinary, will have something of a scale to rest upon; and after a time the degrees of the higher parts in intellectual dynamics may be more nearly attained, though never quite exactly.

Imaginary Conversations, Southey and Porson (1824)

Nowhere, in ancient or modern place, is the education of the critic outlined with greater firmness and accuracy; and those who, by this or that good fortune, have been put through some such a process, may congratulate themselves on having learnt no vulgar art in no vulgar way.

GEORGE SAINTSBURY
A History of Criticism (1904)

LEOFRIC AND GODIVA

GODIVA

There is a dearth in the land, my sweet Leofric! Remember how many weeks of drought we have had, even in the deep pastures of Leicestershire; and how many Sundays we have heard the same prayers for rain, and supplications that it would please the Lord in his mercy to turn aside his anger from the poor pining cattle. You, my dear husband, have imprisoned more than one malefactor for leaving his dead ox in the public way; and other hinds have fled before you out of the traces, in which they and their sons and their daughters, and haply their old fathers and mothers, were dragging the abandoned wain homeward. Although we were accompanied by many brave spearmen and skilful archers, it was perilous to pass the creatures which the farm-yard dogs, driven from the hearth by the poverty of their masters, were tearing and devouring; while others, bitten and lamed, filled the air either with long and deep howls or sharp and quick barkings, as they struggled with hunger and feebleness or were exasperated by heat and pain. Nor could the thyme from the heath, nor the bruised branches of the fir-tree, extinguish or abate the foul odor.

LEOFRIC

And now, Godiva, my darling, thou art afraid we should be eaten up before we enter the gates of Coventry; or perchance that in the gardens there are no roses to greet thee, no sweet herbs for thy mat and pillow.

GODIVA

Leofric, I have no such fears. This is the month of roses: I find them everywhere since my blessed marriage: they, and all other sweet herbs, I know not why, seem to greet me wherever I look at them, as though they knew and expected me. Surely they can not feel that I am fond of them.

LEOFRIC

O light laughing simpleton! But what wouldst thou? I came not hither to pray; and yet if praying would satisfy thee, or remove the drought, I would ride up straightway to Saint Michael's and pray until morning.

GODIVA

I would do the same, O Leofric! but God hath turned away his ear from holier lips than mine. Would my own dear husband hear me, if I implored him for what is easier to accomplish? what he can do like God.

LEOFRIC

How! what is it?

GODIVA

I would not, in the first hurry of your wrath, appeal to you, my loving lord, in behalf of these unhappy men who have offended you.

LEOFRIC

Unhappy! is that all?

GODIVA

Unhappy they must surely be, to have offended you so grievously. What a soft air breathes over us! how quiet and serene and still an evening! how calm are the heavens and the earth! shall none enjoy them? not even we, my Leofric! The sun is ready to set: let it never set, O Leofric, on your anger. These are not my words; they are better than mine; should they lose their virtue from my unworthiness in uttering them!

LEOFRIC

Godiva, wouldst thou plead to me for rebels?

GODIVA

They have then drawn the sword against you! Indeed I knew it not.

LEOFRIC

They have omitted to send me my dues, established by my ancestors, well knowing of our nuptials, and of the charges and festivities they require, and that in a season of such scarcity my own lands are insufficient.

GODIVA

If they were starving as they said they were——

LEOFRIC

Must I starve too? Is it not enough to lose my vassals?

GODIVA

Enough! O God! too much! too much! may you never lose them! Give them life, peace, comfort, contentment. There are those among them who kissed me in my infancy, and who blessed me at the baptismal font. Leofric, Leofric! the first old man I meet I shall think is one of those; and I shall think on the blessing he gave, and (ah me!) on the blessing I bring back to him. My heart will bleed, will burst—and he will weep at it! he will weep, poor soul! for the wife of a cruel lord who denounces vengeance on him, who carries death into his family.

LEOFRIC

We must hold solemn festivals.

GODIVA

We must indeed.

LEOFRIC

Well then.

Is the clamorousness that succeeds the death of God's dumb creatures, are crowded halls, are slaughtered cattle, festivals? are maddening songs and giddy dances, and hireling praises from party-coloured coats? Can the voice of a minstrel tell us better things of ourselves than our own internal one might tell us; or can his breath make our breath softer in sleep? O my beloved! let everything be a joyance to us: it will, if we will. Sad is the day, and worse must follow, when we hear the blackbird in the garden and do not throb with joy. But, Leofric, the high festival is strown by the servant of God upon the heart of man. It is gladness, it is thanksgiving; it is the orphan, the starveling, pressed to the bosom, and bidden as its first commandment to remember its benefactor. We will hold this festival; the guests are ready: we may keep it up for weeks, and months, and years together, and always be the happier and the richer for it. The beverage of this feast, O Leofric, is sweeter than bee or flower or vine can give us: it flows from heaven; and in heaven will it abundantly be poured out again, to him who pours it out here unsparingly.

LEOFRIC

Thou art wild.

GODIVA

I have indeed lost myself. Some Power, some good kind Power, melts me (body and soul and voice) into tenderness and love. O my husband, we must obey it. Look upon me! look upon me! lift your sweet eyes from the ground! I will not cease to supplicate; I dare not.

LEOFRIC

We may think upon it.

GODIVA

Never say that! What! think upon goodness when you can be good? Let not the infants cry for sustenance! The mother of our blessed Lord will hear them; us never, never afterward.

LEOFRIC

Here comes the bishop: we are but one mile from the walls. Why dismountest thou? no bishop can expect it. Godiva! my honour and rank among men are humbled by this: Earl Godwin will hear of it: up! up! the bishop hath seen it: he urgeth his horse onward: dost thou not hear him now upon the solid turf behind thee?

GODIVA

Never, no, never will I rise, O Leofric, until you remit this most impious tax, this tax on hard labour, on hard life.

LEOFRIC

Turn round: look how the fat nag canters, as to the tune of a sinner's psalm, slow and hard-breathing. What reason or right can the people have to complain, while their bishop's steed is so sleek and well caparisoned? Inclination to change, desire to abolish old usages.—Up!

up! for shame! They shall smart for it, idlers! Sir bishop, I must blush for my young bride:

GODIVA

My husband, my husband! will you pardon the city?

LEOFRIC

Sir bishop! I could not think you would have seen her in this plight. Will I pardon? yea, Godiva, by the holy rood, will I pardon the city, when thou ridest naked at noontide through the streets.

GODIVA

O my dear cruel Leofric, where is the heart you gave me! It was not so! can mine have hardened it!

BISHOP

Earl, thou abashest thy spouse; she turneth pale and weepeth. Lady Godiva, peace be with thee.

GODIVA

Thanks, holy man! peace will be with me when peace is with your city. Did you hear my lord's cruel word?

BISHOP

I did, lady.

GODIVA

Will you remember it, and pray against it?

BISHOP

Wilt *thou* forget it, daughter?

GODIVA

I am not offended.

BISHOP

Angel of peace and purity!

GODIVA

But treasure it up in your heart: deem it an incense, good only when it is consumed and spent, ascending with prayer and sacrifice. And now what was it?

BISHOP

Christ save us! that he will pardon the city when thou ridest naked through the streets at noon.·

GODIVA

Did he not swear an oath?

BISHOP

He sware by the holy rood.

GODIVA

My Redeemer! thou hast heard it! save the city!

LEOFRIC

We are now upon the beginning of the pavement: these are the suburbs: let us think of feasting: we may pray afterward: to-morrow we shall rest.

1068

GODIVA

No judgments then to-morrow, Leofric?

LEOFRIC

None: we will carouse.

GODIVA

The saints of heaven have given me strength and confidence: my prayers are heard: the heart of my beloved is now softened.

LEOFRIC (*aside*)

Ay, ay—they shall smart though.

GODIVA

Say, dearest Leofric, is there indeed no other hope, no other mediation?

LEOFRIC

I have sworn: beside, thou hast made me redden and turn my face away from thee, and all the knaves have seen it: this adds to the city's crime.

GODIVA

I have blushed too, Leofric, and was not rash nor obdurate.

LEOFRIC

But thou, my sweetest, art given to blushing; there is no conquering it in thee. I wish thou hadst not alighted so hastily and roughly: it hath shaken down a sheaf of thy hair: take heed thou sit not upon it, lest it anguish thee. Well done! it mingleth now sweetly with the cloth of gold upon the saddle, running here and there, as if it had life and faculties and business, and were working thereupon some newer and cunninger device. O my beauteous Eve! there is a Paradise about thee! the world is refreshed as thou movest and breathest on it. I can not see or think of evil where thou art. I could throw my arms even here about thee. No signs for me! no shaking of sunbeams! no reproof or frown or wonderment—I *will* say it—now then for worse—I could close with my kisses thy half-open lips, ay, and those lovely and loving eyes, before the people.

GODIVA

To-morrow you shall kiss me, and they shall bless you for it. I shall be very pale, for to-night I must fast and pray.

LEOFRIC

I do not hear thee; the voices of the folk are so loud under this archway.

GODIVA (*to herself*)

God help them! good kind souls! I hope they will not crowd about me so to-morrow. O Leofric! could my name be forgotten! and yours alone remembered! But perhaps my innocence may save me from reproach! and how many as innocent are in fear and famine! No eye will open on me but fresh from tears. What a young mother for so large a family! Shall my youth harm me! Under God's hand it gives me courage. Ah, when will the morning come! ah, when will the noon be over!

Imaginary Conversations, Leofric and Godiva (1829)

At the finest Landor's is not only the most substantial but also the most musical of styles. No one has written prose so like poetry and yet so unfailingly true to the laws of prose.

HAVELOCK ELLIS
Introduction to Landor's Imaginary Conversations (1886)

WALTER SAVAGE LANDOR

1 7 7 5 — 1 8 6 4

DIRCE

Stand close around, ye Stygian set,
With Dirce in one boat conveyed!
Or Charon, seeing, may forget
That he is old and she a shade.

(1831)

There is nothing in the language comparable.

ALGERNON CHARLES SWINBURNE
Social Verse (1891)

WALTER SAVAGE LANDOR

1 7 7 5 — 1 8 6 4

EPITAPH

LITERARUM QUÆSIVIT GLORIAM,
VIDET DEI.

He sought the glory of literature and now sees the glory of God.

Citation and Examination of
William Shakespeare (1834)

That most perfect of all epitaphs.

JOHN BAILEY
The Continuity of Letters (1923)

1070

CHARLES LAMB

1 7 7 5 — 1 8 3 4

LONDON

Separate from the pleasure of your company, I don't much care if I never see a mountain in my life. I have passed all my days in London, until I have formed as many and intense local attachments, as any of you mountaineers can have done with dead nature. The Lighted shops of the Strand, . . . the innumerable trades, tradesmen and customers, coaches, waggons, playhouses, all the bustle and wickedness round about Covent Garden, the very women of the Town, the Watchmen, drunken scenes, rattles,—life awake, if you awake, at all hours of the night, the impossibility of being dull in Fleet Street, the crowds, the very dirt & mud, the Sun shining upon houses and pavements, the print shops, the old book stalls, parsons cheap'ning books, coffee houses, steams of soups from kitchens, the pantomimes, London itself a panto-mime and a masquerade,—all these things work themselves into my mind and feed me, without a power of satiating me. The wonder of these sights impells me into night-walks about her crowded streets, and I often shed tears in the motley Strand from fulness of joy at so much Life.

Letter to Wordsworth (January 30, 1801)

The most perfect letter-writer in our language.

WALTER RALEIGH
On Writing and Writers (1926)

JOSEPH BLANCO WHITE

1 7 7 5 — 1 8 4 1

TO NIGHT

Mysterious Night! when our first parent knew
Thee from report divine, and heard thy name,
Did he not tremble for this lovely frame,
This glorious canopy of light and blue?
Yet 'neath a curtain of translucent dew,
Bathed in the rays of the great setting flame,
Hesperus with the host of heaven came,

And lo! Creation widened in man's view.
Who could have thought such darkness lay concealed
Within thy beams, O sun! or who could find,
Whilst fly and leaf and insect stood revealed,
That to such countless orbs thou mad'st us blind!
Why do we then shun death with anxious strife?
If Light can thus deceive, wherefore not Life?

The Bijou (1828)

The finest and most graceful sonnet in our language (at least, it is only in Milton's and Wordsworth's sonnets that I recollect any rival, and this is not my judgment alone, but that of the man χατ' ἐξοχὴν φιλόκαλον, *John Hookham Frere).*

SAMUEL TAYLOR COLERIDGE
Letter to White (November 28, 1827)

JANE AUSTEN

1 7 7 5 — 1 8 1 7

PRIDE AND PREJUDICE

CHAPTER I

It is a truth universally acknowledged, that a single man in possession of a good fortune, must be in want of a wife.

However little known the feelings or views of such a man may be on his first entering a neighbourhood, this truth is so well fixed in the minds of the surrounding families, that he is considered as the rightful property of some one or other of their daughters.

'My dear Mr. Bennet,' said his lady to him one day, 'have you heard that Netherfield Park is let at last?'

Mr. Bennet replied that he had not.

'But it is,' returned she; 'for Mrs. Long has just been here, and she told me all about it.'

Mr. Bennet made no answer.

'Do not you want to know who has taken it?' cried his wife impatiently.

'*You* want to tell me, and I have no objection to hearing it.'

This was invitation enough.

'Why, my dear, you must know, Mrs. Long says that Netherfield is taken by a young man of large fortune from the north of England; that he came down on Monday in a chaise and four to see the place, and was so much delighted with it that he agreed with Mr. Morris immediately; that he is to take possession before Michaelmas, and some of his servants are to be in the house by the end of next week.'

'What is his name?'

'Bingley.'

'Is he married or single?'

'Oh! single, my dear, to be sure! A single man of large fortune; four or five thousand a year. What a fine thing for our girls!'

'How so? how can it affect them?'

'My dear Mr. Bennet,' replied his wife, 'how can you be so tiresome! You must know that I am thinking of his marrying one of them.'

'Is that his design in settling here?'

'Design! nonsense, how can you talk so! But it is very likely that he *may* fall in love with one of them, and therefore you must visit him as soon as he comes.'

'I see no occasion for that. You and the girls may go, or you may send them by themselves, which perhaps will be still better, for as you are as handsome as any of them, Mr. Bingley might like you the best of the party.'

'My dear, you flatter me. I certainly *have* had my share of beauty, but I do not pretend to be any thing extraordinary now. When a woman has five grown up daughters, she ought to give over thinking of her own beauty.'

'In such cases, a woman has not often much beauty to think of.'

'But, my dear, you must indeed go and see Mr. Bingley when he comes into the neighbourhood.'

'It is more than I engage for, I assure you.'

'But consider your daughters. Only think what an establishment it would be for one of them. Sir William and Lady Lucas are determined to go, merely on that account, for in general you know they visit no new comers. Indeed you must go, for it will be impossible for *us* to visit him, if you do not.'

'You are over scrupulous surely. I dare say Mr. Bingley will be very glad to see you; and I will send a few lines by you to assure him of my hearty consent to his marrying which ever he chuses of the girls; though I must throw in a good word for my little Lizzy.'

'I desire you will do no such thing. Lizzy is not a bit better than the others; and I am sure she is not half so handsome as Jane, nor half so good humoured as Lydia. But you are always giving *her* the preference.'

'They have none of them much to recommend them,' replied he; 'they are all silly and ignorant like other girls; but Lizzy has something more of quickness than her sisters.'

'Mr. Bennet, how can you abuse your own children in such a way?

You take delight in vexing me. You have no compassion on my poor nerves.'

'You mistake me, my dear. I have a high respect for your nerves. They are my old friends. I have heard you mention them with consideration these twenty years at least.'

'Ah! you do not know what I suffer.'

'But I hope you will get over it, and live to see many young men of four thousand a year come into the neighbourhood.'

'It will be no use to us, if twenty such should come since you will not visit them.'

'Depend upon it, my dear, that when there are twenty, I will visit them all.'

Mr. Bennet was so odd a mixture of quick parts, sarcastic humour, reserve, and caprice, that the experience of three and twenty years had been insufficient to make his wife understand his character. *Her* mind was less difficult to develop. She was a woman of mean understanding, little information, and uncertain temper. When she was discontented she fancied herself nervous. The business of her life was to get her daughters married; its solace was visiting and news.

(1813)

Possibly the shortest, wittiest, and most workmanlike first chaper in English fiction.

GERALD BULLETT
Readings in English Literature (1945)

THOMAS CAMPBELL

1 7 7 7 — 1 8 4 4

HOHENLINDEN

On Linden, when the sun was low,
All bloodless lay the untrodden snow,
And dark as winter was the flow
    Of Iser, rolling rapidly.

But Linden saw another sight
When the drum beat at dead of night,
Commanding fires of death to light
    The darkness of her scenery.

By torch and trumpet fast arrayed,
Each horseman drew his battle blade,
And furious every charger neighed
    To join the dreadful revelry.

Then shook the hills with thunder riven,
Then rushed the steed to battle driven,
And louder than the bolts of heaven
    Far flashed the red artillery.

But redder yet that light shall glow
On Linden's hills of stainèd snow,
And bloodier yet the torrent flow
    Of Iser, rolling rapidly.

'Tis morn, but scarce yon level sun
Can pierce the war-clouds, rolling dun,
Where furious Frank and fiery Hun
    Shout in their sulphurous canopy.

The combat deepens. On, ye brave,
Who rush to glory, or the grave!
Wave, Munich! all thy banners wave,
    And charge with all thy chivalry!

Few, few shall part where many meet!
The snow shall be their winding-sheet,
And every turf beneath their feet
    Shall be a soldier's sepulchre.

                  (1803)

The BATTLE OF HOHENLINDEN *is of all modern compositions the most lyrical in spirit and in sound.*

WILLIAM HAZLITT
The Spirit of the Age (1825)

THOMAS MOORE

1 7 7 9 — 1 8 5 2

I WISH I WAS BY THAT DIM LAKE

I wish I was by that dim Lake,
Where sinful souls their farewell take
Of this vain world, and half-way lie
In death's cold shadow, ere they die.

1075

There, there, far from thee,
Deceitful world, my home should be;
Where, come what might of gloom and pain,
False hope should ne'er deceive again.

The lifeless sky, the mournful sound
Of unseen waters falling round;
The dry leaves, quivering o'er my head,
Like man, unquiet even when dead!
These, ay, these shall wean
My soul from life's deluding scene,
And turn each thought, o'ercharged with gloom,
Like willows, downward towards the tomb.

As they, who to their couch at night
Would win repose, first quench the light,
So must the hopes, that keep this breast
Awake, be quenched, ere it can rest.
Cold, cold, this heart must grow,
Unmoved by either joy or woe,
Like freezing founts, where all that's thrown
Within their current turns to stone.

(1824)

It has been the fashion, of late days, to deny Moore imagination, while granting him fancy—a distinction originating with Coleridge—than whom no man more fully comprehended the great powers of Moore. The fact is, that the fancy of this poet so far predominates over all his other faculties, and over the fancy of all other men, as to have induced, very naturally, the idea that he is fanciful ONLY. *But never was there a greater mistake. Never was a grosser wrong done the fame of a true poet. In the compass of the English language I can call to mind no poem more profoundly—more weirdly* IMAGINATIVE, *in the best sense, than the lines commencing—'I would I were by that dim lake'—which are the composition of Thomas Moore. I regret that I am unable to remember them.*

EDGAR ALLAN POE
The Poetic Principle (1850)

FRÉTILLON

Francs amis des bonnes filles,
Vous connaissez Frétillon:
Ses charmes aux plus gentilles
Ont fait baisser pavillon.
 Ma Frétillon, (*bis.*)
  Cette fille
  Qui frétille,
N'a pourtant qu'un cotillon.

Deux fois elle eut équipage,
Dentelles et diamants,
Et deux fois mit tout en gage
Pour quelques fripons d'amants.
 Ma Frétillon,
  Cette fille
  Qui frétille,
Reste avec un cotillon.

Point de dame qui la vaille:
Cet hiver, dans son taudis,
Couché presque sur la paille,
Mes sens étaient engourdis;
 Ma Frétillon,
  Cette fille
  Qui frétille,
Mit sur moi son cotillon.

Mais que vient-on de m'apprendre?
Quoi! le peu qui lui restait,
Frétillon a pu le vendre
Pour un fat qui la battait!
 Ma Frétillon,
  Cette fille
  Qui frétille,
A vendu son cotillon.

En chemise, à la croisée,
Il lui faut tendre ses lacs.
A travers la toile usée
Amour lorgne ses appas.

Ma Frétillon,
Cette fille
Qui frétille,
Est si bien sans cotillon.

Seigneurs, banquiers et notaires
La feront encor briller;
Puis encor des mousquetaires
Viendront la déshabiller.
Ma Frétillon,
Cette fille
Qui frétille,
Mourra sans un cotillon.

Hearty friend of good girls, you know Frétillon! Her charms cause
the prettiest girls to confess defeat; my Frétillon, my Frétillon, the girl
with a frisk, has still but one petticoat. Twice she had a coach, laces
and diamonds, and twice she pawned them all for some rascally lovers.
My Frétillon, the girl with a frisk, has only one petticoat left. No lady
equals her. This winter in her hovel I was lying almost on straw. My
senses were numb, but Frétillon, the girl with a frisk, threw her petticoat over me. But what have I just heard? What! the little that remains
to her, Frétillon dared to sell for a fop who beat her! My Frétillon, the
girl with a frisk, sold her petticoat. She stands in her shift at the window
and spreads her snare; love espies her charms through the worn fabric
of her shift. My Frétillon, the girl with a frisk, looks so well without a
petticoat! Lords, bankers and notaries will make her shine again; then
the rough soldiers will come to undress her. My Frétillon, the girl with
a frisk, will die without a petticoat!

*Frétillon gives us the perfection of the purely wanton spirit. **It is the
light trifle, the mere nothing, sprightly and free in all its grace.***

C.-A. SAINTE-BEUVE
Causeries du lundi (1850)

THOMAS DE QUINCEY

1 7 8 5 — 1 8 5 9

LEVANA AND OUR LADIES OF SORROW

Oftentimes at Oxford I saw Levana in my dreams. I knew her by
her Roman symbols. Who is Levana? Readers, that do not pretend to
have leisure for very much scholarship, you will not be angry with me

for telling you. Levana was the Roman goddess that performed for the new-born infant the earliest office of ennobling kindness,—typical, by its mode, of that grandeur which belongs to man everywhere, and of that benignity in powers invisible which even in Pagan worlds sometimes descends to sustain it. At the very moment of birth, just as the infant tasted for the first time the atmosphere of our troubled planet, it was laid on the ground. That might bear different interpretations. But immediately, lest so grand a creature should grovel there for more than one instant, either the paternal hand, as proxy for the goddess Levana, or some near kinsman, as proxy for the father, raised it upright, bade it look erect as the king of all this world, and presented its forehead to the stars, saying, perhaps, in his heart, "Behold what is greater than yourselves!" This symbolic act represented the function of Levana. And that mysterious lady, who never revealed her face (except to me in dreams), but always acted by delegation, had her name from the Latin verb (as still it is the Italian verb) levare, to raise aloft.

This is the explanation of Levana. And hence it has arisen that some people have understood by Levana the tutelary power that controls the education of the nursery. She, that would not suffer at his birth even a prefigurative or mimic degradation for her awful ward, far less could be supposed to suffer the real degradation attaching to the non-development of his powers. She therefore watches over human education. Now, the word educo, with the penultimate short, was derived (by a process often exemplified in the crystallization of languages) from the word educo, with the penultimate long. Whatsoever educes, or develops, educates. By the education of Levana, therefore, is meant,—not the poor machinery that moves by spelling-books and grammars, but that mighty system of central forces hidden in the deep bosom of human life, which by passion, by strife, by temptation, by the energies of resistance, works forever upon children,—resting not day or night, any more than the mighty wheel of day and night themselves, whose moments, like restless spokes, are glimmering forever as they revolve.

If, then, these are the ministries by which Levana works, how profoundly must she reverence the agencies of grief! But you, reader! think, —that children generally are not liable to grief such as mine. There are two senses in the word generally,—the sense of Euclid, where it means universally (or in the whole extent of the genus), and a foolish sense of this world, where it means usually. Now, I am far from saying that children universally are capable of grief like mine. But there are more than you ever heard of who die of grief in this island of ours. I will tell you a common case. The rules of Eton require that a boy on the foundation should be there twelve years: he is superannuated at eighteen, consequently he must come at six. Children torn away from mothers and sisters at that age not unfrequently die. I speak of what I know. The complaint is not entered by the registrar as grief; but that it is.

Grief of that sort, and at that age, has killed more than ever have been counted amongst its martyrs.

Therefore it is that Levana often communes with the powers that shake man's heart: therefore it is that she dotes upon grief. "These ladies," said I softly to myself, on seeing the ministers with whom Levana was conversing, "these are the Sorrows; and they are three in number, as the Graces are three, who dress man's life with beauty; the Parcæ are three, who weave the dark arras of man's life in their mysterious loom always with colours sad in part, sometimes angry with tragic crimson and black; the Furies are three, who visit with retributions called from the other side of the grave offences that walk upon this; and once even the Muses were but three, who fit the harp, the trumpet, or the lute, to the great burdens of man's impassioned creations. These are the Sorrows, all three of whom I know." The last words I say now; but in Oxford I said, "one of whom I know, and the others too surely I shall know." For already, in my fervent youth, I saw (dimly relieved upon the dark back-ground of my dreams) the imperfect lineaments of the awful sisters. These sisters—by what name shall we call them?

If I say simply, "The Sorrows," there will be a chance of mistaking the term; it might be understood of individual sorrow,—separate cases of sorrow,—whereas I want a term expressing the mighty abstractions that incarnate themselves in all individual sufferings of man's heart; and I wish to have these abstractions presented as impersonations, that is, as clothed with human attributes of life, and with functions pointing to flesh. Let us call them, therefore, Our Ladies of Sorrow. I know them thoroughly, and have walked in all their kingdoms. Three sisters they are, of one mysterious household; and their paths are wide apart; but of their dominion there is no end. Them I saw often conversing with Levana, and sometimes about myself. Do they talk, then? O, no! Mighty phantoms like these disdain the infirmities of language. They may utter voices through the organs of man when they dwell in human hearts, but amongst themselves is no voice nor sound; eternal silence reigns in their kingdoms. They spoke not, as they talked with Levana; they whispered not; they sang not; though oftentimes methought they might have sung: for I upon earth had heard their mysteries oftentimes deciphered by harp and timbrel, by dulcimer and organ. Like God, whose servants they are, they utter their pleasure not by sounds that perish, or by words that go astray, but by signs in heaven, by changes on earth, by pulses in secret rivers, heraldries painted on darkness, and hieroglyphics written on the tablets of the brain. They wheeled in mazes; I spelled the steps. They telegraphed from afar; I read the signals. They conspired together; and on the mirrors of darkness my eye traced the plots. Theirs were the symbols; mine are the words.

What is it the sisters are? What is it that they do? Let me describe their form, and their presence; if form it were that still fluctuated in its outline; or presence it were that forever advanced to the front, or forever receded amongst shades.

The eldest of the three is named Mater Lachrymarum, Our Lady of Tears. She it is that night and day raves and moans, calling for vanished faces. She stood, in Rama, where a voice was heard of lamentation,—Rachel weeping for her children, and refused to be comforted. She it was that stood in Bethlehem on the night when Herod's sword swept its nurseries of Innocents, and the little feet were stiffened forever, which, heard at times as they tottered along floors overhead, woke pulses of love in household hearts that were not unmarked in heaven.

Her eyes are sweet and subtile, wild and sleepy, by turns; oftentimes rising to the clouds, oftentimes challenging the heavens. She wears a diadem round her head. And I knew by childish memories that she could go abroad upon the winds, when she heard that sobbing of litanies, or the thundering of organs, and when she beheld the mustering of summer clouds. This sister, the elder, it is that carries keys more than papal at her girdle, which open every cottage and every palace. She, to my knowledge, sat all last summer by the bedside of the blind beggar, him that so often and so gladly I talked with, whose pious daughter, eight years old, with the sunny countenance, resisted the temptations of play and village mirth to travel all day long on dusty roads with her afflicted father. For this did God send her a great reward. In the springtime of the year, and whilst yet her own spring was budding, he recalled her to himself. But her blind father mourns forever over her; still he dreams at midnight that the little guiding hand is locked within his own; and still he wakens to a darkness that is now within a second and a deeper darkness. This Mater Lachrymarum also has been sitting all this winter of 1844-5 within the bedchamber of the Czar, bringing before his eyes a daughter (not less pious) that vanished to God not less suddenly, and left behind her a darkness not less profound. By the power of her keys it is that Our Lady of Tears glides a ghostly intruder into the chambers of sleepless men, sleepless woman, sleepless children, from Ganges to the Nile, from Nile to Mississippi. And her, because she is the first-born of her house, and has the widest empire, let us honour with the title of "Madonna."

The second sister is called Mater Suspiriorum, Our Lady of Sighs. She never scales the clouds nor walks abroad upon the winds. She wears no diadem. And her eyes, if they were ever seen, would be neither sweet nor subtile; no man could read their story; they would be found filled with perishing dreams, and with wrecks of forgotten delirium. But she raises not her eyes; her head, on which sits a dilapidated turban, droops forever, forever fastens on the dust. She weeps not. She groans not. But she sighs inaudibly at intervals. Her sister Madonna is oftentimes stormy and frantic, raging in the highest against heaven, and demanding back her darlings. But Our Lady of Sighs never clamours, never defies, dreams not of rebellious aspirations. She is humble to abjectness. Hers is the meekness that belongs to the hopeless. Murmur she may, but it is in her sleep. Whisper she may, but it is to herself in the twilight. Mutter she does at times, but it is in solitary places that are desolate as she is desolate, in ruined cities, and when the sun has gone down to his rest. This sister is the visitor of the Pariah, of the Jew, of the bondsman to the oar in the Mediterranean galleys; of the English criminal in Norfolk Island, blotted out from the books of remembrance in sweet far-off England; of the baffled penitent reverting his eyes forever upon a solitary grave, which to him seems the altar overthrown of some past and bloody sacrifice, on which altar no oblations can now be availing, whether towards pardon that he might implore, or towards reparation that he might attempt. Every slave that at noonday looks up to the tropical sun with timid reproach, as he points with one hand to the earth, our general mother, but for him a step-mother,—as he points with the other hand to the Bible, our general teacher, but against him sealed and sequestered; every woman sitting in darkness, without love to shelter her head, or hope to illumine her solitude, because the heaven-born instincts kindling in her nature germs of holy affections, which God implanted in her womanly bosom, having been stifled by social necessities, now burn sullenly to waste, like sepulchral lamps amongst the ancients; every nun defrauded of her unreturning May-time by wicked kinsman, whom God will judge; every captive in every dungeon; all that are betrayed, and all that are rejected; outcasts by traditionary law and children of hereditary disgrace,—all these walk with Our Lady of Sighs. She also carries a key; but she needs it little. For her kingdom is chiefly amongst the tents of Shem, and the houseless vagrant of every clime. Yet in the very highest ranks of man she finds chapels of her own; and even in glorious England there are some that, to the world, carry their heads as proudly as the reindeer, who yet secretly have received her mark upon their foreheads.

But the third sister, who is also the youngest——! Hush! whisper whilst we talk of her! Her kingdom is not large, or else no flesh should live; but within that kingdom all power is hers. Her head, turreted like that of Cybèle, rises almost beyond the reach of sight. She droops not; and her eyes rising so high might be hidden by distance. But, being what they are, they cannot be hidden; through the treble veil of crape which she wears, the fierce light of a blazing misery, that rests not for matins or for vespers, for noon of day or noon of night, for ebbing or for flowing tide, may be read from the very ground. She is the defier of God. She also is the mother of lunacies, and the suggestress of suicides. Deep lie the roots of her power; but narrow is the nation that she rules. For she can approach only those in whom a profound nature has been upheaved by central convulsions; in whom the heart trembles and the brain rocks under conspiracies of tempest from without and tempest from within.

Madonna moves with uncertain steps, fast or slow, but still with tragic grace. Our Lady of Sighs creeps timidly and stealthily. But this youngest sister moves with incalculable motions, bounding, and with a tiger's leaps. She carries no key; for, though coming rarely amongst men, she storms all doors at which she is permitted to enter at all. And her name is Mater Tenebrarum,—Our Lady of Darkness.

These were the Semnai Theai, or Sublime Goddesses, these were the Eumenides, or Gracious Ladies (so called by antiquity in shuddering propitiation) of my Oxford dreams. Madonna spoke. She spoke by her mysterious hand. Touching my head, she beckoned to Our Lady of Sighs; and what she spoke, translated out of the signs which (except in dreams) no man reads, was this:

"Lo! here is he, whom in childhood I dedicated to my altars. This is he that once I made my darling. Him I led astray, him I beguiled, and from heaven I stole away his young heart to mine. Through me did he become idolatrous; and through me it was, by languishing desires, that he worshipped the worm, and prayed to the wormy grave. Holy was the grave to him; lovely was its darkness; saintly its corruption. Him, this young idolator, I have seasoned for thee, dear gentle Sister of Sighs! Do thou take him now to thy heart, and season him for our dreadful sister. And thou,"—turning to the Mater Tenebrarum, she said,— "wicked sister, that temptest and hatest, do thou take him from her. See that thy sceptre lie heavy on his head. Suffer not woman and her tenderness to sit near him in his darkness. Banish the frailties of hope, wither the relenting of love, scorch the fountains of tears, curse him as only thou canst curse. So shall he be accomplished in the furnace, so shall he see the things that ought not to be seen, sights that are abominable, and secrets that are unutterable. So shall he read elder truths, sad truths, grand truths, fearful truths. So shall he rise again before he dies. And so shall our commission be accomplished which from God we had,— to plague his heart until we had unfolded the capacities of his spirit."

Suspiria de Profundis (1845)

A master of English prose, he stands alone.

R. BRIMLEY JOHNSON
in Craik's English Prose (1911)

THOMAS LOVE PEACOCK

THE WAR-SONG OF DINAS VAWR

The mountain sheep are sweeter,
But the valley sheep are fatter;
We therefore deemed it meeter
To carry off the latter.
We made an expedition;
We met a host, and quelled it;
We forced a strong position,
And killed the men who held it.

On Dyfed's richest valley,
Where herds of kine were browsing,
We made a mighty sally,
To furnish our carousing.
Fierce warriors rushed to meet us;
We met them, and o'erthrew them:
They struggled hard to beat us;
But we conquered them, and slew them.

As we drove our prize at leisure,
The king marched forth to catch us:
His rage surpassed all measure,
But his people could not match us.
He fled to his hall-pillars;
And, ere our force we led off,
Some sacked his house and cellars,
While others cut his head off.

We there, in strife bewild'ring,
Spilt blood enough to swim in:
We orphaned many children,
And widowed many women.
The eagles and the ravens
We glutted with our foemen;
The heroes and the cravens,
The spearmen and the bowmen.

We brought away from battle,
And much their land bemoaned them,
Two thousand head of cattle,
And the head of him who owned them:

Ednyfed, king of Dyfed,
His head was borne before us;
His wine and beasts supplied our feasts,
And his overthrow, our chorus.

(1829)

The quintessence of all the war-songs that ever were written, and the
sum and substance of all the appetencies, tendencies, and consequences
of military glory.

THOMAS LOVE PEACOCK
The Misfortunes of Elphin (1829)

LUDWIG UHLAND

1 7 8 7 — 1 8 6 2

DER GUTE KAMERAD

Ich hatt' einen Kameraden,
Einen bessern findst du nit.
Die Trommel schlug zum Streite,
Er ging an meiner Seite
In gleichem Schritt und Tritt.

Eine Kugel kam geflogen;
Gilt's mir oder gilt es dir?
Ihn hat es weggerissen,
Er liegt mir vor den Füssen,
Als wär's ein Stück von mir.

Will mir die Hand noch reichen,
Derweil ich eben lad':
"Kann dir die Hand nicht geben,
Bleib du im ew'gen Leben
Mein guter Kamerad!"

THE GOOD COMRADE

I had a trusty comrade
No better man you'll see.
We heard the bugles blowing,
To war together going
Still side by side were we.

Then came a bullet flying;
For you, or me alone?
From me it tears him dying.
Now at my feet he's lying,
Oh, part of me is gone!

His hand is held toward me,
But I must load anew;
'Your hand I cannot hold, lad,
But bide you as of old, lad,
In heaven my comrade true!'

Translated by Norman Macleod

*Uhland was a great student of earlier German literature and a great
master of the narrative ballad, a form in which the folk-singers had not
been particularly successful. In the pure lyric style he wrote one masterpiece, "Der gute Kamerad."*

NORMAN MACLEOD
German Lyric Poetry (1930)

GEORGE GORDON, LORD BYRON

1 7 8 8 — 1 8 2 4

GRIEF

The all of thine that cannot die
Through dark and dread Eternity
    Returns again to me,
And more thy buried love endears
Than aught except its living years.

And Thou art Dead as
Young and Fair (1812)

*I do not know, of its own kind, a more superb monument of grief. . . .
Is not this great poetry? I think that it is. There is no falsehood here.*

EDITH SITWELL
A Poet's Notebook (1943)

GEORGE GORDON, LORD BYRON

1788 — 1824

THE DESTRUCTION OF SENNACHERIB

I

The Assyrian came down like the wolf on the fold,
And his cohorts were gleaming in purple and gold;
And the sheen of their spears was like stars on the sea,
When the blue wave rolls nightly on deep Galilee.

II

Like the leaves of the forest when Summer is green,
That host with their banners at sunset were seen:
Like the leaves of the forest when Autumn hath blown,
That host on the morrow lay wither'd and strown.

III

For the Angel of Death spread his wings on the blast,
And breathed in the face of the foe as he pass'd;
And the eyes of the sleepers wax'd deadly and chill,
And their hearts but once heaved, and for ever grew still!

IV

And there lay the steed with his nostril all wide,
But through it there roll'd not the breath of his pride;
And the foam of his gasping lay white on the turf,
And cold as the spray of the rock-beating surf.

V

And there lay the rider distorted and pale,
With the dew on his brow, and the rust on his mail:
And the tents were all silent, the banners alone,
The lances unlifted, the trumpet unblown.

VI

And the widows of Ashur are loud in their wail,
And the idols are broke in the temple of Baal;
And the might of the Gentile, unsmote by the sword,
Hath melted like snow in the glance of the Lord!

(1815)

GEORGE GORDON, LORD BYRON

1 7 8 8 — 1 8 2 4

THE SHIPWRECK

Then rose from sea to sky the wild farewell—
    Then shriek'd the timid, and stood still the brave—
Then some leap'd overboard with dreadful yell,
    As eager to anticipate their grave;
And the sea yawn'd around her like a hell,
    And down she suck'd with her the whirling wave,
Like one who grapples with his enemy,
And strives to strangle him before he die.

And first one universal shriek there rush'd,
    Louder than the loud ocean, like a crash
Of echoing thunder; and then all was hush'd,
    Save the wild wind and the remorseless dash
Of billows; but at intervals there gush'd,
    Accompanied with a convulsive splash,
A solitary shriek, the bubbling cry
Of some strong swimmer in his agony.

Don Juan (1819–24)

GEORGE GORDON, LORD BYRON

1 7 8 8 — 1 8 2 4

TRIPLE RHYME

But—Oh! ye lords of ladies intellectual,
Inform us truly, have they not hen-pecked you all?

Don Juan (1819–24)

The happiest triple rhyme, perhaps, that ever was written.

JAMES HENRY LEIGH HUNT
Imagination and Fancy (1845)

GEORGE GORDON, LORD BYRON

1 7 8 8 — 1 8 2 4

WHERE HE GAZED A GLOOM PERVADED

But bringing up the rear of this bright host
A Spirit of a different aspect waved
His wings, like thunder-clouds above some coast
Whose barren beach with frequent wrecks is paved;
His brow was like the deep when tempest-tossed;
Fierce and unfathomable thoughts engraved
Eternal wrath on his immortal face,
And *where* he gazed a gloom pervaded space.

The Vision of Judgment (1821)

I read to him THE VISION OF JUDGMENT. *He enjoyed it like a child, but his criticism went little beyond the exclamatory:* 'TOLL! GAR ZU GROSS! HIMMLISCH! UNÜBERTREFFLICH!' *etc. In general, the most strongly peppered passages pleased the best. . . . The stanza 24 he declared to be sublime.*

JOHANN WOLFGANG VON GOETHE
in Henry Crabb Robinson's On Books and Their Writers,
edited by E. J. Morley (1938)

EDWARD CRAVEN HAWTREY

1789 — 1862

HELEN ON THE WALLS OF TROY
LOOKING FOR HER BROTHERS

"Clearly the rest I behold of the dark-ey'd Sons of Achaia,
Known to me well are the Faces of all; their Names I remember;
Two—two only remain, whom I see not among the Commanders,
Kastor fleet in the Car—Polydeykës brave with the Cestus—
Own dear Brethren of mine—one Parent lov'd us as Infants.
Are they not here in the Host, from the Shores of lov'd Lakedaimon,
Or, tho' they came with the Rest in Ships that bound thro' the Waters,
Dare they not enter the Fight or stand in the Council of Heroes,
All for Fear of the Shame and Taunts my Crime has awaken'd?"
So said she;—long since they in Earth's soft Arms were reposing,
There, in their own dear Land, their Father-Land, Lakedaimon.

Translations of Two Passages of the Iliad (1843)

"νῦν δ' ἄλλους μὲν πάντας ὁρῶ ἑλίκωπας Ἀχαιούς,
οὕς κεν ἐὺ γνοίην καί τ' οὔνομα μυθησαίμην·
δοιὼ δ' οὐ δύναμαι ἰδέειν κοσμήτορε λαῶν,
Κάστορά θ' ἱππόδαμον καὶ πὺξ ἀγαθὸν Πολυδεύκεα,
αὐτοκασιγνήτω, τώ μοι μία γείνατο μήτηρ·
ἢ οὐχ ἑσπέσθην Λακεδαίμονος ἐξ ἐρατεινῆς,
ἢ δεύρω μὲν ἕποντο νέεσσ' ἔνι ποντοπόροισι,
νῦν αὖτ' οὐκ ἐθέλουσι μάχην καταδύμεναι ἀνδρῶν
αἴσχεα δειδιότες καὶ ὀνείδεα πόλλ', ἅ μοί ἐστιν."
ὣς φάτο, τοὺς δ' ἤδη κάτεχεν φυσίζοος αἶα
ἐν Λακεδαίμονι αὖθι, φίλῃ ἐν πατρίδι γαίῃ.

Iliad, iii, 234-44

*The most successful attempt hitherto made at rendering Homer into
English, the attempt in which Homer's general effect has been best
retained, is an attempt made in the hexameter measure. . . . it is the
one version of any part of the* ILIAD *which in some degree reproduces
for me the original effect of Homer: it is the best, and it is in hexameters.*

MATTHEW ARNOLD
On Translating Homer (1861)

HYMNE À LA DOULEUR

Frappe encore, ô Douleur, si tu trouves la place!
Frappe! ce cœur saignant t'abhorre et te rend grâce,
Puissance qui ne sais plaindre ni pardonner!
Quoique mes yeux n'aient plus de pleurs à te donner,
Il est peut-être en moi quelque fibre sonore
Qui peut sous ton regard se torturer encore,
Comme un serpent coupé, sur le chemin gisant,
Dont le tronçon se tord sous le pied du passant,
Quand l'homme, ranimant une rage assouvie,
Cherche encor la douleur où ne bat plus la vie!
Il est peut-être encor dans mon cœur déchiré
Quelque cri plus profond et plus inespéré
Que tu n'as pas encor tiré d'un âme humaine,
Musique ravissante aux transports de ta haine!
Cherche! je m'abandonne à ton regard jaloux,
Car mon cœur n'a plus rien à sauver de tes coups.

Souvent, pour prolonger ma vie et ma souffrance,
Tu visitas mon sein d'un rayon d'espérance,
Comme on aisse reprendre haleine aux voyageurs,
Pour les mener plus loin au sentier des douleurs;
Souvent, dans cette nuit qu'un éclair entrecoupe,
De la félicité tu me tendis la coupe,
Et quand elle écumait sous mes désirs ardents,
Ta main me la brisait pleine contre les dents,
Et tu me déchirais, dans tes cruels caprices,
La lèvre aux bords sanglants du vase des délices!
Et maintenant, triomphe! Il n'est plus dans mon cœur
Une fibre qui n'ait résonné sa douleur;
Pas un cheveu blanchi de ma tête penchée
Qui n'ait été broyé comme une herbe fauchée,
Pas un amour en moi qui n'ait été frappé,
Un espoir, un désir, qui n'ait péri trompé!
Et je cherche une place en mon cœur qui te craigne;
Mais je ne trouve plus en lui rien qui ne saigne!

Et cependant j'hésite, et mon cœur suspendu
Flotte encore incertain sur le nom qui t'est dû!

Ma bouche te maudit; mais n'osant te maudire,
Mon âme en gémissant te respecte et t'admire!
Tu fais l'homme, ô Douleur! oui, l'homme tout entier,
Comme le creuset l'or, et la flamme l'acier;
Comme le grès, noirci des débris qu'il enlève,
En déchirant le fer fait un tranchant au glaive.
Qui ne te connut point ne sait rien d'ici-bas;
Il foule mollement la terre, il n'y vit pas;
Comme sur un nuage il flotte sur la vie;
Rien n'y marque pour lui la route en vain suivie;
La sueur de son front n'y mouille pas sa main,
Son pied n'y heurte pas les cailloux du chemin;
Il n'y sait pas, à l'heure où faiblissent ses armes,
Retremper ses vertus aux flots brûlants des larmes,
Il n'y sait point combattre avec son propre cœur
Ce combat douloureux dont gémit le vainqueur,
Élever vers le ciel un cri qui le supplie,
S'affermir par l'effort sur son genou qui plie,
Et dans ses désespoirs, dont Dieu seul est témoin,
S'appuyer sur l'obstacle et s'élancer plus loin!

Pour moi, je ne sais pas à quoi tu me prépares,
Mais tes mains de leçons ne me sont point avares;
Tu me traites sans doute en favori des cieux,
Car tu n'épargnes pas les larmes à mes yeux.
Eh bien! je les reçois comme tu les envoies:
Tes maux seront mes biens, et tes soupirs mes joies.
Je sens qu'il est en toi, sans avoir combattu,
Une vertu divine au lieu de ma vertu;
Que tu n'es pas la mort de l'âme, mais sa vie;
Que ton bras, en frappant, guérit et vivifie,
Toi donc que ma souffrance a souvent accusé,
Toi, devant qui ce cœur s'est tant de fois brisé,
Reçois, Dieu trois fois saint, cet encens dont tout fume!
Oui, c'est le seul bûcher que la terre t'allume,
C'est le charbon divin dont tu brûles nos sens.
Quand l'autel est souillé, la douleur est l'encens!

HYMN TO SORROW

Strike again, O Sorrow, if you find the place! Strike! My bleeding
heart abhors and thanks you, O power incapable of commiseration or
forgiveness! Though my eyes have no more tears to give you, there is

in me, perhaps, some responding fiber that under your glance can suffer anew; like a cut serpent, prostrate on the road, whose stump twists under the foot of a passerby. When man, reviving a satiated rage, still seeks to inflict pain where life no longer throbs, there is perhaps still in my grief-torn heart some cry, deeper and more unexpected, that you have not yet drawn from a human soul, ravishing music to the raptures of your hate! Seek! I submit myself to your jealous glance, for my heart has nothing more to save from your blows. Often, to prolong my life and suffering, you visited my breast with a ray of hope, as travelers are allowed to recover their breath, in order to lead them further along the path of sorrow. Often, in the lightning-torn night, you tendered me the cup of happiness, and when it was brimming over with my warm desires, your hand smashed it full against my teeth, and you tore my lips in your cruel caprices, at the bloody rim of the vase of delight! And now, triumph! My heart no longer has a fiber that has not resounded with sorrow; not a whitened hair of my bent head that has not been crushed like cut grass, not one of my loves that has not been shattered, a hope, a desire, that has not perished in deception! And I seek a place in my heart that fears you, but I find nothing in it that does not bleed! Nevertheless, I hesitate, and in my suspense my heart still wavers uncertainly over the name that is due you! My lips curse you, but, not daring to curse you, my moaning soul respects and admires you! You make the man, O sorrow! Yes! the whole man, as the crucible makes the gold, and flame the steel; as the whetstone, blackened by the fragments it rubs off, sharpens the sword by cutting the iron. He who knew you not, knows nothing here below; he treads the earth softly, he does not live there. He drifts over life as on a cloud; nothing marks for him the path vainly followed, the sweat of his brow does not dampen his hand, his feet do not strike against the pebbles of the road. When his vigor flags, he does not know how to strengthen his virtues in the burning waters of tears, he does not know how to fight with his own heart the dolorous fight which makes the winner groan. He does not know how to beseech heaven, how to grow stronger by his own effort on his weakening knee, and in his despair, that God alone witnesses, how to brace himself on obstacles, and bound ahead. As for myself, I do not know for what you prepare me, but your hands are not sparing of lessons to me. You treat me, without doubt, as heaven's favorite, for you do not spare my eyes any tears. So be it! I receive them as you send them; your unhappiness will be my happiness and your sighs my joys. I feel that there is in you, without having fought, a divine virtue in place of my virtue; that you are not the death of the soul, but its life; that your arm, in striking, heals and vivifies. You, whom my suffering often has accused, you before whom this heart has been broken so many times, receive, God thrice-holy, this incense sent up by the world! Yes, it is the only pyre that the earth kindles for you; it is the divine fuel with which you burn our senses. When the altar is defiled, sorrow is the incense!

The masterpiece of moral poetry and gnomic verse.

ALBERT THIBAUDET
Histoire de la littérature française (1936)

ALPHONSE DE LAMARTINE

1 7 9 0 — 1 8 6 9

LE LAC

Ainsi, toujours poussés vers de nouveaux rivages,
Dans la nuit éternelle emportés sans retour,
Ne pourrons-nous jamais sur l'océan des âges
    Jeter l'ancre un seul jour?

O lac! l'année à peine a fini sa carrière,
Et près des flots chéris qu'elle devait revoir,
Regarde! je viens seul m'asseoir sur cette pierre
    Où tu la vis s'asseoir!

Tu mugissais ainsi sous ces roches profondes;
Ainsi tu te brisais sur leurs flancs déchirés:
Ainsi le vent jetait l'écume de tes ondes
    Sur ses pieds adorés.

Un soir, t'en souvient-il? nous voguions en silence;
On n'entendait au loin, sur l'onde et sous les cieux,
Que le bruit des rameurs qui frappaient en cadence
    Tes flots harmonieux.

Tout à coup des accents inconnus à la terre
Du rivage charmé frappèrent les échos;
Le flot fut attentif, et la voix qui m'est chère
    Laissa tomber ces mots:

'O temps, suspends ton vol! et vous, heures propices,
    Suspendez votre cours!
Laissez-nous savourer les rapides délices
    Des plus beaux de nos jours!

'Assez de malheureux ici-bas vous implorent:
　　Coulez, coulez pour eux;
Prenez avec leurs jours les soins qui les dévorent;
　　Oubliez les heureux.

'Mais je demande en vain quelques moments encore,
　　Le temps m'échappe et fuit;
Je dis à cette nuit: "Sois plus lente"; et l'aurore
　　Va dissiper la nuit.

'Aimons donc, aimons donc! de l'heure fugitive,
　　Hâtons-nous, jouissons!
L'homme n'a point de port, le temps n'a point de rive;
　　Il coule, et nous passons!'

Temps jaloux, se peut-il que ces moments d'ivresse,
Où l'amour à longs flots nous verse le bonheur,
S'envolent loin de nous de la même vitesse
　　Que les jours de malheur?

Hé quoi! n'en pourrons-nous fixer au moins la trace?
Quoi! passés pour jamais? quoi! tout entiers perdus?
Ce temps qui les donna, ce temps qui les efface,
　　Ne nous les rendra plus?

Éternité, néant, passé, sombres abîmes,
Que faites-vous des jours que vous engloutissez?
Parlez: nous rendrez-vous ces extases sublimes
　　Que vous nous ravissez?

O lac! rochers muets! grottes! forêt obscure!
Vous que le temps épargne ou qu'il peut rajeunir,
Gardez de cette nuit, gardez, belle nature,
　　Au moins le souvenir!

Qu'il soit dans ton repos, qu'il soit dans tes orages,
Beau lac, et dans l'aspect de tes riants coteaux,
Et dans ces noirs sapins, et dans ces rocs sauvages
　　Qui pendent sur tes eaux!

Qu'il soit dans le zéphyr qui frémit et qui passe,
Dans les bruits de tes bords par tes bords répétés,
Dans l'astre au front d'argent qui blanchit ta surface
　　De ses molles clartés!

Que le vent qui gémit, le roseau qui soupire,
Que les parfums légers de ton air embaumé,
Que tout ce qu'on entend, l'on voit ou l'on respire,
　　Tout dise: 'Ils ont aimé!'

THE LAKE

Still tow'rd new shores we wend our unreturning way,
Into th' eternal night borne off before the blast;
May we then never on the ages' ocean cast
    Anchor for one sole day?

The year hath scarce attained its term and now alone,
By thy beloved waves, which she should see again,
O lake, behold, I come to sit upon this stone,
    Where she to sit was fain.

Thou murmurest then as now against thy rocky steep;
As now thou brok'st in foam upon thy sheltered sides;
And at her feet adored the breeze, as now, did sweep
    The spray from off thy tides.

One night, rememberest thou? in silence did we float;
Nought in the water heard or air was far and near,
Except the rowers' stroke, whose oars in cadence smote
    Upon thy waters clear;

When accents, all at once, unknown to mortal ear,
Th' enchanted echoes woke, and earth, air, water, all,
Straight hearkened, as the voice of her I held so dear
    These pregnant words let fall;

"O Time, suspend thy flight; and you, propitious hours,
    Your course a moment stay!
Let us the swift delights taste of this day of ours,
    Of this our fairest day!

Unfortunates enough on earth implore your power;
    For them alone flow yet!
Bear with their days away the cares that them devour
    And happy folk forget.

But I implore in vain a moment of delay;
    Time 'scapes me, still a-flight;
Unto the night I say, "Be slower!" And the day
    Will soon disperse the night.

Let us then love, love still and haste the hour that flees
    Now to enjoy. Alas!
Man hath no port and Time no shore hath its seas;
    It lapses and we pass.

Can't be, O jealous Time, that these our hours so sweet,
Wherein, by long-drawn draughts, Love pours us happiness,
With the same breathless speed away from us do fleet
    As the days distress?

What! May we not avail at least to fix their trace?
Are they, then, wholly past and lost for evermore?
Will time, that gave them us and doth them now efface,
    Them ne'er to us restore?

Death, Past, Eternity, ye black abysmal seas,
What do ye with the days ye swallow thus?
Say, will you give us back those rapturous ecstasies
    That you bear off from us?

O lake, O grottoes dumb, rocks, forests dark and deep,
You that Time spares or young can cause again to be,
Keep off this knight of ours, O goodly Nature, keep
    At least the memory!

Be't in thy stormy days or in thy restful nights,
Fair lake, in the aspect of those thy bright hillsides,
Or in those somber pines or in those wilding heights,
    That overhang thy tides,

Be't in the breeze that sighs and passes on its way,
In the sounds by thy shores echoed from place to place,
In yonder argent star, that with its dulcet ray
    Silvers thy smiling face.

Let, let the wind that moans, let, let the reed that sighs,
The perfumes light that float in thine enbalsamed air,
Let all one hears and sees and breathes beneath the skies
    Still "They have loved!" declare.

             Translated by John Payne

Unhoped-for perfection.

        C.-A. SAINTE-BEUVE
       Portraits contemporains (1832)

THE BURIAL OF
SIR JOHN MOORE AFTER CORUNNA

Not a drum was heard, not a funeral note,
   As his corse to the rampart we hurried;
Not a soldier discharged his farewell shot
   O'er the grave where our hero we buried.

We buried him darkly at dead of night,
   The sods with our bayonets turning,
By the struggling moonbeam's misty light
   And the lanthorn dimly burning.

No useless coffin enclosed his breast,
   Not in sheet or in shroud we wound him;
But he lay like a warrior taking his rest
   With his martial cloak around him.

Few and short were the prayers we said,
   And we spoke not a word of sorrow;
But we steadfastly gazed on the face that was dead,
   And we bitterly thought of the morrow.

We thought, as we hollow'd his narrow bed
   And smooth'd down his lonely pillow,
That the foe and the stranger would tread o'er his head,
   And we far away on the billow!

Lightly they'll talk of the spirit that's gone,
   And o'er his cold ashes upbraid him—
But little he'll reck, if they let him sleep on
   In the grave where a Briton has laid him.

But half of our heavy task was done
   When the clock struck the hour for retiring;
And we heard the distant and random gun
   That the foe was sullenly firing.

Slowly and sadly we laid him down,
   From the field of his fame fresh and gory;
We carved not a line, and we raised not a stone,
   But we left him alone with his glory.

(1817)

The one poem in which he is perfectly successful is no happy and in-explicable accident, but the culmination of all his qualities as an artist. . . . There is in this poem, which is one of the most simple and direct poems of the kind in any language, a touch which links it with the characteristic Irish lyric.

The Romantic Movement in English Poetry (1909)

PERCY BYSSHE SHELLEY

1 7 9 2 — 1 8 2 2

SPIRIT OF PLATO

Eagle! why soarest thou above that tomb?
To what sublime and star-ypaven home
　　Floatest thou?—
I am the image of swift Plato's spirit,
Ascending heaven; Athens doth inherit
　　His corpse below.

α.　Αἰετέ, τίπτε βέβηκας ὑπὲρ τάφον; ἢ τίνος, εἰπέ,
　　　ἀστερόεντα θεῶν οἶκον ἀποσκοπέεις;
β.　Ψυχῆς εἰμὶ Πλάτωνος ἀποπταμένης ἐς Ὄλυμπον
　　　εἰκών· σῶμα δὲ γῆ γηγενὲς Ἀτθὶς ἔχει.
　　　　　　　　　　　　　　　　The Greek Anthology, vii, 62

The fruits of this occupation with Greek, Italian, Spanish, and German were Shelley's translations from Homer and Euripides, from Dante, from Calderon's MAGICO PRODIGIOSO, and from FAUST, translations which have never been surpassed for beauty of form and complete transfusion of the spirit of one literature into the language of another.

Shelley (1879)

PERCY BYSSHE SHELLEY

1792 — 1822

LOVE'S PHILOSOPHY

I

The fountains mingle with the river
And the rivers with the Ocean,
The winds of Heaven mix for ever
With a sweet emotion;
Nothing in the world is single;
All things by a law divine
In one spirit meet and mingle.
Why not I with thine?—

II

See the mountains kiss high Heaven
And the waves clasp one another;
No sister-flower would be forgiven
If it disdained its brother;
And the sunlight clasps the earth
And the moonbeams kiss the sea:
What is all this sweet work worth
If thou kiss not me?

(1819)

This poem, one of the most beautiful love-songs in our language, is technically miraculous. Those sounds of sparkling waters rippling and falling together are gained in part by the absence of any words beginning with a hard consonant (excepting, in the second verse, the words "brother," "clasp" and "kiss"—these being given to add ecstasy to the sweetness of the music)—partly by the almost invariable use of female rhymes in the first verse—(six out of the eight lines have female endings, the other two have exquisite bright vowels like the light shining through fountains before they reach the ground). The effect is gained, too, by the exquisite and flawless interweaving of two-syllabled words and one-syllabled words.

In the second verse we have the echo—or not so much echo as reinforcement, of the first line in the first verse; the vowel-scheme gives this echo—a little displaced in the line. In the last quatrain of the second verse there are no female endings, and this gives a greater poignancy and

depth than the exquisite lightness of the last quatrain in the first verse,
in which lines A and C are female, lines B and D are not.

The Pleasures of Poetry, Second Series (1931)

PERCY BYSSHE SHELLEY

1 7 9 2 — 1 8 2 2

VOICE IN THE AIR, SINGING

Life of Life! thy lips enkindle
  With their love the breath between them;
And thy smiles before they dwindle
  Make the cold air fire; then screen them
In those looks, where whoso gazes
Faints, entangled in their mazes.

Child of Light! thy limbs are burning
  Through the vest which seems to hide them;
As the radiant lines of morning
  Through the clouds ere they divide them;
And this atmosphere divinest
Shrouds thee wheresoe'er thou shinest.

Fair are others; none beholds thee,
  But thy voice sounds low and tender
Like the fairest, for it folds thee
  From the sight, that liquid splendour,
And all feel, yet see thee never,
As I feel now, lost for ever!

Lamp of Earth! where'er thou movest
  Its dim shapes are clad with brightness,
And the souls of whom thou lovest
  Walk upon the winds with lightness,
Till they fail, as I am failing,
Dizzy, lost, yet unbewailing!

Prometheus Unbound (1820)
Act ii, Scene v

This poem is probably the most wonderful example known of magic
wrought by a transcendental vowel-technique. I do not know any poem
where we are so conscious of the different wave-lengths of the changing

and *shifting vowels. Shelley's variety, and his incomparable mastery over that variety, is not to be equalled.*

EDITH SITWELL
The Pleasures of Poetry, Second Series (1931)

PERCY BYSSHE SHELLEY

ADONAIS

I

I weep for Adonais—he is dead!
O, weep for Adonais! though our tears
Thaw not the frost which binds so dear a head!
And thou, sad Hour, selected from all years
To mourn our loss, rouse thy obscure compeers,
And teach them thine own sorrow, say: 'With me
Died Adonais; till the Future dares
Forget the Past, his fate and fame shall be
An echo and a light unto eternity!'

II

Where wert thou, mighty Mother, when he lay,
When thy Son lay, pierced by the shaft which flies
In darkness? where was lorn Urania
When Adonais died? With veilèd eyes,
'Mid listening Echoes, in her Paradise
She sate, while one, with soft enamoured breath,
Rekindled all the fading melodies,
With which, like flowers that mock the corse beneath,
He had adorned and hid the coming bulk of Death.

III

Oh, weep for Adonais—he is dead!
Wake, melancholy Mother, wake and weep!
Yet wherefore? Quench within their burning bed
Thy fiery tears, and let thy loud heart keep
Like his, a mute and uncomplaining sleep;
For he is gone, where all things wise and fair
Descend;—oh, dream not that the amorous Deep
Will yet restore him to the vital air;
Death feeds on his mute voice, and laughs at our despair.

IV

Most musical of mourners, weep again!
Lament anew, Urania!—He died,
Who was the Sire of an immortal strain,
Blind, old, and lonely, when his country's pride,
The priest, the slave, and the liberticide,
Trampled and mocked with many a loathèd rite
Of lust and blood; he went, unterrified,
Into the gulf of death; but his clear Sprite
Yet reigns o'er earth; the third among the sons of light.

V

Most musical of mourners, weep anew!
Not all to that bright station dared to climb;
And happier they their happiness who knew,
Whose tapers yet burn through that night of time
In which suns perished; others more sublime,
Struck by the envious wrath of man or God,
Have sunk, extinct in their refulgent prime;
And some yet live, treading the thorny road,
Which leads, through toil and hate, to Fame's serene abode.

VI

But now, thy youngest, dearest one, has perished—
The nursling of thy widowhood, who grew,
Like a pale flower by some sad maiden cherished,
And fed with true-love tears, instead of dew;
Most musical of mourners, weep anew!
Thy extreme hope, the loveliest and the last,
The bloom, whose petals nipped before they blew
Died on the promise of the fruit, is waste;
The broken lily lies—the storm is overpast.

VII

To that high Capital, where kingly Death
Keeps his pale court in beauty and decay,
He came; and bought, with price of purest breath,
A grave among the eternal.—Come away!
Haste, while the vault of blue Italian day
Is yet his fitting charnel-roof! while still
He lies, as if in dewy sleep he lay;
Awake him not! surely he takes his fill
Of deep and liquid rest, forgetful of all ill.

VIII

He will awake no more, oh, never more!—
Within the twilight chamber spreads apace
The shadow of white Death, and at the door
Invisible Corruption waits to trace
His extreme way to her dim dwelling-place;
The eternal Hunger sits, but pity and awe
Soothe her pale rage, nor dares she to deface
So fair a prey, till darkness, and the law
Of change, shall o'er his sleep the mortal curtain draw.

IX

Oh, weep for Adonais!—The quick Dreams,
The passion-wingèd ministers of thought,
Who were his flocks, whom near the living streams
Of his young spirit he fed, and whom he taught
The love which was its music, wander not,—
Wander no more, from kindling brain to brain,
But droop there, whence they sprung; and mourn their lot
Round the cold heart, where, after their sweet pain,
They ne'er will gather strength, or find a home again.

X

And one with trembling hands clasps his cold head,
And fans him with her moonlight wings, and cries;
'Our love, our hope, our sorrow, is not dead;
See, on the silken fringe of his faint eyes,
Like dew upon a sleeping flower, there lies
A tear some Dream has loosened from his brain.'
Lost Angel of a ruined Paradise!
She knew not 'twas her own; as with no stain
She faded, like a cloud which had outwept its rain.

XI

One from a lucid urn of starry dew
Washed his light limbs as if embalming them;
Another clipped her profuse locks, and threw
The wreath upon him, like an anadem,
Which frozen tears instead of pearls begem;
Another in her wilful grief would break
Her bow and wingèd reeds, as if to stem
A greater loss with one which was more weak;
And dull the barbèd fire against his frozen cheek.

XII

Another Splendour on his mouth alit,
That mouth, whence it was wont to draw the breath
Which gave it strength to pierce the guarded wit,
And pass into the panting heart beneath
With lightning and with music: the damp death
Quenched its caress upon his icy lips;
And, as a dying meteor stains a wreath
Of moonlight vapour, which the cold night clips,
It flushed through his pale limbs, and passed to its eclipse.

XIII

And others came . . . Desires and Adorations,
Wingèd Persuasions and veiled Destinies,
Splendours, and Glooms, and glimmering Incarnations
Of hopes and fears, and twilight Phantasies;
And Sorrow, with her family of Sighs,
And Pleasure, blind with tears, led by the gleam
Of her own dying smile instead of eyes,
Came in slow pomp;—the moving pomp might seem
Like pageantry of mist on an autumnal stream.

XIV

All he had loved, and moulded into thought,
From shape, and hue, and odour, and sweet sound,
Lamented Adonais. Morning sought
Her eastern watch-tower, and her hair unbound,
Wet with the tears which should adorn the ground,
Dimmed the aëreal eyes that kindle day;
Afar the melancholy thunder moaned,
Pale Ocean in unquiet slumber lay,
And the wild Winds flew round, sobbing in their dismay.

XV

Lost Echo sits amid the voiceless mountains,
And feeds her grief with his remembered lay,
And will no more reply to winds or fountains,
Or amorous birds perched on the young green spray,
Or herdsman's horn, or bell at closing day;
Since she can mimic not his lips, more dear
Than those for whose disdain she pined away
Into a shadow of all sounds:—a drear
Murmur, between their songs, is all the woodmen hear.

XVI

Grief made the young Spring wild, and she threw down
Her kindling buds, as if she Autumn were,
Or they dead leaves; since her delight is flown,
For whom should she have waked the sullen year?
To Phoebus was not Hyacinth so dear
Nor to himself Narcissus, as to both
Thou, Adonais: wan they stand and sere
Amid the faint companions of their youth,
With dew all turned to tears; odour, to sighing ruth.

XVII

Thy spirit's sister, the lorn nightingale
Mourns not her mate with such melodious pain;
Not so the eagle, who like thee could scale
Heaven, and could nourish in the sun's domain
Her mighty youth with morning, doth complain,
Soaring and screaming round her empty nest,
As Albion wails for thee: the curse of Cain
Light on his head who pierced thy innocent breast,
And scared the angel soul that was its earthly guest!

XVIII

Ah, woe is me! Winter is come and gone,
But grief returns with the revolving year;
The airs and streams renew their joyous tone;
The ants, the bees, the swallows reappear;
Fresh leaves and flowers deck the dead Seasons' bier;
The amorous birds now pair in every brake,
And build their mossy homes in field and brere;
And the green lizard, and the golden snake,
Like unimprisoned flames, out of their trance awake.

XIX

Through wood and stream and field and hill and Ocean
A quickening life from the Earth's heart has burst
As it has ever done, with change and motion,
From the great morning of the world when first
God dawned on Chaos; in its stream immersed,
The lamps of Heaven flash with a softer light;
All baser things pant with life's sacred thirst;
Diffuse themselves; and spend in love's delight,
The beauty and the joy of their renewèd might.

XX

The leprous corpse, touched by this spirit tender,
Exhales itself in flowers of gentle breath;
Like incarnations of the stars, when splendour
Is changed to fragrance, they illumine death
And mock the merry worm that wakes beneath;
Naught we know, dies. Shall that alone which knows
Be as a sword consumed before the sheath
By sightless lightning?—the intense atom glows
A moment, then is quenched in a most cold repose.

XXI

Alas! that all we loved of him should be,
But for our grief, as if it had not been,
And grief itself be mortal! Woe is me!
Whence are we, and why are we? of what scene
The actors or spectators? Great and mean
Meet massed in death, who lends what life must borrow.
As long as skies are blue, and fields are green,
Evening must usher night, night urge the morrow,
Month follow month with woe, and year wake year to sorrow.

XXII

He will awake no more, oh, never more!
'Wake thou,' cried Misery, 'childless Mother, rise
Out of thy sleep, and slake, in thy heart's core,
A wound more fierce than his, with tears and sighs.'
And all the Dreams that watched Urania's eyes,
And all the Echoes whom their sister's song
Had held in holy silence, cried: 'Arise!'
Swift as a Thought by the snake Memory stung,
From her ambrosial rest the fading Splendour sprung.

XXIII

She rose like an autumnal Night, that springs
Out of the East, and follows wild and drear
The golden Day, which, on eternal wings,
Even as a ghost abandoning a bier,
Had left the Earth a corpse. Sorrow and fear
So struck, so roused, so rapped Urania;
So saddened round her like an atmosphere
Of stormy mist; so swept her on her way
Even to the mournful place where Adonais lay.

XXIV

Out of her secret Paradise she sped,
Through camps and cities rough with stone, and steel,
And human hearts, which to her aery tread
Yielding not, wounded the invisible
Palms of her tender feet where'er they fell:
And barbèd tongues, and thoughts more sharp than they,
Rent the soft Form they never could repel,
Whose sacred blood, like the young tears of May,
Paved with eternal flowers that undeserving way.

XXV

In the death-chamber for a moment Death,
Shamed by the presence of that living Might,
Blushed to annihilation, and the breath
Revisited those lips, and Life's pale light
Flashed through those limbs, so late her dear delight.
'Leave me not wild and drear and comfortless,
As silent lightning leaves the starless night!
Leave me not!' cried Urania: her distress
Roused Death: Death rose and smiled, and met her vain caress.

XXVI

'Stay yet awhile! speak to me once again;
Kiss me, so long but as a kiss may live;
And in my heartless breast and burning brain
That word, that kiss, shall all thoughts else survive,
With food of saddest memory kept alive,
Now thou art dead, as if it were a part
Of thee, my Adonais! I would give
All that I am to be as thou now art!
But I am chained to Time, and cannot thence depart!

XXVII

'O gentle child, beautiful as thou wert,
Why didst thou leave the trodden paths of men
Too soon, and with weak hands though mighty heart
Dare the unpastured dragon in his den?
Defenceless as thou wert, oh, where was then
Wisdom the mirrored shield, or scorn the spear?
Or hadst thou waited the full cycle, when
Thy spirit should have filled its crescent sphere,
The monsters of life's waste had fled from thee like deer.

XXVIII

'The herded wolves, bold only to pursue;
The obscene ravens, clamorous o'er the dead;
The vultures to the conqueror's banner true
Who feed where Desolation first has fed,
And whose wings rain contagion;—how they fled,
When, like Apollo, from his golden bow
The Pythian of the age one arrow sped
And smiled!—The spoilers tempt no second blow,
They fawn on the proud feet that spurn them lying low.

XXIX

'The sun comes forth, and many reptiles spawn;
He sets, and each ephemeral insect then
Is gathered into death without a dawn,
And the immortal stars awake again;
So is it in the world of living men:
A godlike mind soars forth, in its delight
Making earth bare and veiling heaven, and when
It sinks, the swarms that dimmed or shared its light
Leave to its kindred lamps the spirit's awful night.'

XXX

Thus ceased she: and the mountain shepherds came,
Their garlands sere, their magic mantles rent;
The Pilgrim of Eternity, whose fame
Over his living head like Heaven is bent,
An early but enduring monument,
Came, veiling all the lightnings of his song
In sorrow; from her wilds Ierne sent
The sweetest lyrist of her saddest wrong,
And Love taught Grief to fall like music from his tongue.

XXXI

Midst others of less note, came one frail Form,
A phantom among men; companionless
As the last cloud of an expiring storm
Whose thunder is its knell; he, as I guess,
Had gazed on Nature's naked loveliness,
Actaeon-like, and now he fled astray
With feeble steps o'er the world's wilderness,
And his own thoughts, along that rugged way,
Pursued, like raging hounds, their father and their prey.

XXXII

A pardlike Spirit beautiful and swift—
A Love in desolation masked;—a Power
Girt round with weakness;—it can scarce uplift
The weight of the superincumbent hour;
It is a dying lamp, a falling shower,
A breaking billow;—even whilst we speak
Is it not broken? On the withering flower
The killing sun smiles brightly: on a cheek
The life can burn in blood, even while the heart may break.

XXXIII

His head was bound with pansies overblown,
And faded violets, white, and pied, and blue;
And a light spear topped with a cypress cone,
Round whose rude shaft dark ivy-tresses grew
Yet dripping with the forest's noonday dew,
Vibrated, as the ever-beating heart
Shook the weak hand that grasped it; of that crew
He came the last, neglected and apart;
A herd-abandoned deer struck by the hunter's dart.

XXXIV

All stood aloof, and at his partial moan
Smiled through their tears; well knew that gentle band
Who in another's fate now wept his own,
As in the accents of an unknown land
He sung new sorrow; sad Urania scanned
The Stranger's mien, and murmured: 'Who art thou?'
He answered not, but with a sudden hand
Made bare his branded and ensanguined brow,
Which was like Cain's or Christ's—oh! that it should be so!

XXXV

What softer voice is hushed over the dead?
Athwart what brow is that dark mantle thrown?
What form leans sadly o'er the white death-bed,
In mockery of monumental stone,
The heavy heart heaving without a moan?
If it be He, who, gentlest of the wise,
Taught, soothed, loved, honoured the departed one,
Let me not vex, with inharmonious sighs,
The silence of that heart's accepted sacrifice.

XXXVI

Our Adonais has drunk poison—oh!
What deaf and viperous murderer could crown
Life's early cup with such a draught of woe?
The nameless worm would now itself disown:
It felt, yet could escape, the magic tone
Whose prelude held all envy, hate, and wrong,
But what was howling in one breast alone,
Silent with expectation of the song,
Whose master's hand is cold, whose silver lyre unstrung.

XXXVII

Live thou, whose infamy is not thy fame!
Live! fear no heavier chastisement from me,
Thou noteless blot on a remembered name!
But be thyself, and know thyself to be!
And ever at thy season be thou free
To spill the venom when thy fangs o'erflow:
Remorse and Self-contempt shall cling to thee;
Hot Shame shall burn upon thy secret brow,
And like a beaten hound tremble thou shalt—as now.

XXXVIII

Nor let us weep that our delight is fled
Far from these carrion kites that scream below;
He wakes or sleeps with the enduring dead;
Thou canst not soar where he is sitting now.—
Dust to the dust! but the pure spirit shall flow
Back to the burning fountain whence it came,
A portion of the Eternal, which must glow
Through time and change, unquenchably the same,
Whilst thy cold embers choke the sordid hearth of shame.

XXXIX

Peace, peace! he is not dead, he doth not sleep—
He hath awakened from the dream of life—
'Tis we, who lost in stormy visions, keep
With phantoms an unprofitable strife,
And in mad trance, strike with our spirit's knife
Invulnerable nothings.—*We* decay
Like corpses in a charnel; fear and grief
Convulse us and consume us day by day,
And cold hopes swarm like worms within our living clay.

XL

He has outsoared the shadow of our night;
Envy and calumny and hate and pain,
And that unrest which men miscall delight,
Can touch him not and torture not again;
From the contagion of the world's slow stain
He is secure, and now can never mourn
A heart grown cold, a head grown gray in vain;
Nor, when the spirit's self has ceased to burn,
With sparkless ashes load an unlamented urn.

XLI

He lives, he wakes—'tis Death is dead, not he;
Mourn not for Adonais.—Thou young Dawn,
Turn all thy dew to splendour, for from thee
The spirit thou lamentest is not gone;
Ye caverns and ye forests, cease to moan!
Cease, ye faint flowers and fountains, and thou Air,
Which like a mourning veil thy scarf hadst thrown
O'er the abandoned Earth, now leave it bare
Even to the joyous stars which smile on its despair!

XLII

He is made one with Nature: there is heard
His voice in all her music, from the moan
Of thunder, to the song of night's sweet bird;
He is a presence to be felt and known
In darkness and in light, from herb and stone,
Spreading itself where'er that Power may move
Which has withdrawn his being to its own;
Which wields the world with never-wearied love,
Sustains it from beneath, and kindles it above.

XLIII

He is a portion of the loveliness
Which once he made more lovely: he doth bear
His part, while the one Spirit's plastic stress
Sweeps through the dull dense world, compelling there,
All new successions to the forms they wear;
Torturing th' unwilling dross that checks its flight
To its own likeness, as each mass may bear;
And bursting in its beauty and its might
From trees and beasts and men into the Heaven's light.

XLIV

The splendours of the firmament of time
May be eclipsed, but are extinguished not;
Like stars to their appointed height they climb,
And death is a low mist which cannot blot
The brightness it may veil. When lofty thought
Lifts a young heart above its mortal lair,
And love and life contend in it, for what
Shall be its earthly doom, the dead live there
And move like winds of light on dark and stormy air.

XLV

The inheritors of unfulfilled renown
Rose from their thrones, built beyond mortal thought,
Far in the Unapparent. Chatterton
Rose pale,—his solemn agony had not
Yet faded from him; Sidney, as he fought
And as he fell and as he lived and loved
Sublimely mild, a Spirit without spot,
Arose; and Lucan, by his death approved:
Oblivion as they rose shrank like a thing reproved.

XLVI

And many more, whose names on Earth are dark,
But whose transmitted effluence cannot die
So long as fire outlives the parent spark,
Rose, robed in dazzling immortality.
'Thou art become as one of us,' they cry,
'It was for thee yon kingless sphere has long
Swung blind in unascended majesty,
Silent alone amid an Heaven of Song.
Assume thy wingèd throne, thou Vesper of our throng!'

XLVII

Who mourns for Adonais? Oh, come forth,
Fond wretch! and know thyself and him aright.
Clasp with thy panting soul the pendulous Earth;
As from a centre, dart thy spirit's light
Beyond all worlds, until its spacious might
Satiate the void circumference: then shrink
Even to a point within our day and night;
And keep thy heart light lest it make thee sink
When hope has kindled hope, and lured thee to the brink.

XLVIII

Or go to Rome, which is the sepulchre,
Oh, not of him, but of our joy: 'tis naught
That ages, empires, and religions there
Lie buried in the ravage they have wrought;
For such as he can lend,—they borrow not
Glory from those who made the world their prey;
And he is gathered to the kings of thought
Who waged contention with their time's decay,
And of the past are all that cannot pass away.

XLIX

Go thou to Rome,—at once the Paradise,
The grave, the city, and the wilderness;
And where its wrecks like shattered mountains rise,
And flowering weeds, and fragrant copses dress
The bones of Desolation's nakedness
Pass, till the spirit of the spot shall lead
Thy footsteps to a slope of green access
Where, like an infant's smile, over the dead
A light of laughing flowers along the grass is spread;

L

And gray walls moulder round, on which dull Time
Feeds, like slow fire upon a hoary brand;
And one keen pyramid with wedge sublime,
Pavilioning the dust of him who planned
This refuge for his memory, doth stand
Like flame transformed to marble; and beneath,
A field is spread, on which a newer band
Have pitched in Heaven's smile their camp of death,
Welcoming him we lose with scarce extinguished breath.

LI

Here pause: these graves are all too young as yet
To have outgrown the sorrow which consigned
Its charge to each; and if the seal is set,
Here, on one fountain of a mourning mind,
Break it not thou! too surely shalt thou find
Thine own well full, if thou returnest home,
Of tears and gall. From the world's bitter wind
Seek shelter in the shadow of the tomb.
What Adonais is, why fear we to become?

LII

The One remains, the many change and pass;
Heaven's light forever shines, Earth's shadows fly;
Life, like a dome of many-coloured glass,
Stains the white radiance of Eternity,
Until Death tramples it to fragments.—Die,
If thou wouldst be with that which thou dost seek!
Follow where all is fled!—Rome's azure sky,
Flowers, ruins, statues, music, words, are weak
The glory they transfuse with fitting truth to speak.

LIII

Why linger, why turn back, why shrink, my Heart?
Thy hopes are gone before: from all things here
They have departed; thou shouldst now depart!
A light is passed from the revolving year,
And man, and woman; and what still is dear
Attracts to crush, repels to make thee wither.
The soft sky smiles,—the low wind whispers near:
'Tis Adonais calls! oh, hasten thither,
No more let Life divide what Death can join together.

LIV

That Light whose smile kindles the Universe,
That Beauty in which all things work and move,
That Benediction which the eclipsing Curse
Of birth can quench not, that sustaining Love
Which through the web of being blindly wove
By man and beast and earth and air and sea,
Burns bright or dim, as each are mirrors of
The fire for which all thirst; now beams on me,
Consuming the last clouds of cold mortality.

LV

The breath whose might I have invoked in song
Descends on me; my spirit's bark is driven,
Far from the shore, far from the trembling throng
Whose sails were never to the tempest given;
The massy earth and spherèd skies are riven!
I am borne darkly, fearfully, afar;
Whilst, burning through the inmost veil of Heaven,
The soul of Adonais, like a star,
Beacons from the abode where the Eternal are.   (1821)

An elegy only equalled in our language by LYCIDAS,* *and in the point of passionate eloquence even superior to Milton's youthful lament for his friend.*

JOHN ADDINGTON SYMONDS
Shelley (1879)

JOHN KEATS

1 7 9 5 — 1 8 2 1

FROM THE SONNET TO HOMER

There is a budding morrow in midnight.

(1818?)

One of the finest lines in all poetry.

DANTE GABRIEL ROSSETTI
Quoted, H. Buxton Forman
The Complete Works of John Keats (1901)

JOHN KEATS

1 7 9 5 — 1 8 2 1

ARS GRATIA ARTIS

"None can usurp this height," return'd that shade,
"But those to whom the miseries of the world
"Are misery, and will not let them rest.
"All else who find a haven in the world,
"Where they may thoughtless sleep away their days,
"If by a chance into this fane they come,
"Rot on the pavement where thou rotted'st half."

The Fall of Hyperion: A Dream (1819)

In the words of Moneta in the VISION, *we find the most searing condemnation of Art for Art's Sake in English literature.*

ALBERT GUÉRARD
Art for Art's Sake (1936)

---

* For *Lycidas,* see page 712.

LA BELLE DAME SANS MERCI

I

O what can ail thee, Knight-at-arms,
  Alone and palely loitering?
The sedge has wither'd from the lake,
  And no birds sing!

II

O what can ail thee, Knight-at-arms,
  So haggard, and so woe-begone?
The squirrel's granary is full
  And the harvest's done.

III

I see a lilly on thy brow
  With anguish moist and fever dew;
And on thy cheeks a fading rose
  Fast withereth too.

IV

I met a lady in the meads,
  Full beautiful, a faery's child;
Her hair was long, her foot was light
  And her eyes were wild.

V

I made a garland for her head,
  And bracelets too, and fragrant zone;
She look'd at me as she did love,
  And made sweet moan.

VI

I set her on my pacing steed,
  And nothing else saw all day long;
For sidelong would she bend, and sing
  A faery's song.

VII

She found me roots of relish sweet,
 And honey wild, and manna dew;
And sure in language strange she said,
 I love thee true.

VIII

She took me to her elfin grot,
 And there she wept and sigh'd full sore,
And there I shut her wild wild eyes—
 With kisses four.

IX

And there she lulled me asleep,
 And there I dream'd, Ah woe betide!
The latest dream I ever dreamt
 On the cold hill side.

X

I saw pale kings and princes too,
 Pale warriors, death-pale were they all;
Who cried—"La belle Dame sans merci
 Hath thee in thrall!"

XI

I saw their starv'd lips in the gloam
 With horrid warning gaped wide,
And I awoke, and found me here
 On the cold hill's side.

XII

And this is why I sojourn here
 Alone and palely loitering;
Though the sedge is wither'd from the lake
 And no birds sing.

(1820)

Probably the very finest lyric in the English language.

COVENTRY PATMORE
Principle in Art (1889)

JOHN KEATS

1 7 9 5 — 1 8 2 1

ODE TO A NIGHTINGALE

I

My heart aches, and a drowsy numbness pains
   My sense, as though of hemlock I had drunk,
Or emptied some dull opiate to the drains
   One minute past, and Lethe-wards had sunk:
'Tis not through envy of thy happy lot,
   But being too happy in thine happiness,—
      That thou, light-winged Dryad of the trees,
         In some melodious plot
Of beechen green, and shadows numberless,
   Singest of summer in full-throated ease.

II

O, for a draught of vintage! that hath been
   Cool'd a long age in the deep-delved earth,
Tasting of Flora and the country green,
   Dance, and Provençal song, and sunburnt mirth!
O for a beaker full of the warm South,
   Full of the true, the blushful Hippocrene,
      With beaded bubbles winking at the brim,
         And purple-stained mouth;
That I might drink, and leave the world unseen,
   And with thee fade away into the forest dim:

III

Fade far away, dissolve, and quite forget
   What thou among the leaves hast never known,
The weariness, the fever, and the fret
   Here, where men sit and hear each other groan;
Where palsy shakes a few, sad, last gray hairs,
   Where youth grows pale, and spectre-thin, and dies;
      Where but to think is to be full of sorrow
         And leaden-eyed despairs,
Where beauty cannot keep her lustrous eyes,
   Or new Love pine at them beyond to-morrow.

IV

Away! away! for I will fly to thee,
   Not charioted by Bacchus and his pards,
But on the viewless wings of Poesy,
   Though the dull brain perplexes and retards:
Already with thee! tender is the night,
   And haply the Queen-Moon is on her throne,
     Cluster'd around by all her starry Fays;
       But here there is no light,
   Save what from heaven is with the breezes blown
     Through verdurous glooms and winding mossy ways.

V

I cannot see what flowers are at my feet,
   Nor what soft incense hangs upon the boughs,
But, in embalmed darkness, guess each sweet
   Wherewith the seasonable month endows
The grass, the thicket, and the fruit-tree wild;
   White hawthorn, and the pastoral eglantine;
     Fast fading violets cover'd up in leaves;
       And mid-May's eldest child,
   The coming musk-rose, full of dewy wine,
     The murmurous haunt of flies on summer eves.

VI

Darkling I listen; and, for many a time
   I have been half in love with easeful Death,
Call'd him soft names in many a mused rhyme,
   To take into the air my quiet breath;
Now more than ever seems it rich to die,
   To cease upon the midnight with no pain,
     While thou art pouring forth thy soul abroad
       In such an ecstasy!
   Still wouldst thou sing, and I have ears in vain—
     To thy high requiem become a sod.

VII

Thou wast not born for death, immortal Bird!
   No hungry generations tread thee down;
The voice I hear this passing night was heard
   In ancient days by emperor and clown:

Perhaps the self-same song that found a path
    Through the sad heart of Ruth, when, sick for home,
        She stood in tears amid the alien corn;
            The same that oft-times hath
        Charm'd magic casements, opening on the foam
    Of perilous seas, in faery lands forlorn.

VIII

Forlorn! the very word is like a bell
    To toll me back from thee to my sole self!
Adieu! the fancy cannot cheat so well
    As she is fam'd to do, deceiving elf.
Adieu! adieu! thy plaintive anthem fades
    Past the near meadows, over the still stream,
        Up the hill-side; and now 'tis buried deep
            In the next valley-glades:
        Was it a vision, or a waking dream?
        Fled is that music:—do I wake or sleep?

(1820)

One of the final masterpieces of human work in all time and for all ages.
ALGERNON CHARLES SWINBURNE
Miscellanies (1886)

JOHN KEATS

1 7 9 5 — 1 8 2 1

ODE TO PSYCHE

O Goddess! hear these tuneless numbers, wrung
    By sweet enforcement and remembrance dear,
And pardon that thy secrets should be sung
    Even into thine own soft-conched ear:
Surely I dreamt to-day, or did I see
    The winged Psyche with awaken'd eyes?
I wander'd in a forest thoughtlessly,
    And, on the sudden, fainting with surprise,
Saw two fair creatures, couched side by side
    In deepest grass, beneath the whisp'ring roof
    Of leaves and trembled blossoms, where there ran
        A brooklet, scarce espied:

1121

'Mid hush'd, cool-rooted flowers, fragrant-eyed,
   Blue, silver-white, and budded Tyrian,
They lay calm-breathing on the bedded grass;
   Their arms embraced, and their pinions too;
   Their lips touch'd not, but had not bade adieu,
As if disjoined by soft-handed slumber,
And ready still past kisses to outnumber
   At tender eye-dawn of aurorean love:
      The winged boy I knew;
   But who wast thou, O happy, happy dove?
   His Psyche true!

O latest born and loveliest vision far
   Of all Olympus' faded hierarchy!
Fairer than Phœbe's sapphire-region'd star,
   Or Vesper, amorous glow-worm of the sky;
Fairer than these, though temple thou hast none,
      Nor altar heap'd with flowers;
Nor virgin-choir to make delicious moan
      Upon the midnight hours;
No voice, no lute, no pipe, no incense sweet
   From chain-swung censer teeming;
No shrine, no grove, no oracle, no heat
   Of pale-mouth'd prophet dreaming.

O brightest! though too late for antique vows,
   Too, too late for the fond believing lyre,
When holy were the haunted forest boughs,
   Holy the air, the water, and the fire;
Yet even in these days so far retir'd
   From happy pieties, thy lucent fans,
   Fluttering among the faint Olympians,
I see, and sing, by my own eyes inspir'd.
So let me be thy choir, and make a moan
      Upon the midnight hours;
Thy voice, thy lute, thy pipe, thy incense sweet
   From swinged censer teeming;
Thy shrine, thy grove, thy oracle, thy heat
   Of pale-mouth'd prophet dreaming.

Yes, I will be thy priest, and build a fane
   In some untrodden region of my mind,
Where branched thoughts, new grown with pleasant pain,
   Instead of pines shall murmur in the wind:

Far, far around shall those dark-cluster'd trees
    Fledge the wild-ridged mountains steep by steep;
And there by zephyrs, streams, and birds, and bees,
    The moss-lain Dryads shall be lull'd to sleep;
And in the midst of this wide quietness
A rosy sanctuary will I dress
With the wreath'd trellis of a working brain,
    With buds, and bells, and stars without a name,
With all the gardener Fancy e'er could feign,
    Who breeding flowers, will never breed the same:
And there shall be for thee all soft delight
    That shadowy thought can win,
A bright torch, and a casement ope at night,
    To let the warm Love in!

                                    (1820)

ODE ON A GRECIAN URN

I

Thou still unravish'd bride of quietness,
    Thou foster-child of silence and slow time,
Sylvan historian, who canst thus express
    A flowery tale more sweetly than our rhyme:
What leaf-fring'd legend haunts about thy shape
    Of deities or mortals, or of both,
        In Tempe or the dales of Arcady?
    What men or gods are these? What maidens loth?
What mad pursuit? What struggle to escape?
        What pipes and timbrels? What wild ecstasy?

II

Heard melodies are sweet, but those unheard
    Are sweeter; therefore, ye soft pipes, play on;
Not to the sensual ear, but, more endear'd,
    Pipe to the spirit ditties of no tone:
Fair youth, beneath the trees, thou canst not leave
    Thy song, nor ever can those trees be bare;
        Bold Lover, never, never canst thou kiss,
Though winning near the goal—yet, do not grieve;
    She cannot fade, though thou hast not thy bliss,
        For ever wilt thou love, and she be fair!

Ah, happy, happy boughs! that cannot shed
　　Your leaves, nor ever bid the Spring adieu;
And, happy melodist, unwearied,
　　For ever piping songs for ever new;
More happy love! more happy, happy love!
　　For ever warm and still to be enjoy'd,
　　　For ever panting, and for ever young;
All breathing human passion far above,
　　That leaves a heart high-sorrowful and cloy'd,
　　　A burning forehead, and a parching tongue.

IV

Who are these coming to the sacrifice?
　　To what green altar, O mysterious priest,
Lead'st thou that heifer lowing at the skies,
　　And all her silken flanks with garlands drest?
What little town by river or sea shore,
　　Or mountain-built with peaceful citadel,
　　　Is emptied of this folk, this pious morn?
And, little town, thy streets for evermore
　　Will silent be; and not a soul to tell
　　　Why thou art desolate, can e'er return.

V

O Attic shape! Fair attitude! with brede
　　Of marble men and maidens overwrought,
With forest branches and the trodden weed;
　　Thou, silent form, dost tease us out of thought
As doth eternity: Cold Pastoral!
　　When old age shall this generation waste,
　　　Thou shalt remain, in midst of other woe
Than ours, a friend to man, to whom thou say'st,
　　"Beauty is truth, truth beauty,"—that is all
　　　Ye know on earth, and all ye need to know.

(1820)

Poems which for perfect apprehension and execution of all attainable in their own sphere would weight down all the world of poetry.

ALGERNON CHARLES SWINBURNE
Essays and Studies (1875)

JOHN KEATS

1 7 9 5 — 1 8 2 1

SONNET

Written on a Blank Page in Shakespeare's Poems,
facing "A Lover's Complaint."

Bright star, would I were stedfast as thou art—
    Not in lone splendour hung aloft the night
And watching, with eternal lids apart,
    Like nature's patient, sleepless Eremite,
The moving waters at their priestlike task
    Of pure ablution round earth's human shores,
Or gazing on the new soft-fallen mask
    Of snow upon the mountains and the moors—
No—yet still stedfast, still unchangeable,
    Pillow'd upon my fair love's ripening breast,
To feel for ever its soft fall and swell,
    Awake for ever in a sweet unrest,
Still, still to hear her tender-taken breath,
And so live ever—or else swoon to death.

(1820)

Perhaps the most beautiful single sonnet in the English language.

HENRI PEYRE
Writers and Their Critics (1944)

JOHN KEATS

1 7 9 5 — 1 8 2 1

WIDE-SPREADED NIGHT

As men talk in a dream, so Corinth all,
Throughout her palaces imperial,
And all her populous streets and temples lewd,
Mutter'd, like tempest in the distance brew'd,
To the wide-spreaded night above her towers.
Men, women, rich and poor, in the cool hours,

Shuffled their sandals o'er the pavement white,
Companion'd or alone; while many a light
Flared, here and there, from wealthy festivals,
And threw their moving shadows on the walls,
Or found them cluster'd in the corniced shade
Of some arch'd temple door, or dusky colonnade.

Lamia (1820)

*A masterpiece of descriptive imagination scarce to be surpassed in the
whole range of our poetry.*

SIDNEY COLVIN
John Keats (1920)

JOHN KEATS

1 7 9 5 — 1 8 2 1

THE EVE OF ST. AGNES

I.

St. Agnes' Eve—Ah, bitter chill it was!
The owl, for all his feathers, was a-cold;
The hare limp'd trembling through the frozen grass,
And silent was the flock in woolly fold:
Numb were the Beadsman's fingers, while he told
His rosary, and while his frosted breath,
Like pious incense from a censer old,
Seem'd taking flight for heaven, without a death,
Past the sweet Virgin's picture, while his prayer he saith.

II.

His prayer he saith, this patient, holy man;
Then takes his lamp, and riseth from his knees,
And back returneth, meagre, barefoot, wan,
Along the chapel aisle by slow degrees:
The sculptur'd dead, on each side, seem to freeze,
Emprison'd in black, purgatorial rails:
Knights, ladies, praying in dumb orat'ries,
He passeth by; and his weak spirit fails
To think how they may ache in icy hoods and mails.

III

Northward he turneth through a little door,
And scarce three steps, ere Music's golden tongue
Flatter'd to tears this aged man and poor;
But no—already had his deathbell rung;
The joys of all his life were said and sung:
His was harsh penance on St. Agnes' Eve:
Another way he went, and soon among
Rough ashes sat he for his soul's reprieve,
And all night kept awake, for sinners' sake to grieve.

IV.

That ancient Beadsman heard the prelude soft;
And so it chanc'd, for many a door was wide,
From hurry to and fro. Soon, up aloft,
The silver, snarling trumpets 'gan to chide:
The level chambers, ready with their pride,
Were glowing to receive a thousand guests:
The carved angels, ever eager-eyed,
Star'd, where upon their heads the cornice rests,
With hair blown back, and wings put cross-wise on their breasts.

V.

At length burst in the argent revelry,
With plume, tiara, and all rich array,
Numerous as shadows haunting fairily
The brain, new stuff'd, in youth, with triumphs gay
Of old romance. These let us wish away,
And turn, sole-thoughted, to one Lady there,
Whose heart had brooded, all that wintry day,
On love, and wing'd St. Agnes' saintly care,
As she had heard old dames full many times declare.

VI.

They told her how, upon St. Agnes' Eve,
Young virgins might have visions of delight,
And soft adorings from their loves receive
Upon the honey'd middle of the night,
If ceremonies due they did aright;
As, supperless to bed they must retire,
And couch supine their beauties, lily white;
Nor look behind, nor sideways, but require
Of Heaven with upward eyes for all that they desire.

VII

Full of this whim was thoughtful Madeline:
The music, yearning like a God in pain,
She scarcely heard: her maiden eyes divine,
Fix'd on the floor, saw many a sweeping train
Pass by—she heeded not at all: in vain
Came many a tiptoe, amorous cavalier,
And back retir'd; not cool'd by high disdain,
But she saw not: her heart was otherwhere:
She sigh'd for Agnes' dreams, the sweetest of the year.

VIII.

She danc'd along with vague, regardless eyes,
Anxious her lips, her breathing quick and short:
The hallow'd hour was near at hand: she sighs
Amid the timbrels, and the throng'd resort
Of whisperers in anger, or in sport;
'Mid looks of love, defiance, hate, and scorn,
Hoodwink'd with faery fancy; all amort,
Save to St. Agnes and her lambs unshorn,
And all the bliss to be before to-morrow morn.

IX.

So, purposing each moment to retire,
She linger'd still. Meantime, across the moors,
Had come young Porphyro, with heart on fire
For Madeline. Beside the portal doors,
Buttress'd from moonlight, stands he, and implores
All saints to give him sight of Madeline,
But for one moment in the tedious hours,
That he might gaze and worship all unseen;
Perchance speak, kneel, touch, kiss—in sooth such things have been.

X.

He ventures in: let no buzz'd whisper tell:
All eyes be muffled, or a hundred swords
Will storm his heart, Love's fev'rous citadel:
For him, those chambers held barbarian hordes,
Hyena foemen, and hot-blooded lords,
Whose very dogs would execrations howl
Against his lineage: not one breast affords
Him any mercy, in that mansion foul,
Save one old beldame, weak in body and in soul.

XI.

Ah, happy chance! the aged creature came,
Shuffling along with ivory-headed wand,
To where he stood, hid from the torch's flame,
Behind a broad hall-pillar, far beyond
The sound of merriment and chorus bland:
He startled her; but soon she knew his face,
And grasp'd his fingers in her palsied hand,
Saying, "Mercy, Porphyro! hie thee from this place;
"They are all here to-night, the whole blood-thirsty race!

XII.

"Get hence! get hence! there's dwarfish Hildebrand;
"He had a fever late, and in the fit
"He cursed thee and thine, both house and land:
"Then there's that old Lord Maurice, not a whit
"More tame for his gray hairs—Alas me! flit!
"Flit like a ghost away."—"Ah, Gossip dear,
"We're safe enough; here in this arm-chair sit,
"And tell me how"—"Good Saints! not here, not here;
"Follow me, child, or else these stones will be thy bier."

XIII.

He follow'd through a lowly arched way,
Brushing the cobwebs with his lofty plume,
And as she mutter'd "Well-a—well-a-day!"
He found him in a little moonlight room,
Pale, lattic'd, chill, and silent as a tomb.
"Now tell me where is Madeline," said he,
"O tell me, Angela, by the holy loom
"Which none but secret sisterhood may see,
"When they St. Agnes' wool are weaving piously."

XIV.

"St. Agnes! Ah! it is St. Agnes' Eve—
"Yet men will murder upon holy days:
"Thou must hold water in a witch's sieve,
"And be liege-lord of all the Elves and Fays,
"To venture so: it fills me with amaze
"To see thee, Porphyro!—St. Agnes' Eve!
"God's help! my lady fair the conjuror plays
"This very night: good angels her deceive!
"But let me laugh awhile, I've mickle time to grieve."

Feebly she laugheth in the languid moon,
While Porphyro upon her face doth look,
Like puzzled urchin on an aged crone
Who keepeth clos'd a wond'rous riddle-book,
As spectacled she sits in chimney nook.
But soon his eyes grew brilliant, when she told
His lady's purpose; and he scarce could brook
Tears, at the thought of those enchantments cold
And Madeline asleep in lap of legends old.

XVI.

Sudden a thought came like a full-blown rose,
Flushing his brow, and in his pained heart
Made purple riot: then doth he propose
A stratagem, that makes the beldame start:
"A cruel man and impious thou art:
"Sweet lady, let her pray, and sleep, and dream
"Alone with her good angels, far apart
"From wicked men like thee. Go, go!—I deem
"Thou canst not surely be the same that thou didst seem."

XVII.

"I will not harm her, by all saints I swear,"
Quoth Porphyro: "O may I ne'er find grace
"When my weak voice shall whisper its last prayer,
"If one of her soft ringlets I displace,
"Or look with ruffian passion in her face:
"Good Angela, believe me by these tears;
"Or I will, even in a moment's space,
"Awake, with horrid shout, my foemen's ears,
"And beard them, though they be more fang'd than wolves and bears."

XVIII.

"Ah! why wilt thou affright a feeble soul?
"A poor, weak, palsy-stricken, churchyard thing,
"Whose passing-bell may ere the midnight toll;
"Whose prayers for thee, each morn and evening,
"Were never miss'd."—Thus plaining, doth she bring
A gentler speech from burning Porphyro;
So woful, and of such deep sorrowing,
That Angela gives promise she will do
Whatever he shall wish, betide her weal or woe.

XIX.

Which was, to lead him, in close secrecy,
Even to Madeline's chamber, and there hide
Him in a closet, of such privacy
That he might see her beauty unespied,
And win perhaps that night a peerless bride,
While legion'd fairies pac'd the coverlet,
And pale enchantment held her sleepy-eyed.
Never on such a night have lovers met,
Since Merlin paid his Demon all the monstrous debt.

XX.

"It shall be as thou wishest," said the Dame:
"All cates and dainties shall be stored there
"Quickly on this feast-night: by the tambour frame
"Her own lute thou wilt see: no time to spare,
"For I am slow and feeble, and scarce dare
"On such a catering trust my dizzy head.
"Wait here, my child, with patience; kneel in prayer
"The while: Ah! thou must needs the lady wed,
"Or may I never leave my grave among the dead."

XXI.

So saying, she hobbled off with busy fear.
The lover's endless minutes slowly pass'd;
The dame return'd, and whisper'd in his ear
To follow her; with aged eyes aghast
From fright of dim espial. Safe at last,
Through many a dusky gallery, they gain
The maiden's chamber, silken, hush'd, and chaste;
Where Porphyro took covert, pleas'd amain.
His poor guide hurried back with agues in her brain.

XXII.

Her falt'ring hand upon the balustrade,
Old Angela was feeling for the stair,
When Madeline, St. Agnes' charmed maid,
Rose, like a mission'd spirit, unaware:
With silver taper's light, and pious care,
She turn'd, and down the aged gossip led
To a safe level matting. Now prepare,
Young Porphyro, for gazing on that bed;
She comes, she comes again, like ring-dove fray'd and fled.

XXIII.

Out went the taper as she hurried in;
Its little smoke, in pallid moonshine, died:
She clos'd the door, she panted, all akin
To spirits of the air, and visions wide:
No uttered syllable, or, woe betide!
But to her heart, her heart was voluble,
Paining with eloquence her balmy side;
As though a tongueless nightingale should swell
Her throat in vain, and die, heart-stifled, in her dell.

XXIV.

A casement high and triple-arch'd there was,
All garlanded with carven imag'ries
Of fruits, and flowers, and bunches of knot-grass,
And diamonded with panes of quaint device,
Innumerable of stains and splendid dyes,
As are the tiger-moth's deep-damask'd wings;
And in the midst, 'mong thousand heraldries,
And twilight saints, and dim emblazonings,
A shielded scutcheon blush'd with blood of queens and kings.

XXV.

Full on this casement shone the wintry moon,
And threw warm gules on Madeline's fair breast,
As down she knelt for heaven's grace and boon;
Rose-bloom fell on her hands, together prest,
And on her silver cross soft amethyst,
And on her hair a glory, like a saint:
She seem'd a splendid angel, newly drest,
Save wings, for heaven:—Porphyro grew faint:
She knelt, so pure a thing, so free from mortal taint.

XXVI.

Anon his heart revives: her vespers done,
Of all its wreathed pearls her hair she frees;
Unclasps her warmed jewels one by one;
Loosens her fragrant boddice; by degrees
Her rich attire creeps rustling to her knees:
Half-hidden, like a mermaid in sea-weed,
Pensive awhile she dreams awake, and sees,
In fancy, fair St. Agnes in her bed,
But dares not look behind, or all the charm is fled.

XXVII.

Soon, trembling in her soft and chilly nest,
In sort of wakeful swoon, perplex'd she lay,
Until the poppied warmth of sleep oppress'd
Her soothed limbs, and soul fatigued away;
Flown, like a thought, until the morrow-day;
Blissfully haven'd both from joy and pain;
Clasp'd like a missal where swart Paynims pray;
Blinded alike from sunshine and from rain,
As though a rose should shut, and be a bud again.

XXVIII.

Stol'n to this paradise, and so entranced,
Porphyro gazed upon her empty dress,
And listen'd to her breathing, if it chanced
To wake into a slumberous tenderness;
Which when he heard, that minute did he bless,
And breath'd himself: then from the closet crept,
Noiseless as fear in a wide wilderness,
And over the hush'd carpet, silent, stept,
And 'tween the curtains peep'd, where, lo!—how fast she slept.

XXIX.

Then by the bed-side, where the faded moon
Made a dim, silver twilight, soft he set
A table, and, half anguish'd, threw thereon
A cloth of woven crimson, gold, and jet:—
O for some drowsy Morphean amulet!
The boisterous, midnight, festive clarion,
The kettle-drum, and far-heard clarionet,
Affray his ears, though but in dying tone:—
The hall door shuts again, and all the noise is gone.

XXX.

And still she slept an azur-lidded sleep,
In blanched linen, smooth, and lavender'd,
While he from forth the closet brought a heap
Of candied apple, quince, and plum, and gourd
With jellies soother than the creamy curd,
And lucent syrops, tinct with cinnamon;
Manna and dates, in argosy transferr'd
From Fez; and spiced dainties, every one,
From silken Samarcand to cedar'd Lebanon.

XXXI.

These delicates he heap'd with glowing hand
On golden dishes and in baskets bright
Of wreathed silver: sumptuous they stand
In the retired quiet of the night,
Filling the chilly room with perfume light.—
"And now, my love, my seraph fair, awake!
"Thou art my heaven, and I thine eremite:
"Open thine eyes, for meek St. Agnes' sake,
"Or I shall drowse beside thee, so my soul doth ache.'

XXXII.

Thus whispering, his warm, unnerved arm
Sank in her pillow. Shaded was her dream
By the dusk curtains:—'twas a midnight charm
Impossible to melt as iced stream:
The lustrous salvers in the moonlight gleam;
Broad golden fringe upon the carpet lies:
It seem'd he never, never could redeem
From such a stedfast spell his lady's eyes;
So mus'd awhile, entoil'd in woofed phantasies.

XXXIII.

Awakening up, he took her hollow lute,—
Tumultuous,—and, in chords that tenderest be,
He play'd an ancient ditty, long since mute,
In Provence call'd, "La belle dame sans mercy:"
Close to her ear touching the melody;—
Wherewith disturb'd, she utter'd a soft moan:
He ceased—she panted quick—and suddenly
Her blue affrayed eyes wide open shone:
Upon his knees he sank, pale as smooth-sculptured stone.

XXXIV.

Her eyes were open, but she still beheld,
Now wide awake, the vision of her sleep:
There was a painful change, that nigh expell'd
The blisses of her dream so pure and deep
At which fair Madeline began to weep,
And moan forth witless words with many a sigh;
While still her gaze on Porphyro would keep;
Who knelt, with joined hands and piteous eye,
Fearing to move or speak, she look'd so dreamingly.

XXXV.

"Ah, Porphyro!" said she, "but even now
"Thy voice was at sweet tremble in mine ear,
"Made tuneable with every sweetest vow;
"And those sad eyes were spiritual and clear:
"How chang'd thou art! how pallid, chill, and drear!
"Give me that voice again, my Porphyro,
"Those looks immortal, those complainings dear!
"Oh leave me not in this eternal woe,
"For if thou diest, my Love, I know not where to go."

XXXVI.

Beyond a mortal man impassion'd far
At these voluptuous accents, he arose,
Ethereal, flush'd, and like a throbbing star
Seen mid the sapphire heaven's deep repose
Into her dream he melted, as the rose
Blendeth its odour with the violet,—
Solution sweet: meantime the frost-wind blows
Like Love's alarum pattering the sharp sleet
Against the window-panes; St. Agnes' moon hath set.

XXXVII.

'Tis dark: quick pattereth the flaw-blown sleet:
"This is no dream, my bride, my Madeline!"
'Tis dark: the iced gusts still rave and beat:
"No dream, alas! alas! and woe is mine!
"Porphyro will leave me here to fade and pine.—
"Cruel! what traitor could thee hither bring?
"I curse not, for my heart is lost in thine
"Though thou forsakest a deceived thing;—
"A dove forlorn and lost with sick unpruned wing."

XXXVIII.

"My Madeline! sweet dreamer! lovely bride!
"Say, may I be for aye thy vassal blest?
"Thy beauty's shield, heart-shap'd and vermeil dyed?
"Ah, silver shrine, here will I take my rest
"After so many hours of toil and quest,
"A famish'd pilgrim,—saved by miracle.
"Though I have found, I will not rob thy nest
"Saving of thy sweet self; if thou think'st well
"To trust, fair Madeline, to no rude infidel."

XXXIX.

"Hark! 'tis an elfin-storm from faery land,
"Of haggard seeming, but a boon indeed:
"Arise—arise! the morning is at hand;—
"The bloated wassaillers will never heed:—
"Let us away, my love, with happy speed;
"There are no ears to hear, or eyes to see,—
"Drown'd all in Rhenish and the sleepy mead:
"Awake! Arise! my love, and fearless be,
"For o'er the southern moors I have a home for thee."

XL.

She hurried at his words, beset with fears,
For there were sleeping dragons all around,
At glaring watch, perhaps, with ready spears—
Down the wide stairs a darkling way they found.—
In all the house was heard no human sound.
A chain-droop'd lamp was flickering by each door;
The arras, rich with horseman, hawk, and hound,
Flutter'd in the besieging wind's uproar;
And the long carpets rose along the gusty floor.

XLI.

They glide, like phantoms, into the wide hall;
Like phantoms, to the iron porch, they glide;
Where lay the Porter, in uneasy sprawl,
With a huge empty flaggon by his side:
The wakeful bloodhound rose, and shook his hide,
But his sagacious eye an inmate owns:
By one, and one, the bolts full easy slide:—
The chains lie silent on the footworn stones;—
The key turns, and the door upon its hinges groans.

XLII.

And they are gone: ay, ages long ago
These lovers fled away into the storm.
That night the Baron dreamt of many a woe,
And all his warrior-guests, with shade and form
Of witch, and demon, and large coffin-worm,
Were long be-nightmar'd. Angela the old
Died palsy-twitch'd, with meagre face deform;
The Beadsman, after thousand aves told,
For aye unsought for slept among his ashes cold.   (1820)

Sᴛ. ᴀɢɴᴇs's ᴇᴠᴇ, *that unsurpassed example—nay, must we not rather call it unequalled?—of the pure charm of coloured and romantic narrative in English verse.*

SIDNEY COLVIN
Keats (1904)

J O H N   K E A T S

1 7 9 5 — 1 8 2 1

THE KERNEL OF THE GRAVE

She gaz'd into the fresh-thrown mould, as though
    One glance did fully all its secrets tell;
Clearly she saw, as other eyes would know
    Pale limbs at bottom of a crystal well;
Upon the murderous spot she seem'd to grow,
    Like to a native lilly of the dell:
Then with her knife, all sudden, she began
To dig more fervently than misers can.

Soon she turn'd up a soiled glove, whereon
    Her silk had play'd in purple phantasies,
She kiss'd it with a lip more chill than stone,
    And put it in her bosom, where it dries
And freezes utterly unto the bone
    Those dainties made to still an infant's cries:
Then 'gan she work again; nor stay'd her care,
But to throw back at times her veiling hair.

That old nurse stood beside her wondering,
    Until her heart felt pity to the core
At sight of such a dismal labouring,
    And so she kneeled, with her locks all hoar,
And put her lean hands to the horrid thing:
    Three hours they labour'd at this travail sore;
At last they felt the kernel of the grave,
And Isabella did not stamp and rave.

Isabella (1820)

Two Florentines, merchants, discovering that their sister Isabella has placed her affections upon Lorenzo, a young factor in their employ, when they had hopes of procuring for her a noble match, decoy Lorenzo, under pretence of a ride, into a wood, where they suddenly stab and bury him. . . . Returning to their sister, they delude her with a story of their having sent Lorenzo abroad to look after their merchandises; but the spirit of her lover appears to Isabella in a dream, and discovers how and where he was stabbed, and the spot where they have buried him. To ascertain the truth of the vision, she sets out to the place, accompanied by her old nurse, ignorant as yet of her wild purpose. . . . There is nothing more awfully simple in diction, more nakedly grand and moving in sentiment, in Dante, in Chaucer, or in Spenser.

CHARLES LAMB

in The New Times (July 19, 1820)

AUGUST GRAF VON PLATEN

1 7 9 6 — 1 8 3 5

DER PILGRIM VOR ST. JUST

Nacht ist's, und Stürme sausen für und für;
Hispanische Mönche, schliesst mir auf die Tür!

Lasst hier mich ruhn, bis Glockenton mich weckt,
Der zum Gebet euch in die Kirche schreckt!

Bereitet mir, was euer Haus vermag,
Ein Ordenskleid und einen Sarkophag!

Gönnt mir die kleine Zelle, weiht mich ein!
Mehr als die Hälfte dieser Welt war mein.

Das Haupt, das nun der Schere sich bequemt,
Mit mancher Krone ward's bediademt.

Die Schulter, die der Kutte nun sich bückt,
Hat kaiserlicher Hermelin geschmückt.

Nun bin ich vor dem Tod den Toten gleich
Und fall' in Trümmer wie das alte Reich.

THE PILGRIM BEFORE ST. JUST

'Tis night, and tempests roar unceasingly:
O Spanish monks, unlock your gates for me!

Here let me rest, until the pealing bell
Shall drive you chapelwards your beads to tell.

1138

Nought but your Order's common gifts I crave,
A friar's raiment and a friar's grave.

Grant me a cell, receive me at your shrine,
More than the half of all the world was mine.

This head that meekly to the tonsure bows,
Has borne full many a crown upon its brows.

This shoulder, bending low the cowl to don,
Imperial ermine wore in days agone.

Like to the dead am I before death calls,
And fall in ruins as my Empire falls.
Translated by Norman Macleod

Platen and Eichendorff were both spiritual sons of Goethe, in whom classical and Romantic influences were uniquely harmonised, and Goethe had given the watchword "Grace and Dignity," which Platen tried to exemplify. His contemporaries were quick to detect a coldness and lack of sympathy in him, and, finding literary life in Germany uncongenial, he turned to Italy for inspiration. His sonnets are among the most perfectly finished in German, and one poem, "The Pilgrim [i.e. the Emperor Charles V] before the Monastery of St. Just," is in all German anthologies.

NORMAN MACLEOD
German Lyric Poetry (1930)

ALFRED DE VIGNY

1 7 9 7 — 1 8 6 3

MY TORN HEART

Sur mon cœur déchiré viens poser ta main pure,
Ne me laisse jamais seul avec la Nature;
Car je la connais trop pour n'en pas avoir peur.

Elle me dit: . . .

"Je roule avec dédain, sans voir et sans entendre,
A côté des fourmis les populations;
Je ne distingue pas leur terrier de leur cendre,
J'ignore en les portant les noms des nations.

On me dit une mère, et je suis une tombe.
Mon hiver prend vos morts comme son hécatombe,
Mon printemps ne sent pas vos adorations.

Avant vous, j'étais belle et toujours parfumée,
J'abandonnais au vent mes cheveux tout entiers,
Je suivais dans les cieux ma route accoutumée,
Sur l'axe harmonieux des divins balanciers,
Après vous, traversant l'espace où tout s'élance,
J'irai seule et sereine, en un chaste silence
Je fendrai l'air du front et de mes seins altiers."

On my torn heart come and place thy pure hand, never leave me
alone with nature, for I know her too well not to fear her. She says to me:
. . . "I whirl round contemptuously, unseeing and unhearing, the peoples
of the earth side by side with the ants; I do not distinguish their dwelling from their ashes, and as I carry them I am ignorant of the names of
the nations. I am called a mother and I am a tomb. My winter takes your
dead as its hecatomb, my spring does not hear your adorations. Before
your day I was beautiful and always perfumed, I abandoned to the wind
my whole hair, I followed my accustomed way in the heavens on the
harmonious axis of the divine scales. After your departure, I shall go on
alone and serene, traversing in a chaste silence the space through which
all things move; I shall cleave the air with my brow and my haughty
breasts."

La Maison du berger (1844)
Translated by A. W. Evans

*An expression of a sombre and pathetic philosophy unsurpassed in pain-
ful eloquence.*

ANATOLE FRANCE
La Vie littéraire (1888–92)

ALFRED DE VIGNY

1 7 9 7 — 1 8 6 3

LA COLÈRE DE SAMSON

Le désert est muet, la tente est solitaire.
Quel pasteur courageux la dressa sur la terre
Du sable et des lions?—La nuit n'a pas calmé
La fournaise du jour dont l'air est enflammé.

Un vent léger s'élève à l'horizon et ride
Les flots de la poussière ainsi qu'un lac limpide.
Le lin blanc de la tente est bercé mollement;
L'œuf d'autruche, allumé, veille paisiblement,
Des voyageurs voilés intérieure étoile,
Et jette longuement deux ombres sur la toile.

L'une est grande et superbe, et l'autre est à ses pieds:
C'est Dalila l'esclave, et ses bras sont liés
Aux genoux réunis du maître jeune et grave
Dont la force divine obéit à l'esclave.
Comme un doux léopard, elle est souple et répand
Ses cheveux dénoués aux pieds de son amant.
Ses grands yeux, entr'ouverts comme s'ouvre l'amande,
Sont brûlants du plaisir que son regard demande,
Et jettent, par éclats, leurs mobiles lueurs.

Ses bras fins tout mouillés de tièdes sueurs,
Ses pieds voluptueux qui sont croisés sous elle,
Ses flancs, plus élancés que ceux de la gazelle,
Pressés de bracelets, d'anneaux, de boucles d'or,
Sont bruns, et, comme il sied aux filles de Hatsor,
Ses deux seins, tout chargés d'amulettes anciennes,
Sont chastement pressés d'étoffes syriennes.

Les genoux de Samson fortement sont unis
Comme les deux genoux du colosse Anubis.
Elle s'endort sans force et riante et bercée
Par la puissante main sous sa tête placée.
Lui, murmure le chant funèbre et douloureux
Prononcé dans la gorge avec des mots hébreux.
Elle ne comprend pas la parole étrangère,
Mais le chant verse un somme en sa tête légère.

"Une lutte éternelle en tout temps, en tout lieu,
Se livre sur la terre, en présence de Dieu,
Entre la bonté d'Homme et la ruse de Femme,
Car la femme est un être impur de corps et d'âme.

"L'Homme a toujours besoin de caresse et d'amour;
Sa mère l'en abreuve alors qu'il vient au jour,
Et ce bras le premier l'engourdit, le balance
Et lui donne un désir d'amour et d'indolence.
Troublé dans l'action, troublé dans le dessein,
Il rêvera partout à la chaleur du sein,
Aux chansons de la nuit, aux baisers de l'aurore,
A la lèvre de feu que sa lèvre dévore,

Aux cheveux dénoués qui roulent sur son front,
Et les regrets du lit, en marchant, le suivront.
Il ira dans la ville, et, là, les vierges folles
Le prendront dans leurs lacs aux premières paroles.
Plus fort il sera né, mieux il sera vaincu,
Car plus le fleuve est grand et plus il est ému.
Quand le combat que Dieu fit pour la créature
Et contre son semblable et contre la nature
Force l'Homme à chercher un sein où reposer,
Quand ses yeux sont en pleurs, il lui faut un baiser.
Mais il n'a pas encor fini toute sa tâche:
Vient un autre combat plus secret, traître et lâche;
Sous son bras, sous son cœur se livre celui-là;
Et, plus ou moins, la femme est toujours DALILA.

"Elle rit et triomphe; en sa froideur savante,
Au milieu de ses sœurs elle attend et se vante
De ne rien éprouver des atteintes du feu.
A sa plus belle amie elle en a fait l'aveu:
Elle se fait aimer sans aimer elle-même;
Un Maître lui fait peur. C'est le plaisir qu'elle aime;
L'Homme est rude et le prend sans savoir le donner.
Un sacrifice illustre et fait pour étonner
Rehausse mieux que l'or, aux yeux de ses pareilles,
La beauté qui produit tant d'étranges merveilles
Et d'un sang précieux sait arroser ses pas.
—Donc, ce que j'ai voulu, Seigneur, n'existe pas!—
Celle à qui va l'amour et de qui vient la vie,
Celle-là, par orgueil, se fait notre ennemie.
La Femme est, à présent, pire que dans ces temps
Où, voyant les Humains, Dieu dit: "Je me repens!"
Bientôt, se retirant dans un hideux royaume,
La Femme aura Gomorrhe et l'Homme aura Sodôme;
Et, se jetant, de loin, un regard irrité,
Les deux sexes mourront chacun de son côté.

"Éternel! Dieu des forts! vous savez que mon âme
N'avait pour aliment que l'amour d'une femme,
Puisant dans l'amour seul plus de sainte vigueur
Que mes cheveux divins n'en donnaient à mon cœur.
—Jugez-nous. —La voilà sur mes pieds endormie.
Trois fois elle a vendu mes secrets et ma vie,
Et trois fois a versé des pleurs fallacieux
Qui n'ont pu me cacher la rage de ses yeux;
Honteuse qu'elle était plus encor qu'étonnée
De se voir découverte ensemble et pardonnée,

Car la bonté de l'Homme est forte, et sa douceur
Écrase, en l'absolvant, l'être faible et menteur.

"Mais enfin je suis las. J'ai l'âme si pesante,
Que mon corps gigantesque et ma tête puissante
Qui soutiennent le poids des colonnes d'airain
Ne la peuvent porter avec tout son chagrin.
   Toujours voir serpenter la vipère dorée
Qui se traîne en sa fange et s'y croit ignorée;
Toujours ce compagnon dont le cœur n'est pas sûr,
La Femme, enfant malade et douze fois impur!
Toujours mettre sa force à garder sa colère
Dans son cœur offensé, comme en un sanctuaire
D'où le feu s'échappant irait tout dévorer,
Interdire à ses yeux de voir ou de pleurer,
C'est trop! Dieu, s'il le veut, peut balayer ma cendre.
J'ai donné mon secret, Dalila va le vendre.
Qu'ils seront beaux, les pieds de celui qui viendra
Pour m'annoncer la mort!—Ce qui sera, sera!"

Il dit, et s'endormit près d'elle jusqu'à l'heure
Où les guerriers, tremblants d'être dans sa demeure,
Payant au poids de l'or chacun de ses cheveux,
Attachèrent ses mains et brûlèrent ses yeux,
Le traînèrent sanglant et chargé d'une chaîne
Que douze grands taureaux ne tiraient qu'avec peine,
Le placèrent debout, silencieusement,
Devant Dagon, leur Dieu, qui gémit sourdement
Et deux fois, en tournant, recula sur sa base
Et fit pâlir deux fois ses prêtres en extase,
Allumèrent l'encens, dressèrent un festin
Dont le bruit s'entendait du mont le plus lointain,
Et près de la génisse aux pieds du Dieu tuée
Placèrent Dalila, pâle prostituée,
Couronnée, adorée et reine du repas,
Mais tremblante et disant: Il ne me verra pas!

————————

Terre et ciel! avez-vous tressailli d'allégresse
Lorsque vous avez vu la menteuse maîtresse
Suivre d'un œil hagard les yeux tachés de sang
Qui cherchaient le soleil d'un regard impuissant?
Et quand enfin Samson, secouant les colonnes
Qui faisaient le soutien des immenses Pylônes,
Écrasa d'un seul coup, sous les débris mortels,
Ses trois mille ennemis, leurs dieux et leurs autels?

Terre et ciel! punissez par de telles justices
La trahison ourdie en des amours factices,
Et la délation du secret de nos cœurs
Arraché dans nos bras par des baisers menteurs!

THE ANGER OF SAMSON

The desert is mute, the tent is solitary. What courageous shepherd pitched it in the land of sand and lions? Night has not stilled the fiery furnace of the day, the air of which is ablaze. A light wind rises on the horizon and ripples the waves of dust like a clear lake. The white linen of the tent sways softly; the lighted ostrich-egg lamp keeps vigil peacefully, like a star within for veiled travelers, and throws two long shadows on the canvas. One shadow is tall and proud, and the other is at its feet: It is the slave, Delilah, and her arms are linked about the knees of the young, grave master whose divine strength yields to the slave. She is lithe as a smooth leopard, and she spreads her unbound hair at the feet of her lover. Her large eyes, half-open like an almond shell, flash brilliantly and restlessly, burning with the pleasure that her glance demands. Her arms are slim and tepidly moist, her voluptuous feet crossed under her, her dark thighs, more slender than those of a gazelle —all covered with bracelets, rings, and golden buckles. As becomes the daughters of Hatsor, her breasts, laden with ancient amulets, are chastely bound with Syrian fabrics. The knees of Samson are firmly joined like the two knees of the colossus Anubis. She falls asleep exhausted, laughing and cradled by the strong hand placed under her head. He murmurs deep in his throat a funereal and mournful Hebrew song. She does not understand the strange tongue, but the chant pours sleep into her light head. "An eternal conflict is fought always and everywhere on earth, in the presence of God, between the goodness of Man and the wiles of Woman, for Woman is a being impure in body and in soul. Man always needs caresses and love; his mother steeps him in them when he comes into the world, and her arm first benumbs him, rocks him and gives him a desire for love and for indolence. Troubled in action, troubled in plans, he will dream always of the warmth of the breast, of the songs of the night, of the kisses of the dawn, of lips of fire which his lips devour, of loosened hair which rolls on his forehead, and longings for the bed will pursue him as he travels. He will go into the town, and there the Foolish Virgins will bind him fast with their first words. The stronger he is at birth the more easily he will be conquered, for the greater the river, the stronger the current. When the conflict that God arranged for his Creature both against his fellowman and against nature forces Man to search for a breast on which he may repose, when his eyes are filled with tears, he needs a kiss. But he has not completed all his task: Another more secret combat is now fought, treacherous and cowardly; it is one fought within his arms, in his heart; and, to some extent the woman is always DELILAH. She laughs and exults; in her knowing coldness she waits among her sisters and boasts of feeling nothing from the onslaughts of the fire. To her best friend she confesses it: She wins love without loving herself; a master frightens her. It is pleasure that she loves. Man is coarse and takes love without knowing how to bestow it. In the eyes of her companions, a striking and astonishing sacrifice enhances beauty more than gold, that beauty which produces so many strange marvels, and whose steps are sprinkled with precious blood.—Ultimately, what I desired, Lord, does not exist!—She to whom our love goes and from whom comes life, she, through pride, becomes our enemy. Woman is, today, worse than in times past when, seeing mankind, God said: 'I repent!' Soon, withdrawing into a hideous realm, Woman will have Gomorrah and Man will have Sodom; and casting an irritated glance at each other from afar, the two sexes will die, each on its own side. Eternal God! God of the strong! You know that my soul was only fed by the love of a woman, drawing from love alone more holy vigor than my divine hair gave to my heart.—Judge us.—She is there, asleep at my feet. Three times she has sold my secrets and my life, and three times she has shed false tears which have not been able to hide from me the rage in her eyes; ashamed as she was, even more than astonished, to see herself at once discovered and pardoned. For the goodness of Man is strong, and its gentleness crushes, as it absolves, the weak and false being. But at last I am tired. My heart is so heavy that my gigantic body and my powerful head, which bear the weight of bronze columns, cannot carry it with all its weight of grief. Always to see writhing the gilded viper which drags itself in its slime and believes itself unseen; always this companion whose heart is not true, Woman, sick child and twelve times unclean! Always to put one's strength into guarding one's anger within an injured heart, as in a sanctuary whence, escaping, fire would devour all; to forbid one's eyes to see or cry, it is too much! God, if he wills, may sweep away my ashes. I have given up my secret, Delilah goes to sell it. How beautiful will be the feet of the one who comes to announce my death to me!— What must be, will be!" He finished speaking and fell asleep close to her until the hour when the warriors, trembling at being in his dwelling, paying in weight of gold for each one of the hairs of his head, bound his hands and burnt out his eyes, dragged him bleeding and weighed down with a chain that twelve great bullocks could only drag with difficulty, stood him upright, silently, before Dagon, their God, who groaned dully, and twice, in turning, fell back on his pedestal and twice made his priests turn pale in ecstasy. They lighted the incense, prepared a banquet the noise of which was heard as far as the farthest mountain, and, near the heifer killed at the feet of the god they placed the pale prostitute, Delilah, crowned, adored, and queen of the feast, but trembling and saying: He will not see me! Heaven and Earth! Did you quiver with joy when you saw the false mistress follow with a haggard eye the eyes stained with blood which searched for the sun with a helpless look? And when at last Samson, shaking the columns which supported the immense pylons, crushed at one blow his three thousand enemies, their gods and their altars under the mortal debris? Heaven and Earth! Punish by such justice treachery plotted in artificial love, and the betrayal of the secret of our hearts, extorted in our arms by false kisses!

(1839)

Nothing in nineteenth-century verse surpasses it in power.

ERNEST DUPUY
Les Origines Littéraires d'Alfred de Vigny
(Revue d'Histoire Littéraire de la France, 1903)

ALFRED DE VIGNY

1 7 9 7 — 1 8 6 3

LES DESTINÉES

Depuis le premier jour de la création,
Les pieds lourds et puissants de chaque Destinée
Pesaient sur chaque tête et sur toute action.

Chaque front se courbait et traçait sa journée,
Comme le front d'un bœuf creuse un sillon profond
Sans dépasser la pierre où sa ligne est bornée.

Ces froides déités liaient le joug de plomb
Sur le crâne et les yeux des Hommes leurs esclaves,
Tous errants, sans étoile, en un désert sans fond;

Levant avec effort leurs pieds chargés d'entraves;
Suivant le doigt d'airain dans le cercle fatal,
Le doigt des Volontés inflexibles et graves.

Tristes divinités du monde oriental,
Femmes au voile blanc, immuables statues,
Elles nous écrasaient de leur poids colossal.

Comme un vol de vautours sur le sol abattues,
Dans un ordre éternel, toujours en nombre égal
Aux têtes des mortels sur la terre épandues,

Elles avaient posé leur ongle sans pitié
Sur les cheveux dressés des races éperdues,
Traînant la femme en pleurs et l'homme humilié.

Un soir, il arriva que l'antique planète
Secoua sa poussière.—Il se fit un grand cri:
"Le Sauveur est venu, voici le jeune athlète,

"Il a le front sanglant et le côté meurtri,
"Mais la Fatalité meurt aux pieds du Prophète;
"La Croix monte et s'étend sur nous comme un abri!"

Avant l'heure où, jadis, ces choses arrivèrent,
Tout Homme était courbé, le front pâle et flétri;
Quand ce cri fut jeté, tous ils se relevèrent.

Détachant les nœuds lourds du joug de plomb du Sort,
Toutes les Nations à la fois s'écrièrent:
"O Seigneur! est-il vrai? le Destin est-il mort?"

Et l'on vit remonter vers le ciel, par volées,
Les filles du Destin, ouvrant avec effort
Leurs ongles qui pressaient nos races désolées;

Sous leur robe aux longs plis voilant leurs pieds d'airain,
Leur main inexorable et leur face inflexible;
Montant avec lenteur en innombrable essaim,

D'un vol inaperçu, sans ailes, insensible,
Comme apparaît au soir, vers l'horizon lointain,
D'un nuage orageux l'ascension paisible.

—Un soupir de bonheur sortit du cœur humain;
La Terre frissonna dans son orbite immense,
Comme un cheval frémit délivré de son frein.

Tous les astres émus restèrent en silence,
Attendant avec l'Homme, en la même stupeur,
Le suprême décret de la Toute-Puissance,

Quand ces filles du Ciel, retournant au Seigneur,
Comme ayant retrouvé leurs régions natales,
Autour de Jéhovah se rangèrent en chœur,

D'un mouvement pareil levant leurs mains fatales,
Puis chantant d'une voix leur hymne de douleur,
Et baissant à la fois leurs fronts calmes et pâles:

"Nous venons demander la Loi de l'avenir.
"Nous sommes, ô Seigneur, les froides Destinées
"Dont l'antique pouvoir ne devait point faillir.

"Nous roulions sous nos doigts les jours et les années;
"Devons-nous vivre encore ou devons-nous finir,
"Des Puissances du ciel, nous, les fortes aînées?

"Vous détruisez d'un coup le grand piège du Sort
"Où tombaient tour à tour les races consternées.
"Faut-il combler la fosse et briser le ressort?

"Ne mènerons-nous plus ce troupeau faible et morne,
"Ces hommes d'un moment, ces condamnés à mort,
"Jusqu'au bout du chemin dont nous posions la borne?

"Le moule de la vie était creusé par nous.
"Toutes les passions y répandaient leur lave,
"Et les événements venaient s'y fondre tous.

"Sur les tables d'airain où notre loi se grave,
"Vous effacez le nom de la FATALITÉ,
"Vous déliez les pieds de l'Homme notre esclave.

"Qui va porter le poids dont s'est épouvanté
"Tout ce qui fut créé? ce poids sur la pensée,
"Dont le nom est en bas: RESPONSABILITÉ?"

Il se fit un silence, et la Terre affaissée
S'arrêta comme fait la barque sans rameurs
Sur les flots orageux dans la nuit balancée.

Une voix descendit, venant de ces hauteurs
Où s'engendrent sans fin les mondes dans l'espace;
Cette voix de la terre emplit les profondeurs:

"Retournez en mon nom, Reines, je suis la Grâce.
"L'Homme sera toujours un nageur incertain
"Dans les ondes du temps qui se mesure et passe.

"Vous toucherez son front, ô filles du Destin!
"Son bras ouvrira l'eau, qu'elle soit haute ou basse,
"Voulant trouver sa place et deviner sa fin.

"Il sera plus heureux, se croyant maître et libre,
"En luttant contre vous dans un combat mauvais
"Où moi seule d'en haut je tiendrai l'équilibre.

"De moi naîtra son souffle et sa force à jamais.
"Son mérite est le mien, sa loi perpétuelle:
"Faire ce que je veux pour venir où JE SAIS."

———————

Et le chœur descendit vers sa proie éternelle
Afin d'y ressaisir sa domination
Sur la race timide, incomplète et rebelle.

On entendit venir la sombre Légion
Et retomber les pieds des femmes inflexibles,
Comme sur nos caveaux tombe un cercueil de plomb.

Chacune prit chaque homme en ses mains invisibles.
—Mais, plus forte à présent, dans ce sombre duel,
Notre âme en deuil combat ces Esprits impassibles.

Nous soulevons parfois leur doigt faux et cruel.
La Volonté transporte à des hauteurs sublimes
Notre front éclairé par un rayon du ciel.

Cependant sur nos caps, sur nos rocs, sur nos cimes,
Leur doigt rude et fatal se pose devant nous,
Et, d'un coup, nous renverse au fond des noirs abîmes.

Oh! dans quel désespoir nous sommes encor tous!
Vous avez élargi le COLLIER qui nous lie,
Mais qui donc tient la chaîne?—Ah! Dieu juste, est-ce vous?

Arbitre libre et fier des actes de sa vie,
Si notre cœur s'entr'ouvre au parfum des vertus,
S'il s'embrase à l'amour, s'il s'élève au génie,

Que l'ombre des Destins, Seigneur, n'oppose plus
A nos belles ardeurs une immuable entrave,
A nos efforts sans fin des coups inattendus!

O sujet d'épouvante à troubler le plus brave!
Question sans réponse où vos Saints se sont tus!
O mystère! ô tourment de l'âme forte et grave!

Notre mot éternel est-il: C'ÉTAIT ÉCRIT?
SUR LE LIVRE DE DIEU, dit l'Orient esclave;
Et l'Occident répond: SUR LE LIVRE DU CHRIST.

THE FATES

Since the first day of creation, the strong and heavy tread of the
Fates threatened each head and every action. Each head was bowed,
and mapped out its day's work as the ox plows a deep furrow without
going beyond the stone which is its boundary line. These cold deities
bound the yoke of lead on the skull and the eyes of their slaves, Men,
who were all wandering, without a guiding star, in a boundless desert.

With an effort they lifted their shackled feet, and followed the brazen finger in its fatal circle, the finger of the inexorable and grave Fates. Melancholy divinities of the oriental world, white veiled women, unchanging statues, they were crushing us with their colossal weight. Like a flight of vultures brought down to earth in an eternal order, always equal in number to the mortals scattered over the world. They had laid their claws pitilessly on the bristling hair of the distracted races, dragging off tearful Woman and humiliated Man. One evening the ancient planet quaked— It gave a great cry: "The Saviour has come, here is the young athlete, his forehead is bleeding and his side is wounded, but Fate dies at the feet of the Prophet; the Cross ascends and covers us like a shelter!" Before the time in the olden days when these things took place, every man was bowed down, with a pale and wasted face; when this cry was uttered, they all arose. Untying the heavy knots of the leaden yoke of Destiny, all the Nations cried out at once: "Oh Lord! Is it true? Is Destiny dead?" And one saw the daughters of Destiny reascending to Heaven in flocks, opening with an effort their talons which were gripping our disconsolate races. Their feet of brass they concealed under the long folds of their robes; their hands were unrelenting and their faces inflexible. They ascended slowly in an innumerable swarm, gliding imperceptibly, wingless, insensibly, like the peaceful ascent of a thunder cloud on a far horizon at evening. A sigh of happiness issued from the human heart; the Earth shivered in its immense orbit as a horse quivers when released from his bridle. All the stars, deeply moved, kept silence, waiting with Man, in the same stupor, for the supreme decree of the Almighty. When the daughters of Heaven, returning to the Lord, rediscovering the regions of their birth, stood all together around Jehovah, they raised their fatal hands with an identical movement, and sang in unison their hymn of grief, bowing their calm, pale faces: "We have come to ask the Law for the future. Oh Lord, we are the cold Fates whose ancient power was not meant to fail. We made the days and years revolve under our fingers. Are we to live on or are we to end our lives, we who are by far the eldest of the Heavenly powers? You are destroying at a blow the great snare of Fate into which the dismayed races of men fell one after another. Is it necessary to fill in the pit and break the spring of the trap? Will we no longer lead this feeble and dejected flock, these men of a moment, condemned to death, to the end of the road whose boundary stone we fix? The mould of life was hollowed out by us. All the passions poured out their lava in it, and events came there to blend themselves. On the tables of bronze where our law is engraved, you are erasing Fate's name, you unfetter the feet of our slave, Man. Who will bear the burden which has terrified every creature? Who will bear the weight on the conscience whose name is written below: RESPONSIBILITY"? There was a silence, and the Earth, giving way, stopped, as a boat without rowers rocks on stormy waves in the night. A voice came down from the heights where the worlds are begotten endlessly in space; the voice filled the depths of the earth: "Return in my name, oh Queens, I am the Saving Grace. Man will always be an uncertain swimmer in the seas of time, time which measures itself out and passes on. You will touch him on the forehead, oh daughters of Destiny! Wishing to find his place and foresee his end, his arm will cleave the water, whether the tide is high or low. He will be happier believing himself his own master and free, while struggling against you in a losing battle, where I alone will maintain the balance from on high. From me will spring his strength and his breath forever. His merit is mine; his eternal law: 'Do my will in order that you may come only I know whither.'" And the chorus descended to its eternal prey in order to recapture its domination over the timid, imperfect and rebellious race of men. The dark legion was heard coming, and the feet of those inflexible women were heard falling again with a noise like a leaden coffin dropping down into our burial vaults. Each one of the Fates took a man in her invisible hands.—In the sombre duel, our souls, in mourning but stronger now, combat those impassive spirits. We sometimes lift up their treacherous and cruel fingers. Will transports to sublime heights our brow lighted by a ray from heaven. On capes and rocks and mountain tops, however, the severe finger of Fate appears in front of us and, at one blow, strikes us down into the depths of the black chasms. In what great despair we still live! You have loosened the COLLAR which binds us, but who holds the chain?—Ah, just God, is it you? As free and proud arbiters of the actions of our lives, if our hearts are half opened to the fragrance of virtue, if they are enkindled by love, if they rise to genius, may the shadow of the Fates, oh Lord, no longer oppose an unalterable obstacle to our noble ardors, and deal unforeseen blows to our endless efforts! Oh frightening matters troubling the bravest! Unanswerable question in the face of which even the saints are silent! Mystery! Torment of the strong and earnest soul! Our eternal motto is: IT WAS WRITTEN IN THE BOOK OF GOD, the enslaved Orient says; and the Occident answers: IN THE BOOK OF CHRIST.

(1849)

Nothing in French literature can be compared with the slow, forceful, inexorable movement of these rugged tercets.

ÉMILE LAUVRIÈRE
Alfred de Vigny: Sa vie et son œuvre (1909)

HEINRICH HEINE

1 7 9 7 — 1 8 5 6

GAZELLES

Es hüpfen herbei und lauschen
Die frommen, klugen Gazelln;
Und in der Ferne rauschen
Des heiligen Stromes Welln.

Gazelles come bounding from the brake,
And pause, and look shyly round;
And the waves of the sacred river make
A far-off slumb'rous sound.

Lyrisches Intermezzo (1822–23)
Translated by Sir Theodore Martin

This is an immortal stanza.

GEORG BRANDES
Main Currents in Nineteenth Century Literature (1905)

HEINRICH HEINE

1 7 9 7 — 1 8 5 6

EIN FICHTENBAUM STEHT EINSAM

Ein Fichtenbaum steht einsam
Im Norden auf kahler Höh'.
Ihn schläfert; mit weisser Decke
Umhüllen ihn Eis und Schnee.

Er träumt von einer Palme,
Die fern im Morgenland
Einsam und schweigend trauert
Auf brennender Felsenwand.

A LONELY PINE IS STANDING

A lonely pine is standing
  In the North where high winds blow.
He sleeps; and the whitest blanket
  Wraps him in ice and snow.

He dreams—dreams of a palm-tree
That far in an Orient land
Languishes, lonely and drooping,
Upon the burning sand.

Lyrisches Intermezzo (1822–23)
Translated by Louis Untermeyer

The loveliest poem of eight lines in the literature of the world.

MICHAEL MONAHAN
Heinrich Heine (1923)

GIACOMO LEOPARDI

1798 — 1837

THE INFINITE

Sempre caro mi fu quest' ermo colle,
E questa siepe, che da tanta parte
Dell' ultimo orizzonte il guardo esclude.
Ma sedendo e mirando, interminati
Spazi di la da quella, e sovrumani
Silenzi, e profondissima quiete
Io nel pensier mi fingo, ove per poco
Il cor non si spaura. E come il vento
Odo stormir tra queste piante, io quello
Infinito silenzio e questa voce
Vo comparando, e mi sovvien l' eterno,
E le morte stagioni, e la presente
E viva, e il suon di lei. Così tra questa
Immensita s' annega il pensier mio,
E il naufragar m' è dolce in questo mare.

Dear to me ever was this lonely hill,
This hedge, that from mine eyes shuts off so much
Of the horizon's far immensity.
I sit and gaze, and in my mind are born
Unbounded space, unearthly silences,
And quietness profound, so that my heart
Leaps on the brink of fear. And as the wind

1153

Murmurs among these leaves, this kindly voice
With that eternal silence I compare,
Think on infinity and the dead years,
Until the living present seems more near,
More sweet its sound. Thus are my thoughts submerged
In this immensity, and in this sea
'Tis happiness voluptuously to drown.

Translated by Romilda Rendel

Leopardi's blank verse is the finest in Italian literature.

RICHARD GARNETT
A History of Italian Literature (1928)

HONORÉ DE BALZAC

1 7 9 9 — 1 8 5 0

THE MAISON VAUQUER

This apartment is in all its lustre at the moment when, toward seven o'clock in the morning, Madame Vauquer's cat precedes his mistress, jumping on the sideboards, smelling at the milk contained in several basins covered with plates, and giving forth his matutinal purr. Presently the widow appears, decked out in her tulle cap, under which hangs a crooked band of false hair; as she walks she drags along her wrinkled slippers. Her little plump elderly face, from the middle of which protrudes a nose like a parrot's beak; her little fat dimpled hands, her whole person, rounded like a church-rat, the waist of her gown, too tight for its contents, which flaps over it, are all in harmony with this room, where misfortune seems to ooze, where speculation lurks in corners, and of which Madame Vauquer inhales the warm, fetid air without being nauseated. Her countenance, fresh as a first autumn frost, her wrinkled eyes, whose expression passes from the smile prescribed to *danseuses* to the acrid scowl of the discounter—her whole person, in short, is an explanation of the boarding-house, as the boarding-house is an implication of her person. . . . Her worsted petticoat, which falls below her outer skirt, made of an old dress, and with the wadding coming out of the slits in the stuff, which is full of them, resumes the parlour, the dining-room, the yard, announces the kitchen, and gives a presentiment of the boarders.

Le Père Goriot (1834)

In this musty and mouldy little boarding-house the Père Goriot is the
senior resident. Certain students in law and medicine, from the Quartier
Latin, hard by, subscribe to the dinner, where Maman Vauquer glares
at them when she watches them cut their slice from the loaf. When the
Père Goriot dies horribly, at the end of the tragedy, the kindest thing
said of him, as the other boarders unfold their much-crumpled napkins,
is, "Well, he won't sit and sniff his bread any more!" and the speaker
imitates the old man's favourite gesture. The portrait of the Maison
Vauquer and its inmates is one of the most portentous settings of the
scene in all the literature of fiction. In this case there is nothing super-
fluous; there is a profound correspondence between the background
and the action.

HENRY JAMES
French Poets and Novelists (1878)

THOMAS HOOD

1 7 9 9 — 1 8 4 5

THE HAUNTED HOUSE

A ROMANCE

Part I

Some dreams we have are nothing else but dreams,
Unnatural, and full of contradictions;
Yet others of our most romantic schemes
Are something more than fictions.

It might be only on enchanted ground;
It might be merely by a thought's expansion;
But in the spirit, or the flesh, I found
An old deserted Mansion.

A residence for woman, child, and man,
A dwelling-place,—and yet no habitation;
A House,—but under some prodigious ban
Of excommunication.

Unhinged the iron gates half open hung,
Jarr'd by the gusty gales of many winters,
That from its crumbled pedestal had flung
One marble globe in splinters.

No dog was at the threshold, great or small;
No pigeon on the roof—no household creature—
No cat demurely dozing on the wall—
Not one domestic feature.

No human figure stirr'd, to go or come,
No face look'd forth from shut or open casement;
No chimney smoked—there was no sign of Home
From parapet to basement.

With shatter'd panes the grassy court was starr'd;
The time-worn coping-stone had tumbled after!
And thro' the ragged roof the sky shone, barr'd
With naked beam and rafter.

O'er all there hung a shadow and a fear;
A sense of mystery the spirit daunted
And said, as plain as whisper in the ear,
The place is Haunted!

The flow'r grew wild and rankly as the weed,
Roses with thistles struggled for espial,
And vagrant plants of parasitic breed
Had overgrown the Dial.

But gay or gloomy, steadfast or infirm,
No heart was there to heed the hour's duration;
All times and tides were lost in one long term
Of stagnant desolation.

The wren had built within the Porch, she found
Its quiet loneliness so sure and thorough;
And on the lawn,—within its turfy mound,—
The rabbit made its burrow.

The rabbit wild and gray, that flitted thro'
The shrubby clumps, and frisk'd, and sat, and vanish'd,
But leisurely and bold, as if he knew
His enemy was banish'd.

The wary crow,—the pheasant from the woods—
Lull'd by the still and everlasting sameness,
Close to the Mansion, like domestic broods,
Fed with a 'shocking tameness.'

The coot was swimming in the reedy pond,
Beside the water-hen, so soon affrighted;
And in the weedy moat the heron, fond
Of solitude, alighted.

The moping heron, motionless and stiff,
That on a stone, as silently and stilly,
Stood, an apparent sentinel, as if
To guard the water-lily.

No sound was heard except, from far away,
The ringing of the Whitwall's shrilly laughter,
Or, now and then, the chatter of the jay,
That Echo murmur'd after.

But Echo never mock'd the human tongue;
Some weighty crime, that Heaven could not pardon,
A secret curse on that old Building hung,
And its deserted Garden.

The beds were all untouch'd by hand or tool;
No footstep mark'd the damp and mossy gravel,
Each walk as green as is the mantled pool,
For want of human travel.

The vine unprun'd, and the neglected peach,
Droop'd from the wall with which they used to grapple;
And on the canker'd tree, in easy reach,
Rotted the golden apple.

But awfully the truant shunn'd the ground,
The vagrant kept aloof, and daring Poacher,
In spite of gaps that thro' the fences round
Invited the encroacher.

For over all there hung a cloud of fear,
A sense of mystery the spirit daunted,
And said, as plain as whisper in the ear,
The place is Haunted!

The pear and quince lay squander'd on the grass;
The mould was purple with unheeded showers
Of bloomy plums—a Wilderness it was
Of fruits, and weeds, and flowers!

The marigold amidst the nettles blew,
The gourd embraced the rose bush in its ramble.
The thistle and the stock together grew,
The holly-hock and bramble.

The bear-bine with the lilac interlaced,
The sturdy bur-dock choked its slender neighbour,
The spicy pink. All tokens were effac'd
Of human care and labour.

The very yew Formality had train'd
To such a rigid pyramidal stature,
For want of trimming had almost regain'd
The raggedness of nature.

The Fountain was a-dry—neglect and time
Had marr'd the work of artisan and mason,
And efts and croaking frogs, begot of slime,
Sprawl'd in the ruin'd bason.

The Statue, fallen from its marble base,
Amidst the refuse leaves, and herbage rotten,
Lay like the Idol of some bygone race,
Its name and rites forgotten.

On ev'ry side the aspect was the same,
All ruin'd, desolate, forlorn, and savage:
No hand or foot within the precinct came
To rectify or ravage.

For over all there hung a cloud of fear,
A sense of mystery the spirit daunted,
And said as plain as whisper in the ear,
The place is Haunted!

Part II

O, very gloomy is the House of Woe,
Where tears are falling while the bell is knelling,
With all the dark solemnities which show
That Death is in the dwelling!

O very, very dreary is the room
Where Love, domestic Love, no longer nestles,
But smitten by the common stroke of doom,
The Corpse lies on the trestles!

But House of Woe, and hearse, and sable pall,
The narrow home of the departed mortal,
Ne'er look'd so gloomy as that Ghostly Hall,
With its deserted portal!

The centipede along the threshold crept,
The cobweb hung across in mazy tangle,
And in its winding-sheet the maggot slept,
At every nook and angle.

1158

The keyhole lodged the earwig and her brood,
The emmets of the steps had old possession,
And march'd in search of their diurnal food
In undisturbed procession.

As undisturb'd as the prehensile cell
Of moth or maggot, or the spider's tissue,
For never foot upon that threshold fell,
To enter or to issue.

O'er all there hung the shadow of a fear,
A sense of mystery the spirit daunted,
And said, as plain as whisper in the ear,
The place is Haunted!

Howbeit, the door I pushed—or so I dream'd—
Which slowly, slowly gaped,—the hinges creaking
With such a rusty eloquence, it seem'd
That Time himself was speaking.

But Time was dumb within that Mansion old,
Or left his tale to the heraldic banners,
That hung from the corroded walls, and told
Of former men and manners:—

Those tatter'd flags, that with the open'd door,
Seem'd the old wave of battle to remember,
While fallen fragments danced upon the floor,
Like dead leaves in December.

The startled bats flew out—bird after bird—
The screech-owl overhead began to flutter,
And seem'd to mock the cry that she had heard
Some dying victim utter!

A shriek that echo'd from the joisted roof,
And up the stair, and further still and further,
Till in some ringing chamber far aloof
It ceased its tale of murther!

Meanwhile the rusty armour rattled round,
The banner shudder'd, and the ragged streamer;
All things the horrid tenor of the sound
Acknowledged with a tremor.

The antlers, where the helmet hung and belt,
Stirr'd as the tempest stirs the forest branches,
Or as the stag had trembled when he felt
The blood-hound at his haunches.

The window jingled in its crumbled frame,
And thro' its many gaps of destitution
Dolorous moans and hollow sighings came,
Like those of dissolution.

The wood-louse dropped and rolled into a ball,
Touch'd by some impulse occult or mechanic;
And nameless beetles ran along the wall
In universal panic.

The subtle spider, that from overhead
Hung like a spy on human guilt and error,
Suddenly turn'd, and up its slender thread
Ran with a nimble terror.

The very stains and fractures on the wall
Assuming features solemn and terrific,
Hinted some tragedy of that old Hall,
Lock'd up in Hieroglyphic.

Some tale that might, perchance, have solved the doubt,
Wherefore amongst those flags so dull and livid,
The banner of the Bloody Hand shone out
So ominously vivid.

Some key to that inscrutable appeal,
Which made the very frame of Nature quiver;
And every thrilling nerve and fibre feel
So ague-like a shiver.

For over all there hung a cloud of fear,
A sense of mystery the spirit daunted,
And said, as plain as whisper in the ear,
The place is Haunted!

If but a rat had lingered in the house,
To lure the thought into a social channel!
But not a rat remain'd, or tiny mouse,
To squeak behind the panel.

Huge drops roll'd down the walls, as if they wept;
And where the cricket used to chirp so shrilly,
The toad was squatting, and the lizard crept
On that damp hearth and chilly.

For years no cheerful blaze had sparkled there,
Or glanc'd on coat of buff or knightly metal;
The slug was crawling on the vacant chair,—
The snail upon the settle.

The floor was redolent of mould and must,
The fungus in the rotten seams had quicken'd;
While on the oaken table coats of dust
Perennially had thicken'd.

No mark of leathern jack or metal can,
No cup—no horn—no hospitable token—
All social ties between that board and Man
Had long ago been broken.

There was so foul a rumour in the air,
The shadow of a Presence so atrocious;
No human creature could have feasted there,
Even the most ferocious.

For over all there hung a cloud of fear,
A sense of mystery the spirit daunted,
And said, as plain as whisper in the ear,
The place is Haunted!

Part III

'Tis hard for human actions to account,
Whether from reason or from impulse only—
But some internal prompting bade me mount
The gloomy stairs and lonely.

Those gloomy stairs, so dark, and damp, and cold,
With odours as from bones and relics carnal,
Deprived of rite, and consecrated mould,
The chapel vault, or charnel.

Those dreary stairs, where with the sounding stress
Of ev'ry step so many echoes blended,
The mind, with dark misgivings, fear'd to guess
How many feet ascended.

The tempest with its spoils had drifted in,
Till each unwholesome stone was darkly spotted,
As thickly as the leopard's dappled skin,
With leaves that rankly rotted.

The air was thick—and in the upper gloom
The bat—or something in its shape—was winging,
And on the wall, as chilly as a tomb,
The Death's Head moth was clinging.

That mystic moth, which, with a sense profound
Of all unholy presence, augurs truly;
And with a grim significance flits round
The taper burning bluely.

Such omens in the place there seem'd to be,
At ev'ry crooked turn, or on the landing,
The straining eyeball was prepared to see
Some Apparition standing.

For over all there hung a cloud of fear,
A sense of mystery the spirit daunted,
And said, as plain as whisper in the ear,
The place is Haunted!

Yet no portentous Shape the sight amaz'd;
Each object plain, and tangible, and valid;
But from their tarnish'd frames dark Figures gaz'd,
And Faces spectre-pallid.

Not merely with the mimic life that lies
Within the compass of Art's simulation;
Their souls were looking thro' their painted eyes
With awful speculation.

On every lip a speechless horror dwelt;
On ev'ry brow the burthen of affliction;
The old Ancestral Spirits knew and felt
The House's malediction.

Such earnest woe their features overcast,
They might have stirr'd, or sigh'd, or wept, or spoken;
But, save the hollow moaning of the blast,
The stillness was unbroken.

No other sound or stir of life was there,
Except my steps in solitary clamber,
From flight to flight, from humid stair to stair,
From chamber into chamber.

Deserted rooms of luxury and state,
That old magnificence had richly furnish'd
With pictures, cabinets of ancient date,
And carvings gilt and burnish'd.

Rich hangings, storied by the needle's art,
With scripture history, or classic fable;
But all had faded, save one ragged part,
Where Cain was slaying Abel.

The silent waste of mildew and the moth
Had marr'd the tissue with a partial ravage;
But undecaying frown'd upon the cloth
Each feature stern and savage.

The sky was pale; the cloud a thing of doubt;
Some hues were fresh, and some decay'd and duller;
But still the BLOODY HAND shone strangely out
With vehemence of colour!

The BLOODY HAND that with a lurid stain
Shone on the dusty floor, a dismal token,
Projected from the casement's painted pane,
Where all beside was broken.

The BLOODY HAND significant of crime,
That glaring on the old heraldic banner,
Had kept its crimson unimpair'd by time,
In such a wondrous manner!

O'er all there hung the shadow of a fear,
A sense of mystery the spirit daunted,
And said, as plain as whisper in the ear,
The place is Haunted!

The Death Watch tick'd behind the panel'd oak,
Inexplicable tremors shook the arras,
And echoes strange and mystical awoke,
The fancy to embarrass.

Prophetic hints that filled the soul with dread,
But thro' one gloomy entrance pointing mostly,
The while some secret inspiration said
That Chamber is the Ghostly!

Across the door no gossamer festoon
Swung pendulous—no web—no dusty fringes,
No silky chrysalis or white cocoon
About its nooks and hinges.

The spider shunn'd the interdicted room,
The moth, the beetle, and the fly were banish'd,
And where the sunbeam fell athwart the gloom,
The very midge had vanish'd.

One lonely ray that glanc'd upon a Bed,
As if with awful aim direct and certain,
To show the BLOODY HAND in burning red
Embroider'd on the curtain.

And yet no gory stain was on the quilt—
The pillow in its place had slowly rotted;
The floor alone retain'd the trace of guilt,
Those boards obscurely spotted.

Obscurely spotted to the door, and thence
With mazy doubles to the grated casement—
Oh what a tale they told of fear intense,
Of horror and amazement!

What human creature in the dead of night
Had coursed like hunted hare that cruel distance?
Had sought the door, the window in his flight,
Striving for dear existence?

What shrieking Spirit in that bloody room
Its mortal frame had violently quitted?—
Across the sunbeam, with a sudden gloom,
A ghostly Shadow flitted.

Across the sunbeam, and along the wall,
But painted on the air so very dimly,
It hardly veil'd the tapestry at all,
Or portrait frowning grimly.

O'er all there hung the shadow of a fear,
A sense of mystery the spirit daunted,
And said, as plain as whisper in the ear,
The place is Haunted!

(1844)

One of the truest poems ever written—one of the TRUEST—*one of the most unexceptionable—one of the most thoroughly artistic, both in its theme and in its execution. It is, moreover, powerfully ideal—imaginative.*

EDGAR ALLAN POE
The Poetic Principle (1850)

THOMAS HOOD

1 7 9 9 — 1 8 4 5

RHYMES

Still, for all slips of hers,
One of Eve's family—
Wipe those poor lips of hers
Oozing so clammily.

The Bridge of Sighs (1844)

1164

Hood is one of the great artists in English verse, especially in his serious play with double and treble endings. No one else could have written such a stanza.

ARTHUR SYMONS
The Romantic Movement in English Poetry (1909)

JOHN HENRY NEWMAN

1 8 0 1 — 1 8 9 0

BLESSED VISION OF PEACE

Such were the thoughts concerning the "Blessed Vision of Peace," of one whose long-continued petition had been that the Most Merciful would not despise the work of His own Hands, nor leave him to himself;—while yet his eyes were dim, and his breast laden, and he could but employ Reason in the things of Faith. And now, dear Reader, time is short, eternity is long. Put not from you what you have here found; regard it not as mere matter of present controversy; set not out resolved to refute it, and looking about for the best way of doing so; seduce not yourself with the imagination that it comes of disappointment, or disgust, or restlessness, or wounded feeling, or undue sensibility, or other weakness. Wrap not yourself round in the associations of years past; nor determine that to be truth which you wish to be so, nor make an idol of cherished anticipations. Time is short, eternity is long.

NUNC DIMITTIS SERVUM TUUM, DOMINE,

SECUNDUM VERBUM TUUM IN PACE:

QUIA VIDERUNT OCULI MEI SALUTARE TUUM.

An Essay on the Development
of Christian Doctrine (1845)

It will be remembered as long as the English language endures.

PAUL ELMER MORE
The Drift of Romanticism (1913)

VICTOR HUGO

1 8 0 2 — 1 8 8 5

LIGHT AND LIFE

Oui, ce soleil est beau. Ses rayons,—les derniers!—
Sur le front du Taunus posent une couronne;
Le fleuve luit; le bois de splendeurs s'environne;
Les vitres du hameau, là-bas, sont tout en feu;
Que c'est beau! que c'est grand! que c'est charmant, mon Dieu!
La nature est un flot de vie et de lumière! . . .

    'Tis true, the sun is beautiful. Its rays—
    The last—do set a crown on Taunus' brow.
    The river gleams, the forests are engirt
    With brilliancy. The windows in yon burg
    Are all on fire. How beautiful it is!
    How grand! how lovely. O Almighty God!
    All nature is a flood of light and life!—

Les Burgraves, Part i, Scene iii (1843)
Translated by George Burnham Ives

LOVE

De ma vie, ô mon Dieu! cette heure est la première.
Devant moi tout un monde, un monde de lumière,
Comme ces paradis qu'en songe nous voyons,
S'entr'ouvre en m'inondant de vie et de rayons!
Partout en moi, hors moi, joie, extase et mystère,
Et l'ivresse, et l'orgueil, et ce qui, sur la terre,
Se rapproche le plus de la divinité,
L'amour dans la puissance et dans la majesté!

    In all my life, oh God,
  This hour stands first. Before me is a world,
  A world of light, as if the paradise
  We dream about had open'd wide and fill'd
  My being with new life and brilliancy!
  In me, around me, everywhere is joy,
  Intoxication, mystery, and delight,
  And pride, and that one thing that on the earth
  Approaches most divinity, love—love,
  In majesty and power.

Ruy Blas, Act iii, Scene iv (1838)
Translated by Mrs. Newton Crosland

OH, THOU, MY LOVER

Tout s'est éteint, flambeaux et musique de fête;
Rien que la nuit et nous! Félicité parfaite!
Dis, ne le crois-tu pas? sur nous, tout en dormant,
La nature à demi veille amoureusement.
La lune est seule aux cieux, qui comme nous repose,
Et respire avec nous l'air embaumé de rose!
Regarde: plus de feux, plus de bruit. Tout se tait.
La lune tout à l'heure à l'horizon montait;
Tandis que tu parlais, sa lumière qui tremble
Et ta voix, toutes deux m'allaient au cœur ensemble;
Je me sentais joyeuse et calme, ô mon amant!
Et j'aurais bien voulu mourir en ce moment.

        All now is o'er, the torches out,
The music done. Night only is with us.
Felicity most perfect! Think you not
That now while all is still and slumbering,
Nature, half waking, watches us with love?
No cloud is in the sky. All things like us
Are now at rest. Come, breathe with me the air
Perfumed by roses. Look, there is no light,
Nor hear we any noise. Silence prevails.
The moon just now from the horizon rose
E'en while you spoke to me; her trembling light
And thy dear voice together reached my heart.
Joyous and softly calm I felt, oh, thou
My lover! And it seemed that I would then
Most willingly have died.

          Hernani, Act v, Scene iii (1830)
         Translated by Mrs. Newton Crosland

---

*Drama can rise to the most sublime lyric flights, and as witness of this
we need only turn to the plays of Victor Hugo.*
        THÉODORE DE BANVILLE
        Petit Traité de poésie française (1871)

TRISTESSE D'OLYMPIO

Que peu de temps suffit pour changer toutes choses!
Nature au front serein, comme vous oubliez!
Et comme vous brisez dans vos métamorphoses
Les fils mystérieux où nos cœurs sont liés!

Nos chambres de feuillage en halliers sont changées;
L'arbre où fut notre chiffre est mort ou renversé,
Nos roses dans l'enclos ont été ravagées
Par les petits enfants qui sautent le fossé!

Un mur clôt la fontaine où, par l'heure échauffée,
Folâtre elle buvait en descendant des bois:
Elle prenait de l'eau dans sa main, douce fée,
Et laissait retomber des perles de ses doigts!

On a pavé la route âpre et mal aplanie,
Où, dans le sable pur se dessinant si bien
Et de sa petitesse étalant l'ironie,
Son pied charmant semblait rire à côté du mien!

La borne du chemin, qui vit des jours sans nombre,
Où jadis pour m'attendre elle aimait à s'asseoir,
S'est usée en heurtant, lorsque la route est sombre,
Les grands chars gémissants qui reviennent le soir.

La forêt ici manque et là est agrandie.
De tout ce qui fut nous presque rien n'est vivant;
Et, comme un tas de cendre éteinte et refroidie,
L'amas des souvenirs se disperse à tout vent!

N'existons-nous donc plus? Avons-nous eu notre heure?
Rien ne la rendra-t-il à nos cris superflus?
L'air joue avec la branche au moment où je pleure,
Ma maison me regarde et ne me connaît plus.

D'autres vont maintenant passer où nous passâmes.
Nous y sommes venus, d'autres vont y venir;
Et le songe qu'avaient ébauché nos deux âmes,
Ils le continueront sans pouvoir le finir!

Car personne ici-bas ne termine et n'achève;
Les pires des humains sont comme les meilleurs,
Nous nous réveillons tous au même endroit du rêve:
Tout commence en ce monde et tout finit ailleurs.

Oui, d'autres à leur tour viendront, couples sans tache,
Puiser dans cet asile heureux, calme, enchanté,
Tout ce que la nature à l'amour qui se cache
Mêle de rêverie et de solennité!

D'autres auront nos champs, nos sentiers, nos retraites;
Ton bois, ma bien-aimée, est à des inconnus.
D'autres femmes viendront, baigneuses indiscrètes,
Troubler le flot sacré qu'ont touché tes pieds nus!

Quoi donc! c'est vainement qu'ici nous nous aimâmes!
Rien ne nous restera de ces coteaux fleuris
Où nous fondions notre être en y mêlant nos flammes!
L'impassible nature a déjà tout repris!

Oh! dites-moi, ravins, frais ruisseaux, treilles mûres,
Rameaux chargés de nids, grottes, forêts, buissons,
Est-ce que vous ferez pour d'autres vos murmures?
Est-ce que vous direz à d'autres vos chansons?

Nous vous comprenions tant! doux, attentifs, austères,
Tous nos échos s'ouvraient si bien à votre voix!
Et nous prêtions si bien, sans troubler vos mystères,
L'oreille aux mots profonds que vous dites parfois!

Répondez, vallon pur; répondez, solitude;
O nature abritée en ce désert si beau,
Lorsque nous dormirons tous deux dans l'attitude
Que donne aux morts pensifs la forme du tombeau,

Est-ce que vous serez à ce point insensible
De nous savoir couchés, morts avec nos amours,
Et de continuer votre fête paisible,
Et de toujours sourire et de chanter toujours?

Est-ce que, nous sentant errer dans vos retraites,
Fantômes reconnus par vos monts et vos bois,
Vous ne nous direz pas de ces choses secrètes
Qu'on dit en revoyant des amis d'autrefois?

Est-ce que vous pourrez, sans tristesse et sans plainte,
Voir nos ombres flotter où marchèrent nos pas,
Et la voir m'entraîner, dans une morne étreinte,
Vers quelque source en pleurs qui sanglote tout bas?

Et, s'il est quelque part, dans l'ombre où rien ne veille,
Deux amants sous vos fleurs abritant leurs transports,
Ne leur irez-vous pas murmurer à l'oreille:
—Vous qui vivez, donnez une pensée aux morts!

Dieu nous prête un moment les prés et les fontaines,
Les grands bois frissonnants, les rocs profonds et sourds,
Et les cieux azurés et les lacs et les plaines,
Pour y mettre nos cœurs, nos rêves, nos amours!

Puis il nous les retire; il souffle notre flamme;
Il plonge dans la nuit l'antre où nous rayonnons;
Et dit à la vallée où s'imprima notre âme
D'effacer notre trace et d'oublier nos noms.

Eh bien, oubliez-nous, maison, jardin, ombrages!
Herbe, use notre seuil! ronce, cache nos pas!
Chantez, oiseaux! ruisseaux, coulez! croissez, feuillages!
Ceux que vous oubliez ne vous oublieront pas!

Car vous êtes pour nous l'ombre de l'amour même!
Vous êtes l'oasis qu'on rencontre en chemin!
Vous êtes, ô vallon! la retraite suprême
Où nous avons pleuré nous tenant par la main!

Toutes les passions s'éloignent avec l'âge,
L'une emportant son masque et l'autre son couteau,
Comme un essaim chantant d'histrions en voyage
Dont le groupe décroît derrière le coteau.

Mais toi, rien ne t'efface, Amour, toi qui nous charmes!
Toi qui, torche ou flambeau, luis dans notre brouillard!
Tu nous tiens par la joie et surtout par les larmes!
Jeune homme on te maudit, on t'adore vieillard.

Dans ces jours où la tête au poids des ans s'incline,
Où l'homme, sans projets, sans but, sans visions,
Sent qu'il n'est déjà plus qu'une tombe en ruine
Où gisent ses vertus et ses illusions;

Quand notre âme en rêvant descend dans nos entrailles,
Comptant dans notre cœur, qu'enfin la glace atteint,
Comme on compte les morts sur un champ de bataille,
Chaque douleur tombée et chaque songe éteint;

Comme quelqu'un qui cherche en tenant une lampe,
Loin des objets réels, loin du monde rieur,
Elle arrive à pas lents par une obscure rampe
Jusqu'au fond désolé du gouffre intérieur;

Et là, dans cette nuit qu'aucun rayon n'étoile,
L'âme, en un repli sombre où tout semble finir,
Sent quelque chose encor palpiter sous un voile . . .
C'est toi qui dors dans l'ombre, ô sacré souvenir!

THE SADNESS OF OLYMPIO

How short a time suffices to estrange
   Thy face, calm Nature! How dost thou forget!
How dost thou sever by continual change
   The strings unseen that take us in the net!

The tree that bore our names is felled, or dead;
   Our green-clad bowers are grown to thickets brown;
The little boys who jump the ditch, and tread
   The unwatched close, have torn our roses down.

Where once athirst, descending from the wood,
   Gaily she drank, the little waterfall
Her hands enchaliced, and in fairy mood
   Showered for pearls, is prisoned by a wall.

'Tis metalled now, the rough uneven road,
   Where printing on the sand a clear-cut line,
Her little steps in humorous contrast showed
   Their footmarks laughing by the side of mine.

The immemorial stone beside the way,
   Where she would sit, and wait for me to come,
Is worn by jostlings at the close of day
   From the great carts, that creaked as they went home.

The forest here has shrunk, and there has spread;
   Little survives wherein we had our share;
And like a heap of ashes cold and dead
   Our memories are scattered by the air.

Is all then over? Have we lived our day?
   Is crying unavailing to restore?
Winds, as I grieve, among the tree-tops play;
   My dwelling fronts me, knowing me no more.

Others must now be passing where we passed,
   The paths we traced be traced by others' feet,
The dream of life by our two hearts forecast
   Others perhaps continue—not complete.

For none on earth can fully end or make
   What they would compass, be it worst or best;
Just when the dream seems fairest, we awake;
   Here the beginning—somewhere else the rest.

Yes, other innocent lovers in their bliss
   Will come to taste what Nature's fount supplies
Of awe, of magic in a spot like this
   To love that hides itself from curious eyes.

Leave we to others fields and paths and glades,
    And your own wood by strangers to be trod,
And trampled be by other barefoot maids
    The wave made holy round your feet unshod.

That in this spot we loved was all in vain.
    Nothing to us, who here blent soul with soul,
Of all these flowering hillsides may remain.
    Passionless Nature has resumed the whole.

Tell me O forest, rivulet and brake,
    Nest-laden boughs, caves, thickets, fruits that hang,
Speak ye to others as to us ye spake?
    Sing ye for others as for us ye sang?

We knew your language. Docile, grave, intent,
    Our hearts responded to the tale you told.
We reverenced your mysteries; we lent
    Ears to the deeper secrets you unfold.

Answer chaste valley, and thou solitude,
    Thou Nature shrined within a scene so fair,
When we shall sleep, to that calm form subdued
    Shaped by the tomb for those who slumber there,

Will you be still so mindless as to see
    Us dead together, loving and beloved,
And to continue your mild ecstasy,
    And to smile on, and to sing on, unmoved?

If you then mark us in our wanderings,
    Ghosts by your woods and banks once known so well,
Will you not tell us some of those fond things
    We, when we meet an old acquaintance, tell?

Will you ungrieving, unbewailing see
    Our phantoms flitting where in life we went,
And her with sad embraces drawing me
    Down to some streamlet vocal in lament?

And if some dusky nook, where nothing stirs,
    To hide their bliss two lovers shall have sped,
Will you not go and whisper in their ears
    "Think, you who live, one moment on the dead"?

God for an instant lends us park and brake,
    Tall shivering trees, dark rocks and running streams,
The deep blue sky, the meadow and the lake,
    Wherein to rest our hearts, our hopes, our dreams.

Then He withdraws them; makes the circle dark
    Lit by our tapers; He blows our our flames,
And bids the valley where we set our mark
    Efface our soul-prints, and forget our names.

Be it so, forget us, dwelling, garden, shade!
    Weeds, blur our threshold! Thorns, blot out our trace!
Sing, ye birds; flow, ye rills! Leaves, sprout and fade!
    Those you forget will not forget your face.

You, to our eyes, were love's own counterfeit;
    An oasis amidst our waste of sand;
Thou, O lone valley, wert the last retreat
    Where we shed tears together hand in hand.

Our passions leave us as our feelings grow,
    One with its mask, another with its knife;
Like strolling actors, singing as they go,
    They disappear behind the hills of life.

But thee, O Love, whom every thought endears,
    Our light in darkness, nothing can destroy;
Thou hold'st us by our joys, yea by our tears,
    Idol of age, the torment of the boy.

Now, when the head with weight of years is bent,
    When aimless, nerveless, all our visions fled,
We feel ourselves the ruined monument
    Wherein our hopes and energies lie dead;

When the soul sinks within us, while again
    It numbers, in a heart just touched by frost,
As on a battlefield men count the slain,
    Each out-worn sorrow, each illusion lost;

When even as one searching with a light,
    Far from broad day, far from the world's gay din,
At last it reaches by a winding flight
    The ungarnished basement of the void within;

There, in that night unstarred by any spark,
    Upon some confine of existence, thee
It finds yet stirring, breathing through the dark,
    Veiled and asleep—O sacred memory!

Les Rayons et les ombres (1840)
Translated by Sir George Young

VICTOR HUGO

1 8 0 2 — 1 8 8 5

FROM *LES CONTEMPLATIONS*

Une terre au flanc maigre, âpre, avare, inclément,
Où les vivants pensifs travaillent tristement,
Et qui donne à regret à cette race humaine
Un peu de pain pour tant de labeur et de peine;
Des hommes durs, éclos sur ces sillons ingrats;
Des cités d'où s'en vont, en se tordant les bras,
La charité, la paix, la foi, sœurs vénérables;
L'orgueil chez les puissants et chez les misérables;
La haine au cœur de tous; la mort, spectre sans yeux,
Frappant sur les meilleurs des coups mystérieux;
Sur tous les hauts sommets, des brumes répandues;
Deux vierges, la justice et la pudeur, vendues;
Toutes les passions engendrant tous les maux;
Des forêts abritant des loups sous leurs rameaux;
Là le désert torride, ici les froids polaires;
Des océans, émus de subites colères,
Pleins de mâts frissonnants qui sombrent dans la nuit;
Des continents couverts de fumée et de bruit,
Où, deux torches aux mains, rugit la guerre infâme,
Où toujours quelque part fume une ville en flamme,
Où se heurtent sanglants les peuples furieux;—

Et que tout cela fasse un astre dans les cieux!

BRIGHT STARS AND DARK

A meagre soil, arid and harsh and rude,
Furrowed by man with dull solicitude,
Yielding with grudging to the labouring swains
A little bread for all their pangs and pains;

Dour peasants, bending o'er ungrateful lands;
Crammed cities whence depart, wringing their hands,
The sisters grave, Peace, Faith, and Charity;
Pride in the homes of high and low degree,
Hate in all bosoms; Death, an eyeless guest,
Aiming clandestine buffets at the best;
Mists over all the lofty summits rolled;
Two virgins, Modesty and Justice, sold;

Men's passions all, begetters of all woes;
Here the parched desert, there the polar snows;
The forest sheltering wolves beneath its trees;
Lashed into sudden fits of rage, the seas
Shivering with masts that founder in the night;
Continents overspread with smoke and fright,
Where Discord fell, a torch in either hand,
Shrieks, where a flame goes up from land on land,
Where bleeding nations meet in frenzied jar,
—Strange that all this should go to make a star!

(1840)
Translated by Sir George Young

A wholly sublime composition.

C H A R L E S   R E N O U V I E R
Victor Hugo le poète (1907)

VICTOR HUGO

1 8 0 2 — 1 8 8 5

FROM *PAROLES SUR LA DUNE*

Et je reste parfois couché sans me lever
    Sur l'herbe rare de la dune,
Jusqu'à l'heure où l'on voit apparaître et rêver
    Les yeux sinistres de la lune.

Elle monte, elle jette un long rayon dormant
    A l'espace, au mystère, au gouffre;
Et nous nous regardons tous les deux fixement,
    Elle qui brille et moi qui souffre.

Où donc s'en sont allés mes jours évanouis?
Est-il quelqu'un qui me connaisse?
Ai-je encor quelque chose en mes yeux éblouis,
De la clarté de ma jeunesse?

At times I lie stretched out, and never rise,
Upon the scant grass of the moor,
Until I see the moon's ill-omened eyes,
As in a dream, their glances pour.

Rising, she casts a long and sleepy ray
On space, the deep, and mystery;
And we each other with fixt eyes survey—
She shining bright, and I who sigh.

Where, then, have fled away my vanished years?
My face, is there a soul who knows?
Say, in my eyes if one last glance appears,
Which of my life's glad morning shows?

(1854)
Translated by Henry Carrington

Pure and miraculous poetry.

FERNAND GREGH
Étude sur Victor Hugo (1905)

VICTOR HUGO

1 8 0 2 — 1 8 8 5

BEYOND DREAMS

Il descend, réveillé, l'autre côté du rêve.

Awakened, he descends the far side of dreams.

Ce Que Dit la bouche d'ombre (1855)

This extraordinary line, so weighted with such a beautiful image, so pulsating with both emotion and thought, that you would seek vainly anywhere else than in Hugo for its equal.

ANDRÉ GIDE
Interviews Imaginaires (1943)

VICTOR HUGO

1 8 0 2 — 1 8 8 5

FROM *BOOZ ENDORMI*

Quel dieu, quel moissonneur de l'éternel été
Avait, en s'en allant, négligemment jeté
Cette faucille d'or dans le champ des étoiles.

What God, what harvester of eternal summer, in departing, had negli-
gently thrown that golden sickle into the field of stars.

La Légende des siècles (1857)

There is no art more knowing, nor more exquisite.

ÉMILE FAGUET
Dix-neuvième Siècle: Études littéraires (1887)

VICTOR HUGO

1 8 0 2 — 1 8 8 5

LES ENFANTS PAUVRES

Prenez garde à ce petit être;
Il est bien grand; il contient Dieu.
Les enfants sont, avant de naître,
Des lumières dans le ciel bleu.

Dieu nous les offre en sa largesse;
Ils viennent; Dieu nous en fait don;
Dans leur rire il met sa sagesse
Et dans leur baiser son pardon.

Leur douce clarté nous effleure.
Hélas, le bonheur est leur droit.
S'ils ont faim, le paradis pleure,
Et le ciel tremble, s'ils ont froid.

La misère de l'innocence
Accuse l'homme vicieux.
L'homme tient l'ange en sa puissance.
Oh! quel tonnerre au fond des cieux,

Quand Dieu, cherchant ces êtres frêles
Que dans l'ombre où nous sommeillons
Il nous envoie avec des ailes,
Les retrouve avec des haillons!

THE CHILDREN OF THE POOR

Take heed of this small child of earth;
   He is great: he hath in him God most high.
Children before their fleshly birth
   Are lights alive in the blue sky.

In our light bitter world of wrong
   They come; God gives us them awhile.
His speech is in their stammering tongue,
   And his forgiveness in their smile.

Their sweet light rests upon our eyes.
   Alas! their right to joy is plain.
If they are hungry, Paradise
   Weeps, and, if cold, Heaven thrills with pain.

The want that saps their sinless flower
   Speaks judgment on sin's ministers.
Man holds an angel in his power.
   Ah! deep in Heaven what thunder stirs,

When God seeks out these tender things
   Whom in the shadow where we sleep
He sends us clothed about with wings,
   And finds them ragged babes that weep!

Translated by Algernon Charles Swinburne

There is one other poem of even more astonishing power, the five stanzas about the children of the poor, which Mr. Swinburne's incomparable rendering has made familiar to all lovers of English poetry. Perhaps the translator has even surpassed his original, treachery as he would hold it that we should say so: still, in any case the ineffable tenderness of the poem is not his, but Hugo's. There is nothing quite like it so far as I know in all poetry.

JOHN C. BAILEY
The Claims of French Poetry (1907)

VICTOR HUGO

1 8 0 2 — 1 8 8 5

FROM *TOUTE LA LYRE*

Passons, car c'est la loi; nul ne peut s'y soustraire;
Tout penche, et ce grand siècle, avec tous ses rayons,
Entre en cette ombre immense où, pâles, nous fuyons.
Oh! quel farouche bruit font dans le crépuscule
Les chênes qu'on abat pour le bûcher d'Hercule!
Les chevaux de la Mort se mettent à hennir
Et sont joyeux, car l'âge éclatant va finir;
Ce siècle altier, qui sut dompter le vent contraire,
Expire . . . O Gautier! toi, leur égal et leur frère,
Tu pars après Dumas, Lamartine et Musset.
L'onde antique est tarie où l'on rajeunissait;
Comme il n'est plus de Styx, il n'est plus de Jouvence.
Le dur faucheur avec sa large lame avance,
Pensif et pas à pas, vers le reste du blé;
C'est mon tour; et la nuit emplit mon œil troublé
Qui, devinant, hélas! l'avenir des colombes,
Pleure sur des berceaux et sourit à des tombes.

Let us pass on, for it is the law which no one can evade. Everything declines, and our great century, with all its rays of light, enters into that boundless shadow where, pale, we flee. What a savage noise the trees, which are felled for the funeral pyre of Hercules, make as they crash down in the twilight! The horses of Death begin to neigh and are joyful, because the brilliant age is ending; our proud century which knew how to subdue contrary winds, is expiring. . . . You, Gautier, are departing after Dumas, Lamartine and Musset, your equals and brothers. The fountains of the ancient world where one grew young again have run dry; there is no longer a river Styx, nor fountain of youth. The cruel reaper advances with his broad blade, pensively, step by step towards the rest of the wheat. It is my turn; and darkness fills my dimmed eyes, which, guessing, alas, at the future of the doves, weep over cradles and smile at graves.

À Théophile Gautier (1872)

Victor Hugo is the man who wrote the best French verse. No poetry at times is more beautiful or more virile than his. His virtuosity is incomparable.

PAUL VALÉRY
In conversation with Dorothy Bussy
Some Recollections of Paul Valéry (Horizon, May, 1946)

VICTOR HUGO

NOUVELLE CHANSON
SUR UN VIEIL AIR

S'il est un charmant gazon
  Que le ciel arrose,
Où brille en toute saison
  Quelque fleur éclose,
Où l'on cueille à pleine main
Lis, chèvrefeuille et jasmin,
J'en veux faire le chemin
  Où ton pied se pose!

S'il est un sein bien aimant
  Dont l'honneur dispose,
Dont le ferme dévouement
  N'ait rien de morose;
Si toujours ce noble sein
Bat pour un digne dessein,
J'en veux faire le coussin
  Où ton front se pose!

S'il est un rêve d'amour,
  Parfumé de rose,
Où l'on trouve chaque jour
  Quelque douce chose,
Un rêve que Dieu bénit,
Où l'âme à l'âme s'unit,
Oh! j'en veux faire le nid
  Où ton cœur se pose!

NEW SONG TO AN OLD AIR

Is there a tuft of grass,
  Nought to deface it,
Where, in their tiny mass,
  Sunny flowers grace it;
Where purple, gold, and red,
Mix in their scented bed?
Under her fairy tread
  Softly I'd place it.

Is there a loving breast,
    Fond as the willow
Watching the stream at rest,
    Pure as its billow;
Filled with great thoughts, and free
From all infirmity?
Sweet, such were meant for thee,
    Meant for thy pillow.

Is there a loving dream,
    Perfumed with roses,
Where every sunny beam
    Fresh charms discloses,
Love-dream which God has blest
Where fond souls meet, and rest?
Then upon such a nest
    Thy heart reposes.

                              Translated by Harry Curwen

How it sings, every word of it, sets itself to music, and dances to its own tune! There are deeper songs in the world of poetry, songs whose time is beaten for them by the droppings of human tears, and some of them come from Victor Hugo: but where shall we find one in which the delightfulness of love's assurance gets more gracious utterance? Unless indeed it be this which follows it:

AUTRE CHANSON

L'aube naît, et ta porte est close!
Ma belle, pourquoi sommeiller?
A l'heure où s'éveille la rose
Ne vas-tu pas te réveiller?

            O ma charmante!
            Écoute ici
            L'amant qui chante
            Et pleure aussi!

Tout frappe à ta porte bénie;
L'aurore dit: Je suis le jour!
L'oiseau dit: Je suis l'harmonie!
Et mon cœur dit: Je suis l'amour!

O ma charmante!
Écoute ici
L'amant qui chante
Et pleure aussi!

Je t'adore ange et t'aime femme.
Dieu, qui par toi m'a complété,
A fait mon amour pour ton âme
Et mon regard pour ta beauté!

O ma charmante!
Écoute ici
L'amant qui chante
Et pleure aussi!

ANOTHER SONG

Though heaven's gate of light uncloses,
    Thou stirr'st not—thou'rt laid to rest,
Waking are thy sister roses,
    One only dreameth on thy breast.

    Hear me, sweet dreamer!
    Tell me all thy fears,
    Trembling in song,
    But to break in tears.

Lo! to greet thee, spirits pressing,
    Soft music brings the gentle dove,
And fair light falleth like a blessing,
    While my poor heart can bring thee only love.

Worship thee, angels love thee, sweet woman?
    Yes; for that love perfects my soul.
None the less of heaven that my heart is human,
    Blent in one exquisite, harmonious whole.

Les Chants du crépuscule (1835)
Translated by H. B. Favnie

Is not the poise and balance of that refrain, as it seems to hang in the air, lingering to enjoy its own delightfulness, one of the greatest triumphs which the art of making music out of human speech has ever achieved?

JOHN C. BAILEY
The Claims of French Poetry (1907)

VICTOR HUGO

1 8 0 2 — 1 8 8 5

FROM *CHOSES DU SOIR*

On voit sur la mer des chasse-marées;
Le naufrage guette un mât frissonnant;
Le vent dit: demain! l'eau dit: maintenant!
Les voix qu'on entend sont désespérées. . . .

Le coche qui va d'Avranche à Fougère
Fait claquer son fouet comme un vif éclair;
Voici le moment où flottent dans l'air
Tous ces bruits confus que l'ombre exagère. . . .

Des flaques d'argent tremblent sur les sables;
L'orfraie est au bord des talus crayeux;
Le pâtre, à travers le vent, suit des yeux
Le vol monstrueux et vague des diables. . . .

Un panache gris sort des cheminées;
Le bûcheron passe avec son fardeau;
On entend, parmi le bruit des cours d'eau,
Des frémissements de branches traînées. . . .

La faim fait rêver les grands loups moroses;
La rivière court, le nuage fuit;
Derrière la vitre où la lampe luit,
Les petits enfants ont des têtes roses.

Some coasting vessels can be seen on the ocean; the wreck lies in wait for a shivering mast; the wind says, Tomorrow! the water says, Now! The voices heard are desperate. The coachman on the road from Avranche to Fougère cracks his whip like a vivid flash; this is the moment when all the confused noises that darkness exaggerates float in the air. Silver splashes tremble on the sands, the osprey stands on the chalky slopes; the shepherd, through the wind, follows with his eyes the vague and monstrous flight of devils. A gray plume winds from the chimneys; the woodcutter passes with his burden; one hears, midst the noise of flowing water, the rustle of the dragged branches. Hunger makes the big, morose wolves dream; the river hurries, the cloud passes; behind the window, where the lamp shines, the little children have rosy heads.

L'Art d'être grand-père (1877)

A pure masterpiece.

ÉMILE FAGUET
Dix-neuvième Siècle: Études littéraires (1887)

RALPH WALDO EMERSON

1 8 0 3 — 1 8 8 2

WHAT IS THIS TRUTH?

Gentlemen, I have ventured to offer you these considerations upon the scholar's place and hope, because I thought that standing, as many of you now do, on the threshold of this College, girt and ready to go and assume tasks, public and private, in your country, you would not be sorry to be admonished of those primary duties of the intellect whereof you will seldom hear from the lips of your new companions. You will hear every day the maxims of a low prudence. You will hear that the first duty is to get land and money, place and name. "What is this Truth you seek? what is this Beauty?" men will ask, with derision. If nevertheless God have called any of you to explore truth and beauty, be bold, be firm, be true. When you shall say, "As others do, so will I: I renounce, I am sorry for it, my early visions; I must eat the good of the land and let learning and romantic expectations go, until a more convenient season;"——then dies the man in you; then once more perish the buds of art, and poetry, and science, as they have died already in a thousand thousand men. The hour of that choice is the crisis of your history, and see that you hold yourself fast by the intellect. It is this domineering temper of the sensual world that creates the extreme need of the priests of science. . . . Be content with a little light, so it be your own. Explore, and explore. Be neither chided nor flattered out of your position of perpetual inquiry. Neither dogmatize, nor accept another's dogmatism. Why should you renounce your right to traverse the star-lit deserts of truth, for the premature comforts of an acre, house, and barn? Truth also has its roof, and bed, and board. Make yourself necessary to the world, and mankind will give you bread, and if not store of it, yet such as shall not take away your property in all men's possessions, in all men's affections, in art, in nature, and in hope.

Literary Ethics (1838)

Every word is still printed on my memory: I can see the left-hand page and read again that divine message: I make no excuse for quoting it almost word for word.

FRANK HARRIS
My Life and Loves (1922–27)

RALPH WALDO EMERSON

1 8 0 3 — 1 8 8 2

ALONE

Every god is there sitting in his sphere. The young mortal enters the hall of the firmament; there is he alone with them alone, they pouring on him benedictions and gifts, and beckoning him up to their thrones. On the instant, and incessantly, fall snowstorms of illusions. He fancies himself in a vast crowd which sways this way and that, and whose movements and doings he must obey; he fancies himself poor, orphaned, insignificant. The mad crowd drives hither and thither, now furiously commanding this thing to be done, now that. What is he that he should resist their will, and think or act for himself? Every moment new changes and new showers of deceptions to baffle and distract him. And when, by and by, for an instant, the air clears and the cloud lifts a little, there are the gods still sitting around him on their thrones—they alone with him alone.

Illusions (1857)

That Emerson had within him the soul of a poet no one will question, but his poems are expressed in prose forms. There are passages in his early addresses which can be matched in English only by bits from Sir Thomas Browne or Milton, or from the great poets. Heine might have written the . . . parable into verse, but it could not have been finer. It comes from the very bottom of Emerson's nature. It is his uttermost. Infancy and manhood and old age, the first and the last of him, speak in it.

JOHN JAY CHAPMAN
Emerson and Other Essays (1898)

THOMAS LOVELL BEDDOES

1 8 0 3 — 1 8 4 9

DIRGE

If thou wilt ease thine heart
Of love and all its smart,
Then sleep, dear, sleep;

And not a sorrow
    Hang any tear on your eyelashes;
        Lie still and deep,
    Sad soul, until the sea-wave washes
The rim o' th' sun to-morrow,
        In eastern sky.

                    Death's Jest-Book, Act ii, Scene ii (1833)

DREAM-PEDLARY

If there were dreams to sell,
    What would you buy?
Some cost a passing bell;
    Some a light sigh,
That shakes from Life's fresh crown
Only a roseleaf down.
If there were dreams to sell,
Merry and sad to tell,
And the crier rung the bell,
    What would you buy?

                            Poems (1829–44)

This [dirge] is perfect, and when we come to what should be the universally known first stanza of "Dream-Pedlary" what words can possibly do justice to its movement and music? what prosody of the very greatest that we have cited or referred to, in this voyage through the realms of gold, can be held superior to it? The selection of stanza; the arrangement of the rhymes; the framing of single lines to suit their sense; the utter inevitableness of the diction—how shall we acknowledge them rightly? There is nothing for it but to borrow those great and final words for which, even if Hazlitt's many sins were more than they are and his many virtues fewer, he should be canonised as a critic: "It is something worth living for to write, or even read, such poetry as this, or to know that it has been written." And, once more, beyond all question, though not beyond all difference in estimate of proportion, the prosody is a mighty part of this inestimable poetry.

One might quote many more, but this is not an anthology, and after the pair just quoted it is not necessary. Not even in Shelley before, or in Tennyson after, is there anything more significant of the recovered mastery of prosodic music—of the unlocking of the forgotten treasury where the harps and horns of Elfland had hung so long unused.

                        GEORGE SAINTSBURY
                A History of English Prosody (1910)

NATHANIEL HAWTHORNE

1 8 0 4 — 1 8 6 4

HESTER PRYNNE

Hester Prynne, gazing steadfastly at the clergyman, felt a dreary influence come over her, but wherefore or whence she knew not; unless that he seemed so remote from her own sphere, and utterly beyond her reach. One glance of recognition, she had imagined, must needs pass between them. She thought of the dim forest, with its little dell of solitude, and love, and anguish, and the mossy tree-trunk, where, sitting hand in hand, they had mingled their sad and passionate talk with the melancholy murmur of the brook. How deeply had they known each other then! And was this the man? She hardly knew him now! He, moving proudly past, enveloped, as it were, in the rich music, with the procession of majestic and venerable fathers; he, so unattainable in his worldly position, and still more so in that far vista of his unsympathizing thoughts, through which she now beheld him! Her spirit sank with the idea that all must have been a delusion, and that, vividly as she had dreamed it, there could be no real bond betwixt the clergyman and herself. And thus much of woman was there in Hester, that she could scarcely forgive him,—least of all now, when the heavy footstep of their approaching Fate might be heard, nearer, nearer, nearer!—for being able so completely to withdraw himself from their mutual world; while she groped darkly, and stretched forth her cold hands, and found him not.

The Scarlet Letter (1850)

In such a passage as one I have marked for quotation from THE SCARLET LETTER *there is the stamp of the genius of style.*

HENRY JAMES
Hawthorne (1879)

EDUARD MÖRIKE

1 8 0 4 — 1 8 7 5

DAS VERLASSENE MÄGDLEIN

Früh, wann die Hähne krähn,
Eh' die Sternlein verschwinden,
Muss ich am Herde stehn,
Muss Feuer zünden.

Schön ist der Flammen Schein,
Es springen die Funken;
Ich schaue so drein,
In Leid versunken.

Plötzlich, da kommt es mir,
Treuloser Knabe,
Dass ich die Nacht von dir
Geträumet habe.

Träne auf Träne dann
Stürzet hernieder;
So kommt der Tag heran—
O ging' er wieder!

THE DESERTED MAIDEN

When the cocks craw,
Or the wee stars are gane,
I maun kindle the fire
On the cauld hearthstane.

The sparks flee up,
And the lowe blinks bonnie,
I glower at the licht
Mair waefu' than ony.

Then it comes ower me,
Fause lad! my sorrow!
I did but dream o' ye
A' the nicht thorow.

Fast fa' the tears,
On the hard hearthstane,
And the day's here, but O
Gin it were gane!

Translated by Norman Macleod

*One of the great things in German song—recalling folk-poetry, but with
greater intensity and higher art.*

NORMAN MACLEOD
German Lyric Poetry (1930)

THE BROKEN OAR

Once upon Iceland's solitary strand
 A poet wandered with his book and pen,
 Seeking some final word, some sweet Amen,
 Wherewith to close the volume in his hand.
The billows rolled and plunged upon the sand,
 The circling sea-gulls swept beyond his ken,
 And from the parting cloud-rack now and then
 Flashed the red sunset over sea and land.
Then by the billows at his feet was tossed
 A broken oar; and carved thereon he read:
 "Oft was I weary, when I toiled at thee;"
And like a man, who findeth what was lost,
 He wrote the words, then lifted up his head,
 And flung his useless pen into the sea.

A Book of Sonnets (1875)

This has the gnomic quality of romantic poetry at its best.

HOWARD MUMFORD JONES
in American Writers on American Literature (1931)

WAIL OF THE FOREST

While from its rocky caverns the deep-voiced, neighboring ocean,
Speaks, and in accents disconsolate answers the wail of the forest.

Evangeline (1847)

Hexameters, by the way, as sonorous and rhythmical as any in the language.

PAUL ELMER MORE
Shelburne Essays, Fifth Series (1908)

EDGAR ALLAN POE

1809 — 1849

TO HELEN

Helen, thy beauty is to me
  Like those Nicean barks of yore,
That gently, o'er a perfumed sea,
    The weary, wayworn wanderer bore
    To his own native shore.

On desperate seas long wont to roam,
  Thy hyacinth hair, thy classic face,
Thy Naiad airs have brought me home
  To the glory that was Greece,
And the grandeur that was Rome.

Lo! in yon brilliant window-niche
  How statue-like I see thee stand,
  The agate lamp within thy hand!
Ah, Psyche, from the regions which
  Are Holy Land!

One of the most ripely perfect and spiritually charming poems ever written. . . . The two closing lines of the middle stanza have passed into the body of choice distillations of language reserved for immortality; and there is assuredly nothing more exquisite in its kind in English literature than the last stanza. To have written such verses is to have done a perfect thing.

J. M. ROBERTSON
New Essays Towards a Critical Method (1897)

ABRAHAM LINCOLN

1809 — 1865

THE GETTYSBURG ADDRESS

Four score and seven years ago our fathers brought forth on this continent, a new nation, conceived in Liberty, and dedicated to the proposition that all men are created equal.

Now we are engaged in a great civil war, testing whether that nation, or any nation so conceived and so dedicated, can long endure. We are

1190

met on a great battlefield of that war. We have come to dedicate a portion of that field, as a final resting place for those who here gave their lives that that nation might live. It is altogether fitting and proper that we should do this.

But, in a larger sense, we can not dedicate—we can not consecrate—we can not hallow—this ground. The brave men, living and dead, who struggled here have consecrated it, far above our poor power to add or detract. The world will little note, nor long remember what we say here, but it can never forget what they did here. It is for us the living, rather, to be dedicated here to the unfinished work which they who fought here have thus far so nobly advanced. It is rather for us to be here dedicated to the great task remaining before us—that from these honored dead we take increased devotion to that cause for which they gave the last full measure of devotion—that we here highly resolve that these dead shall not have died in vain—that this nation, under God, shall have a new birth of freedom—and that government of the people, by the people, for the people, shall not perish from the earth.

(1863)

His brief speech at Gettysburg will not easily be surpassed by words on any recorded occasion.

RALPH WALDO EMERSON
Miscellanies (1878)

EDWARD FITZGERALD

1 8 0 9 — 1 8 8 3

RUBÁIYÁT OF OMAR KHAYYÁM

I.

Wake! For the Sun who scatter'd into flight
The Stars before him from the Field of Night,
    Drives Night along with them from Heav'n, and strikes
The Sultán's Turret with a Shaft of Light.

II.

Before the phantom of False morning died,
Methought a Voice within the Tavern cried,
    "When all the Temple is prepared within,
"Why nods the drowsy Worshipper outside?"

III.

And, as the Cock crew, those who stood before
The Tavern shouted—"Open then the Door!
  "You know how little while we have to stay,
"And, once departed, may return no more."

IV.

Now the New Year reviving old Desires,
The thoughtful Soul to Solitude retires,
  Where the WHITE HAND OF MOSES on the Bough
Puts out, and Jesus from the Ground suspires.

V.

Iram indeed is gone with all his Rose,
And Jamshyd's Sev'n-ring'd Cup where no one knows;
  But still a Ruby kindles in the Vine,
And many a Garden by the Water blows.

VI.

And David's lips are lockt; but in divine
High-piping Pehleví, with "Wine! Wine! Wine!
  "Red Wine!"—the Nightingale cries to the Rose
That sallow cheek of her's to' incarnadine.

VII.

Come, fill the Cup, and in the fire of Spring
Your Winter-garment of Repentance fling:
  The Bird of Time has but a little way
To flutter—and the Bird is on the Wing.

VIII.

Whether at Naishápúr or Babylon,
Whether the Cup with sweet or bitter run,
  The Wine of Life keeps oozing drop by drop,
The Leaves of Life keep falling one by one.

IX.

Each Morn a thousand Roses brings, you say;
Yes, but where leaves the Rose of Yesterday?
  And this first Summer month that brings the Rose
Shall take Jamshyd and Kaikobád away.

X.

Well, let it take them! What have we to do
With Kaikobád the Great, or Kaikhosrú?
    Let Zál and Rustum bluster as they will,
Or Hátim call to Supper—heed not you.

XI.

With me along the strip of Herbage strown
That just divides the desert from the sown,
    Where name of Slave and Sultán is forgot—
And Peace to Mahmúd on his golden Throne!

XII.

A Book of Verses underneath the Bough,
A Jug of Wine, a Loaf of Bread—and Thou
    Beside me singing in the Wilderness—
Oh, Wilderness were Paradise enow!

XIII.

Some for the Glories of This World; and some
Sigh for the Prophet's Paradise to come;
    Ah, take the Cash, and let the Credit go,
Nor heed the rumble of a distant Drum!

XIV.

Look to the blowing Rose about us—"Lo,
"Laughing," she says, "into the world I blow,
    "At once the silken tassel of my Purse
"Tear, and its Treasure on the Garden throw."

XV.

And those who husbanded the Golden grain,
And those who flung it to the winds like Rain,
    Alike to no such aureate Earth are turn'd
As, buried once, Men want dug up again.

XVI.

The Worldly Hope men set their Hearts upon
Turns Ashes—or it prospers; and anon,
    Like Snow upon the Desert's dusty Face,
Lighting a little hour or two—was gone.

XVII.

Think, in this batter'd Caravanserai
Whose Portals are alternate Night and Day,
  How Sultán after Sultán with his Pomp
Abode his destin'd Hour, and went his way.

XVIII.

They say the Lion and the Lizard keep
The Courts where Jamshyd gloried and drank deep:
  And Bahrám, that great Hunter—the Wild Ass
Stamps o'er his Head, but cannot break his Sleep.

XIX.

I sometimes think that never blows so red
The Rose as where some buried Cæsar bled;
  That every Hyacinth the Garden wears
Dropt in her Lap from some once lovely Head.

XX.

And this reviving Herb whose tender Green
Fledges the River-Lip on which we lean—
  Ah, lean upon it lightly! for who knows
From what once lovely Lip it springs unseen!

XXI.

Ah, my Belovéd, fill the Cup that clears
To-day of past Regret and future Fears:
  To-morrow!—Why, To-morrow I may be
Myself with Yesterday's Sev'n thousand Years.

XXII.

For some we loved, the loveliest and the best
That from his Vintage rolling Time hath prest,
  Have drunk their Cup a Round or two before,
And one by one crept silently to rest.

XXIII.

And we, that now make merry in the Room
They left, and Summer dresses in new bloom,
  Ourselves must we beneath the Couch of Earth
Descend—ourselves to make a Couch—for whom?

XXIV.

Ah, make the most of what we yet may spend,
Before we too into the Dust descend;
   Dust into Dust, and under Dust, to lie,
Sans Wine, sans Song, sans Singer, and—sans End!

XXV.

Alike for those who for To-day prepare,
And those that after some To-morrow stare,
   A Muezzín from the Tower of Darkness cries,
"Fools! your Reward is neither Here nor There."

XXVI.

Why, all the Saints and Sages who discuss'd
Of the Two Worlds so wisely—they are thrust
   Like foolish Prophets forth; their Words to Scorn
Are scatter'd, and their Mouths are stopt with Dust.

XXVII.

Myself when young did eagerly frequent
Doctor and Saint, and heard great argument
   About it and about: but evermore
Came out by the same door where in I went.

XXVIII.

With them the seed of Wisdom did I sow,
And with mine own hand wrought to make it grow;
   And this was all the Harvest that I reap'd—
"I came like Water, and like Wind I go."

XXIX.

Into this Universe, and *Why* not knowing
Nor *Whence*, like Water willy-nilly flowing;
   And out of it, as Wind along the Waste,
I know not *Whither*, willy-nilly blowing.

XXX.

What, without asking, hither hurried *Whence?*
And, without asking, *Whither* hurried hence!
   Oh, many a Cup of this forbidden Wine
Must drown the memory of that insolence!

1195

XXXI.

Up from Earth's Centre through the Seventh Gate
I rose, and on the Throne of Saturn sate,
   And many a Knot unravel'd by the Road;
But not the Master-knot of Human Fate.

XXXII.

There was the Door to which I found no Key;
There was the Veil through which I might not see:
   Some little talk awhile of ME and THEE
There was—and then no more of THEE and ME.

XXXIII.

Earth could not answer; nor the Seas that mourn
In flowing Purple, of their Lord forlorn;
   Nor rolling Heaven, with all his Signs reveal'd
And hidden by the sleeve of Night and Morn.

XXXIV.

Then of the THEE IN ME who works behind
The Veil, I lifted up my hands to find
   A Lamp amid the Darkness; and I heard,
As from Without—"THE ME WITHIN THEE BLIND!"

XXXV.

Then to the Lip of this poor earthen Urn
I lean'd, the Secret of my Life to learn:
   And Lip to Lip it murmur'd—"While you live,
"Drink!—for, once dead, you never shall return."

XXXVI.

I think the Vessel, that with fugitive
Articulation answer'd, once did live,
   And drink; and Ah! the passive Lip I kiss'd,
How many Kisses might it take—and give!

XXXVII.

For I remember stopping by the way
To watch a Potter thumping his wet Clay:
   And with its all-obliterated Tongue
It murmur'd—"Gently, Brother, gently, pray!"

XXXVIII.

And has not such a Story from of Old
Down Man's successive generations roll'd
    Of such a clod of saturated Earth
Cast by the Maker into Human mould?

XXXIX.

And not a drop that from our Cups we throw
For Earth to drink of, but may steal below
    To quench the fire of Anguish in some Eye
There hidden—far beneath, and long ago.

XL.

As then the Tulip for her morning sup
Of Heav'nly Vintage from the soil looks up,
    Do you devoutly do the like, till Heav'n
To Earth invert you—like an empty Cup.

XLI.

Perplext no more with Human or Divine,
To-morrow's tangle to the winds resign,
    And lose your fingers in the tresses of
The Cypress-slender Minister of Wine.

XLII.

And if the Wine you drink, the Lip you press,
End in what All begins and ends in—Yes;
    Think then you are To-day what Yesterday
You were—To-morrow you shall not be less.

XLIII.

So when the Angel of the darker Drink
At last shall find you by the river-brink,
    And, offering his Cup, invite your Soul
Forth to your Lips to quaff—you shall not shrink.

XLIV.

Why, if the Soul can fling the Dust aside,
And naked on the Air of Heaven ride,
    Wer't not a Shame—wer't not a Shame for him
In this clay carcase crippled to abide?

XLV.

'Tis but a Tent where takes his one day's rest
A Sultán to the realm of Death addrest;
  The Sultán rises, and the dark Ferrásh
Strikes, and prepares it for another Guest.

XLVI.

And fear not lest Existence closing your
Account, and mine, should know the like no more;
  The Eternal Sákí from that Bowl has pour'd
Millions of Bubbles like us, and will pour.

XLVII.

When You and I behind the Veil are past,
Oh, but the long, long while the World shall last,
  Which of our Coming and Departure heeds
As the Sea's self should heed a pebble-cast.

XLVIII.

A Moment's Halt—a momentary taste
Of BEING from the Well amid the Waste—
  And Lo!—the phantom Caravan has reacht
The NOTHING it set out from—Oh, make haste!

XLIX.

Would you that spangle of Existence spend
About THE SECRET—quick about it, Friend!
  A Hair perhaps divides the False and True—
And upon what, prithee, does life depend?

L.

A Hair perhaps divides the False and True;
Yes; and a single Alif were the clue—
  Could you but find it—to the Treasure-house,
And peradventure to THE MASTER too;

LI.

Whose secret Presence, through Creation's veins
Running Quicksilver-like eludes your pains;
  Taking all shapes from Máh to Máhi; and
They change and perish all—but He remains;

LII.

A moment guess'd—then back behind the Fold
Immerst of Darkness round the Drama roll'd
   Which, for the Pastime of Eternity,
He doth Himself contrive, enact, behold.

LIII.

But if in vain, down on the stubborn floor
Of Earth, and up to Heav'n's unopening Door,
   You gaze To-DAY, while You are You—how then
To-MORROW, You when shall be You no more?

LIV.

Waste not your Hour, nor in the vain pursuit
Of This and That endeavour and dispute;
   Better be jocund with the fruitful Grape
Than sadden after none, or bitter, Fruit.

LV.

You know, my Friends, with what a brave Carouse
I made a Second Marriage in my house;
   Divorced old barren Reason from my Bed,
And took the Daughter of the Vine to Spouse.

LVI.

For "Is" and "Is-NOT" though with Rule and Line,
And "UP-AND-DOWN" by Logic I define,
   Of all that one should care to fathom, I
Was never deep in anything but—Wine.

LVII.

Ah, but my Computations, People say,
Reduced the Year to better reckoning?—Nay,
   'Twas only striking from the Calendar
Unborn To-morrow, and dead Yesterday.

LVIII.

And lately, by the Tavern Door agape,
Came shining through the Dusk an Angel Shape
   Bearing a Vessel on his Shoulder; and
He bid me taste of it; and 'twas—the Grape!

LIX.

The Grape that can with Logic absolute
The Two-and-Seventy jarring Sects confute:
   The sovereign Alchemist that in a trice
Life's leaden metal into Gold transmute:

LX.

The mighty Mahmúd, Allah-breathing Lord,
That all the misbelieving and black Horde
   Of Fears and Sorrows that infest the Soul
Scatters before him with his whirlwind Sword.

LXI.

Why, be this Juice the growth of God, who dare
Blaspheme the twisted tendril as a Snare?
   A Blessing, we should use it, should we not?
And if a Curse—why, then, Who set it there?

LXII.

I must abjure the Balm of Life, I must,
Scared by some After-reckoning ta'en on trust,
   Or lured with Hope of some Diviner Drink,
To fill the Cup—when crumbled into Dust!

LXIII.

Oh threats of Hell and Hopes of Paradise!
One thing at least is certain—*This* Life flies;
   One thing is certain and the rest is Lies;
The Flower that once has blown for ever dies.

LXIV.

Strange, is it not? that of the myriads who
Before us pass'd the door of Darkness through,
   Not one returns to tell us of the Road,
Which to discover we must travel too.

LXV.

The Revelations of Devout and Learn'd
Who rose before us, and as Prophets burn'd,
   Are all but Stories, which, awoke from Sleep
They told their comrades, and to Sleep return'd.

LXVI.

I sent my Soul through the Invisible,
Some letter of that After-life to spell:
    And by and by my Soul return'd to me,
And answer'd "I Myself am Heav'n and Hell:"

LXVII.

Heav'n but the Vision of fulfill'd Desire,
And Hell the Shadow from a Soul on fire
    Cast on the Darkness into which Ourselves,
So late emerg'd from, shall so soon expire.

LXVIII.

We are no other than a moving row
Of Magic Shadow-shapes that come and go
    Round with the Sun-illumin'd Lantern held
In Midnight by the Master of the Show;

LXIX.

But helpless Pieces of the Game He plays
Upon this Chequer-board of Nights and Days;
    Hither and thither moves, and checks, and slays,
And one by one back in the Closet lays.

LXX.

The Ball no question makes of Ayes and Noes,
But Here or There as strikes the Player goes;
    And He that toss'd you down into the Field,
He knows about it all—HE knows—HE knows!

LXXI.

The Moving Finger writes; and, having writ,
Moves on: nor all your Piety nor Wit
    Shall lure it back to cancel half a Line,
Nor all your Tears wash out a Word of it.

LXXII.

And that inverted Bowl they call the Sky,
Whereunder crawling coop'd we live and die,
    Lift not your hands to *It* for help—for It
As impotently moves as you or I.

LXXIII.

With Earth's first Clay They did the Last Man knead,
And there of the Last Harvest sow'd the Seed:
    And the first Morning of Creation wrote
What the Last Dawn of Reckoning shall read.

LXXIV.

YESTERDAY *This* Day's Madness did prepare;
To-MORROW'S Silence, Triumph, or Despair:
    Drink! for you know not whence you came, nor why:
Drink! for you know not why you go, nor where.

LXXV.

I tell you this—When, started from the Goal,
Over the flaming shoulders of the Foal
    Of Heav'n Parwín and Mushtarí they flung,
In my predestin'd Plot of Dust and Soul

LXXVI.

The Vine had struck a fibre: which about
If clings my Being—let the Dervish flout;
    Of my Base metal may be filed a Key,
That shall unlock the Door he howls without.

LXXVII.

And this I know: whether the one True Light
Kindle to Love, or Wrath-consume me quite,
    One Flash of It within the Tavern caught
Better than in the Temple lost outright.

LXXVIII.

What! out of senseless Nothing to provoke
A conscious Something to resent the yoke
    Of unpermitted Pleasure, under pain
Of Everlasting Penalties, if broke!

LXXIX.

What! from his helpless Creature be repaid
Pure Gold for what he lent him dross-allay'd—
    Sue for a Debt we never did contract,
And cannot answer—Oh the sorry trade!

LXXX.

Oh Thou, who didst with pitfall and with gin
Beset the Road I was to wander in,
    Thou wilt not with Predestin'd Evil round
Enmesh, and then impute my Fall to Sin!

LXXXI.

Oh Thou, who Man of baser Earth didst make,
And ev'n with Paradise devise the Snake:
    For all the Sin wherewith the Face of Man
Is blacken'd—Man's forgiveness give—and take!

.   .   .   .   .   .

LXXXII.

As under cover of departing Day
Slunk hunger-stricken Ramazán away,
    Once more within the Potter's house alone
I stood, surrounded by the Shapes of Clay.

LXXXIII.

Shapes of all Sorts and Sizes, great and small,
That stood along the floor and by the wall;
    And some loquacious Vessels were; and some
Listen'd perhaps, but never talk'd at all.

LXXXIV.

Said one among them—"Surely not in vain
My substance of the common Earth was ta'en
    And to this Figure moulded, to be broke,
Or trampled back to shapeless Earth again."

LXXXV.

Then said a Second—"Ne'er a peevish Boy
"Would break the Bowl from which he drank in joy;
    "And He that with his hand the Vessel made
"Will surely not in after Wrath destroy."

LXXXVI.

After a momentary silence spake
Some Vessel of a more ungainly Make;
    "They sneer at me for leaning all awry:
"What! did the Hand then of the Potter shake?"

LXXXVII.

Whereat some one of the loquacious Lot—
I think a Súfi pipkin—waxing hot—
   "All this of Pot and Potter—Tell me then,
"Who is the Potter, pray, and who the Pot?"

LXXXVIII.

"Why," said another, "Some there are who tell
"Of one who threatens he will toss to Hell
   "The luckless Pots he marr'd in making—Pish!
"He's a Good Fellow, and 't will all be well."

LXXXIX.

"Well," murmur'd one, "Let whoso make or buy,
"My Clay with long Oblivion is gone dry:
   "But fill me with the old familiar Juice,
"Methinks I might recover by and by."

XC.

So while the Vessels one by one were speaking,
The little Moon look'd in that all were seeking:
   And then they jogg'd each other, "Brother! Brother!
"Now for the Porter's shoulder-knot a-creaking!"

    .   .   .   .   .   .

XCI.

Ah, with the Grape my fading Life provide,
And wash the Body whence the Life has died,
   And lay me, shrouded in the living Leaf,
By some not unfrequented Garden-side.

XCII.

That ev'n my buried Ashes such a snare
Of Vintage shall fling up into the Air
   As not a True-believer passing by
But shall be overtaken unaware.

XCIII.

Indeed the Idols I have loved so long
Have done my credit in this World much wrong:
   Have drown'd my Glory in a shallow Cup,
And sold my Reputation for a Song.

XCIV.

Indeed, indeed, Repentance oft before
I swore—but was I sober when I swore?
    And then and then came Spring, and Rose-in-hand
My thread-bare Penitence apieces tore.

XCV.

And much as Wine has play'd the Infidel,
And robb'd me of my Robe of Honour—Well,
    I wonder often what the Vintners buy
One half so precious as the stuff they sell.

XCVI.

Yet Ah, that Spring should vanish with the Rose!
That Youth's sweet-scented manuscript should close!
    The Nightingale that in the branches sang,
Ah whence, and whither flown again, who knows!

XCVII.

Would but the Desert of the Fountain yield
One glimpse—if dimly, yet indeed, reveal'd,
    To which the fainting Traveller might spring,
As springs the trampled herbage of the field!

XCVIII.

Would but some wingéd Angel ere too late
Arrest the yet unfolded Roll of Fate,
    And make the stern Recorder otherwise
Enregister, or quite obliterate!

XCIX.

Ah Love! could you and I with Him conspire
To grasp this sorry Scheme of Things entire,
    Would not we shatter it to bits—and then
Re-mould it nearer to the Heart's Desire!

.   .   .   .   .   .

C.

Yon rising Moon that looks for us again—
How oft hereafter will she wax and wane;
    How oft hereafter rising look for us
Through this same Garden—and for *one* in vain!

CI.

And when like her, oh Sákí, you shall pass
Among the Guests Star-scatter'd on the Grass,
  And in your joyous errand reach the spot
Where I made One—turn down an empty Glass!

TAMÁM.

(1879)

Omar's theme, the unconquered mystery of life and death, the flux, beyond arrest, of human things, the sorrowful and swift flight of beauty and joy, was a theme old as the world itself. . . . Nor is it likely to lose its power, so subtly does it render the bitter-sweet of reflective existence, the thought of beauty that must be loved and yet must be relinquished, the uneasy fear, never wholly to be banished from the hearts of men, that their exile from the joys of conscious being will be without return, that the only affections they have known can never again be known. It may well remain, while the language lasts, its most finished expression of the spirit's darker broodings, its most searching music in the minor key.

W.   MACNEILE DIXON and H.   J.   C.   GRIERSON
The English Parnassus (1916)

ALFRED LORD TENNYSON

1 8 0 9 — 1 8 9 2

THE VISION OF SIN

I

I had a vision when the night was late:
A youth came riding toward a palace-gate.
He rode a horse with wings, that would have flown,
But that his heavy rider kept him down.
And from the palace came a child of sin,
And took him by the curls, and led him in,
Where sat a company with heated eyes,
Expecting when a fountain should arise:
A sleepy light upon their brows and lips—
As when the sun, a crescent of eclipse,

Dreams over lake and lawn, and isles and capes—
Suffused them, sitting, lying, languid shapes,
By heaps of gourds, and skins of wine, and piles of grapes.

II

Then methought I heard a mellow sound,
Gathering up from all the lower ground;
Narrowing in to where they sat assembled
Low voluptuous music winding trembled,
Wov'n in circles: they that heard it sigh'd,
Panted hand in hand with faces pale,
Swung themselves, and in low tones replied;
Till the fountain spouted, showering wide
Sleet of diamond-drift and pearly hail;
Then the music touch'd the gates and died;
Rose again from where it seem'd to fail,
Storm'd in orbs of song, a growing gale;
Till thronging in and in, to where they waited,
As 'twere a hundred-throated nightingale,
The strong tempestuous treble throbb'd and palpitated;
Ran into its giddiest whirl of sound,
Caught the sparkles, and in circles,
Purple gauzes, golden hazes, liquid mazes,
Flung the torrent rainbow round:
Then they started from their places,
Moved with violence, changed in hue,
Caught each other with wild grimaces,
Half-invisible to the view,
Wheeling with precipitate paces
To the melody, till they flew,
Hair, and eyes, and limbs, and faces,
Twisted hard in fierce embraces,
Like to Furies, like to Graces,
Dash'd together in blinding dew:
Till, kill'd with some luxurious agony,
The nerve-dissolving melody
Flutter'd headlong from the sky.

III

And then I look'd up toward a mountain-tract,
That girt the region with high cliff and lawn:
I saw that every morning, far withdrawn
Beyond the darkness and the cataract,

God made Himself an awful rose of dawn,
Unheeded: and detaching, fold by fold,
From those still heights, and, slowly drawing near,
A vapour heavy, hueless, formless, cold,
Came floating on for many a month and year,
Unheeded: and I thought I would have spoken,
And warn'd that madman ere it grew too late:
But, as in dreams, I could not. Mine was broken,
When that cold vapour touch'd the palace-gate,
And link'd again. I saw within my head
A grey and gap-tooth'd man as lean as death,
Who slowly rode across a wither'd heath,
And lighted at a ruin'd inn, and said:

IV

'Wrinkled ostler, grim and thin!
    Here is custom come your way;
Take my brute, and lead him in,
    Stuff his ribs with mouldy hay.

'Bitter barmaid, waning fast!
    See that sheets are on my bed;
What! the flower of life is past:
    It is long before you wed.

'Slip-shod waiter, lank and sour,
    At the Dragon on the heath!
Let us have a quiet hour,
    Let us hob-and-nob with Death.

'I am old, but let me drink;
    Bring me spices, bring me wine;
I remember, when I think,
    That my youth was half divine.

'Wine is good for shrivell'd lips,
    When a blanket wraps the day,
When the rotten woodland drips,
    And the leaf is stamp'd in clay.

'Sit thee down, and have no shame,
    Cheek by jowl, and knee by knee:
What care I for any name
    What for order or degree?

'Let me screw thee up a peg:
  Let me loose thy tongue with wine:
Callest thou that thing a leg?
  Which is thinnest? thine or mine?

'Thou shalt not be saved by works:
  Thou hast been a sinner too:
Ruin'd trunks on wither'd forks,
  Empty scarecrows, I and you!

'Fill the cup, and fill the can:
  Have a rouse before the morn:
Every moment dies a man,
  Every moment one is born.

'We are men of ruin'd blood;
  Therefore comes it we are wise.
Fish are we that love the mud,
  Rising to no fancy-flies.

'Name and fame! to fly sublime
  Thro' the courts, the camps, the schools,
Is to be the ball of Time,
  Bandied by the hands of fools.

'Friendship!—to be two in one—
  Let the canting liar pack!
Well I know, when I am gone,
  How she mouths behind my back.

'Virtue!—to be good and just—
  Every heart, when sifted well,
Is a clot of warmer dust,
  Mix'd with cunning sparks of hell.

'O! we two as well can look
  Whited thought and cleanly life
As the priest, above his book
  Leering at his neighbour's wife.

'Fill the cup, and fill the can:
  Have a rouse before the morn:
Every moment dies a man,
  Every moment one is born.

'Drink, and let the parties rave:
  They are fill'd with idle spleen;
Rising, falling, like a wave,
  For they know not what they mean.

'He that roars for liberty
  Faster binds a tyrant's power;
And the tyrant's cruel glee
  Forces on the freer hour.

'Fill the can, and fill the cup:
  All the windy ways of men
Are but dust that rises up,
  And is lightly laid again.

'Greet her with applausive breath,
  Freedom, gaily doth she tread;
In her right a civic wreath,
  In her left a human head.

'No, I love not what is new;
  She is of an ancient house:
And I think we know the hue
  Of that cap upon her brows.

'Let her go! her thirst she slakes
  Where the bloody conduit runs:
Then her sweetest meal she makes
  On the first-born of her sons.

'Drink to lofty hopes that cool—
  Visions of a perfect State:
Drink we, last, the public fool,
  Frantic love and frantic hate.

'Chant me now some wicked stave,
  Till thy drooping courage rise,
And the glow-worm of the grave
  Glimmer in thy rheumy eyes.

'Fear not thou to loose thy tongue;
  Set thy hoary fancies free;
What is loathsome to the young
  Savours well to thee and me.

'Change, reverting to the years,
  When thy nerves could understand
What there is in loving tears,
  And the warmth of hand in hand.

'Tell me tales of thy first love—
  April hopes, the fools of chance;
Till the graves begin to move,
  And the dead begin to dance.

'Fill the can, and fill the cup:
  All the windy ways of men
Are but dust that rises up,
  And is lightly laid again.

'Trooping from their mouldy dens
  The chap-fallen circle spreads:
Welcome, fellow-citizens,
  Hollow hearts and empty heads!

'You are bones, and what of that?
  Every face, however full,
Padded round with flesh and fat,
  Is but modell'd on a skull.

'Death is king, and Vivat Rex!
  Tread a measure on the stones,
Madam—if I know your sex,
  From the fashion of your bones.

'No, I cannot praise the fire
  In your eye—nor yet your lip:
All the more do I admire
  Joints of cunning workmanship.

'Lo! God's likeness—the ground-plan—
  Neither modell'd, glazed, or framed:
Buss me, thou rough sketch of man,
  Far too naked to be shamed!

'Drink to Fortune, drink to Chance,
  While we keep a little breath!
Drink to heavy Ignorance!
  Hob-and-nob with brother Death!

'Thou art mazed, the night is long,
  And the longer night is near:
What! I am not all as wrong
  As a bitter jest is dear.

'Youthful hopes, by scores, to all,
  When the locks are crisp and curl'd;
Unto me my maudlin gall
  And my mockeries of the world.

'Fill the cup, and fill the can!
  Mingle madness, mingle scorn!
Dregs of life, and lees of man:
  Yet we will not die forlorn.'

The voice grew faint: there came a further change:
Once more uprose the mystic mountain-range:
Below were men and horses pierced with worms,
And slowly quickening into lower forms;
By shards and scurf of salt, and scum of dross,
Old plash of rains, and refuse patch'd with moss.
Then some one spake: 'Behold! It was a crime
Of sense avenged by sense that wore with time.'
Another answer'd 'But a crime of sense?
Give him new nerves with old experience.'
Another said: 'The crime of sense became
The crime of malice, and is equal blame.'
And one: 'He had not wholly quench'd his power;
A little grain of conscience made him sour'
At last I heard a voice upon the slope
Cry to the summit, 'Is there any hope?'
To which an answer peal'd from that high land,
But in a tongue no man could understand;
And on the glimmering limit far withdrawn
God made Himself an awful rose of dawn.   (1842)

*There are few more prosodically perfect examples in English of what
Johnson calls "the greater ode."*

GEORGE SAINTSBURY
A History of English Prosody (1910)

ALFRED LORD TENNYSON

1 8 0 9 — 1 8 9 2

THE DAYS THAT ARE NO MORE

Tears, idle tears, I know not what they mean,
Tears from the depth of some divine despair
Rise in the heart, and gather to the eyes,
In looking on the happy Autumn-fields,
And thinking of the days that are no more.

Fresh as the first beam glittering on a sail,
That brings our friends up from the underworld,
Sad as the last which reddens over one
That sinks with all we love below the verge;
So sad, so fresh, the days that are no more.

Ah, sad and strange as in dark summer dawns
The earliest pipe of half-awaken'd birds
To dying ears, when unto dying eyes
The casement slowly grows a glimmering square;
So sad, so strange, the days that are no more.

Dear as remember'd kisses after death,
And sweet as those by hopeless fancy feign'd
On lips that are for others; deep as love,
Deep as first love, and wild with all regret;
O Death in Life, the days that are no more.

The Princess (1847)

From Alfred Tennyson—although in perfect sincerity I regard him as the noblest poet that ever lived—I have left myself time to cite only a very brief specimen. I call him, and THINK *him the noblest of poets—*NOT *because the impressions he produces are, at* ALL *times, the most profound—*NOT *because the poetical excitement which he induces is, at* ALL *times, the most intense—but because it* IS, *at all times, the most ethereal —in other words, the most elevating and the most pure. No poet is so little of the earth, earthy.*

EDGAR ALLAN POE
The Poetic Principle (1850)

ALFRED LORD TENNYSON

1 8 0 9 — 1 8 9 2

SIR JOHN FRANKLIN

ON THE CENOTAPH IN WESTMINSTER ABBEY

Not here! the white North has thy bones; and thou,
    Heroic sailor-soul,
Art passing on thine happier voyage now
    Toward no earthly pole.

(1877)

The finest [epitaph] that exists in English verse.

JOHN BAILEY
The Continuity of Letters (1923)

EARLY SPRING

I

Once more the Heavenly Power
  Makes all things new,
And domes the red-plow'd hills
  With loving blue;
The blackbirds have their wills,
  The throstles too.

II

Opens a door in Heaven;
  From skies of glass
A Jacob's ladder falls
  On greening grass,
And o'er the mountain-walls
  Young angels pass.

III

Before them fleets the shower,
  And burst the buds,
And shine the level lands,
  And flash the floods;
The stars are from their hands
  Flung thro' the woods,

IV

The woods with living airs
  How softly fann'd,
Light airs from where the deep,
  All down the sand,
Is breathing in his sleep,
  Heard by the land.

V

O follow, leaping blood,
　The season's lure!
O heart, look down and up
　Serene, secure,
Warm as the crocus cup,
　Like snowdrops, pure!

VI

Past, Future glimpse and fade
　Thro' some slight spell,
A gleam from yonder vale,
　Some far blue fell,
And sympathies, how frail,
　In sound and smell!

VII

Till at thy chuckled note,
　Thou twinkling bird,
The fairy fancies range,
　And, lightly stirr'd,
Ring little bells of change
　From word to word.

VIII

For now the Heavenly Power
　Makes all things new,
And thaws the cold, and fills
　The flower with dew;
The blackbirds have their wills,
　The poets too.

(1885)

If a man who had derived great happiness from the observation of nature were stricken with blindness or confined for the rest of his life to a sick-room, and if he were condemned to lose his recollection of all poets but one, Tennyson's is the poetry he should choose to keep.

A. C. BRADLEY
A Miscellany (1929)

NAPOLÉON PEYRAT

1 8 0 9 — 1 8 7 9

ROLAND

L'Arabie, en nos champs, des rochers espagnols
S'abattit; le printemps a moins de rossignols
    Et l'été moins d'épis de seigle.
Blonds étaient les chevaux dont le vent soulevait
La crinière argentée, et leur pied grêle avait
    Des poils comme des plumes d'aigle.

Ces Mores mécréants, ces maudits Sarrasins
Buvaient l'eau de nos puits et mangeaient nos raisins
    Et nos figues, et nos grenades,
Suivaient dans les vallons les vierges à l'œil noir
Et leur parlaient d'amour, à la lune, le soir,
    Et leur faisaient des sérénades.

Pour eux, leurs grands yeux noirs, pour eux, leurs beaux seins bruns,
Pour eux, leurs longs baisers, leur bouche aux doux parfums,
    Pour eux, leur belle joue ovale;
Et quand elles pleuraient, criant: "Fils des démons!"
Ils les mettaient en croupe et par-dessus les monts
    Ils faisaient sauter leur cavale.

Arabia, in our fields threw down her Spanish rocks; spring has fewer
nightingales and summer fewer blades of rye. Fair were the horses whose
silvered manes were tossed by the wind, and their slender legs had hairs
like an eagle's feathers. These unbelieving Moors, these cursed Saracens,
drank the water of our wells and ate our grapes, and our figs, and our
pomegranates, followed the black-eyed maidens in the valleys, and spoke
to them of love in the evenings by moonlight, and serenaded them. For
them their large eyes were dark, for them their brown bosoms were fair,
for them their kisses were long, the odour of their mouths was sweet,
for them their fair cheeks were rounded; and when they wept, crying:
'Sons of demons!' they put them on their cruppers and galloped across
the mountains.

Translated by A. W. Evans

The most beautiful and most finished masterpiece of the art of his age.

ANATOLE FRANCE
La Vie littéraire (1888–92)

ALFRED DE MUSSET

1 8 1 0 — 1 8 5 7

CHANSON DE FORTUNIO

Si vous croyez que je vais dire
    Qui j'ose aimer,
Je ne saurais, pour un empire,
    Vous la nommer.

Nous allons chanter à la ronde,
    Si vous voulez,
Que je l'adore et qu'elle est blonde
    Comme les blés.

Je fais ce que sa fantaisie
    Veut m'ordonner,
Et je puis, s'il lui faut ma vie,
    La lui donner.

Du mal qu'une amour ignorée
    Nous fait souffrir,
J'en porte l'âme déchirée
    Jusqu'à mourir.

Maïs j'aime trop pour que je die
    Qui j'ose aimer,
Et je veux mourir pour ma mie
    Sans la nommer.

FORTUNIO'S SONG

So sweet my love, her face so fair,
    So pure her fame,
Not for a kingdom would I dare
    To tell her name.

We'll sing our loves, each lover his,
    And I'll sing mine,
How blithe she is, how blond she is,
    How blue her eyne.

Whate'er she asks me, I will give
    Without a sigh;
It is for her alone I live,
    For her I'd die.

Though love that worships unconfessed
　　Is grievous woe,
Yet will I hide mine in my breast
　　And fain die so.

Too fond am I my love to tell
　　Lest I should shame
Her whom I love and love too well
　　To breathe her name.

Le Chandelier (1836), Act ii
Translated by William Frederic Giese

*Some of his lyrics are perfect; the famous song of Fortunio in itself
entitles him to a high place among the masters of the language.*

LYTTON STRACHEY
Landmarks in French Literature (1923)

ALFRED DE MUSSET

1 8 1 0 — 1 8 5 7

À LA MALIBRAN

STANCES

I

Sans doute il est trop tard pour parler encor d'elle;
Depuis qu'elle n'est plus quinze jours sont passés,
Et dans ce pays-ci quinze jours, je le sais,
Font d'une mort récente une vieille nouvelle.
De quelque nom d'ailleurs que le regret s'appelle,
L'homme, par tout pays, en a bien vite assez.

II

O Maria-Félicia! le peintre et le poëte
Laissent, en expirant, d'immortels héritiers;
Jamais l'affreuse nuit ne les prend tout entiers:
A défaut d'action, leur grande âme inquiète
De la mort et du temps entreprend la conquête,
Et, frappés dans la lutte, ils tombent en guerriers.

III

Celui-là sur l'airain a gravé sa pensée;
Dans un rhythme doré l'autre l'a cadencée;
Du moment qu'on l'écoute, on lui devient ami
Sur sa toile, en mourant, Raphaël l'a laissée;
Et, pour que le néant ne touche point à lui,
C'est assez d'un enfant sur sa mère endormi.

IV

Comme dans une lampe une flamme fidèle,
Au fond du Parthénon le marbre inhabité
Garde de Phidias la mémoire éternelle,
Et la jeune Vénus, fille de Praxitèle,
Sourit encor, debout dans sa divinité,
Aux siècles impuissants qu'a vaincus sa beauté.

V

Recevant d'âge en âge une nouvelle vie,
Ainsi s'en vont à Dieu les gloires d'autrefois;
Ainsi le vaste écho de la voix du génie
Devient du genre humain l'universelle voix . . .
Et de toi, morte hier, de toi, pauvre Marie,
Au fond d'une chapelle il nous reste une croix!

VI

Une croix! et l'oubli, la nuit et le silence!
Écoutez! c'est le vent, c'est l'Océan immense;
C'est un pêcheur qui chante au bord du grand chemin.
Et de tant de beauté, de gloire et d'espérance,
De tant d'accords si doux d'un instrument divin,
Pas un faible soupir, pas un écho lointain!

VII

Une croix, et ton nom écrit sur une pierre,
Non pas même le tien, mais celui d'un époux,
Voilà ce qu'après toi tu laisses sur la terre;
Et ceux qui t'iront voir à ta maison dernière,
N'y trouvant pas ce nom qui fut aimé de nous,
Ne sauront pour prier ou poser les genoux.

VIII

O Ninette! où sont-ils, belle muse adorée,
Ces accents pleins d'amour, de charme et de terreur,
Qui voltigeaient le soir sur ta lèvre inspirée,
Comme un parfum léger sur l'aubépine en fleur?
Où vibre maintenant cette voix éplorée,
Cette harpe vivante attachée à ton cœur?

IX

N'était-ce pas hier, fille joyeuse et folle,
Que ta verve railleuse animait Corilla,
Et que tu nous lançais avec la Rosina
La roulade amoureuse et l'œillade espagnole?
Ces pleurs sur tes bras nus, quand tu chantais *le Saule*,
N'était-ce pas hier, pâle Desdemona?

X

N'était-ce pas hier qu'à le fleur de ton âge
Tu traversais l'Europe, une lyre à la main;
Dans la mer, en riant, te jetant à la nage,
Chantant la tarentelle au ciel napolitain,
Cœur d'ange et de lion, libre oiseau de passage,
Espiègle enfant ce soir, sainte artiste demain?

XI

N'était-ce pas hier qu'enivrée et bénie
Tu traînais à ton char un peuple transporté,
Et que Londre et Madrid, la France et l'Italie,
Apportaient à tes pieds cet or tant convoité,
Cet or deux fois sacré qui payait ton génie,
Et qu'à tes pieds souvent laissa ta charité?

XII

Qu'as-tu fait pour mourir, ô noble créature,
Belle image de Dieu, qui donnais en chemin
Au riche un peu de joie, au malheureux du pain?
Ah! qui donc frappe ainsi dans la mère nature,
Et quel faucheur aveugle, affamé de pâture,
Sur les meilleurs de nous ose porter la main?

XIII

Ne suffit-il donc pas à l'ange des ténèbres
Qu'à peine de ce temps il nous reste un grand nom?
Que Géricault, Cuvier, Schiller, Gœthe et Byron
Soient endormis d'hier sous les dalles funèbres,
Et que nous ayons vu tant d'autres morts célèbres
Dans l'abîme entr'ouvert suivre Napoléon?

XIV

Nous faut-il perdre encor nos têtes les plus chères,
Et venir en pleurant leur fermer les paupières,
Dès qu'un rayon d'espoir a brillé dans leurs yeux?
Le ciel de ses élus devient-il envieux?
Ou faut-il croire, hélas! ce que disaient nos pères,
Que lorsqu'on meurt si jeune on est aimé des dieux?

XV

Ah! combien, depuis peu, sont partis pleins de vie!
Sous les cyprès anciens que de saules nouveaux!
La cendre de Robert à peine refroidie,
Bellini tombe et meurt!—Une lente agonie
Traîne Carrel sanglant à l'éternel repos.
Le seuil de notre siècle est pavé de tombeaux.

XVI

Que nous restera-t-il si l'ombre insatiable,
Dès que nous bâtissons, vient tout ensevelir?
Nous qui sentons déjà le sol si variable,
Et, sur tant de débris, marchons vers l'avenir,
Si le vent, sous nos pas, balaye ainsi le sable,
De quel deuil le Seigneur veut-il donc nous vêtir?

XVII

Hélas! Marietta, tu nous restais encore.
Lorsque, sur le sillon, l'oiseau chante à l'aurore,
Le laboureur s'arrête, et, le front en sueur,
Aspire dans l'air pur un souffle de bonheur.
Ainsi nous consolait ta voix fraîche et sonore,
Et tes chants dans les cieux emportaient la douleur.

1221

XVIII

Ce qu'il nous faut pleurer sur ta tombe hâtive,
Ce n'est pas l'art divin, ni ses savants secrets;
Quelque autre étudiera cet art que tu créais:
C'est ton âme, Ninette, et ta grandeur naïve,
C'est cette voix du cœur qui seule au cœur arrive,
Que nul autre, après toi, ne nous rendra jamais.

XIX

Ah! tu vivrais encor sans cette âme indomptable.
Ce fut là ton seul mal, et le secret fardeau
Sous lequel ton beau corps plia comme un roseau.
Il en soutint longtemps la lutte inexorable.
C'est le Dieu tout-puissant, c'est la Muse implacable
Qui dans ses bras en feu t'a portée au tombeau.

XX

Que ne l'étouffais-tu, cette flamme brûlante
Que ton sein palpitant ne pouvait contenir!
Tu vivrais, tu verrais te suivre et t'applaudir
De ce public blasé la foule indifférente,
Qui prodigue aujourd'hui sa faveur inconstante
A des gens dont pas un, certes, n'en doit mourir.

XXI

Connaissais-tu si peu l'ingratitude humaine?
Quel rêve as-tu donc fait de te tuer pour eux!
Quelques bouquets de fleurs te rendaient-ils si vaine,
Pour venir nous verser de vrais pleurs sur la scène,
Lorsque tant d'histrions et d'artistes fameux,
Couronnés mille fois, n'en ont pas dans les yeux?

XXII

Que ne détournais-tu la tête pour sourire,
Comme on en use ici quand on feint d'être ému?
Hélas! on t'aimait tant, qu'on n'en aurait rien vu.
Quand tu chantais *le Saule*, au lieu de ce délire,
Que ne t'occupais-tu de bien porter ta lyre?
La Pasta fait ainsi: que ne l'imitais-tu?

XXIII

Ne savais-tu donc pas, comédienne imprudente,
Que ces cris insensés qui te sortaient du cœur
De ta joue amaigrie augmentaient la pâleur?
Ne savais-tu donc pas que, sur ta tempe ardente,
Ta main de jour en jour se posait plus tremblante,
Et que c'est tenter Dieu que d'aimer la douleur?

XXIV

Ne sentais-tu donc pas que ta belle jeunesse
De tes yeux fatigués s'écoulait en ruisseaux,
Et de ton noble cœur s'exhalait en sanglots?
Quand de ceux qui t'aimaient tu voyais la tristesse,
Ne sentais-tu donc pas qu'une fatale ivresse
Berçait ta vie errante à ses derniers rameaux?

XXV

Oui, oui, tu le savais, qu'au sortir du théâtre,
Un soir dans ton linceul il faudrait te coucher.
Lorsqu'on te rapportait plus froide que l'albâtre,
Lorsque le médecin, de ta veine bleuâtre,
Regardait goutte à goutte un sang noir s'épancher,
Tu savais quelle main venait de te toucher.

XXVI

Oui, oui, tu le savais, et que, dans cette vie,
Rien n'est bon que d'aimer, n'est vrai que de souffrir.
Chaque soir dans tes chants tu te sentais pâlir.
Tu connaissais le monde, et la foule et l'envie,
Et, dans ce corps brisé concentrant ton génie,
Tu regardais aussi la Malibran mourir.

XXVII

Meurs donc! ta mort est douce et ta tâche est remplie.
Ce que l'homme ici-bas appelle le génie,
C'est le besoin d'aimer; hors de là tout est vain.
Et, puisque tôt ou tard l'amour humain s'oublie,
Il est d'une grande âme et d'un heureux destin
D'expirer comme toi pour un amour divin!

MALIBRAN

STANZAS

I

It is too late—of her has all been said;
She is no more, and fifteen days are fled;
And in our land a fortnight, I am told,
A recent death but makes an item old.
Whatever means, besides, regret translate,
It soon in every land us men doth sate.

II

O Maria! The painter and the poet high
Leave heirs immortal when at last they die;
Never does frightful night take them entire;
They can not act; but their great souls aspire
Of death, of time, the conquest seek to try,
And in the figh* both bard and painter die.

III

The one on **bronze** his thought to grave has sought,
To golden rhythm the other cadence brought;
At first we listen, then become his friend;
To canvas dying Raphael thought would lend;
And, too, that nothingness might come not near,
Enough the child asleep on mother dear.

IV

As in the lamp the faithful flame may shine,
The empty Parthenon, the marble shrine,
Phidias, eternal memory, guards and sees;
Young Venus, daughter of Praxiteles,
Still smiles in her divinity alone,
On feebler ages by her beauty won.

V

From age to age, receiving life anon,
So more toward God the glories all foregone;
So the wide echo of the genius' voice
Is voice of universal human choice.
Of thee, poor Marie, yesterday bereft,
To us a chapel and a cross is left!

VI

A cross, oblivion, silence in the night!
Oh, listen! 'Tis the wind—'tis ocean's night.
A fisher sings upon the grand highway,
Of all that beauty, glory, hope's bright day;
Of sweetest strains of instrument divine,
No feeble sighs, no far-off echoes pine.

VII

A cross! and thy name carved upon a stone,
A husband's name, not even name thy own.
And this is all on earth that thou may'st leave,
And they who go at thy last home to grieve,
Find not that name by all mankind caressed,
And, praying, see no place where knee may rest.

VIII

Ninette, where are they, beauteous muse above,
Those accents full of charm, of dread and love,
Which fluttered with the lip's inspiring power
Like light perfume from out the hawthorn flower?
Where vibrates now the voice's wailing sound,
That living harp to all thy heart-strings bound?

IX

Was it not yesterday, with maddening thrill
Thy mocking rapture quickened fair Corille,
And with Rosina flung at us again
The amorous roulade, sweet leer of Spain?
Those tears upon thy arm when Willow rang,
'Twas yesterday, and Desdemona sang.

X

But yesterday in life's bright flower and fire,
Thou went'st o'er Europe, in thy hand a lyre,
As thou didst swim in seas with laughing cry,
And sing the tarantella 'neath Naples' sky,
Thou angel lion-heart, bird without rest,
At eve a child, the morrow artist blest!

XI

But yesterday elate with happy joy,
Thy charm could the enraptured crowds decoy,
And London, Madrid, France, Italia old,
Brought to thy feet what we men covet—gold;
The gold twice-sacred, need of thy sweet song,
So often charity's, but thine not long.

XII

What hadst thou done to die, O noble heart,
Image of God, who didst while here impart
To rich men some delight, bread to the poor?
Ah, tell, who strikes so in mother nature,
And what blind reaper and his famished hand
Upon the best of us dare to lay their hand?

XIII

Is't not enough for that dark angel wan
To leave us in our day not one great man?
That Géricault, Cuvier, Goethe, Byron,
Sank yesterday beneath the funeral stone;
That we have seen so many dead, well known,
In the abyss succeed Napoleon?

XIV

Is it our fate our dearest ones to lose,
And weeping come, and eyelids for them close,
As soon as hope has sparkled in their eyes?
Of their elect, so jealous are the skies?
Or shall we say the word of ancient seer,
That he who dieth young to God is dear?

XV

How many full of life to death have sprung!
Beneath the ancient cypress, willows young,
The ashes of Robert are hardly cold,
Bellini falls and dies. Slow torture hold
And drag Carrel, bleeding, to his last rest;
The portal of our age with tombs is dressed.

XVI

What shall remain to us but funeral pall!
To-day we build, to-morrow bury all;
We, who can feel the soil already shake,
And o'er the dust onward our passage make;
And if beneath our feet winds sweep the sand,
What mourning wear we at the Lord's command?

XVII

Alas! Maria, thou wast with us still;
When birds on furrows sing Aurora's will,
The plowman stops and wipes his sweaty brow,
Breathes in the air a breath of pleasure now;
Thy voice consoled us; fresh, sonorous strain,
Thy songs to Heaven bore our heavy pain.

XVIII

What we must weep on thy untimely grave,
Is not the art divine the secret wisdom gave;
Some one may read the art thou couldst create;
It is thy soul, Ninette, so simply great;
Heart's voice alone can every heart obtain,
And none shall give it back to us again.

XIX

Thou mightest live without the undaunted soul;
This was thy only ill, the burden whole,
'Neath which thy frame was bending like a reed:
It bore the strife inexorable indeed.
The Muse implacable, all-powerful God,
With arms of fire laid thee beneath the sod.

XX

Thou couldst not stifle that enduring flame
Which throbbing breast of thine could never tame.
Thou might'st be living, hear the plaudits loud
Of hardened public, cool, indifferent crowd,
Which lavishes to-day a fickle boon
On folks of whom not one shall die so soon.

XXI

Knewest thou, so ill, human ingratitude?
What dream was thine to die for things so rude?
What clustering flowers could render thee so vain,
And make thee shed true tears upon our Seine,
When actors, artists of most famous guise,
Though crowned a thousand times, have yet dry eyes?

XXII

Why turned I not my head to smile again,
As we do here when we emotion feign?
Alas! such love as men had never seen.
When singing Willow in that wild, glad mien;
'Twere better hold the lyre in graceful state.
Pasta does so: couldst not her imitate?

XXIII

Didst thou not know, my sweet comedienne,
That all those cries that touched the hearts of men
Increased thy pallor and thy cheeks made thin?
And that upon thy temple's burning skin
From day to day thou laid'st a trembling hand,
That, choosing pain, can we our God withstand?

XXIV

And then didst thou not feel that thy fair youth
From thy tired eyes was flowing, tears of ruth,
And from thy noble heart exhaled in sobs?
And hearing thou thy loved ones' saddened throbs,
Didst thou not feel some fatal, frenzied strife,
Would wear thee out, and still thy wandering life?

XXV

Yes, yes, thou knowest, after triumph sweet,
Some night they'd lay thee in a winding sheet!
They brought thee, like to alabaster cold;
The surgeon would the bluish veinlet hold,
And watch the blood in drops so dark to see;
And well thou knewest what was touching thee.

XXVI

Thou knew'st that in this weary, transient hour,
Naught's good but love, naught true but suffering's power.
Each night amid thy songs thou feltest pale;
The world thou knewest, and foul envy's bale;
Gathering thy genius in a broken frame,
Thou sawest, Malibran, thy dying flame.

XXVII

Die, then! Thy death is sweet, thy task fulfil;
Now, what we men on earth call genius still,
Is need of loving—all beyond is vain,
Since human love is quickly lost again.
It is a great soul's happy destiny
For some high love divine like thee to die.

(1836)
Translated by Marie Agathe Clarke

Perfection.

HENRY JAMES
French Poets and Novelists (1878)

WILLIAM MAKEPEACE THACKERAY

1 8 1 1 — 1 8 6 3

TELMESSUS

There should have been a poet in our company to describe that charming little bay of Glaucus, into which we entered on the 26th of September, in the first steamboat that ever disturbed its beautiful waters. You can't put down in prose that delicious episode of natural poetry; it ought to be done in a symphony, full of sweet melodies and swelling harmonies; or sung in a strain of clear crystal iambics, such as Milnes knows how to write. A mere map, drawn in words, gives the mind no notion of that exquisite nature. What do mountains become in type, or rivers in Mr. Vizetelly's best brevier? Here lies the sweet bay, gleaming peaceful in the rosy sunshine; green islands dip here and there in its waters; purple mountains swell circling round it; and towards them, rising from the bay, stretches a rich green plain, fruitful with herbs and various foliage, in the midst of which the white houses twinkle. I can see a little minaret, and some spreading palm trees; but, beyond these, the description would answer as well for Bantry Bay as for Makri. You could write so far, nay, much more particularly and grandly, without seeing the place at all, and after reading Beaufort's *Caramania*, which gives you not the least notion of it.

Suppose the great hydrographer of the admiralty himself can't describe it, who surveyed the place; suppose Mr. Fellowes, who discovered it afterwards—suppose, I say, Sir John Fellowes, Knt., can't do it (and I defy any man of imagination to get an impression from his book)—can you, vain man, hope to try? The effect of the artist, as I take it, ought to be, to produce upon his hearer's mind, by his art, an effect something similar to that produced on his own by the sight of the natural object. Only music, or the best poetry, can do this. Keats's *Ode to the Grecian Urn* is the best description I know of that sweet, old, silent ruin of Telmessus. After you have once seen it, the remembrance remains with you, like a tune from Mozart, which he seems to have caught out of heaven, and which rings sweet harmony in your ears for ever after! It's a benefit for all after life! You have but to shut your eyes, and think, and recall it, and the delightful vision comes smiling back to your order! —the divine air—the delicious little pageant, which nature set before you on this lucky day.

Here is the entry made in the note-book on the eventful day;—"In the morning steamed into the bay of Glaucus—landed at Makri—cheerful old desolate village—theatre by the beautiful seashore—great fertility, oleanders—a palm-tree in the midst of the village, spreading out like a Sultan's aigrette—sculptured caverns, or tombs, up the mountain—camels over the bridge."

Perhaps it is best for a man of fancy to make his own landscape out of these materials: to group the couched camels under the plane-trees; the little crowd of wandering, ragged heathens come down to the calm water, to behold the nearing steamer; to fancy a mountain, in the sides of which some scores of tombs are rudely carved; pillars and porticoes, and Doric entablatures. But it is of the little theatre that he must make the most beautiful picture, a charming little place of festival, lying out on the shore, and looking over the sweet bay and the swelling purple islands. No theatre-goer ever looked out on a fairer scene. It encourages poetry, idleness, delicious sensual reverie. O Jones! friend of my heart! would you not like to be a white-robed Greek, lolling languidly on the cool benches here, and pouring compliments in the Ionic dialect into the rosy ears of Neæra? Instead of Jones your name should be Ionides; instead of a silk hat, you should wear a chaplet of roses in your hair: you would not listen to the choruses they were singing on the stage, for the voice of the fair one would be whispering a rendezvous for the *mesonuktiais horais,* and my Ionides would have no ear for aught beside.

Yonder, in the mountain, they would carve a Doric cave temple, to receive your urn when all was done; and you would be accompanied thither by a dirge of the surviving Ionidæ. The caves of the dead are empty now, however, and their place knows them not any more among the festal haunts of the living.

A Journey from Cornhill (1846)

THE ARCH OF DEATH

There came a day when the round of decorous pleasures and solemn gaieties in which Mr. Joseph Sedley's family indulged, was interrupted by an event which happens in most houses. As you ascend the staircase of your house from the drawing towards the bedroom floors, you may have remarked a little arch in the wall right before you which at once gives light to the stair which leads from the second story to the third, where the nursery and servants' chambers commonly are, and serves for another purpose of utility, of which the undertaker's men can give you a notion. They rest the coffins upon that arch, or pass them through it so as not to disturb in any unseemly manner the cold tenant slumbering within the black arch.

That second-floor arch in a London house, looking up and down the well of the staircase, and commanding the main thoroughfare by which the inhabitants are passing; by which the cook lurks down before daylight to scour her pots and pans in the kitchen; by which the young master stealthily ascends, having left his boots in the hall, and let himself in after dawn from a jolly night at the club; down which miss comes rustling in fresh ribbons and spreading muslins, brilliant and beautiful, and prepared for conquest and the ball; or master Tommy slides, preferring the bannisters for a mode of conveyance, and disdaining danger and the stair; down which the mother is fondly carried smiling in her strong husband's arms, as he steps steadily step by step, and followed by the monthly nurse, on the day when the medical man has pronounced that the charming patient may go down-stairs; up which John lurks to bed, yawning with a sputtering tallow candle, and to gather up before sunrise the boots which are awaiting him in the passages;—that stair, up or down which babies are carried, old people are helped, guests are marshalled to the ball, the parson walks to the christening, the doctor to the sickroom, and the undertaker's men to the upper floor; what a memento of life, death, and vanity it is—that arch and stair—if you choose to consider it, and sit on the landing, looking up and down the well! The doctor will come up to us for the last time there, my friend in motley. The nurse will look in at the curtains, and you take no notice; and then she will fling open the windows for a little, and let in the air. Then they will pull down all the front blinds of the house and live in the back

1231

rooms; then they will send for the lawyer and other men in black, etc. Your comedy and mine will have been played then, and we shall be removed, O how far, from the trumpets, and the shouting, and the posture-making. If we are gentlefolks they will put hatchments over our late domicile, with gilt cherubim, and mottoes stating that there is "Quiet in Heaven." Your son will new furnish the house, or perhaps let it, and go into a more modern quarter; your name will be among the "Members Deceased," in the lists of your clubs next year. However much you may be mourned, your widow will like to have her weeds neatly made; the cook will send or come up to ask about dinner; the survivors will soon bear to look at your picture over the mantelpiece, which will presently be deposed from the place of honour, to make way for the portrait of the son who reigns.

Vanity Fair (1847–48)

When I say that I hardly know any master of English prose-rhythm greater, in his way, than Thackeray, and that I certainly do not know any one with so various and pervasive a command, I may seem to provoke the answer, "Oh! you are, if not a maniac, at any rate a MANIAQUE. *The obsession of Titmarsh blinds and deafens you." Nevertheless, I say it; and will maintain it. That he seldom—perhaps never—tried diploma-pieces of the most elaborate kind may, of course, be admitted; the cap-and-bells, which he never wholly laid aside for more than a minute or two, forbade that. Yet the first of the two long passages which I have selected is not in this way far behind—some may think that it is at least on a level with—the most greatly-intending scenes of description that we have had or shall have; and the second, as a piece of reflection, will be hard to beat in sermon or essay, history or tractate, from Raleigh to Newman. But the most remarkable thing about Thackeray, in our connection—a thing impossible fully to illustrate here,—is his mastery of that mixed style "*SHOT *with rhythm" which has been noticed. Even in his earliest and most grotesque extravaganzas you will rarely find a discordant sentence—the very vulgarisms and mis-spellings come like solecisms from a pair of pretty lips and uttered in a musical voice. As there never was a much hastier writer, it is clear that the man thought in rhythm—that the words, as they flowed from his pen, brought the harmony with them.*

GEORGE SAINTSBURY
A History of English Prose Rhythm (1922)

THÉOPHILE GAUTIER

1 8 1 1 — 1 8 7 2

FROM *LE TRIOMPHE DE PÉTRARQUE*

Sur l'autel idéal entretenez la flamme,
Guidez le peuple au bien par le chemin du beau,
Par l'admiration et l'amour de la femme.

Comme un vase d'albâtre où l'on cache un flambeau,
Mettez l'idée au fond de la forme sculptée,
Et d'une lampe ardente éclairez le tombeau.

Que votre douce voix, de Dieu même écoutée,
Au milieu du combat jetant des mots de paix,
Fasse tomber les flots de la foule irritée.

Que votre poésie, aux vers calmes et frais,
Soit pour les cœurs souffrants comme ces cours d'eau vive
Où vont boire les cerfs dans l'ombre des forêts.

Faites de la musique avec la voix plaintive
De la création et de l'humanité,
De l'homme dans la ville et du flot sur la rive.

Puis, comme un beau symbole, un grand peintre vanté
Vous représentera dans une immense toile,
Sur un char triomphal par un peuple escorté:

Et vous aurez au front la couronne et l'étoile!

Let the flame be fed on the altar of the ideal, guide the people to virtue by the path of beauty, by admiration and the love of woman. Like an alabaster vase in which a torch is hidden, place the idea within the sculptured form, and with a burning lamp light up the grave. Let your soft voice, heard by God himself, uttering words of peace in the midst of strife, cause the surge of the angry crowd to subside. Let your poetry, with its calm, fresh lines, be for suffering hearts like running streams, where the deer go to drink in the forest shade. Make music with the plaintive voice of creation and humanity, of man in cities and waves on the shore. Then, like a beautiful symbol, some celebrated painter will depict you on an immense canvas, on a triumphal chariot, escorted by a whole people; and you will have on your forehead the crown and the star.

Poésies diverses (1836)

For the TERZA RIMA, *the poet to read and study always is Théophile Gautier, master and absolute lord of this rhythm, who has pushed it to the uttermost perfection.*

THÉODORE DE BANVILLE
Petit Traité de poésie française (1871)

THÉOPHILE GAUTIER

1 8 1 1 — 1 8 7 2

L'ART

Oui, l'œuvre sort plus belle
D'une forme au travail
    Rebelle,
Vers, marbre, onyx, émail.

Point de contraintes fausses!
Mais que pour marcher droit
    Tu chausses,
Muse, un cothurne étroit.

Fi du rhythme commode,
Comme un soulier trop grand,
    Du mode
Que tout pied quitte et prend!

Statuaire, repousse
L'argile que pétrit
    Le pouce
Quand flotte ailleurs l'esprit.

Lutte avec le carrare,
Avec le paros dur
    Et rare,
Gardiens du contour pur;

Emprunte à Syracuse
Son bronze où fermement
    S'accuse
Le trait fier et charmant;

D'une main délicate
Poursuis dans un filon
    D'agate
Le profil d'Apollon.

Peintre, fuis l'aquarelle,
Et fixe la couleur
    Trop frêle
Au four de l'émailleur.

Fais les sirènes bleues,
Tordant de cent façons
    Leurs queues,
Les monstres des blasons;

Dans son nimbe trilobe
La Vierge et son Jésus,
    Le globe
Avec la croix dessus.

Tout passe.—L'art robuste
Seul a l'éternité.
    Le buste
Survit à la cité,

Et la médaille austère
Que trouve un laboureur
    Sous terre
Révèle un empereur.

Les dieux eux-mêmes meurent,
Mais les vers souverains
    Demeurent
Plus forts que les airains.

Sculpte, lime, cisèle;
Que ton rêve flottant
    Se scelle
Dans le bloc résistant!

ART

All things are doubly fair
If patience fashion them
    And care—
Verse, enamel, marble, gem.

No idle chains endure:
Yet, Muse, to walk aright,
    Lace tight
Thy buskin proud and sure.

Fie on a facile measure,
A shoe where every lout
    At pleasure
Slips his foot in and out!

Sculptor, lay by the clay
On which thy nerveless finger
    May linger,
Thy thoughts flown far away.

Keep to Carrara rare,
Struggle with Paros cold,
    That hold
The subtle line and fair.

Lest haply nature lose
That proud, that perfect line,
    Make thine
The bronze of Syracuse.

And with a tender dread
Upon an agate's face
    Retrace
Apollo's golden head.

Despise a watery hue
And tints that soon expire.
    With fire
Burn thine enamel true.

Twine, twine in artful wise
The blue-green mermaid's arms,
    Mid charms
Of thousand heraldries.

Show in their triple lobe
Virgin and Child, that hold
    Their globe,
Cross-crowned and aureoled.

—All things return to dust
Save beauties fashioned well.
    The bust
Outlasts the citadel.

Oft doth the plowman's heel,
Breaking an ancient clod,
    Reveal
A Cæsar or a god.

The gods, too, die, alas!
But deathless and more strong
Than brass
Remains the sovereign song.

Chisel and carve and file,
Till thy vague dream imprint
Its smile
On the unyielding flint.

Translated by George Santayana

Singularly perfect.

HENRY JAMES
French Poets and Novelists (1878)

JOHN BRIGHT

1 8 1 1 — 1 8 8 9

THE ANGEL OF DEATH

I cannot, I say, but notice that an uneasy feeling exists as to the news which may arrive by the very next mail from the East. I do not suppose that your troops are to be beaten in actual conflict with the foe, or that they will be driven into the sea; but I am certain that many homes in England in which there now exists a fond hope that the distant one may return—many such homes may be rendered desolate when the next mail shall arrive. The angel of death has been abroad throughout the land; you may almost hear the beating of his wings. There is no one, as when the first-born were slain of old, to sprinkle with blood the lintel and the two sideposts of our doors, that he may spare and pass on; he takes his victims from the castle of the noble, the mansion of the wealthy, and the cottage of the poor and the lowly, and it is on behalf of all these classes that I make this solemn appeal.

Speech in The House of Commons (February 23, 1855)

Impassioned writing of the highest quality.

HERBERT J. C. GRIERSON
Rhetoric and English Composition (1945)

CHARLES DICKENS

1812 — 1870

THE MANOR-FARM KITCHEN
ON CHRISTMAS EVE

"How it snows!" said one of the men, in a low tone.

"Snows, does it?" said Wardle.

"Rough, cold night, Sir," replied the man; "and there's a wind got up, that drifts it across the fields, in a thick white cloud."

"What does Jem say?" inquired the old lady. "There a'n't anything the matter, is there?"

"No, no, mother," replied Wardle; "he says there's a snow-drift, and a wind that's piercing cold."

Pickwick Papers (1836–37)

You know this is the introduction to the Tale of Gabriel Grub, an admirable legend which Dickens "farsed" with an obtrusive moral. But I confess that the atmosphere (which to me seems all the wild weather and the wild legend of the north) suggested by those phrases "a thick white cloud," and "a wind that's piercing cold," is in my judgment wholly marvellous.

ARTHUR MACHEN
Hieroglyphics (1923)

CHARLES DICKENS

1812 — 1870

THE DOVER ROAD

For anything I know, I may have had some wild idea of running all the way to Dover, when I gave up the pursuit of the young man with the donkey-cart, and started for Greenwich. My scattered senses were soon collected as to that point, if I had; for I came to a stop in the Kent Road, at a terrace with a piece of water before it, and a great foolish image in the middle, blowing a dry shell. Here I sat down on a doorstep, quite spent and exhausted with the efforts I had already made, and with hardly breath enough to cry for the loss of my box and half-guinea.

It was by this time dark; I heard the clocks strike ten, as I sat resting. But it was a summer night, fortunately, and fine weather. When I had recovered my breath, and had got rid of a stifling sensation in my throat, I rose up and went on. In the midst of my distress, I had no notion of going back. I doubt if I should have had any, though there had been a Swiss snow-drift in the Kent Road.

But my standing possessed of only three-halfpence in the world (and I am sure I wonder how *they* came to be left in my pocket on a Saturday night!) troubled me none the less because I went on. I began to picture to myself, as a scrap of newspaper intelligence, my being found dead in a day or two, under some hedge; and I trudged on miserably, though as fast as I could, until I happened to pass a little shop, where it was written up that ladies' and gentlemen's wardrobes were bought, and that the best price was given for rags, bones, and kitchen-stuff. The master of this shop was sitting at the door in his shirt-sleeves, smoking; and as there were a great many coats and pairs of trousers dangling from the low ceiling, and only two feeble candles burning inside to show what they were, I fancied that he looked like a man of a revengeful disposition, who had hung all his enemies, and was enjoying himself.

My late experiences with Mr. and Mrs. Micawber suggested to me that here might be a means of keeping off the wolf for a little while. I went up the next bye-street, took off my waistcoat, rolled it neatly under my arm, and came back to the shop-door. "If you please, sir," I said, "I am to sell this for a fair price."

Mr. Dolloby—Dolloby was the name over the shop-door, at least—took the waistcoat, stood his pipe on its head against the door-post, went into the shop, followed by me, snuffed the two candles with his fingers, spread the waistcoat on the counter, and looked at it there, held it up against the light, and looked at it there, and ultimately said:

"What do you call a price, now, for this here little weskit?"

"Oh! you know best, sir," I returned modestly.

"I can't be buyer and seller too," said Mr. Dolloby. "Put a price on this here little weskit."

"Would eighteenpence be?"—I hinted, after some hesitation.

Mr. Dolloby rolled it up again, and gave it me back. "I should rob my family," he said, "if I was to offer ninepence for it."

This was a disagreeable way of putting the business; because it imposed upon me, a perfect stranger, the unpleasantness of asking Mr. Dolloby to rob his family on my account. My circumstances being so very pressing, however, I said I would take ninepence for it, if he pleased. Mr. Dolloby, not without some grumbling, gave ninepence. I wished him goodnight, and walked out of the shop, the richer by that sum, and the poorer by a waistcoat. But when I buttoned my jacket, that was not much.

Indeed, I foresaw pretty clearly that my jacket would go next, and that I should have to make the best of my way to Dover in a shirt and a pair of trousers, and might deem myself lucky if I got there even in

that trim. But my mind did not run so much on this as might be supposed. Beyond a general impression of the distance before me, and of
the young man with the donkey-cart having used me cruelly, I think I
had no very urgent sense of my difficulties when I once again set off
with my ninepence in my pocket.

A plan had occurred to me for passing the night, which I was going
to carry into execution. This was, to lie behind the wall at the back of
my old school, in a corner where there used to be a haystack. I imagined
it would be a kind of company to have the boys, and the bedroom where
I used to tell the stories, so near me: although the boys would know
nothing of my being there, and the bedroom would yield me no shelter.

I had had a hard day's work, and was pretty well jaded when I came
climbing out, at last, upon the level of Blackheath. It cost me some
trouble to find out Salem House; but I found it, and I found a haystack
in the corner, and I lay down by it; having first walked round the wall,
and looked up at the windows, and seen that all was dark and silent
within. Never shall I forget the lonely sensation of first lying down,
without a roof above my head!

Sleep came upon me as it came on many other outcasts, against whom
house-doors were locked, and house-dogs barked, that night—and I
dreamed of lying on my old school-bed, talking to the boys in my room;
and found myself sitting upright, with Steerforth's name upon my lips,
looking wildly at the stars that were glistening and glimmering above me.
When I remembered where I was at that untimely hour, a feeling stole
upon me that made me get up, afraid of I don't know what, and walk
about. But the fainter glimmering of the stars, and the pale light in the
sky where the day was coming, reassured me: and my eyes being very
heavy, I lay down again, and slept—though with a knowledge in my
sleep that it was cold—until the warm beams of the sun, and the ringing
of the getting-up bell at Salem House, awoke me. If I could have hoped
that Steerforth was there, I would have lurked about until he came out
alone; but I knew he must have left long since. Traddles still remained,
perhaps, but it was very doubtful; and I had not sufficient confidence
in his discretion or good luck, however strong my reliance was on his
good-nature, to wish to trust him with my situation. So I crept away
from the wall as Mr. Creakle's boys were getting up, and struck into
the long dusty track which I had first known to be the Dover Road when
I was one of them, and when I little expected that any eyes would ever
see me the wayfarer I was now, upon it.

What a different Sunday morning from the old Sunday morning at
Yarmouth! In due time I heard the church-bells ringing, as I plodded
on; and I met people who were going to church; and I passed a church
or two where the congregation were inside, and the sound of singing
came out into the sunshine, while the beadle sat and cooled himself in
the shade of the porch, or stood beneath the yew-tree, with his hand

1240

to his forehead, glowering at me going by. But the peace and rest of the old Sunday morning were on everything, except me. That was the difference. I felt quite wicked in my dirt and dust, with my tangled hair. But for the quiet picture I had conjured up, of my mother in her youth and beauty, weeping by the fire, and my aunt relenting to her, I hardly think I should have had the courage to go on until next day. But it always went before me, and I followed.

I got, that Sunday, through three-and-twenty miles on the straight road, though not very easily, for I was new to that kind of toil. I see myself, as evening closes in, coming over the bridge at Rochester, foot-sore and tired, and eating bread that I had bought for supper. One or two little houses, with the notice, "Lodgings for Travellers," hanging out, had tempted me; but I was afraid of spending the few pence I had, and was even more afraid of the vicious looks of the trampers I had met or overtaken. I sought no shelter, therefore, but the sky; and toiling into Chatham,—which, in the night's aspect, is a mere dream of chalk, and drawbridges, and mastless ships in a muddy river, roofed like Noah's arks,—crept, at last, upon a sort of grass-grown battery overhanging a lane, where a sentry was walking to and fro. Here I lay down, near a cannon; and, happy in the society of the sentry's footsteps, though he knew no more of my being above him than the boys of Salem House had known of my lying by the wall, slept soundly until morning.

Very stiff and sore of foot I was in the morning, and quite dazed by the beating of drums and marching of troops, which seemed to hem me in on every side when I went down towards the long narrow street. Feeling that I could go but a very little way that day, if I were to re-serve any strength for getting to my journey's end, I resolved to make the sale of my jacket its principal business. Accordingly, I took the jacket off, that I might learn to do without it; and carrying it under my arm, began a tour of inspection of the various slop-shops.

It was a likely place to sell a jacket in; for the dealers in second-hand clothes were numerous, and were, generally speaking, on the look-out for customers at their shop-doors. But, as most of them had, hanging up among their stock, an officer's coat or two, epaulettes and all, I was rendered timid by the costly nature of their dealings, and walked about for a long time without offering my merchandise to any one.

This modesty of mine directed my attention to the marine-store shops, and such shops as Mr. Dolloby's, in preference to the regular dealers. At last I found one that I thought looked promising, at the corner of a dirty lane, ending in an inclosure full of stinging-nettles, against the palings of which some second-hand sailors' clothes, that seemed to have overflowed the shop, were fluttering among some cots, and rusty guns, and oilskin hats, and certain trays full of so many old rusty keys of so many sizes that they seemed various enough to open all the doors in the world.

Into this shop, which was low and small, and which was darkened rather than lighted by a little window, overhung with clothes, and was descended into by some steps, I went with a palpitating heart; which was not relieved when an ugly old man, with the lower part of his face all covered with a stubbly grey beard, rushed out of a dirty den behind it, and seized me by the hair of my head. He was a dreadful old man to look at, in a filthy flannel waistcoat, and smelling terribly of rum. His bedstead, covered with a tumbled and ragged piece of patchwork, was in the den he had come from, where another little window showed a prospect of more stinging-nettles, and a lame donkey.

"Oh, what do you want?" grinned this old man, in a fierce, monotonous whine. "Oh, my eyes and limbs, what do you want? Oh, my lungs and liver, what do you want? Oh, goroo, goroo!"

I was so much dismayed by these words, and particularly by the repetition of the last unknown one, which was a kind of rattle in his throat, that I could make no answer; hereupon the old man, still holding me by the hair, repeated:

"Oh, what do you want? Oh, my eyes and limbs, what do you want? Oh, my lungs and liver, what do you want? Oh, goroo!"—which he screwed out of himself, with an energy that made his eyes start in his head.

"I wanted to know," I said, trembling, "if you would buy a jacket?"

"Oh, let's see the jacket!" cried the old man. "Oh, my heart on fire, show the jacket to us! Oh, my eyes and limbs, bring the jacket out!"

With that he took his trembling hands, which were like the claws of a great bird, out of my hair; and put on a pair of spectacles, not at all ornamental to his inflamed eyes.

"Oh, how much for the jacket?" cried the old man, after examining it. "Oh—goroo!—how much for the jacket?"

"Half-a-crown," I answered, recovering myself.

"Oh, my lungs and liver," cried the old man, "no! Oh, my eyes, no! Oh, my limbs, no! Eighteenpence. Goroo!"

Every time he uttered this ejaculation, his eyes seemed to be in danger of starting out; and every sentence he spoke, he delivered in a sort of tune, always exactly the same, and more like a gust of wind, which begins low, mounts up high, and falls again, than any other comparison I can find for it.

"Well," said I, glad to have closed the bargain, "I'll take eighteenpence."

"Oh, my liver!" cried the old man, throwing the jacket on a shelf. "Get out of the shop! Oh, my lungs, get out of the shop! Oh, my eyes and limbs—goroo!—don't ask for money; make it an exchange."

I never was so frightened in my life, before or since; but I told him humbly that I wanted money, and that nothing else was of any use to me, but that I would wait for it, as he desired, outside, and had no wish to hurry him. So I went outside, and sat down in the shade in a corner. And I sat there so many hours, that the shade became sunlight, and the sunlight shade again, and still I sat there waiting for the money.

There never was such another drunken madman in that line of business, I hope. That he was well known in the neighbourhood, and enjoyed the reputation of having sold himself to the devil, I soon understood from the visits he received from the boys, who continually came skirmishing about the shop, shouting that legend, and calling to him to bring out his gold. "You ain't poor, you know, Charley, as you pretend. Bring out your gold. Bring out some of the gold you sold yourself to the devil for. Come! It's in the lining of the mattress, Charley. Rip it open and let's have some!" This, and many offers to lend his a knife for the purpose, exasperated him to such a degree, that the whole day was a succession of rushes on his part, and flights on the part of the boys. Sometimes in his rage he would take me for one of them, and come at me, mouthing as if he were going to tear me in pieces; then, remembering me just in time, would dive into the shop, and lie upon his bed, as I thought from the sound of his voice, yelling in a frantic way, to his own windy tune, the Death of Nelson; with an Oh! before every line, and innumerable Goroos interspersed. As if this were not bad enough for me, the boys, connecting me with the establishment, on account of the patience and perserverance with which I sat outside, half-dressed, pelted me, and used me very ill all day.

He made many attempts to induce me to consent to an exchange; at one time coming out with a fishing-rod, at another with a fiddle, at another with a cocked hat, at another with a flute. But I resisted all these overtures, and sat there in desperation; each time asking him, with tears in my eyes, for my money or my jacket. At last he began to pay me in half-pence at a time; and was full two hours at getting by easy stages to a shilling.

"Oh, my eyes and limbs!" he then cried, peeping hideously out of the shop, after a long pause, "will you go for twopence more?"

"I can't," I said, "I shall be starved."

"Oh, my lungs and liver, will you go for threepence?"

"I would go for nothing, if I could," I said, "but I want the money badly."

"Oh, go—roo!" (it is really impossible to express how he twisted this ejaculation out of himself, as he peeped round the doorpost at me, showing nothing but his crafty old head); "will you go for fourpence?"

I was so faint and weary that I closed with this offer; and taking the money out of his claw, not without trembling, went away more hungry and thirsty than I had ever been, a little before sunset. But at an expense of threepence I soon refreshed myself completely; and, being in better spirits then, limped seven miles upon my road.

My bed at night was under another haystack where I rested comfortably, after having washed my blistered feet in a stream, and dressed them as well as I was able, with some cool leaves. When I took the road again next morning, I found that it lay through a succession of hop-grounds and orchards. It was sufficiently late in the year for the orchards to be ruddy with ripe apples; and in a few places the hop-pickers were already at work. I thought it all extremely beautiful, and made up my mind to sleep among the hops that night; imagining some cheerful companionship in the long perspectives of poles, with the graceful leaves twining round them.

The trampers were worse than ever that day, and inspired me with a dread that is yet quite fresh in my mind. Some of them were most ferocious-looking ruffians, who stared at me as I went by; and stopped, perhaps, and called after me to come back and speak to them, and when I took to my heels, stoned me. I recollect one young fellow—a tinker, I suppose, from his wallet and brazier—who had a woman with him, and who faced about and stared at me thus; and then roared at me in such a tremendous voice to come back, that I halted and looked round.

"Come here, when you're called," said the tinker, "or I'll rip your young body open."

I thought it best to go back. As I drew nearer to them, trying to propitiate the tinker by my looks, I observed that the woman had a black eye.

"Where are you going?" said the tinker, gripping the bosom of my shirt with his blackened hand.

"I am going to Dover," I said.

"Where do you come from?" asked the tinker, giving his hand another turn in my shirt, to hold me more securely.

"I come from London," I said.

"What lay are you upon?" asked the tinker. "Are you a prig?"

"N—— no," I said.

"Ain't you, by G——? If you make a brag of your honesty to me," said the tinker, "I'll knock your brains out."

With his disengaged hand he made a menace of striking me, and then looked at me from head to foot.

"Have you got the price of a pint of beer about you?" said the tinker. "If you have, out with it, afore I take it away!"

I should certainly have produced it, but that I met the woman's look, and saw her very slightly shake her head, and form "No!" with her lips.

"I am very poor," I said, attempting to smile, "and have got no money."

"Why, what do you mean?" said the tinker, looking so sternly at me, that I almost feared he saw the money in my pocket.

"Sir!" I stammered.

"What do you mean," said the tinker, "by wearing my brother's silk

1244

handkerchief! Give it over here!" And he had mine off my neck in a moment, and tossed it to the woman.

The woman burst into a fit of laughter, as if she thought this a joke, and tossed it back to me, nodded once, as slightly as before, and made the word "Go!" with her lips. Before I could obey, however, the tinker seized the handkerchief out of my hand with a roughness that threw me away like a feather, and putting it loosely round his own neck, turned upon the woman with an oath, and knocked her down. I never shall forget seeing her fall backward on the hard road, and lie there with her bonnet tumbled off, and her hair all whitened in the dust; nor, when I looked back from a distance, seeing her sitting on the pathway, which was a bank by the roadside, wiping the blood from her face with a corner of her shawl, while he went on ahead.

This adventure frightened me so, that, afterwards, when I saw any of these people coming, I turned back until I could find a hiding-place, where I remained until they had gone out of sight; which happened so often, that I was very seriously delayed. But under this difficulty, as under all the other difficulties of my journey, I seemed to be sustained and led on by my fanciful picture of my mother in her youth, before I came into the world. It always kept me company. It was there, among the hops, when I lay down to sleep: it was with me on my waking in the morning; it went before me all day. I have associated it, ever since, with the sunny street of Canterbury, dozing as it were in the hot light; and with the sight of its old houses and gateways, and the stately, grey Cathedral, with the rooks sailing round the towers. When I came, at last, upon the bare wide downs near Dover, it relieved the solitary aspect of the scene with hope; and not until I reached that first great aim of my journey, and actually set foot in the town itself, on the sixth day of my flight, did it desert me. But then, strange to say, when I stood with my ragged shoes, and my dusty, sunburnt, half-clothed figure, in the place so long desired, it seemed to vanish like a dream, and to leave me helpless and dispirited.

David Copperfield (1849–50)

As good a piece of narrative prose as can be found in English.

GEORGE GISSING
Charles Dickens (1898)

THE LOST MISTRESS

I

All's over, then: does truth sound bitter
　　As one at first believes?
Hark, 'tis the sparrows' good-night twitter
　　About your cottage eaves!

II

And the leaf-buds on the vine are woolly,
　　I noticed that, to-day;
One day more bursts them open fully
　　—You know the red turns grey.

III

To-morrow we meet the same then, dearest?
　　May I take your hand in mine?
Mere friends are we,—well, friends the merest
　　Keep much that I resign:

IV

For each glance of the eye so bright and black,
　　Though I keep with heart's endeavour,—
Your voice, when you wish the snowdrops back,
　　Though it stay in my soul forever!—

V

Yet I will but say what mere friends say,
　　Or only a thought stronger;
I will hold your hand but as long as all may,
　　Or so very little longer!

　　　　　　　　　　　　　　　　(1845)

*This is one of those love-songs which we cannot but consider among the
noblest of such songs in all Love's language.*

ARTHUR SYMONS
An Introduction to the Study of Browning (1906)

TO DRIVE LIFE INTO A CORNER

I went to the woods because I wished to live deliberately, to front only the essential facts of life, and see if I could not learn what it had to teach, and not, when I came to die, discover that I had not lived. I did not wish to live what was not life, living is so dear; nor did I wish to practise resignation, unless it was quite necessary. I wanted to live deep and suck out all the marrow of life, to live so sturdily and Spartan-like as to put to rout all that was not life, to cut a broad swath and shave close, to drive life into a corner, and reduce it to its lowest terms, and, if it proved to be mean, why then to get the whole and genuine mean-ness of it, and publish its meanness to the world; or if it were sublime, to know it by experience, and be able to give a true account of it in my next excursion. For most men, it appears to me, are in a strange uncer-tainty about it, whether it is of the devil or of God, and have *somewhat hastily* concluded that it is the chief end of man here to "glorify God and enjoy him forever."

Walden, or Life in the Woods (1854)

What had proved so heartening to Emerson's contemporaries was his insistence that life for Americans no longer needed to be starved. The most intense expression of that conviction, perhaps the most intense single passage in American writing, is Thoreau's.

F. O. MATTHIESSEN
Henry James: The Major Phase (1944)

TR-R-R-R-OONK

And then the frogs, bullfrogs; they are the more sturdy spirits of an-cient wine-bibbers and wassailers, still unrepentant, trying to sing a catch in their Stygian lakes. They would fain keep up the hilarious good fellowship and all the rules of their old round tables, but they have waxed hoarse and solemnly grave and serious their voices, mocking at mirth, and their wine has lost its flavor and is only liquor to distend

their paunches, and never comes sweet intoxication to drown the memory
of the past, but mere saturation and water-logged dullness and disten-
sion. Still the most aldermanic, and with his chin upon a pad, which
answers for a napkin to his drooling chaps, under the eastern shore quaffs
a deep draught of the once scorned water, and passes round the cup with
the ejaculation *tr-r-r-r-r-oonk, tr-r-r-r-r-oonk, tr-r-r-r-r-oonk!* and straightway comes over the water from some distant cove the selfsame password,
where the next in seniority and girth has gulped down to his mark; and
when the strain has made the circuit of the shores, then ejaculates the
master of ceremonies with satisfaction *tr-r-r-r-oonk!* and each in turn repeats the sound, down to the least distended, leakiest, flabbiest
paunched, that there be no mistake; and the bowl goes round again,
until the sun dispels the morning mist, and only the patriarch is not
under the pond, but vainly bellowing *troonk* from time to time, pausing
for a reply.

The Journal (August, 1845)

*Where will one turn for a more superbly Rabelaisian picture than this
wassail scene of the woods.*

PAUL ELMER MORE
Selected Shelburne Essays (1935)

EMILY BRONTË

1 8 1 8 — 1 8 4 8

THE THREE HEADSTONES
BY THE MOOR

I lingered round them, under that benign sky: watched the moths
fluttering among the heath and hare-bells; listened to the soft wind
breathing through the grass; and wondered how any one could ever
imagine unquiet slumbers for the sleepers in that quiet earth.

Wuthering Heights (1847)

Among the greatest masters of our prose.

HERBERT READ
A Coat of Many Colours (1945)

FROM *QAÏN*

Thogorma dans ses yeux vit monter des murailles
De fer d'où s'enroulaient des spirales de tours
Et de palais cerclés d'airain sur des blocs lourds;
Ruche énorme, géhenne aux lugubres entrailles
Où s'engouffraient les Forts, princes des anciens jours.

Ils s'en venaient de la montagne et de la plaine,
Du fond des sombres bois et du désert sans fin,
Plus massifs que le cèdre et plus hauts que le pin,
Suants, échevelés, soufflant leur rude haleine
Avec leur bouche épaisse et rouge, et pleins de faim.

C'est ainsi qu'ils rentraient, l'ours velu des cavernes
A l'épaule, ou le cerf, ou le lion sanglant.
Et les femmes marchaient, géantes, d'un pas lent,
Sous les vases d'airain qu'emplit l'eau des citernes,
Graves, et les bras nus, et les mains sur le flanc.

Elles allaient, dardant leurs prunelles superbes,
Les seins droits, le col haut, dans la sérénité
Terrible de la force et de la liberté,
Et posant tour à tour dans la ronce et les herbes
Leurs pieds fermes et blancs avec tranquillité.

Le vent respectueux, parmi leurs tresses sombres,
Sur leur nuque de marbre errait en frémissant,
Tandis que les parois des rocs couleur de sang,
Comme de grands miroirs suspendus dans les ombres,
De la pourpre du soir baignaient leur dos puissant.

Les ânes de Khamos, les vaches aux mamelles
Pesantes, les boucs noirs, les taureaux vagabonds
Se hâtaient, sous l'épieu, par files et par bonds;
Et de grands chiens mordaient le jarret des chamelles;
Et les portes criaient en tournant sur leurs gonds.

Et les éclats de rire et les chansons féroces
Mêlés aux beuglements lugubres des troupeaux,
Tels que le bruit des rocs secoués par les eaux,
Montaient jusques aux tours où, le poing sur leurs crosses,
Des vieillards regardaient, dans leurs robes de peaux;

Spectres de qui la barbe, inondant leurs poitrines,
De son écume errante argentait leurs bras roux,
Immobiles, de lourds colliers de cuivre aux cous,
Et qui, d'en haut, dardaient, l'orgueil plein les narines,
Sur leur race des yeux profonds comme des trous.

Thogorma in his imagination saw walls of iron arise, from which spiral towers wound upwards, and palaces belted with bronze and resting on heavy blocks; an enormous hive, a gehenna with dismal entrails, where the strong ones, princes of ancient times, were swallowed up as by a chasm. They came from the mountain and from the plain, from the depths of somber forests and from the boundless desert, more massive than the cedar, and taller than pines, sweating, disheveled, blowing their rough breath, with their thick, red mouths, full of hunger. Thus they came home, the shaggy cave-bear on their shoulders, or a deer or a blood-dripping lion. And the gigantic women walked with slow step, under bronze vases filled with cistern water, solemn, with bare arms, and hands on hips. Darting glances from their superb eyes as they walked, firm-breasted, high-necked, with the terrible serenity of strength and freedom, and tranquilly putting down their firm, white feet on briars and grass in turn. The considerate wind, in their somber tresses, wandered tremblingly over their marmoreal napes, while the walls of blood-colored rock, like large mirrors suspended in the shadows, bathed their powerful backs with the purple light of sunset. The asses of Khamos, the cows with heavy udders, the black goats, the wandering bulls hasten, under the goad, single file and leaping, and great dogs bit the she-camel's hocks; and the doors shrieked turning on their hinges. And shouts of laughter and fierce songs mixed with the dismal bellowing of the herds, like the noise of rocks shaken by waters, rose to the towers where, hands on their crooks, old men looked on, in their skin garments. Specters whose beards, flooding over their chests, shed the silver of its wandering foam over their red arms, motionless, with heavy copper necklaces on their necks, and who from on high, with nostrils full of pride, darted over their race glances from eyes deep as holes.

Poèmes barbares (1862)

The most perfect model of what may be conceded to be today the epic style.

THÉODORE DE BANVILLE
Petit Traité de poésie française (1871)

LE MANCHY

Sous un nuage frais de claire mousseline,
    Tous les dimanches, au matin,
Tu venais à la ville en manchy de rotin,
    Par les rampes de la colline.

La cloche de l'église alertement tintait;
    Le vent de mer berçait les cannes:
Comme une grêle d'or, aux pointes des savanes,
    Le feu du soleil crépitait.

Le bracelet aux poings, l'anneau sur la cheville,
    Et le mouchoir jaune aux chignons,
Deux Telingas portaient, assidus compagnons,
    Ton lit aux nattes de Manille.

Ployant leur jarret maigre et nerveux, et chantant,
    Souples dans leurs tuniques blanches,
Le bambou sur l'épaule et les mains sur les hanches,
    Ils allaient le long de l'Étang.

Le long de la chaussée et des varangues basses
    Où les vieux créoles fumaient,
Par les groupes joyeux des Noirs, ils s'animaient
    Au bruit des bobres Madécasses.

Dans l'air léger flottait l'odeur des tamarins;
    Sur les houles illuminées
Au large, les oiseaux, en d'immenses traînées,
    Plongeaient dans les brouillards marins.

Et, tandis que ton pied, sorti de la babouche,
    Pendait, rose, au bord du manchy,
A l'ombre des Bois-noirs touffus, et du Letchi
    Aux fruits moins pourprés que ta bouche;

Tandis qu'un papillon, les deux ailes en fleur,
    Teinté d'azur et d'écarlate,
Se posait par instants sur ta peau délicate
    En y laissant de sa couleur;

On voyait, au travers du rideau de batiste,
  Tes boucles dorer l'oreiller;
Et, sous leurs cils mi-clos, feignant de sommeiller,
  Tes beaux yeux de sombre améthyste.

Tu t'en venais ainsi, par ces matins si doux,
  De la montagne à la grand'messe,
Dans ta grâce naïve et ta rose jeunesse,
  Au pas rythmé de tes Hindous.

Maintenant, dans le sable aride de nos grèves,
  Sous les chiendents, au bruit des mers,
Tu reposes parmi les morts qui me sont chers,
  O charme de mes premiers rêves!

THE MANCHY

Clothed in your filmy muslin gown,
  Every Sunday morning, you
  Would come in your manchy of bamboo
Down the footpaths to the town.

The church-bell rang out noisily;
  The salt breeze waved the lofty cane;
  The sun shook out a golden rain
On the savannah's grassy sea.

With rings on wrist and ankle flat,
  And yellow kerchief on the crown,
  Your two telingas carried down
Your litter of Manila mat.

Slim, in tunics white, they sang
  As 'neath the pole of bamboo bent,
  With hands upon their hips, they went
Steadily by the long Etang.

Past banks where Creoles used to come
  To smoke their ancient pipes; past bands
  Of blacks disporting on the sands
To the sound of the Madagascar drum.

The tamarind's breath was on the air;
  Out in the glittering surf the flocks
  Of birds swung through the billow's shocks
And plunged beneath the foaming blare.

While hung—your sandal loosed—the tips
    Of one pink foot at the manchy's side,
    In the shade of the letchi branching wide
With fruit less purple than your lips;

While like a flower, a butterfly
    Of blue and scarlet fluttered on
    Your skin an instant, and was gone,
Leaving his colors in good-by.

We saw between the cambric's mist
    Your earrings on the pillows lain;
    While your long lashes veiled in vain
Your eyes of sombre amethyst.

'Twas thus you came, those mornings sweet,
    With grace so gentle, to High Mass,
    Borne slowly down the mountain pass
By your faithful Hindoos' steady feet.

But now where our dry sand-bar gleams
    Beneath the dog-grass near the sea,
    You rest with dead ones dear to me,
O charm of my first tender dreams!

                    Translated by Thomas Walsh

A masterpiece without an equal.

                    CHARLES BAUDELAIRE
                    Les Poëtes français (1863)

JOHN RUSKIN

1 8 1 9 — 1 9 0 0

MORNING AT VENICE

Between the shafts of the pillars, the morning sky is seen pure and
pale, relieving the grey dome of the church of the Salute; but beside
that vault, and like it, vast thunderclouds heap themselves above the
horizon, catching the light of dawn upon them where they rise, far west-
ward, over the dark roof of the ruined Badia;—but all so massive, that
half-an-hour ago, in the dawn, I scarcely knew the Salute dome and
towers from theirs; while the sea-gulls, rising and falling hither and

thither in clusters above the green water beyond my balcony, tell me
that the south wind is wild on Adria.

Fors Clavigera (November 9, 1876)

*He could not only recover but even better his earlier music; and the
fall of the last ten words is incomparable, quite effacing the faint impression of metre which is twice left by the preceding clauses—I will leave
the reader to discover where.*

OLIVER ELTON
A Survey of English Literature 1780–1880 (1920)

WALT WHITMAN

1819 — 1892

COME SAID THE MUSE

I am the man, I suffer'd, I was there.

Agonies are one of my changes of garments.

Song of Myself (1881)

Now we have met, we have look'd, we are safe.

Out of the Rolling Ocean the Crowd (1867)

Whoever you are, I fear you are walking the walks of dreams.

To You (1881)

For my enemy is dead, a man divine as myself is dead,
I look where he lies white-faced and still in the coffin—I draw near,
Bend down and touch lightly with my lips the white face in the coffin.

Reconciliation (1881)

Come, I will make the continent indissoluble,
I will make the most splendid race the sun ever shone upon,
I will make divine magnetic lands,
   With the love of comrades,
     With the life-long love of comrades.

For You O Democracy (1881)

When lilacs last in the dooryard bloom'd,
And the great star early dropp'd in the western sky in the night,
I mourn'd, and yet shall mourn with ever-returning spring.

Ever-returning spring, trinity sure to me you bring,
Lilac blooming perennial and drooping star in the west,
And thought of him I love.

When Lilacs Last in the Dooryard Bloom'd (1881)

Come said the Muse,
Sing me a song no poet yet has chanted,
Sing me the universal.

Song of the Universal (1881)

One must admit, too, that only once or twice in the course of a fairly long poem would he reach the high plane of memorable expression, but when he reached it, it was as memorable as that of any poet who ever lived, and in a different way. Sometimes all that was memorable was a line, but the line was pregnant as few single lines ever were. . . . On his highest level, his pregnancy and his lyric potency were both unsurpassable and unique.

MARY M. COLUM
From These Roots (1937)

HERMAN MELVILLE

1819 — 1891

THE GREAT SHROUD OF THE SEA

The harpoon was darted; the stricken whale flew forward; with igniting velocity the line ran through the groove;—ran foul. Ahab stooped to clear it; he did clear it; but the flying turn caught him round the neck, and voicelessly as Turkish mutes bowstring their victim, he was shot out of the boat, ere the crew knew he was gone. Next instant, the heavy eye-splice in the rope's final end flew out of the stark-empty tub, knocked down an oarsman, and smiting the sea, disappeared in its depths.

For an instant, the tranced boat's crew stood still; then turned. 'The ship? Great God, where is the ship?' Soon they through dim, bewildering mediums saw her sidelong fading phantom, as in the gaseous Fata Morgana; only the uppermost masts out of water; while fixed by infatuation, or fidelity, or fate, to their once lofty perches, the pagan harpooners still maintained their sinking lookouts on the sea. And now, concentric circles seized the lone boat itself, and all its crew, and each floating oar, and every lance-pole, and spinning, animate and inanimate, all round and round in one vortex, carried the smallest chip of the Pequod out of sight.

But as the last whelmings intermixingly poured themselves over the sunken head of the Indian at the mainmast, leaving a few inches of the erect spar yet visible, together with long streaming yards of the flag, which calmly undulated, with ironical coincidings, over the destroying billows they almost touched;—at that instant, a red arm and a hammer hovered backwardly uplifted in the open air, in the act of nailing the flag faster and yet faster to the subsiding spar. A sky-hawk that tauntingly had followed the main-truck downwards from its natural home among the stars, pecking at the flag, and incommoding Tashtego there; this bird now chanced to intercept its broad fluttering wing between the hammer and the wood; and simultaneously feeling that etherial thrill, the submerged savage beneath, in his death-gasp, kept his hammer frozen there; and so the bird of heaven, with archangelic shrieks, and his imperial beak thrust upwards, and his whole captive form folded in the flag of Ahab, went down with his ship, which, like Satan, would not sink to hell till she had dragged a living part of heaven along with her, and helmeted herself with it.

Now small fowls flew screaming over the yet yawning gulf; a sullen white surf beat against its steep sides; then all collapsed, and the great shroud of the sea rolled on as it rolled five thousand years ago.

Moby-Dick or The Whale (1851)

The greatest seer and poet of the sea for me is Melville. His vision is more real than Swinburne's, because he doesn't personify the sea, and far sounder than Joseph Conrad's, because Melville doesn't sentimentalize the ocean and the sea's unfortunates.

D. H. LAWRENCE
Studies in Classic American Literature (1924)

CHARLES BAUDELAIRE

1 8 2 1 — 1 8 6 7

LE REBELLE

Un Ange furieux fond du ciel comme un aigle,
Du mécréant saisit à plein poing les cheveux,
Et dit, le secouant: "Tu connaîtras la règle!
(Car je suis ton bon Ange, entends-tu?) Je le veux!

Sache qu'il faut aimer, sans faire la grimace,
Le pauvre, le méchant, le tortu, l'hébété,
Pour que tu puisses faire à Jésus, quand il passe,
Un tapis triomphal avec ta charité.

Tel est l'Amour! Avant que ton cœur ne se blase,
A la gloire de Dieu rallume ton extase;
C'est la Volupté vraie aux durables appas!"

Et l'Ange, châtiant autant, ma foi! qu'il aime,
De ses poings de géant torture l'anathème;
Mais le damné répond toujours: "Je ne veux pas!"

THE REBEL

An Angel swoops, like eagle on his prey,
  Grips by the hair the unbelieving wight,
  And furious cries, "O scorner of the right,
  'Tis I, thine angel good, who speaks. Obey!
Know thou shalt love without the least distaste
  The poor, the base, the crooked and the dull;
  So shall the pageant of thy Lord be graced
  With banners by thy love made beautiful.
This is God's love. See that thy soul be fired
  With its pure flame, or e'er thy heart grow tired,
  And thou shalt know the bliss that lasts for aye."
Ah! with what ruthless love that Angel grand
  Tortures and racks the wretch with giant hand!
  But still he answers "Never, till I die."

(1868)

Translated by Cosmo Monkhouse

YEUX DE JAIS

Je te donne ces vers afin que, si mon nom
Aborde heureusement aux époques lointaines
Et fait rêver un soir les cervelles humaines,
Vaisseau favorisé par un grand aquilon,

Ta mémoire, pareille aux fables incertaines,
Fatigue le lecteur ainsi qu'un tympanon,
Et par un fraternel et mystique chaînon
Reste comme pendue à mes rimes hautaines;

Être maudit à qui de l'abîme profond
Jusqu'au plus haut du ciel rien, hors moi, ne répond;
—O toi qui, comme une ombre à la trace éphémère,

Foules d'un pied léger et d'un regard serein
Les stupides mortels qui t'ont jugée amère,
Statue aux yeux de jais, grand ange au front d'airain!

JET EYES

I give you these verses so that, if my name happily reaches distant
times, and causes the human mind to dream some evening, like a ship
favored by a great north wind, your memory, like vague fables, may stun
the reader as a tympanum does, and by a fraternal and mystic link may
remain suspended to my proud rhymes; accursed being to whom, from
the deep abyss to the summit of the sky, nothing answers except myself;
—Oh you who, like a shadow with an ephemeral trace, treads with a
light foot and serene glance, stupid mortals who have judged you bitter,
statue with jet eyes, great angel with forehead of bronze!

(1857)

Masterpieces.

THÉODORE DE BANVILLE
Petit Traité de poésie française (1871)

CHARLES BAUDELAIRE

1 8 2 1 — 1 8 6 7

LES FLEURS DU MAL

Les morts, les pauvres morts ont de grandes douleurs.

The dead, the poor dead, have great sorrows.

Tableaux parisiens (1857)

L'irréparable ronge avec sa dent maudite
Notre âme.

The Irreparable gnaws our soul with his cursed teeth.

L'Irréparable (1857)

La Maladie et la Mort font des cendres
De tout le feu qui pour nous flamboya.

Illness and Death make ashes of all the fire that flamed for us.

Le Portrait (1861)

Ma jeunesse ne fut qu'un ténébreux orage,
Traversé çà et là par de brillants soleils.

My youth was only a tenebrous storm, traversed here and there by brilliant suns.

L'Ennemi (1857)

—O douleur! ô douleur! Le Temps mange la vie,
Et l'obscur Ennemi qui nous ronge le cœur
Du sang que nous perdons croît et se fortifie!

O sorrow, sorrow! Time eats life away, and the obscure Enemy that gnaws our heart, grows and is fortified by the blood we lose.

L'Ennemi (1857)

J'ai plus de souvenirs que si j'avais mille ans.

I have more memories than if I had a thousand years.

Spleen (1857)

Mon triste cerveau.
C'est une pyramide, un immense caveau,
Qui contient plus de morts que la fosse commune.

My sad brain is an immense cave that contains more dead than the potter's field.

Spleen (1857)

Rien n'égale en longueur les boiteuses journées,
Quand sous les lourds flocons des neigeuses années
L'ennui, fruit de la morne incuriosité,
Prend les proportions de l'immortalité.

Nothing equals in length the limping days, when, under the heavy flakes of the snowing years, Ennui, fruit of gloomy incuriosity, takes on the proportions of immortality.

Spleen (1857)
Translated by Mary M. Colum

The Goncourts said that both language and literature had been formed by men who were too healthy and well-balanced to be really representative of humanity. They concluded that the instabilities of the ordinary man, his vagaries, his experiences, his bewilderments, his sins and his suffering, must be expressed in a different style of writing and in a language and syntax susceptible of taking on the coloring of the modern world and the shapes of the many complex human types that compose it.

The Goncourts believed that they themselves were to be the first to accomplish this in prose, for the old Titans of literature had expressed the few and not the many, the uncommon, simple emotions instead of the common, complicated ones. But their contemporary and friend, Baudelaire, was doing it in poetry in their lifetime with a complexity and completeness which no one, either in prose or verse, has since equalled.

MARY M. COLUM
From These Roots (1937)

CHARLES AND EMMA

Quand il rentrait au milieu de la nuit, il n'osait pas la réveiller. La veilleuse de porcelaine arrondissait au plafond une clarté tremblante, et les rideaux fermés du petit berceau faisaient comme une hutte blanche qui se bombait dans l'ombre, au bord du lit. Charles les regardait. Il croyait entendre l'haleine légère de son enfant. Elle allait grandir mainte-nant; chaque saison, vite, amènerait un progrès; il la voyait déjà revenant de l'école à la tombée du jour, toute rieuse, avec sa brassière tachée d'encre, et portant au bras son panier; puis il faudrait la mettre en pension, cela coûterait beaucoup; comment faire? Alors il réfléchis-sait. Il pensait à louer une petite ferme aux environs, et qu'il surveillerait lui-même, tous les matins, en allant voir ses malades. Il en économiserait le revenu, il le placerait à la caisse d'épargne; ensuite il achèterait des actions, quelque part, n'importe où; d'ailleurs la clientèle augmenterait; il y comptait, car il voulait que Berthe fût bien élevée, qu'elle eût des talents, qu'elle apprît le piano. Ah! qu'elle serait jolie, plus tard, à quinze ans, quand, ressemblant à sa mère, elle porterait comme elle, dans l'été, de grands chapeaux de paille! On les prendrait de loin pour les deux sœurs. Il se la figurait travaillant le soir auprès d'eux, sous la lumière de la lampe; elle lui broderait des pantoufles; elle s'occuperait du ménage. . . .

Emma ne dormait pas, elle faisait semblant d'être endormie; et, tandis qu'il s'assoupissait à ses côtés, elle se réveillait en d'autres rêves.

Au galop de quatre chevaux, elle était emportée depuis huit jours vers un pays nouveau, d'où ils ne reviendraient plus. Ils allaient, ils allaient, les bras enlacés, sans parler. Souvent, du haut d'une montagne, ils apercevaient tout à coup quelque cité splendide avec des dômes, des ponts, des navires, des forêts de citronniers et des cathédrales de marbre blanc, dont les clochers aigus portaient des nids de cigognes. On marchait au pas à cause des grandes dalles, et il y avait par terre des bouquets de fleurs que vous offraient des femmes habillées en corset rouge. On entendait sonner des cloches, hennir des mulets, avec le murmure des guitares et le bruit des fontaines, dont la vapeur s'envolant rafraîchissait des tas de fruits, disposés en pyramides au pied des statues pâles, qui souriaient sous les jets d'eau. Et puis ils arrivaient, un soir, dans un village de pêcheurs, où des filets bruns séchaient au vent, le long de la falaise et des cabanes. C'est là qu'ils s'arrêteraient pour vivre: ils habiteraient une maison basse à toit plat, ombragée d'un palmier, au fond d'un golfe, au bord de la mer. Ils se promèneraient en gondole, ils se balanceraient en hamac; et leur existence serait facile et large comme leurs vêtements de soie, toute chaude et étoilée comme les nuits douces qu'ils contempleraient. Cependant, sur l'immensité de cet avenir qu'elle se faisait apparaître, rien de particulier ne surgissait: les jours, tous magnifiques, se ressemblaient comme des flots; et cela se balançait à l'horizon infini, harmonieux, bleuâtre et couvert de soleil. Mais l'enfant se mettait à tousser dans son berceau, ou bien Bovary ronflait plus fort, et Emma ne s'endormait que le matin.

When he came home in the middle of the night, he did not dare to wake her. The porcelain nightlight threw a round trembling gleam upon the ceiling, and the drawn curtains of the little cot formed, as it were, a white hut standing out in the shade, and by the bedside Charles looked at them. He seemed to hear the light breathing of his child. She would grow big now; every season would bring rapid progress. He already saw her coming from school as the day drew in, laughing, with ink-stains on her jacket, and carrying her basket on her arm. Then she would have to be sent to a boarding-school; that would cost much; how was it to be done? Then he reflected. He thought of hiring a small farm in the neighborhood, that he would superintend every morning on his way to his patients. He would save up what he brought in; he would put it in the savings-bank. Then he would buy shares somewhere, no matter where; besides, his practice would increase; he counted upon that, for he wanted Berthe to be well-educated, to be accomplished, to learn to play the piano. Ah! how pretty she would be later on when she was fifteen, when, resembling her mother, she would, like her, wear large straw hats in the summer-time; from a distance they would be taken for two sisters. He pictured her to himself working in the evening by their side beneath the light of the lamp; she would embroider him slippers; she would look after the house. . . .

Emma was not asleep; she pretended to be; and while he dozed off by her side she awakened to other dreams.

To the gallop of four horses she was carried away for a week towards a new land, whence they would return no more. They went on and on, their arms entwined, without a word. Often from the top of a mountain there suddenly glimpsed some splendid city with domes, and bridges, and ships, forests of citron trees, and cathedrals of white marble, on whose pointed steeples were storks' nests. They went at a walking-pace because of the great flag-stones, and on the ground there were bouquets of flowers, offered you by women dressed in red bodices. They heard the chiming of bells, the neighing of mules, together with the murmur of guitars and the noise of fountains, whose rising spray refreshed heaps of fruit arranged like a pyramid at the foot of pale statues that smiled beneath playing waters. And then, one night they came to a fishing village, where brown nets were drying in the wind along the cliffs and in front of the huts. It was there that they would stay; they would live in a low, flat-roofed house, shaded by a palm-tree, in the heart of a gulf, by the sea. They would row in gondolas, swing in hammocks, and their existence would be easy and large as their silk gowns, warm and star-spangled as the nights they would contemplate. However, in the immensity of this future that she conjured up, nothing special stood forth; the days, all magnificent, resembled each other like waves; and it swayed in the horizon, infinite, harmonized, azure, and bathed in sunshine. But the child began to cough in her cot or Bovary snored more loudly, and Emma did not fall asleep till morning.

Madame Bovary (1857)
Translation anonymous

*This is indeed writing; this is finding the style suitable to each object,
each place, each circumstance, each being; and this is picturing through
differences and oppositions of tone the deep and eternal discords which
render beings impenetrable to each other, as far away from each other,
in the light of the same candle, as if an abyss opened between them.
Flaubert is indeed the master of what has been called the artistic style—
the style which paints, which engraves, and the style which sings, which
whispers and which growls; a style which renders sounds as well as
objects and with an equal force of impression.*

ÉMILE FAGUET
Flaubert (1899)
Translated by Mrs. R. L. Devonshire

MATTHEW ARNOLD

1 8 2 2 — 1 8 8 8

THYRSIS

Thus yesterday, to-day, to-morrow come,
They hustle one another and they pass;
But all our hustling morrows only make
The smooth to-day of God.

From LUCRETIUS
an unpublished Tragedy.

How changed is here each spot man makes or fills!
    In the two Hinkseys nothing keeps the same;
        The village-street its haunted mansion lacks,
    And from the sign is gone Sibylla's name,
        And from the roofs the twisted chimney-stacks;
            Are ye too changed, ye hills?

See, 'tis no foot of unfamiliar men
    To-night from Oxford up your pathway strays:
    Here came I often, often, in old days;
Thyrsis and I; we still had Thyrsis then.

Runs it not here, the track by Childsworth Farm,
    Up past the wood, to where the elm-tree crowns
        The hill behind whose ridge the sunset flames?
    The signal-elm, that looks on Ilsley Downs,
        The Vale, the three lone weirs, the youthful Thames?—
            This winter-eve is warm,
    Humid the air; leafless, yet soft as spring,
        The tender purple spray on copse and briers;
        And that sweet City with her dreaming spires,
    She needs not June for beauty's heightening,

Lovely all times she lies, lovely to-night!
    Only, methinks, some loss of habit's power
        Befalls me wandering through this upland dim;
    Once pass'd I blindfold here, at any hour,
        Now seldom come I, since I came with him.
            That single elm-tree bright
    Against the west—I miss it! is it gone?
        We prized it dearly; while it stood, we said,
        Our friend, the Scholar-Gipsy, was not dead;
    While the tree lived, he in these fields lived on.

Too rare, too rare, grow now my visits here!
    But once I knew each field, each flower, each stick;
        And with the country-folk acquaintance made
    By barn in threshing-time, by new-built rick.
        Here, too, our shepherd-pipes we first assay'd.
            Ah me! this many a year
    My pipe is lost, my shepherd's-holiday!
        Needs must I lose them, needs with heavy heart
        Into the world and wave of men depart;
    But Thyrsis of his own will went away.

It irk'd him to be here, he could not rest.
    He loved each simple joy the country yields,
        He loved his mates; but yet he could not keep,
    For that a shadow lower'd on the fields,
        Here with the shepherds and the silly sheep.
            Some life of men unblest

1264

He knew, which made him droop, and fill'd his head.
　　He went; his piping took a troubled sound
　　　Of storms that rage outside our happy ground;
　　He could not wait their passing, he is dead!

So, some tempestuous morn in early June,
　　When the year's primal burst of bloom is o'er,
　　　Before the roses and the longest day—
　　When garden-walks, and all the grassy floor,
　　　With blossoms, red and white, of fallen May,
　　　　And chestnut-flowers are strewn—
　　So have I heard the cuckoo's parting cry,
　　　From the wet field, through the vext garden-trees,
　　　Come with the volleying rain and tossing breeze:
　　The bloom is gone, and with the bloom go I.

Too quick despairer, wherefore wilt thou go?
　　Soon will the high Midsummer pomps come on,
　　　Soon will the musk carnations break and swell,
　　Soon shall we have gold-dusted snapdragon,
　　　Sweet-William with its homely cottage-smell,
　　　　And stocks in fragrant blow;
　　Roses that down the alleys shine afar,
　　　And open, jasmine-muffled lattices,
　　　And groups under the dreaming garden-trees,
　　And the full moon, and the white evening-star.

He hearkens not! light comer, he is flown!
　　What matters it? next year he will return,
　　　And we shall have him in the sweet spring-days,
　　With whitening hedges, and uncrumpling fern,
　　　And blue-bells trembling by the forest-ways,
　　　　And scent of hay new-mown.
　　But Thyrsis never more we swains shall see!
　　　See him come back, and cut a smoother reed,
　　　And blow a strain the world at last shall heed—
　　For Time, not Corydon, hath conquer'd thee.

Alack, for Corydon no rival now!—
　　But when Sicilian shepherds lost a mate,
　　　Some good survivor with his flute would go,
　　Piping a ditty sad for Bion's fate,
　　　And cross the unpermitted ferry's flow,
　　　　And relax Pluto's brow,

And make leap up with joy the beauteous head
    Of Proserpine, among whose crownèd hair
    Are flowers, first open'd on Sicilian air,
And flute his friend, like Orpheus, from the dead.

O easy access to the hearer's grace
    When Dorian shepherds sang to Proserpine!
      For she herself had trod Sicilian fields,
    She knew the Dorian water's gush divine,
      She knew each lily white which Enna yields,
        Each rose with blushing face;
    She loved the Dorian pipe, the Dorian strain.
      But ah, of our poor Thames she never heard!
      Her foot the Cumner cowslips never stirr'd!
    And we should tease her with our plaint in vain.

Well! wind-dispers'd and vain the words will be,
    Yet, Thyrsis, let me give my grief its hour
      In the old haunt, and find our tree-topp'd hill!
    Who, if not I, for questing here hath power?
      I know the wood which hides the daffodil,
        I know the Fyfield tree,
    I know what white, what purple fritillaries
      The grassy harvest of the river-fields,
      Above by Ensham, down by Sandford, yields,
    And what sedg'd brooks are Thames's tributaries;

I know these slopes; who knows them if not I?—
    But many a dingle on the loved hill-side,
      With thorns once studded, old, white-blossom'd trees,
    Where thick the cowslips grew, and, far descried,
      High tower'd the spikes of purple orchises,
        Hath since our day put by
    The coronals of that forgotten time.
      Down each green bank hath gone the ploughboy's team,
      And only in the hidden brookside gleam
    Primroses, orphans of the flowery prime.

Where is the girl, who, by the boatman's door,
    Above the locks, above the boating throng,
      Unmoor'd our skiff, when, through the Wytham flats,
    Red loosestrife and blond meadow-sweet among,
      And darting swallows, and light water-gnats,
        We track'd the shy Thames shore?

Where are the mowers, who, as the tiny swell
   Of our boat passing heav'd the river-grass,
     Stood with suspended scythe to see us pass?—
They all are gone, and thou art gone as well.

Yes, thou art gone! and round me too the night
   In ever-nearing circle weaves her shade.
     I see her veil draw soft across the day,
   I feel her slowly chilling breath invade
     The cheek grown thin, the brown hair sprent with grey;
       I feel her finger light
   Laid pausefully upon life's headlong train;
     The foot less prompt to meet the morning dew,
     The heart less bounding at emotion new,
And hope, once crush'd, less quick to spring again.

And long the way appears, which seem'd so short
   To the unpractis'd eye of sanguine youth;
     And high the mountain-tops, in cloudy air,
   The mountain-tops where is the throne of Truth,
     Tops in life's morning-sun so bright and bare!
       Unbreachable the fort
   Of the long-batter'd world uplifts its wall.
     And strange and vain the earthly turmoil grows,
     And near and real the charm of thy repose,
And night as welcome as a friend would fall.

But hush! the upland hath a sudden loss
   Of quiet;—Look! adown the dusk hill-side,
     A troop of Oxford hunters going home,
   As in old days, jovial and talking, ride!
     From hunting with the Berkshire hounds they come—
       Quick, let me fly, and cross
   Into yon further field!—'Tis done; and see,
     Back'd by the sunset, which doth glorify
     The orange and pale violet evening-sky,
Bare on its lonely ridge, the Tree! the Tree!

I take the omen! Eve lets down her veil,
   The white fog creeps from bush to bush about,
     The west unflushes, the high stars grow bright,
   And in the scatter'd farms the lights come out.
     I cannot reach the Signal-Tree to-night,
       Yet, happy omen, hail!

Hear it from thy broad lucent Arno vale
    (For there thine earth-forgetting eyelids keep
    The morningless and unawakening sleep
Under the flowery oleanders pale),

Hear it, O Thyrsis, still our Tree is there!—
    Ah, vain! These English fields, this upland dim,
    These brambles pale with mist engarlanded,
    That lone, sky-pointing tree, are not for him.
      To a boon southern country he is fled,
        And now in happier air,
Wandering with the great Mother's train divine
    (And purer or more subtle soul than thee,
      I trow, the mighty Mother doth not see!)
Within a folding of the Apennine,

Thou hearest the immortal strains of old.
    Putting his sickle to the perilous grain
      In the hot cornfield of the Phrygian king,
    For thee the Lityerses song again
      Young Daphnis with his silver voice doth sing;
        Sings his Sicilian fold,
His sheep, his hapless love, his blinded eyes;
      And how a call celestial round him rang
      And heavenward from the fountain-brink he sprang,
And all the marvel of the golden skies.

There thou art gone, and me thou leavest here
    Sole in these fields; yet will I not despair;
      Despair I will not, while I yet descry
    'Neath the soft canopy of English air
      That lonely Tree against the western sky.
        Still, still these slopes, 'tis clear,
Our Gipsy-Scholar haunts, outliving thee!
      Fields where soft sheep from cages pull the hay,
      Woods with anemonies in flower till May,
Know him a wanderer still; then why not me?

A fugitive and gracious light he seeks,
    Shy to illumine; and I seek it too.
      This does not come with houses or with gold,
    With place, with honour, and a flattering crew;
      'Tis not in the world's market bought and sold.
      But the smooth-slipping weeks

Drop by, and leave its seeker still untired;
　　Out of the heed of mortals he is gone,
　　　He wends unfollow'd, he must house alone;
　　Yet on he fares, by his own heart inspired.

Thou too, O Thyrsis, on like quest wert bound,
　　Thou wanderedst with me for a little hour;
　　　Men gave thee nothing, but this happy quest,
　　If men esteem'd thee feeble, gave thee power,
　　　If men procured thee trouble, gave thee rest.
　　　　And this rude Cumner ground,
　　Its fir-topped Hurst, its farms, its quiet fields,
　　　Here cam'st thou in thy jocund youthful time,
　　　Here was thine height of strength, thy golden prime;
　　And still the haunt beloved a virtue yields.

What though the music of thy rustic flute
　　Kept not for long its happy, country tone,
　　　Lost it too soon, and learnt a stormy note
　　Of men contention-tost, of men who groan,
　　　Which task'd thy pipe too sore, and tired thy throat—
　　　　It fail'd, and thou wast mute;
　　Yet hadst thou alway visions of our light,
　　　And long with men of care thou couldst not stay,
　　　And soon thy foot resumed its wandering way,
　　Left human haunt, and on alone till night.

Too rare, too rare, grow now my visits here!
　　'Mid city-noise, not, as with thee of yore,
　　　Thyrsis, in reach of sheep-bells is my home!
　　Then through the great town's harsh, heart-wearying roar,
　　　Let in thy voice a whisper often come,
　　　　To chase fatigue and fear:
　　Why faintest thou? I wander'd till I died.
　　　Roam on! the light we sought is shining still.
　　　Dost thou ask proof? Our Tree yet crowns the hill,
　　Our Scholar travels yet the loved hillside.

　　　　　　　　　　　　　　　　　　(1866)

1269

AVE ATQUE VALE

(*In memory of Charles Baudelaire*)

I

Shall I strew on thee rose or rue or laurel,
    Brother, on this that was the veil of thee?
    Or quiet sea-flower moulded by the sea,
Or simplest growth of meadow-sweet or sorrel,
    Such as the summer-sleepy Dryads weave,
    Waked up by snow-soft sudden rains at eve?
Or wilt thou rather, as on earth before,
    Half-faded fiery blossoms, pale with heat
    And full of bitter summer, but more sweet
To thee than gleanings of a northern shore
    Trod by no tropic feet?

II

For always thee the fervid languid glories
    Allured of heavier suns in mightier skies;
    Thine ears knew all the wandering watery sighs
Where the sea sobs round Lesbian promontories,
    The barren kiss of piteous wave to wave
    That knows not where is that Leucadian grave
Which hides too deep the supreme head of song.
    Ah, salt and sterile as her kisses were,
    The wild sea winds her and the green gulfs bear
Hither and thither, and vex and work her wrong,
    Blind gods that cannot spare.

III

Thou sawest, in thine old singing season, brother,
    Secrets and sorrows unbeheld of us:
    Fierce loves, and lovely leaf-buds poisonous,
Bare to thy subtler eye, but for none other
    Blowing by night in some unbreathed-in clime;
    The hidden harvest of luxurious time,

1270

Sin without shape, and pleasure without speech;
      And where strange dreams in a tumultuous sleep
      Make the shut eyes of stricken spirits weep;
And with each face thou sawest the shadow on each,
      Seeing as men sow men reap.

IV

O sleepless heart and sombre soul unsleeping,
      That were athirst for sleep and no more life
      And no more love, for peace and no more strife!
Now the dim gods of death have in their keeping
      Spirit and body and all the springs of song,
      Is it well now where love can do no wrong,
Where stingless pleasure has no foam or fang
      Behind the unopening closure of her lips?
      Is it not well where soul from body slips
And flesh from bone divides without a pang
      As dew from flower-bell drips?

V

It is enough; the end and the beginning
      Are one thing to thee, who art past the end.
      O hand unclasp'd of unbeholden friend,
For thee no fruits to pluck, no palms for winning,
      No triumph and no labour and no lust,
      Only dead yew-leaves and a little dust.
O quiet eyes wherein the light saith naught,
      Whereto the day is dumb, nor any night
      With obscure finger silences your sight,
Nor in your speech the sudden soul speaks thought,
      Sleep, and have sleep for light.

VI

Now all strange hours and all strange loves are over,
      Dreams and desires and sombre songs and sweet,
      Hast thou found place at the great knees and feet
Of some pale Titan-woman like a lover,
      Such as thy vision here solicited,
      Under the shadow of her fair vast head,

1271

The deep division of prodigious breasts,
  The solemn slope of mighty limbs asleep,
  The weight of awful tresses that still keep
The savour and shade of old-world pine-forests
  Where the wet hill-winds weep?

VII

Hast thou found any likeness for thy vision?
  O gardener of strange flowers, what bud, what bloom,
  Hast thou found sown, what gather'd in the gloom?
What of despair, of rapture, of derision,
  What of life is there, what of ill or good?
  Are the fruits grey like dust or bright like blood?
Does the dim ground grow any seed of ours,
  The faint fields quicken any terrene root,
  In low lands where the sun and moon are mute
And all the stars keep silence? Are there flowers
  At all, or any fruit?

VIII

Alas, but though my flying song flies after,
  O sweet strange elder singer, thy more fleet
  Singing, and footprints of thy fleeter feet,
Some dim derision of mysterious laughter
  From the blind tongueless warders of the dead,
  Some gainless glimpse of Proserpine's veil'd head,
Some little sound of unregarded tears
  Wept by effaced unprofitable eyes,
  And from pale mouths some cadence of dead sighs—
These only, these the hearkening spirit hears,
  Sees only such things rise.

IX

Thou art far too far for wings of words to follow,
  Far too far off for thought or any prayer.
  What ails us with thee, who art wind and air?
What ails us gazing where all seen is hollow?
  Yet with some fancy, yet with some desire,
  Dreams pursue death as winds a flying fire,

Our dreams pursue our dead and do not find.
    Still, and more swift than they, the thin flame flies,
    The low light fails us in elusive skies,
Still the foil'd earnest ear is deaf, and blind
    Are still the eluded eyes.

X

Not thee, O never thee, in all time's changes,
    Not thee, but this the sound of thy sad soul,
    The shadow of thy swift spirit, this shut scroll
I lay my hand on, and not death estranges
    My spirit from communion of thy song—
    These memories and these melodies that throng
Veil'd porches of a Muse funereal—
    These I salute, these touch, these clasp and fold
    As though a hand were in my hand to hold,
Or through mine ears a mourning musical
    Of many mourners roll'd.

XI

I among these, I also, in such station
    As when the pyre was charr'd, and piled the sods.
    And offering to the dead made, and their gods,
The old mourners had, standing to make libation,
    I stand, and to the Gods and to the dead
    Do reverence without prayer or praise, and shed
Offering to these unknown, the gods of gloom,
    And what of honey and spice my seed-lands bear,
    And what I may of fruits in this chill'd air,
And lay, Orestes-like, across the tomb
    A curl of sever'd hair.

XII

But by no hand nor any treason stricken,
    Not like the low-lying head of Him, the King,
    The flame that made of Troy a ruinous thing,
Thou liest, and on this dust no tears could quicken.
    There fall no tears like theirs that all men hear
    Fall tear by sweet imperishable tear

Down the opening leaves of holy poets' pages.
    Thee not Orestes, not Electra mourns;
    But bending us-ward with memorial urns
The most high Muses that fulfil all ages
    Weep, and our God's heart yearns.

XIII

For, sparing of his sacred strength, not often
    Among us darkling here the lord of light
    Makes manifest his music and his might
In hearts that open and in lips that soften
    With the soft flame and heat of songs that shine.
    Thy lips indeed he touch'd with bitter wine,
And nourish'd them indeed with bitter bread;
    Yet surely from his hand thy soul's food came,
    The fire that scarr'd thy spirit at his flame
Was lighted, and thine hungering heart he fed
    Who feeds our hearts with fame.

XIV

Therefore he too now at thy soul's sunsetting,
    God of all suns and songs, he too bends down
    To mix his laurel with thy cypress crown,
And save thy dust from blame and from forgetting.
    Therefore he too, seeing all thou wert and art,
    Compassionate, with sad and sacred heart,
Mourns thee of many his children the last dead,
    And hallows with strange tears and alien sighs
    Thine unmelodious mouth and sunless eyes,
And over thine irrevocable head
    Sheds light from the under skies.

XV

And one weeps with him in the ways Lethean,
    And stains with tears her changing bosom chill;
    That obscure Venus of the hollow hill,
That thing transform'd which was the Cytherean,
    With lips that lost their Grecian laugh divine
    Long since, and face no more call'd Erycine—

A ghost, a bitter and luxurious god.
　　　Thee also with fair flesh and singing spell
　　　Did she, a sad and second prey, compel
Into the footless places once more trod,
　　　And shadows hot from hell.

XVI

And now no sacred staff shall break in blossom,
　　　No choral salutation lure to light
　　　A spirit sick with perfume and sweet night
And love's tired eyes and hands and barren bosom.
　　　There is no help for these things; none to mend,
　　　And none to mar; not all our songs, O friend,
Will make death clear or make life durable.
　　　Howbeit with rose and ivy and wild vine
　　　And with wild notes about this dust of thine
At least I fill the place where white dreams dwell
　　　And wreathe an unseen shrine.

XVII ·

Sleep; and if life was bitter to thee, pardon,
　　　If sweet, give thanks; thou hast no more to live;
　　　And to give thanks is good, and to forgive.
Out of the mystic and the mournful garden
　　　Where all day through thine hands in barren braid
　　　Wove the sick flowers of secrecy and shade,
Green buds of sorrow and sin, and remnants grey,
　　　Sweet-smelling, pale with poison, sanguine-hearted,
　　　Passions that sprang from sleep and thoughts that started,
Shall death not bring us all as thee one day
　　　Among the days departed?

XVIII

For thee, O now a silent soul, my brother,
　　　Take at my hands this garland, and farewell.
　　　Thin is the leaf, and chill the wintry smell,
And chill the solemn earth, a fatal mother,
　　　With sadder than the Niobean womb,
　　　And in the hollow of her breasts a tomb.

Content thee, howsoe'er, whose days are done;
     There lies not any troublous thing before,
     Nor sight nor sound to war against thee more,
For whom all winds are quiet as the sun,
     All waters as the shore.

Poems and Ballads, Second Series (1878)

Swinburne modestly wrote "There are in the English language three elegiac poems so great that they eclipse and efface all the elegiac poetry we know, all of Italian, all of Greek." He meant LYCIDAS *and* ADONAIS *and* THYRSIS,* *but we make them four, and include "Ave Atque Vale."*

EDMUND GOSSE
The Life of Algernon Charles Swinburne (1917)

WILLIAM ALLINGHAM

1 8 2 4 — 1 8 8 9

A MEMORY

Four ducks on a pond,
A grass-bank beyond,
A blue sky of spring,
White clouds on the wing:
What a little thing
To remember for years—
To remember with tears!

(1854)

As simple an instance of the art of poetry as we could have.

LASCELLES ABERCROMBIE
The Theory of Poetry. (1926)

---

* See pages 712, 1102, 1263.

GEORGE MEREDITH

1 8 2 8 — 1 9 0 9

KINSHIP WITH THE STARS

Cold as a mountain in its star-pitched tent,
Stood high Philosophy, less friend than foe:
Whom self-caged Passion, from its prison-bars,
Is always watching with a wondering hate.
Not till the fire is dying in the grate,
Look we for any kinship with the stars.

Modern Love (1862), **iv.**

The region of pure poetry.

GEORGE MACAULAY TREVELYAN
The Poetry and Philosophy of George Meredith (1906)

GEORGE MEREDITH

1 8 2 8 — 1 9 0 9

THIS LITTLE MOMENT

We saw the swallows gathering in the sky,
And in the osier-isle we heard them noise.
We had not to look back on summer joys,
Or forward to a summer of bright dye:
But in the largeness of the evening earth
Our spirits grew as we went side by side.
The hour became her husband and my bride.
Love, that had robbed us so, thus blessed our dearth!
The pilgrims of the year waxed very loud
In multitudinous chatterings, as the flood
Full brown came from the West, and like pale blood
Expanded to the upper crimson cloud.

Love, that had robbed us of immortal things,
This little moment mercifully gave,
Where I have seen across the twilight wave
The swan sail with her young beneath her wings.

Modern Love (1862), xlvii

A more perfect piece of writing no man alive has ever turned out.
ALGERNON CHARLES SWINBURNE
Letter to The Spectator (June 7, 1862)

GEORGE MEREDITH

1 8 2 8 — 1 9 0 9

DIRGE IN WOODS

A wind sways the pines,
    And below
Not a breath of wild air;
Still as the mosses that glow
On the flooring and over the lines
Of the roots here and there.
The pine-tree drops its dead;
They are quiet, as under the sea.
Overhead, overhead
Rushes life in a race,
As the clouds the clouds chase;
    And we go,
And we drop like the fruits of the tree,
    Even we,
    Even so.

A Reading of Earth (1888)

Certain of his poems will live as long as the language, and there are pages of his novels, such as the love idyll in RICHARD FEVEREL, *which are of the same quality. Here is a short poem almost as fine as Goethe's best; indeed it is almost a rendering of the magical verse beginning: Ueber allen Gipfeln ist Ruh.*

FRANK HARRIS
Contemporary Portraits, First Series (1920)

JENNY

Lazy laughing languid Jenny,
Fond of a kiss and fond of a guinea,
Whose head upon my knee to-night
Rests for a while, as if grown light
With all our dances and the sound
To which the wild tunes spun you round:
Fair Jenny mine, the thoughtless queen
Of kisses which the blush between
Could hardly make much daintier;
Whose eyes are as blue skies, whose hair
Is countless gold incomparable:
Fresh flower, scarce touched with signs that tell
Of Love's exuberant hotbed:—Nay,
Poor flower left torn since yesterday
Until to-morrow leave you bare;
Poor handful of bright spring-water
Flung in the whirlpool's shrieking face;
Poor shameful Jenny, full of grace
Thus with your head upon my knee;—
Whose person or whose purse may be
The lodestar of your reverie?

This room of yours, my Jenny, looks
A change from mine so full of books,
Whose serried ranks hold fast, forsooth,
So many captive hours of youth,—
The hours they thieve from day and night
To make one's cherished work come right,
And leave it wrong for all their theft,
Even as to-night my work was left:
Until I vowed that since my brain
And eyes of dancing seemed so fain,
My feet should have some dancing too:—
And thus it was I met with you.
Well, I suppose 'twas hard to part,
For here I am. And now, sweetheart,
You seem too tired to get to bed.

It was a careless life I led
When rooms like this were scarce so strange
Not long ago. What breeds the change,—
The many aims or the few years?
Because to-night it all appears
Something I do not know again.

The cloud's not danced out of my brain,—
The cloud that made it turn and swim
While hour by hour the books grew dim.
Why, Jenny, as I watch you there,—
For all your wealth of loosened hair,
Your silk ungirdled and unlac'd
And warm sweets open to the waist,
All golden in the lamplight's gleam,—
You know not what a book you seem,
Half-read by lightning in a dream!
How should you know, my Jenny? Nay,
And I should be ashamed to say:—
Poor beauty, so well worth a kiss!
But while my thought runs on like this
With wasteful whims more than enough,
I wonder what you're thinking of.

If of myself you think at all,
What is the thought?—conjectural
On sorry matters best unsolved?—
Or inly is each grace revolved
To fit me with a lure?—or (sad
To think!) perhaps you're merely glad
That I'm not drunk or ruffianly
And let you rest upon my knee.

For sometimes, were the truth confess'd,
You're thankful for a little rest,—
Glad from the crush to rest within,
From the heart-sickness and the din
Where envy's voice at virtue's pitch
Mocks you because your gown is rich;
And from the pale girl's dumb rebuke,
Whose ill-clad grace and toil-worn look
Proclaim the strength that keeps her weak,
And other nights than yours bespeak;
And from the wise unchildish elf,
To schoolmate lesser than himself

Pointing you out, what thing you are:—
Yes, from the daily jeer and jar,
From shame and shame's outbraving too,
Is rest not sometimes sweet to you?—
But most from the hatefulness of man,
Who spares not to end what he began,
Whose acts are ill and his speech ill,
Who, having used you at his will,
Thrusts you aside, as when I dine
I serve the dishes and the wine.

Well, handsome Jenny mine, sit up:
I've filled our glasses, let us sup,
And do not let me think of you,
Lest shame of yours suffice for two.
What, still so tired? Well, well then, keep
Your head there, so you do not sleep;
But that the weariness may pass
And leave you merry, take this glass.
Ah! lazy lily hand, more bless'd
If ne'er in rings it had been dress'd
Nor ever by a glove conceal'd!

Behold the lilies of the field,
They toil not neither do they spin;
(So doth the ancient text begin,—
Not of such rest as one of these
Can share.) Another rest and ease
Along each summer-sated path
From its new lord the garden hath,
Than that whose spring in blessings ran
Which praised the bounteous husbandman,
Ere yet, in days of hankering breath,
The lilies sickened unto death.

What, Jenny, are your lilies dead?
Aye, and the snow-white leaves are spread
Like winter on the garden-bed.
But you had roses left in May,—
They were not gone too. Jenny, nay,
But must your roses die, and those
Their purfled buds that should unclose?
Even so; the leaves are curled apart,
Still red as from the broken heart,
And here's the naked stem of thorns.

Nay, nay, mere words. Here nothing warns
As yet of winter. Sickness here
Or want alone could waken fear,—
Nothing but passion wrings a tear.
Except when there may rise unsought
Haply at times a passing thought
Of the old days which seem to be
Much older than any history
That is written in any book;
When she would lie in fields and look
Along the ground through the blown grass,
And wonder where the city was,
Far out of sight, whose broil and bale
They told her then for a child's tale.

Jenny, you know the city now.
A child can tell the tale there, how
Some things which are not yet enroll'd
In market-lists are bought and sold
Even till the early Sunday light,
When Saturday night is market-night
Everywhere, be it dry or wet,
And market-night in the Haymarket.
Our learned London children know,
Poor Jenny, all your pride and woe;
Have seen your lifted silken skirt
Advertise dainties through the dirt;
Have seen your coach-wheels splash rebuke
On virtue; and have learned your look
When, wealth and health slipped past, you stare
Along the streets alone, and there,
Round the long park, across the bridge,
The cold lamps at the pavement's edge
Wind on together and apart,
A fiery serpent for your heart.

Let the thoughts pass, an empty cloud!
Suppose I were to think aloud,—
What if to her all this were said?
Why, as a volume seldom read
Being opened halfway shuts again,
So might the pages of her brain
Be parted at such words, and thence
Close back upon the dusty sense.

For is there hue or shape defin'd
In Jenny's desecrated mind,
Where all contagious currents meet,
A Lethe of the middle street?
Nay, it reflects not any face,
Nor sound is in its sluggish pace,
But as they coil those eddies clot,
And night and day remember not.

Why, Jenny, you're asleep at last!—
Asleep, poor Jenny, hard and fast,—
So young and soft and tired; so fair,
With chin thus nestled in your hair,
Mouth quiet, eyelids almost blue
As if some sky of dreams shone through!

Just as another woman sleeps!
Enough to throw one's thoughts in heaps
Of doubt and horror,—what to say
Or think,—this awful secret sway,
The potter's power over the clay!
Of the same lump (it has been said)
For honour and dishonour made,
Two sister vessels. Here is one.

My cousin Nell is fond of fun,
And fond of dress, and change, and praise,
So mere a woman in her ways:
And if her sweet eyes rich in youth
Are like her lips that tell the truth,
My cousin Nell is fond of love.
And she's the girl I'm proudest of.
Who does not prize her, guard her well?
The love of change, in cousin Nell,
Shall find the best and hold it dear:
The unconquered mirth turn quieter
Not through her own, through others' woe:
The conscious pride of beauty glow
Beside another's pride in her,
One little part of all they share.
For Love himself shall ripen these
In a kind soil to just increase
Through years of fertilizing peace.

Of the same lump (as it is said)
For honour and dishonour made,
Two sister vessels. Here is one.

It makes a goblin of the sun.

So pure,—so fall'n! How dare to think
Of the first common kindred link?
Yet, Jenny, till the world shall burn
It seems that all things take their turn;
And who shall say but this fair tree
May need, in changes that may be,
Your children's children's charity?
Scorned then, no doubt, as you are scorn'd!
Shall no man hold his pride forewarn'd
Till in the end, the Day of Days,
At Judgment, one of his own race,
As frail and lost as you, shall rise,—
His daughter, with his mother's eyes?

How Jenny's clock ticks on the shelf!
Might not the dial scorn itself
That has such hours to register?
Yet as to me, even so to her
Are golden sun and silver moon,
In daily largesse of earth's boon,
Counted for life-coins to one tune.
And if, as blindfold fates are toss'd,
Through some one man this life be lost,
Shall soul not somehow pay for soul?

Fair shines the gilded aureole
In which our highest painters place
Some living woman's simple face.
And the stilled features thus descried
As Jenny's long throat droops aside,—
The shadows where the cheeks are thin,
And pure wide curve from ear to chin,—
With Raffael's, Leonardo's hand
To show them to men's souls, might stand,
Whole ages long, the whole world through,
For preachings of what God can do.
What has man done here? How atone,
Great God, for this which man has done?

And for the body and soul which by
Man's pitiless doom must now comply
With lifelong hell, what lullaby
Of sweet forgetful second birth
Remains? All dark. No sign on earth
What measure of God's rest endows
The many mansions of his house.

If but a woman's heart might see
Such erring heart unerringly
For once! But that can never be.

Like a rose shut in a book
In which pure women may not look,
For its base pages claim control
To crush the flower within the soul;
Where through each dead rose-leaf that clings,
Pale as transparent Psyche-wings,
To the vile text, are traced such things
As might make the lady's cheek indeed
More than a living rose to read;
So nought save foolish foulness may
Watch with hard eyes the sure decay;
And so the life-blood of this rose,
Puddled with shameful knowledge, flows
Through leaves no chaste hand may unclose:
Yet still it keeps such faded show
Of when 'twas gathered long ago,
That the crushed petals' lovely grain,
The sweetness of the sanguine stain,
Seen of a woman's eyes, must make
Her pitiful heart, so prone to ache,
Love roses better for its sake:—
Only that this can never be:—
Even so unto her sex is she.

Yet, Jenny, looking long at you,
The woman almost fades from view.
A cipher of man's changeless sum
Of lust, past, present, and to come,
Is left. A riddle that one shrinks
To challenge from the scornful sphinx.

Like a toad within a stone
Seated while Time crumbles on;
Which sits there since the earth was curs'd
For Man's transgression at the first;
Which, living through all centuries,
Not once has seen the sun arise;
Whose life, to its cold circle charmed,
The earth's whole summers have not warmed;
Which always—whitherso the stone
Be flung—sits there, deaf, blind, alone,—
Aye, and shall not be driven out
Till that which shuts him round about
Break at the very Master's stroke,
And the dust thereof vanish as smoke,
And the seed of Man vanish as dust:—
Even so within this world is Lust.

Come, come, what use in thoughts like this?
Poor little Jenny, good to kiss,—
You'd not believe by what strange roads
Thought travels, when your beauty goads
A man to-night to think of toads!
Jenny, wake up. . . . Why, there's the dawn!

And there's an early waggon drawn
To market, and some sheep that jog
Bleating before a barking dog;
And the old streets come peering through
Another night that London knew;
And all as ghostlike as the lamps.

So on the wings of day decamps
My last night's frolic. Glooms begin
To shiver off as lights creep in
Past the gauze curtains half drawn-to,
And the lamp's doubled shade grows blue,—
Your lamp, my Jenny, kept alight,
Like a wise virgin's, all one night!
And in the alcove coolly spread
Glimmers with dawn your empty bed;
And yonder your fair face I see
Reflected lying on my knee,
Where teems with first foreshadowings
Your pier-glass scrawled with diamond rings.

And on your bosom all night worn
Yesterday's rose now droops forlorn,
But dies not yet this summer morn.

And now without, as if some word
Had called upon them that they heard,
The London sparrows far and nigh
Clamour together suddenly;
And Jenny's cage-bird grown awake
Here in their song his part must take,
Because here too the day doth break.

And somehow in myself the dawn
Among stirred clouds and veils withdrawn
Strikes greyly on her. Let her sleep.
But will it wake her if I heap
These cushions thus beneath her head
Where my knee was? No,—there's your bed,
My Jenny, while you dream. And there
I lay among your golden hair
Perhaps the subject of your dreams,
These golden coins.
               For still one deems
That Jenny's flattering sleep confers
New magic on the magic purse,—
Grim web, how clogged with shrivelled flies!
Between the threads fine fumes arise
And shape their pictures in the brain.
There roll no streets in glare and rain,
Nor flagrant man-swine whets his tusk;
But delicately sighs in musk
The homage of the dim boudoir;
Or like a palpitating star
Thrilled into song, the opera-night
Breathes faint in the quick pulse of light;
Or at the carriage-window shine
Rich wares for choice; or, free to dine,
Whirls through its hour of health (divine
For her) the concourse of the Park.
And though in the discounted dark
Her functions there and here are one,
Beneath the lamps and in the sun
There reigns at least the acknowledged belle
Apparelled beyond parallel.
Ah Jenny, yes, we know your dreams.

For even the Paphian Venus seems
A goddess o'er the realms of love,
When silver-shrined in shadowy grove:
Aye, or let offerings nicely plac'd
But hide Priapus to the waist,
And whoso looks on him shall see
An eligible deity.

Why, Jenny, waking here alone
May help you to remember one,
Though all the memory's long outworn
Of many a double-pillowed morn.
I think I see you when you wake,
And rub your eyes for me, and shake
My gold, in rising, from your hair,
A Danaë for a moment there.

Jenny, my love rang true! for still
Love at first sight is vague, until
That tinkling makes him audible.

And must I mock you to the last,
Ashamed of my own shame,—aghast
Because some thoughts not born amiss
Rose at a poor fair face like this?
Well, of such thoughts so much I know:
In my life, as in hers, they show,
By a far gleam which I may near,
A dark path I can strive to clear.

Only one kiss. Good-bye, my dear.

The simple sudden sound of that plain line is as great and rare a thing in the way of verse, as final and superb a proof of absolute poetic power upon words, as any man's work can show.

ALGERNON CHARLES SWINBURNE
Essays and Studies (1875)

HENRY KINGSLEY

1 8 3 0 — 1 8 7 6

LANDSCAPE

Down below in the valley, among the meadows, the lanes and the fords, it was nearly as peaceful and quiet as it was aloft on the mountain-tops; and under the darkening shadows of the rapidly leafing elms you could hear—it was so still—the cows grazing and the trout rising in the river.

Stretton (1869)

As word-painter of landscape he is probably unexcelled by any English novelist; as master of the subtle music of prose, as maker of beautiful phrases, he is unrivalled.

MICHAEL SADLEIR
Things Past (1944)

CHRISTINA GEORGINA ROSSETTI

1 8 3 0 — 1 8 9 4

PASSING AWAY

Passing away, saith the World, passing away:
Chances, beauty and youth sapped day by day:
Thy life never continueth in one stay.
Is the eye waxen dim, is the dark hair changing to grey
That hath won neither laurel nor bay?
I shall clothe myself in Spring and bud in May:
Thou, root-stricken, shalt not rebuild thy decay
On my bosom for aye.
Then I answered: Yea.

Passing away, saith my Soul, passing away:
With its burden of fear and hope, of labour and play,
Hearken what the past doth witness and say:
Rust in thy gold, a moth is in thine array,
A canker is in thy bud, thy leaf must decay.
At midnight, at cockcrow, at morning, one certain day
Lo, the Bridegroom shall come and shall not delay:
Watch thou and pray.
Then I answered: Yea.

1289

Passing away, saith my God, passing away:
Winter passeth after the long delay:
New grapes on the vine, new figs on the tender spray
Turtle calleth turtle in Heaven's May.
Though I tarry, wait for Me, trust Me, watch and pray.
Arise, come away, night is past and lo it is day,
My love, My sister, My spouse, thou shalt hear Me say—
Then I answered: Yea.

(1860)

By God! That's one of the finest things ever written!
ALGERNON CHARLES SWINBURNE

And Swinburne, somewhat contrary to his wont, was right. Purer inspiration, less troubled by worldly motives, than these verses cannot be found.
PAUL ELMER MORE
Selected Shelburne Essays (1935)

EMILY DICKINSON

1 8 3 0 — 1 8 8 6

THE CHARIOT

Because I could not stop for Death,
He kindly stopped for me;
The carriage held but just ourselves
And Immortality.

We slowly drove, he knew no haste,
And I had put away
My labor, and my leisure too,
For his civility.

We passed the school where children played
At wrestling in a ring;
We passed the fields of gazing grain,
We passed the setting sun.

We paused before a house that seemed
A swelling of the ground;
The roof was scarcely visible,
The cornice but a mound.

Since then 'tis centuries; but each
Feels shorter than the day
I first surmised the horses' heads
Were toward eternity.

The Poems of Emily Dickinson (1930)

If the word great means anything in poetry, this poem is one of the greatest in the English language; it is flawless to the last detail. The rhythm charges with movement the pattern of suspended action back of the poem. Every image is precise and, moreover, not merely beautiful, but inextricably fused with the central idea. Every image extends and intensifies every other. The third stanza especially shows Miss Dickinson's power to fuse, into a single order of perception, a heterogeneous series: the children, the grain, and the setting sun (time) have the same degree of credibility; the first subtly preparing for the last. The sharp GAZING *before* GRAIN *instils into nature a kind of cold vitality of which the qualitative richness has infinite depth. The content of death in the poem eludes forever any explicit definition. He is a gentleman taking a lady out for a drive. But note the restraint that keeps the poet from carrying this so far that it is ludicrous and incredible; and note the subtly interfused erotic motive, which the idea of death has presented to every romantic poet, love being a symbol interchangeable with death. The terror of death is objectified through this figure of the genteel driver, who is made ironically to serve the end of Immortality. This is the heart of the poem: she has presented a typical Christian theme in all its final irresolution, without making any final statement about it. There is no solution to the problem; there can be only a statement of it in the full context of intellect and feeling. A construction of the human will, elaborated with all the abstracting powers of the mind, is put to the concrete test of experience: the idea of immortality is confronted with the fact of physical disintegration. We are not told what to think; we are told to look at the situation.*

A L L E N   T A T E

Reactionary Essays On Poetry and Ideas (1936)

WILLIAM MORRIS

1 8 3 4 — 1 8 9 6

GOLDEN WINGS

Midways of a walled garden,
  In the happy poplar land,
  Did an ancient castle stand,
With an old knight for a warden.

Many scarlet bricks there were
  In its walls, and old grey stone;
  Over which red apples shone
At the right time of the year.

On the bricks the green moss grew,
  Yellow lichen on the stone,
  Over which red apples shone;
Little war that castle knew.

Deep green water fill'd the moat,
  Each side had a red-brick lip,
  Green and mossy with the drip
Of dew and rain; there was a boat

Of carven wood, with hangings green
  About the stern; it was great bliss
  For lovers to sit there and kiss
In the hot summer noons, not seen.

Across the moat the fresh west wind
  In very little ripples went;
  The way the heavy aspens bent
Towards it, was a thing to mind.

The painted drawbridge over it
  Went up and down with gilded chains,
  'Twas pleasant in the summer rains
Within the bridge-house there to sit.

There were five swans that ne'er did eat
  The water-weeds, for ladies came
  Each day, and young knights did the same,
And gave them cakes and bread for meat.

They had a house of painted wood,
   A red roof gold-spiked over it,
   Wherein upon their eggs to sit
Week after week; no drop of blood,

Drawn from men's bodies by sword-blows,
   Came over there, or any tear;
   Most certainly from year to year
'Twas pleasant as a Provence rose.

The banners seem'd quite full of ease,
   That over the turret-roofs hung down;
   The battlements could get no frown
From the flower-moulded cornices.

    The Defence of Guenevere and Other Poems (1858)

The best description of happiness in the world.

W. B. YEATS
Essays (1924)

———

W. S. GILBERT

1 8 3 6 — 1 9 1 1

THE FIRST LORD OF THE ADMIRALTY

When I was a lad I served a term
As office boy to an Attorney's firm.
I cleaned the windows and I swept the floor,
And I polished up the handle of the big front door.
   I polished up that handle so carefullee
   That now I am the Ruler of the Queen's Navee!

    CHORUS.—He polished, etc.

As office boy I made such a mark
That they gave me the post of a junior clerk.
I served the writs with a smile so bland,
And I copied all the letters in a big round hand—
   I copied all the letters in a hand so free,
   That now I am the Ruler of the Queen's Navee!

CHORUS.—He copied, etc.

In serving writs I made such a name
That an articled clerk I soon became;
I wore clean collars and a brand-new suit
For the pass examination at the Institute,
 And that pass examination did so well for me,
 That now I am the Ruler of the Queen's Navee!

   CHORUS.—And that pass examination, etc.

Of legal knowledge I acquired such a grip
That they took me into the partnership.
And that junior partnership, I ween,
Was the only ship that I ever had seen.
 But that kind of ship so suited me,
 That now I am the Ruler of the Queen's Navee!

   CHORUS.—But that kind, etc.

I grew so rich that I was sent
By a pocket borough into Parliament.
I always voted at my party's call,
And I never thought of thinking for myself at all.
 I thought so little, they rewarded me
 By making me the Ruler of the Queen's Navee!

   CHORUS.—He thought so little, etc.

Now landsmen all, whoever you may be,
If you want to rise to the top of the tree,
If your soul isn't fettered to an office stool,
Be careful to be guided by this golden rule—
 Stick close to your desks and never go to sea,
 And you all may be Rulers of the Queen's Navee!

   CHORUS.—Stick close, etc.

H.M.S. Pinafore (1878)

The very perfection of farce.

THEODORE WATTS-DUNTON
Poetry and the Renascence of Wonder (1914)

ALGERNON CHARLES SWINBURNE

1 8 3 7 — 1 9 0 9

FROM *LAUS VENERIS*

The thunder of the trumpets of the night.
                    Poems and Ballads (1866)

One of the greatest lines in modern, and English, poetry.
                                        GEORGE SAINTSBURY
                    A History of English Prosody (1910)

ALGERNON CHARLES SWINBURNE

1 8 3 7 — 1 9 0 9

CHORUSES FROM *ATALANTA IN CALYDON*

When the hounds of spring are on winter's traces,
    The mother of months in meadow or plain
Fills the shadows and windy places
    With lisp of leaves and ripple of rain;
And the brown bright nightingale amorous
Is half assuaged for Itylus,
For the Thracian ships and the foreign faces,
    The tongueless vigil, and all the pain.

Come with bows bent and with emptying of quivers,
    Maiden most perfect, lady of light,
With a noise of winds and many rivers,
    With a clamour of waters, and with might;
Bind on thy sandals, O thou most fleet,
Over the splendour and speed of thy feet;
For the faint east quickens, the wan west shivers,
    Round the feet of the day and the feet of the night.

Where shall we find her, how shall we sing to her,
    Fold our hands round her knees, and cling?
O that man's heart were as fire and could spring to her,
    Fire, or the strength of the streams that spring!

For the stars and the winds are unto her
As raiment, as songs of the harp-player;
For the risen stars and the fallen cling to her,
    And the southwest-wind and the west-wind sing.

For winter's rains and ruins are over,
    And all the season of snows and sins;
The days dividing lover and lover,
    The light that loses, the night that wins;
And time remembered is grief forgotten,
And frosts are slain and flowers begotten,
And in green underwood and cover
    Blossom by blossom the spring begins.

The full streams feed on flower of rushes,
    Ripe grasses trammel a travelling foot,
The faint fresh flame of the young year flushes
    From leaf to flower and flower to fruit;
And fruit and leaf are as gold and fire,
And the oat is heard above the lyre,
And the hoofèd heel of a satyr crushes
    The chestnut-husk at the chestnut-root.

And Pan by noon and Bacchus by night,
    Fleeter of foot than the fleet-foot kid,
Follows with dancing and fills with delight
    The Mænad and the Bassarid:
And soft as lips that laugh and hide
The laughing leaves of the trees divide,
And screen from seeing and leave in sight
    The god pursuing, the maiden hid.

The ivy falls with the Bacchanal's hair
    Over her eyebrows hiding her eyes;
The wild vine slipping down leaves bare
    Her bright breast shortening into sighs;
The wild vine slips with the weight of its leaves,
But the berried ivy catches and cleaves
To the limbs that glitter, the feet that scare
    The wolf that follows, the fawn that flies.

Before the beginning of years
    There came to the making of man
Time, with a gift of tears;
    Grief, with a glass that ran;

Pleasure, with pain for leaven;
  Summer, with flowers that fell;
Remembrance fallen from heaven,
  And madness risen from hell;
Strength without hands to smite;
  Love that endures for a breath;
Night, the shadow of light,
  And life, the shadow of death.

And the high gods took in hand
  Fire, and the falling of tears,
And a measure of sliding sand
  From under the feet of the years;
And froth and drift of the sea;
  And dust of the labouring earth;
And bodies of things to be
  In the houses of death and of birth;
And wrought with weeping and laughter,
  And fashioned with loathing and love,
With life before and after
  And death beneath and above,
For a day and a night and a morrow,
  That his strength might endure for a span
With travail and heavy sorrow,
  The holy spirit of man.

From the winds of the north and the south
  They gathered as unto strife;
They breathed upon his mouth,
  They filled his body with life;
Eyesight and speech they wrought
  For the veils of the soul therein,
A time for labour and thought,
  A time to serve and to sin;
They gave him light in his ways,
  And love, and a space for delight,
And beauty and length of days,
  And night, and sleep in the night.
His speech is a burning fire;
  With his lips he travaileth;
In this heart is a blind desire,
  In his eyes foreknowledge of death;
He weaves, and is clothed with derision;
  Sows, and he shall not reap;
His life is a watch or a vision
  Between a sleep and a sleep.

We have seen thee, O Love, thou art fair; thou art goodly, O Love;
Thy wings make light in the air as the wings of a dove.
Thy feet are as winds that divide the stream of the sea;
Earth is thy covering to hide thee, the garment of thee.
Thou art swift and subtle and blind as a flame of fire;
Before thee the laughter, behind thee the tears of desire;
And twain go forth beside thee, a man with a maid;
Her eyes are the eyes of a bride whom delight makes afraid;
As the breath in the buds that stir is her bridal breath:
But Fate is the name of her; and his name is Death.

    For an evil blossom was born
      Of sea-foam and the frothing of blood,
        Blood-red and bitter of fruit,
          And the seed of it laughter and tears,
    And the leaves of it madness and scorn;
      A bitter flower from the bud,
        Sprung of the sea without root,
          Sprung without graft from the years.

    The weft of the world was untorn
      That is woven of the day on the night,
      The hair of the hours was not white
    Nor the raiment of time overworn,
      When a wonder, a world's delight,
    A perilous goddess was born;
      And the waves of the sea as she came
    Clove, and the foam at her feet,
      Fawning, rejoiced to bring forth
    A fleshly blossom, a flame
    Filling the heavens with heat
      To the cold white ends of the north.

    And in air the clamorous birds,
      And men upon earth that hear
    Sweet articulate words
      Sweetly divided apart,
    And in shallow and channel and mere
    The rapid and footless herds,
      Rejoiced, being foolish of heart.

    For all they said upon earth,
      She is fair, she is white like a dove,
      And the life of the world in her breath
    Breathes, and is born at her birth;
      For they knew thee for mother of love,
      And knew thee not mother of death.

What hadst thou to do being born,
　Mother, when winds were at ease,
As a flower of the springtime of corn,
　A flower of the foam of the seas?
For bitter thou wast from thy birth,
　Aphrodite, a mother of strife;
For before thee some rest was on earth,
　　A little respite from tears,
　　A little pleasure of life;
For life was not then as thou art,
　　But as one that waxeth in years
Sweet-spoken, a fruitful wife;
　　Earth had no thorn, and desire
No sting, neither death any dart;
　　What hadst thou to do amongst these,
　　Thou, clothed with a burning fire,
Thou, girt with sorrow of heart,
　　Thou, sprung of the seed of the seas
As an ear from a seed of corn,
　　As a brand plucked forth of a pyre,
As a ray shed forth of the morn,
　　For division of soul and disease,
For a dart and a sting and a thorn?
What ailed thee then to be born?

Was there not evil enough,
　Mother, and anguish on earth
　Born with a man at his birth,
Wastes underfoot, and above
　Storm out of heaven, and dearth
Shaken down from the shining thereof,
　　Wrecks from afar overseas
　And peril of shallow and firth,
　　And tears that spring and increase
　In the barren places of mirth,
That thou, having wings as a dove,
　Being girt with desire for a girth,
　　That thou must come after these,
That thou must lay on him love?

Thou shouldst not so have been born:
　But death should have risen with thee,
　　Mother, and visible fear,
　　Grief, and the wringing of hands,

And noise of many that mourn;
　　The smitten bosom, the knee
　　　　Bowed, and in each man's ear
　　　　A cry as of perishing lands,
A moan as of people in prison,
　　A tumult of infinite griefs;
　　　　And thunder of storm on the sands,
　　　　And wailing of wives on the shore;
And under thee newly arisen
　　Loud shoals and shipwrecking reefs,
　　　　Fierce air and violent light;
　　　　Sail rent and sundering oar,
　　　　Darkness, and noises of night;
Clashing of streams in the sea,
　　Wave against wave as a sword,
　　　　Clamour of currents, and foam;
　　　　Rains making ruin on earth,
　　　　Winds that wax ravenous and roam
As wolves in a wolfish horde;
Fruits growing faint in the tree,
　　　　And blind things dead in their birth;
　　　　Famine, and blighting of corn,
　　　　When thy time was come to be born.

All these we know of; but thee
　　Who shall discern or declare?
In the uttermost ends of the sea
　　The light of thine eyelids and hair,
　　　　The light of thy bosom as fire
　　　　Between the wheel of the sun
And the flying flames of the air?
　　　　Wilt thou turn thee not yet nor have pity,
But abide with despair and desire
　　And the crying of armies undone,
　　　　Lamentation of one with another
　　　　And breaking of city by city;
The dividing of friend against friend,
　　　　The severing of brother and brother;
Wilt thou utterly bring to an end?
　　　　Have mercy, mother!

For against all men from of old
　　Thou hast set thine hand as a curse,
　　　　And cast out gods from their places.
　　　　These things are spoken of thee.

1300

Strong kings and goodly with gold
　　Thou hast found out arrows to pierce,
　　　And made their kingdoms and races
　　　　As dust and surf of the sea.
All these, overburdened with woes
　　And with length of their days waxen weak,
　　　Thou slewest; and sentest moreover
　　　　Upon Tyro an evil thing,
Rent hair and a fetter and blows
　　Making bloody the flower of the cheek,
　　　Though she lay by a god as a lover,
　　　　Though fair, and the seed of a king.
For of old, being full of thy fire,
　　She endured not longer to wear
　　　On her bosom a saffron vest,
　　　　On her shoulder an ashwood quiver;
Being mixed and made one through desire
　　With Enipeus, and all her hair
　　　Made moist with his mouth, and her breast
　　　　Filled full of the foam of the river.

Atalanta in Calydon (1865)

*Nothing so swift had been heard in English poetry before as sounded in
the almost superhuman choruses of* ATALANTA.

EDMUND GOSSE

The Life of Algernon Charles Swinburne (1917)

ALGERNON CHARLES SWINBURNE

1 8 3 7 — 1 9 0 9

FROM *HESPERIA*

Sudden and steady the music, as eight hoofs trample and thunder,
　　Rings in the ear of the low blind wind of the night as we pass.

Poems and Ballads (1866)

*Never in any land has there been such a master in word-music, such
unerring mastership in construction.*

GEORG BRANDES

Creative Spirits of the Nineteenth Century (1923)

Translated by Rasmus B. Anderson

ALGERNON CHARLES SWINBURNE

1 8 3 7 — 1 9 0 9

SUPER FLUMINA BABYLONIS

By the waters of Babylon we sat down and wept,
    Remembering thee,
That for ages of agony hast endured, and slept,
    And wouldst not see.

By the waters of Babylon we stood up and sang,
    Considering thee,
That a blast of deliverance in the darkness rang,
    To set thee free.

And with trumpets and thunderings and with morning song
    Came up the light;
And thy spirit uplifted thee to forget thy wrong
    As day doth night.

And thy sons were dejected not any more, as then
    When thou wast shamed;
When thy lovers went heavily without heart, as men
    Whose life was maimed.

In the desolate distances, with a great desire,
    For thy love's sake,
With our hearts going back to thee, they were filled with fire,
    Were nigh to break.

It was said to us: 'Verily ye are great of heart,
    But ye shall bend;
Ye are bondmen and bondwomen, to be scourged and smart,
    To toil and tend.'

And with harrows men harrowed us, and subdued with spears,
    And crushed with shame;
And the summer and winter was, and the length of years,
    And no change came.

By the rivers of Italy, by the sacred streams,
    By town, by tower,
There was feasting with revelling, there was sleep with dreams,
    Until thine hour.

And they slept and they rioted on their rose-hung beds,
    With mouths on flame,
And with love-locks vine-chapleted, and with rose-crowned heads
    And robes of shame.

And they knew not their forefathers, nor the hills and streams
     And words of power,
Nor the gods that were good to them, but with songs and dreams
     Filled up their hour.

By the rivers of Italy, by the dry streams' beds,
     When thy time came,
There was casting of crowns from them, from their young men's heads,
     The crowns of shame.

By the horn of Eridanus, by the Tiber mouth,
     As thy day rose,
They arose up and girded them to the north and south,
     By seas, by snows.

As a water in January the frost confines,
     Thy kings bound thee;
As a water in April is, in the new-blown vines,
     Thy sons made free.

And thy lovers that looked for thee, and that mourned from far,
     For thy sake dead,
We rejoiced in the light of thee, in the signal star
     Above thine head.

In thy grief had we followed thee, in thy passion loved,
     Loved in thy loss;
In thy shame we stood fast to thee, with thy pangs were moved,
     Clung to thy cross.

By the hillside of Calvary we beheld thy blood,
     Thy bloodred tears,
As a mother's in bitterness, an unebbing flood,
     Years upon years.

And the north was Gethsemane, without leaf or bloom,
     A garden sealed;
And the south was Aceldama, for a sanguine fume
     Hid all the field.

By the stone of the sepulchre we returned to weep,
     From far, from prison;
And the guards by it keeping it we beheld asleep,
     But thou wast risen.

And an angel's similitude by the unsealed grave,
     And by the stone:
And the voice was angelical, to whose words God gave
     Strength like his own.

'Lo, the graveclothes of Italy that are folded up
          In the grave's gloom!
And the guards as men wrought upon with a charmèd cup,
          By the open tomb.

'And her body most beautiful, and her shining head,
          These are not here;
For your mother, for Italy, is not surely dead:
          Have ye no fear.

'As of old time she spake to you, and you hardly heard,
          Hardly took heed,
So now also she saith to you, yet another word,
          Who is risen indeed.

'By my saying she saith to you, in your ears she saith,
          Who hear these things,
Put no trust in men's royalties, nor in great men's breath,
          Nor words of kings.

'For the life of them vanishes and is no more seen,
          Nor no more known;
Nor shall any remember him if a crown hath been,
          Or where a throne.

'Unto each man his handiwork, unto each his crown,
          The just Fate gives;
Whoso takes the world's life on him and his own lays down,
          He, dying so, lives.

'Whoso bears the whole heaviness of the wronged world's weight
          And puts it by,
It is well with him suffering, though he face man's fate;
          How should he die?

'Seeing death has no part in him any more, no power
          Upon his head;
He has bought his eternity with a little hour,
          And is not dead.

'For an hour, if ye look for him, he is no more found,
          For one hour's space;
Then ye lift up your eyes to him and behold him crowned,
          A deathless face.

'On the mountains of memory, by the world's well-springs,
          In all men's eyes,
Where the light of the life of him is on all past things,
          Death only dies.

'Not the light that was quenched for us, nor the deeds that were,
    Nor the ancient days,
Nor the sorrows not sorrowful, nor the face most fair
    Of perfect praise.'

So the angel of Italy's resurrection said,
    So yet he saith;
So the son of her suffering, that from breasts nigh dead
    Drew life, not death.

That the pavement of Golgotha should be white as snow,
    Not red, but white;
That the waters of Babylon should no longer flow,
    And men see light.

Songs Before Sunrise (1871)

*Perhaps the most remarkable case in English literature where a chance
set of words, of quite peculiar rhythm, is taken by a poet, and the rhythm
of those words repeated until it becomes accepted as a perfect and
satisfying pattern, is Swinburne's poem,*

> *By the waters of Babylon we sate down and wept,*
>   *Remembering thee,*
> *That for ages of agony hast lain down and slept,*
>   *And wouldst not see.*

It is a marvel of metrical skill to produce this effect in English.

GILBERT MURRAY
The Classical Tradition in Poetry (1927)

WALTER PATER

1 8 3 9 — 1 8 9 4

LA GIOCONDA

The presence that thus so strangely rose beside the waters is expressive of what in the ways of a thousand years man had come to desire.
Hers is the head upon which all 'the ends of the world are come,' and
the eyelids are a little weary. It is a beauty wrought out from within
upon the flesh, the deposit, little cell by cell, of strange thoughts and
fantastic reveries and exquisite passions. Set it for a moment beside one
of those white Greek goddesses or beautiful women of antiquity, and
how would they be troubled by this beauty, into which the soul with

all its maladies has passed? All the thoughts and experience of the world have etched and moulded there in that which they have of power to refine and make expressive the outward form, the animalism of Greece, the lust of Rome, the reverie of the middle age with its spiritual ambition and imaginative loves, the return of the Pagan world, the sins of the Borgias. She is older than the rocks among which she sits; like the vampire, she has been dead many times, and learned the secrets of the grave; and has been a diver in deep seas, and keeps their fallen day about her; and trafficked for strange webs with Eastern merchants; and, as Leda, was the mother of Helen of Troy, and, as Saint Anne, the mother of Mary; and all this has been to her but as the sound of lyres and flutes, and lives only in the delicacy with which it has moulded the changing lineaments and tinged the eyelids and the hands.

Studies in the History of the Renaissance (1873)

There is hardly a finer passage in English literature than Pater's page on the Mona Lisa.

FRANK HARRIS
My Life and Loves (1922–27)

THOMAS HARDY

1 8 4 0 — 1 9 2 8

MICHAEL HENCHARD'S WILL

'That Elizabeth-Jane Farfrae be not told of my death, or made to grieve on account of me.

'& that I be not bury'd in consecrated ground.

'& that no sexton be asked to toll the bell.

'& that nobody is wished to see my dead body.

'& that no murners walk behind me at my funeral.

'& that no flours be planted on my grave.

'& that no man remember me.

'To this I put my name.

'MICHAEL HENCHARD'
The Mayor of Casterbridge (1886)

Realistic truth and imaginative power here unite [in] Hardy to achieve their most tremendous effect. The plain words are perfectly in character, just what an uneducated farmer like Henchard might write. But Hardy has managed to charge them with all the emotional grandeur of great

1306

*tragedy. He has achieved his purpose of giving a novel the imaginative
force of poetry—and the highest poetry, the poetry of the book of Job.*

DAVID CECIL
Hardy the Novelist (1943)

STÉPHANE MALLARMÉ

1 8 4 2 — 1 8 9 8

SONNET

O si chère de loin et proche et blanche, si
Délicieusement toi, Mary, que je songe
A quelque baume rare émané par mensonge
Sur aucun bouquetier de cristal obscurci.

Le sais-tu, oui! pour moi voici des ans, voici
Toujours que ton sourire éblouissant prolonge
La même rose avec son bel été qui plonge
Dans autrefois et puis dans le futur aussi.

Mon cœur qui dans les nuits parfois cherche à s'entendre
Ou de quel dernier mot t'appeler le plus tendre
S'exalte en celui rien que chuchoté de sœur

N'était, très grand trésor et tête si petite,
Que tu m'enseignes bien toute une autre douceur
Tout bas par le baiser seul dans tes cheveux dite.

From afar so lov'd and near, so cloudless fair, so
Exquisitely thou, my Mary, that I seem
Breathing rarest balm was never but in dream
From vase-crystal lucent like thee—fain it were so!
Know'st thou? Surely. So all time that I recall, so
Always 'neath thy summer's smile doth bloom for aye
This one rose, its gladness wreathing day to day,
Time past one with now—yea, time that cometh, also!
My heart searching in the night account to render
How—by what last name to call thee—name most tender,
Reacheth but to this but falter'd 'sister mine'—
Thou, such treasure in this little head adwelling,
Teachest me the secret—this caressing name of thine—
That alone my kiss breath'd on thy hair, is telling.

Translated by Arthur Ellis

Mallarmé's sonnet is that miracle, an entire poem consciously organized to such a pitch of artistic perfection that the whole is one single, unflawed piece of "pure poetry." In its unobtrusive way, this is one of the most potent spells ever committed to paper. In what does its magic consist? Partly it is a magic of sound. (Note, incidentally, that the magical sound is not concentrated in single words, or phrases, or lines; it is the sound of the poem as a whole.) But mainly it is a magic of grammar, a syntactical magic of the relations of thought with thought. Consider the sextet; it is a grammatical apocalypse. A whole world of ideas is miraculously concentrated by means of the syntax into what is almost a point.

ALDOUS HUXLEY
Texts & Pretexts (1933)

STÉPHANE MALLARMÉ

1 8 4 2 — 1 8 9 8

L'APRÈS-MIDI D'UN FAUNE. ÉGLOGUE

Ces nymphes, je les veux perpétuer.

> *Si clair,*
> *Leur incarnat léger, qu'il voltige dans l'air*
> *Assoupi de sommeils touffus.*

> *Aimai-je un rêve?*

Mon doute, amas de nuit ancienne, s'achève
En maint rameau subtil, qui, demeuré les vrais
Bois mêmes, prouve, hélas! que bien seul je m'offrais
Pour triomphe la faute idéale de roses.
Réfléchissons . . .

> *ou si les femmes dont tu gloses*
> *Figurent un souhait de tes sens fabuleux!*
> *Faune, l'illusion s'échappe des yeux bleus*
> *Et froids, comme une source en pleurs, de la plus chaste:*
> *Mais, l'autre tout soupirs, dis-tu qu'elle contraste*
> *Comme brise du jour chaude dans ta toison!*
> *Que non! par l'immobile et lasse pâmoison*
> *Suffoquant de chaleurs le matin frais s'il lutte,*
> *Ne murmure point d'eau que ne verse ma flûte*

Au bosquet arrosé d'accords; et le seul vent
Hors des deux tuyaux prompt à s'exhaler avant
Qu'il disperse le son dans une pluie aride,
C'est, à l'horizon pas remué d'une ride,
Le visible et serein souffle artificiel
De l'inspiration, qui regagne le ciel.

O bords siciliens d'un calme marécage
Qu'à l'envi des soleils ma vanité saccage,
Tacite sous les fleurs d'étincelles, CONTEZ
'Que je coupais ici les creux roseaux domptés
'Par le talent; quand, sur l'or glauque de lointaines
'Verdures dédiant leur vigne à des fontaines,
'Ondoie une blancheur animale au repos:
'Et qu'au prélude lent où naissent les pipeaux
'Ce vol de cygnes, non! de naïades se sauve
'Ou plonge . . .'

        Inerte, tout brûle dans l'heure fauve
Sans marquer par quel art ensemble détala
Trop d'hymen souhaité de qui cherche le la:
Alors m'éveillerai-je à la ferveur première,
Droit et seul, sous un flot antique de lumière,
Lys! et l'un de vous tous pour l'ingénuité.

Autre que ce doux rien par leur lèvre ébruité,
Le baiser, qui tout bas des perfides assure,
Mon sein, vierge de preuve, atteste une morsure
Mystérieuse, due à quelque auguste dent;

Mais, bast! arcane tel élut pour confident
Le jonc vaste et jumeau dont sous l'azur on joue:
Qui, détournant à soi le trouble de la joue
Rêve, dans un solo long, que nous amusions
La beauté d'alentour par des confusions
Fausses entre elle-même et notre chant crédule;
Et de faire aussi haut que l'amour se module
Évanouir du songe ordinaire de dos
Ou de flanc pur suivis avec mes regards clos,
Une sonore, vaine et monotone ligne.

Tâche donc, instrument des fuites, ô maligne
Syrinx, de refleurir aux lacs où tu m'attends!
Moi, de ma rumeur fier, je vais parler longtemps
Des déesses; et par d'idolâtres peintures,
A leur ombre enlever encore des ceintures:

Ainsi, quand des raisins j'ai sucé la clarté,
Pour bannir un regret par ma feinte écarté,
Rieur, j'élève au ciel d'été la grappe vide
Et, soufflant dans ses peaux lumineuses, avide
D'ivresse, jusqu'au soir je regarde au travers.

O nymphes, regonflons des SOUVENIRS divers.
'Mon œil, trouant les joncs, dardait chaque encolure
'Immortelle, qui noie en l'onde sa brûlure
'Avec un cri de rage au ciel de la forêt;
'Et le splendide bain de cheveux disparaît
'Dans les clartés et les frissons, o pierreries!
'J'accours; quand, à mes pieds, s'entrejoignent (meurtries
'De la langueur goûtée à ce mal d'être deux)
'Des dormeuses parmi leurs seuls bras hasardeux;
'Je les ravis, sans les désenlacer, et vole
'A ce massif, haï par l'ombrage frivole,
'De roses tarissant tout parfum au soleil,
'Où notre ébat au jour consumé soit pareil.'
Je t'adore, courroux des vierges, ô délice
Farouche du sacré fardeau nu qui se glisse
Pour fuir ma lèvre en feu buvant, comme un éclair
Tressaille! la frayeur secrète de la chair:
Des pieds de l'inhumaine au cœur de la timide
Que délaisse à la fois une innocence, humide
De larmes folles ou de moins tristes vapeurs.
'Mon crime, c'est d'avoir, gai de vaincre ces peurs
'Traîtresses, divisé la touffe échevelée
'De baisers que les dieux gardaient si bien mêlée;
'Car, à peine j'allais cacher un rire ardent
'Sous les replis heureux d'une seule (gardant
'Par un doigt simple, afin que sa candeur de plume
'Se teignît à l'émoi de sa sœur qui s'allume,
'La petite, naïve et ne rougissant pas:)
'Que de mes bras, défaits par de vagues trépas,
'Cette proie, à jamais ingrate se délivre
'Sans pitié du sanglot dont j'étais encore ivre.'

Tant pis! vers le bonheur d'autres m'entraîneront
Par leur tresse nouée aux cornes de mon front:
Tu sais, ma passion, que, pourpre et déjà mûre,
Chaque grenade éclate et d'abeilles murmure;
Et notre sang, épris de qui le va saisir,
Coule pour tout l'essaim éternel du désir.

A l'heure où ce bois d'or et de cendres se teinte
Une fête s'exalte en la feuillée éteinte:
Etna! c'est parmi toi visité de Vénus
Sur ta lave posant ses talons ingénus,
Quand tonne un somme triste ou s'épuise la flamme.
Je tiens la reine!

   O sûr châtiment . . .

     Non, mais l'âme

De paroles vacante et ce corps alourdi
Tard succombent au fier silence de midi:
Sans plus il faut dormir en l'oubli du blasphème,
Sur le sable altéré gisant et comme j'aime
Ouvrir ma bouche à l'astre efficace des vins!

Couple, adieu; je vais voir l'ombre que tu devins.

THE AFTERNOON OF A FAUN

I would immortalize these nymphs: so bright
Their sunlit colouring, so airy light,
It floats like drowsing down. Loved I a dream?
My doubts, born of oblivious darkness, seem
A subtle tracery of branches grown
The tree's true self—proving that I have known,
Thinking it love, the blushing of a rose.
But think. These nymphs, their loveliness . . . suppose
They bodied forth your senses' fabulous thirst?
Illusion! which the blue eyes of the first,
As cold and chaste as is the weeping spring,
Beget: the other, sighing, passioning,
Is she the wind, warm in your fleece at noon?
No; through this quiet, when a weary swoon
Crushes and chokes the latest faint essay
Of morning, cool against the encroaching day,
There is no murmuring water, save the gush
Of my clear fluted notes; and in the hush
Blows never a wind, save that which through my reed
Puffs out before the rain of notes can speed
Upon the air, with that calm breath of art
That mounts the unwrinkled zenith visibly,
Where inspiration seeks its native sky.
You fringes of a calm Sicilian lake,
The sun's own mirror which I love to take,

Silent beneath your starry flowers, tell
How here I cut the hollow rushes, well
Tamed by my skill, when on the glaucous gold
Of distant lawns about their fountain cold
A living whiteness stirs like a lazy wave;
And at the first slow notes my panpipes gave
These flocking swans, these naiads, rather, fly
Or dive. Noon burns inert and tawny dry,
Nor marks how clean that Hymen slipped away
From me who seek in song the real A.
Wake, then, to the first ardour and the sight,
O lonely faun, of the old fierce white light,
With, lilies, one of you for innocence.
Other than their lips' delicate pretence,
The light caress that quiets treacherous lovers,
My breast, I know not how to tell, discovers
The bitten print of some immortal's kiss.
But hush! a mystery so great as this
I dare not tell, save to my double reed,
Which, sharer of my every joy and need,
Dreams down its cadenced monologues that we
Falsely confuse the beauties that we see
With the bright palpable shapes our song creates:
My flute, as loud as passion modulates,
Purges the common dream of flank and breast,
Seen through closed eyes and inwardly caressed,
Of every empty and monotonous line.

Bloom then, O Syrinx, in thy flight malign,
A reed once more beside our trysting-lake.
Proud of my music, let me often make
A song of goddesses and see their rape
Profanely done on many a painted shape.
So when the grape's transparent juice I drain,
I quell regret for pleasures past and feign
A new real grape. For holding towards the sky
The empty skin, I blow it tight and lie
Dream-drunk till evening, eyeing it.

                              Tell o'er
Remembered joys and plump the grape once more.
Between the reeds I saw their bodies gleam
Who cool no mortal fever in the stream
Crying to the woods the rage of their desire:
And their bright hair went down in jewelled fire

Where crystal broke and dazzled shudderingly.
I check my swift pursuit: for see where lie,
Bruised, being twins in love, by languor sweet,
Two sleeping girls, clasped at my very feet.
I seize and run with them, nor part the pair,
Breaking this covert of frail petals, where
Roses drink scent of the sun and our light play
'Mid tumbled flowers shall match the death of day.
I love that virginal fury—ah, the wild
Thrill when a maiden body shrinks, defiled,
Shuddering like arctic light, from lips that sear
Its nakedness . . . the flesh in secret fear!
Contagiously through my linked pair it flies
Where innocence in either, struggling, dies,
Wet with fond tears or some less piteous dew.
Gay in the conquest of these fears, I grew
So rash that I must needs the sheaf divide
Of ruffled kisses heaven itself had tied.
For as I leaned to stifle in the hair
Of one my passionate laughter (taking care
With a stretched finger, that her innocence
Might stain with her companion's kindling sense
To touch the younger little one, who lay
Child-like unblushing) my ungrateful prey
Slips from me, freed by passion's sudden death,
Nor heeds the frenzy of my sobbing breath.

Let it pass! others of their hair shall twist
A rope to drag me to those joys I missed.
See how the ripe pomegranates bursting red
To quench the thirst of the mumbling bees have bled;
So too our blood, kindled by some chance fire,
Flows for the swarming legions of desire.
At evening, when the woodland green turns gold
And ashen grey, 'mid the quenched leaves, behold!
Red Etna glows, by Venus visited,
Walking the lava with her snowy tread
Whene'er the flames in thunderous slumber die.
I hold the goddess!

Ah, sure penalty!

But the unthinking soul and body swoon
At last beneath the heavy hush of noon.

Forgetful let me lie where summer's drouth
Sifts fine the sand and then with gaping mouth
Dream planet-struck by the grape's round wine-red star.

Nymphs, I shall see the shade that now you are.

Translated by Aldous Huxley

*It is assuredly the most skilful poem in our language; it is the most
musical and the richest in internal relations.*

PAUL VALÉRY
Les Nouvelles Littéraires (February 28, 1931)

FROM HÉRODIADE

HÉRODIADE

Oui, c'est pour moi, pour moi, que je fleuris, déserte!
Vous le savez, jardins d'améthyste, enfouis
Sans fin dans de savants abîmes éblouis,
Ors ignorés, gardant votre antique lumière
Sous le sombre sommeil d'une terre première,
Vous pierres où mes yeux comme de purs bijoux
Empruntent leur clarté mélodieuse, et vous
Métaux qui donnez à ma jeune chevelure
Une splendeur fatale et sa massive allure!
Quant à toi, femme née en des siècles malins
Pour la méchanceté des antres sibyllins,
Qui parles d'un mortel! selon qui, des calices
De mes robes, arôme aux farouches délices,
Sortirait le frisson blanc de ma nudité,
Prophétise que si le tiède azur d'été,
Vers lui nativement la femme se dévoile,
Me voit dans ma pudeur grelottante d'étoile,
Je meurs!

J'aime l'horreur d'être vierge et je veux
Vivre parmi l'effroi que me font mes cheveux
Pour, le soir, retirée en ma couche, reptile
Inviolé sentir en la chair inutile
Le froid scintillement de ta pâle clarté
Toi qui te meurs, toi qui brûles de chasteté,
Nuit blanche de glaçons et de neige cruelle!

Et ta sœur solitaire, ô ma sœur éternelle
Mon rêve montera vers toi: telle déjà
Rare limpidité d'un cœur qui le songea,

Je me crois seule en ma monotone patrie
Et tout, autour de moi, vit dans l'idolâtrie
D'un miroir qui reflète en son calme dormant
Hérodiade au clair regard de diamant . . .
O charme dernier, oui! je le sens, je suis seule.

LA NOURRICE
Madame, allez-vous donc mourir?

HÉRODIADE
                              Non, pauvre aïeule,
Sois calme et, t'éloignant, pardonne à ce cœur dur
Mais avant, si tu veux, clos les volets, l'azur
Séraphique sourit dans les vitres profondes,
Et je déteste, moi, le bel azur!

                              Des ondes
Se bercent et, là-bas, sais-tu pas un pays
Où le sinistre ciel ait les regards haïs
De Vénus qui, le soir, brûle dans le feuillage;
J'y partirais.

                  Allume encore, enfantillage
Dis-tu, ces flambeaux où la cire au feu léger
Pleure parmi l'or vain quelque pleur étranger
Et . . .

LA NOURRICE
          Maintenant?

HÉRODIADE
                        Adieu.
                  Vous mentez, ô fleur nue
De mes lèvres!

          J'attends une chose inconnue
Ou peut-être, ignorant le mystère et vos cris,
Jetez-vous les sanglots suprêmes et meurtris
D'une enfance sentant parmi les rêveries
Se séparer enfin ses froides pierreries.

HÉRODIADE
To mine own self I am a wilderness.
You know it, amethyst gardens numberless
Enfolded in the flaming, subtle deep,
Strange gold, that through the red earth's heavy sleep
Has cherished ancient brightness like a dream,
Stones whence mine eyes, pure jewels, have their gleam

Of icy and melodious radiance, you,
Metals, which into my young tresses drew
A fatal splendour and their manifold grace!
Thou, woman, born into these evil days
Disastrous to the cavern sibylline,
Who speakest, prophesying not of one divine,
But of a mortal, if from that close sheath,
My robes, rustle the wild enchanted breath
In the white quiver of my nakedness,
If the warm air of summer, O prophetess,
(And woman's body obeys that ancient claim)
Behold me in my shivering starry shame,
I die!
The horror of my virginity
Delights me, and I would envelop me
In the terror of my tresses, that, by night,
Inviolate reptile, I might feel the white
And glimmering radiance of thy frozen fire,
Thou that art chaste and diest of desire,
White night of ice and of the cruel snow!
Eternal sister, my lone sister, lo
My dreams uplifted before thee! now, apart,
So rare a crystal is my dreaming heart,
I live in a monotonous land alone,
And all about me lives but in mine own
Image, the idolatrous mirror of my pride,
Mirroring this Hérodiade diamond-eyed.
I am indeed alone, O charm and curse!

NURSE

O lady, would you die then?

HÉRODIADE

No, poor nurse;
Be calm, and leave me; prithee, pardon me,
But, ere thou go, close-to the casement; see
How the seraphical blue in the dim glass smiles,
But I abhor the blue of the sky!
Yet miles
On miles of rocking waves! Know'st not a land
Where, in the pestilent sky, men see the hand
Of Venus, and her shadow in dark leaves?
Thither I go.
Light thou the wax that grieves
In the swift flame, and sheds an alien tear
Over the vain gold; wilt not say in mere
Childishness?

NURSE

Now?

HÉRODIADE

Farewell. You lie, O flower
Of these chill lips!
I wait the unknown hour,
Or, deaf to your crying and that hour supreme,
Utter the lamentation of the dream
Of childhood seeing fall apart in sighs
The icy chaplet of its reveries.

Translated by Arthur Symons

In these two poems [THE AFTERNOON OF A FAUN *and* HÉRODIADE] *I find Mallarmé at the moment when his own desire achieves itself; when he attains Wagner's ideal, that "the most complete work of the poet should be that which, in its final achievement, becomes a perfect music": every word is a jewel, scattering and recapturing sudden fire, every image is a symbol, and the whole poem is visible music.*

ARTHUR SYMONS
Studies in Two Literatures (1924)

JOSÉ-MARIA DE HEREDIA

1 8 4 2 — 1 9 0 5

THE DEATH OF THE EAGLE

Avec un cri sinistre, il tournoie, emporté
Par la trombe, et crispé, buvant d'un trait sublime
La flamme éparse, il plonge au fulgurant abîme.

Heureux qui pour la Gloire ou pour la Liberté,
Dans l'orgueil de la force et l'ivresse du rêve,
Meurt ainsi, d'une mort éblouissante et brève!

A wild scream, and the vortex whirls him down;
    Sublime, he drinks the flames that round him hiss
    And plunges, shriveled, into the abyss.
What joy, for Liberty and Glory's crown,
In pride of might and ecstasy's uplift,
    To die a death so dazzling and so swift!

Les Trophées (1893)
Translated by John Hervey

1317

HENRY JAMES

1 8 4 3 — 1 9 1 6

THE KISS ON THE STAIRS

Facing him, waving him away, she had taken another upward step; but he sprang to the side of the stairs, and brought his hand, above the banister, down hard on her wrist. "Do you mean to tell me that I must marry a woman I hate?"

From her step she looked down into his raised face. "Ah you see it's not true that you're free!" She seemed almost to exult. "It's not true, it's not true!"

He only, at this, like a buffeting swimmer, gave a shake of his head and repeated his question: "Do you mean to tell me I must marry such a woman?"

Fleda gasped too; he held her fast. "No. Anything's better than that."

"Then in God's name what must I do?"

"You must settle that with Mona. You mustn't break faith. Anything's better than that. You must at any rate be utterly sure. She must love you—how can she help it? *I* wouldn't give you up!" said Fleda. She spoke in broken bits, panting out her words. "The great thing is to keep faith. Where's a man if he doesn't? If he doesn't he may be so cruel. So cruel, so cruel, so cruel!" Fleda repeated. "I couldn't have a hand in that, you know: that's my position—that's mine. You offered her marriage. It's a tremendous thing for her." Then looking at him another moment, "*I* wouldn't give you up!" she said again. He still had hold of her arm; she took in his blank dread. With a quick dip of her face she reached his hand with her lips, pressing them to the back of it with a force that doubled the force of her words. "Never, never, never!" she cried; and before he could succeed in seizing her she had turned and, flashing up the stairs, got away from him even faster than she had got away at Ricks.

The Spoils of Poynton (1908)

WILLIAM SHAKESPEARE

1 5 6 4 — 1 6 1 6

A SINGLE FAMISHED KISS

Iniurious time now with a robbers hast,
Crams his ritch theeu'ry vp, hee knowes not how.
As many farewells as be starres in heauen,
With distinct breath, and consign'd kisses to them,
He fumbles vp into a loose adewe:
And skants vs with a single famisht kisse,
Distasted with the salt of broken teares.

Troilus and Cressida (1609)
Act iv, Scene iv

The most famous kisses in literature.

EDITH WHARTON
A Backward Glance (1934)

HENRY JAMES

1 8 4 3 — 1 9 1 6

THE MADONNA OF THE CHAIR

I suffered him at last to lead me directly to the goal of our journey—
the most tenderly fair of Raphael's virgins, the Madonna of the Chair.
Of all the fine pictures of the world, it was to strike me at once as the
work with which criticism has least to do. None betrays less effort, less
of the mechanism of success and of the irrepressible discord between
conception and result that sometimes faintly invalidates noble efforts.
Graceful, human, near to our sympathies as it is, it has nothing of manner,
of method, nothing almost of style; it blooms there in a softness as
rounded and as instinct with harmony as if it were an immediate exhala-
tion of genius. The figure imposes on the spectator a spell of submission
which he scarce knows whether he has given to heavenly purity or to
earthly charm. He is intoxicated with the fragrance of the tenderest
blossom of maternity that ever bloomed among men.

"That's what I call a fine picture," said my companion after we had
gazed a while in silence. "I've a right to say so, for I've copied it so often
and so carefully that I could repeat it now with my eyes shut. Other
works are of Raphael: this is Raphael himself. Others you can praise,
you can qualify, you can measure, explain, account for: this you can
only love and admire. I don't know in what seeming he walked here

below while this divine mood was upon him; but after it surely he could do nothing but die—this world had nothing more to teach him. Think of it a while, my friend, and you'll admit that I'm not raving. Think of his seeing that spotless image not for a moment, for a day, in a happy dream or a restless fever-fit, not as a poet in a five minutes' frenzy—time to snatch his phrase and scribble his immortal stanza; but for days together, while the slow labour of the brush went on, while the foul vapours of life interposed and the fancy ached with tension, fixed, radiant, distinct, as we see it now! What a master, certainly! But ah what a seer!"

"Don't you imagine," I fear I profanely asked, "that he had a model, and that some pretty young woman—"

"As pretty a young woman as you please! It doesn't diminish the miracle. He took his hint of course, and the young woman possibly sat smiling before his canvas. But meanwhile the painter's idea had taken wings. No lovely human outline could charm it to vulgar fact. He saw the fair form made perfect; he rose to the vision without tremor, without effort of wing; he communed with it face to face and resolved into finer and lovelier truth the purity which completes it as the fragrance completes the rose. That's what they call idealism; the word's vastly abused, but the thing's good. It's my own creed at any rate. Lovely Madonna, model at once and muse, I call you to witness that I too am an idealist!"

"An idealist then"—and I really but wanted to draw him further out—"an idealist is a gentleman who says to Nature in the person of a beautiful girl: 'Go to, you're all wrong! Your fine's coarse, your bright's dim, your grace is *gaucherie*. This is the way you should have done it!' Isn't the chance against him?"

He turned on me at first almost angrily—then saw that I was but sowing the false to reap the true. "Look at that picture," he said, "and cease your irreverent mockery! Idealism is *that*! There's no explaining it; one must feel the flame. It says nothing to Nature, or to any beautiful girl, that they won't both forgive. It says to the fair woman: 'Accept me as your artist-friend, lend me your beautiful face, trust me, help me, and your eyes shall be half my masterpiece.' No one so loves and respects the rich realities of nature as the artist whose imagination intensifies them. He knows what a fact may hold—whether Raphael knew, you may judge by his inimitable portrait, behind us there, of Tommaso Inghirami—but his fancy hovers above it as Ariel in the play hovers above the sleeping prince. There's only one Raphael, but an artist may still be an artist. As I said last night, the days of illumination are gone; visions are rare; we've to look long to have them. But in meditation we may still cultivate the ideal; round it, smooth it, perfect it. The result, the result"—here his voice faltered suddenly and he fixed his eyes for a moment on the picture; when they met my own again they were full of tears—"the result may be less than this, but still it may be good, it may be *great!*" he cried with vehemence. "It may hang somewhere, through all the years, in goodly company, and keep the artist's memory warm. Think of being known to mankind after some such fashion as this; of keeping pace with the restless centuries and the changing world; of living on and on in the cunning of an eye and a hand that belong to the dust of ages, a delight and a law to remote generations; of making beauty more and more a force and purity more and more an example!"

"Heaven forbid," I smiled, "that I should take the wind out of your sails! But doesn't it occur to you that besides being strong in his genius Raphael was happy in a certain good faith of which we've lost the trick? There are people, I know, who deny that his spotless Madonnas are anything more than pretty blondes of that period, enhanced by the Raphaelesque touch, which they declare to be then as calculating and commercial as any other. Be that as it may, people's religious and esthetic needs went arm in arm, and there was, as I may say, a demand for the Blessed Virgin, visible and adorable, which must have given firmness to the artist's hand. I'm afraid there's no demand now."

My friend momentarily stared—he shivered and shook his ears under this bucketful of cold water. But he bravely kept up his high tone. "There's always a demand—that ineffable type is one of the eternal needs of man's heart; only pious souls long for it in silence, almost in shame. Let it appear and their faith grows brave. How *should* it appear in this corrupt generation? It can't be made to order. It could indeed when the order came trumpet-toned from the lips of the Church herself and was addressed to genius panting with inspiration. But it can spring now only from the soil of passionate labour and culture. Do you really fancy that while from time to time a man of complete artistic vision is born into the world such an image can perish? The man who paints it has painted everything. The subject admits of every perfection—form, colour, expression, composition. It can be as simple as you please and yet as rich; as broad and free and yet as full of delicate detail. Think of the chance for flesh in the little naked nestling child, irradiating divinity; of the chance for drapery in the chaste and ample garment of the mother. Think of the great story you compress into that simple theme. Think above all of the mother's face and its ineffable suggestiveness, of the mingled burden of joy and trouble, the tenderness turned to worship and the worship turned to far-seeing pity. Then look at it all in perfect line and lovely colour, breathing truth and beauty and mastery."

The Madonna of the Future (1873)

We should seek English literature vainly for a more beautiful description of Raphael's Madonna, than his VIRGIN OF THE CHAIR.

GEORGE MOORE
Avowals (1926)

ARABIA DESERTA

Now longwhile our black booths had been built upon the sandy stretches, lying before the swelling white Nefûd side: the lofty coast of Irnàn in front, whose cragged breaches, where is any footing for small herbs nourished of this barren atmosphere, are the harbour of wild goats, which never drink. The summer's night at end, the sun stands up as a crown of hostile flames from that huge covert of inhospitable sandstone bergs; the desert day dawns not little and little, but it is noontide in an hour. The sun, entering as a tyrant upon the waste landscape, darts upon us a torment of fiery beams, not to be remitted till the far-off evening.—No matins here of birds; not a rock partridge-cock, calling with blithesome chuckle over the extreme waterless desolation. Grave is that giddy heat upon the crown of the head; the ears tingle with a flickering shrillness, a subtle crepitation it seems, in the glassiness of this sun-stricken nature: the hot sand-blink is in the eyes, and there is little refreshment to find in the tents' shelter; the worsted booths leak to this fiery rain of sunny light. Mountains looming like dry bones through the thin air, stand far around about us: the savage flank of Ybba Moghrair, the high spire and ruinous stacks of el-Jebâl, Chebàd, the coast of Helwàn! Herds of the weak nomad camels waver dispersedly, seeking pasture in the midst of this hollow fainting country, where but lately the swarming locusts have fretted every green thing. This silent air burning about us, we endure breathless till the assr: when the dazing Arabs in the tents revive after their heavy hours. The lingering day draws down to the sun-setting; the herdsmen, weary of the sun, come again with the cattle, to taste in their menzils the first sweetness of mirth and repose.—The day is done, and there rises the nightly freshness of this purest mountain air: and then to the cheerful song and the cup at the common fire. The moon rises ruddy from that solemn obscurity of jebel like a mighty beacon:—and the morrow will be as this day, days deadly drowned in the sun of the summer wilderness.

Travels in Arabia Deserta (1888)

This is the achievement of a pure and deliberate art; very little prose of this assured magnificence has been written in our day; and certainly no other book has been maintained on such a level for centuries. ARABIA DESERTA *is incomparable.*

JOHN MIDDLETON MURRY
Countries of the Mind (1922)

PAUL VERLAINE

1 8 4 4 — 1 8 9 6

CHANSON D'AUTOMNE

Les sanglots longs
Des violons
    De l'automne
Blessent mon cœur
D'une langueur
    Monotone.

Tout suffocant
Et blême, quand
    Sonne l'heure,
Je me souviens
Des jours anciens
    Et je pleure.

Et je m'en vais
Au vent mauvais
    Qui m'emporte
Deçà, delà,
Pareil à la
    Feuille morte.

When a sighing begins
In the violins
Of the autumn-song,
My heart is drowned
In the slow sound
Languorous and long.

Pale as with pain,
Breath fails me when
The hour tolls deep.
My thoughts recover
The days that are over,
And I weep.

1323

And I go
Where the winds know,
Broken and brief,
To and fro,
As the winds blow
A dead leaf.

Poèmes saturniens (1867)
Translated by Arthur Symons

The miraculous song.

FRANÇOIS PORCHÉ
Verlaine tel qu'il fut (1933)

PAUL VERLAINE

1 8 4 4 — 1 8 9 6

CLAIR DE LUNE

Votre âme est un paysage choisi
Que vont charmant masques et bergamasques
Jouant du luth et dansant et quasi
Tristes sous leurs déguisements fantasques.

Tout en chantant sur le mode mineur
L'amour vainqueur et la vie opportune,
Ils n'ont pas l'air de croire à leur bonheur
Et leur chanson se mêle au clair de lune,

Au calme clair de lune triste et beau,
Qui fait rêver les oiseaux dans les arbres
Et sangloter d'extase les jets d'eau,
Les grands jets d'eau sveltes parmi les marbres.

Your soul is a sealed garden, and there go
With masque and bergamasque fair companies
Playing on lutes and dancing and as though
Sad under their fantastic fripperies.

Though they in minor keys go carolling
Of love the conqueror and of life the boon
They seem to doubt the happiness they sing
And the song melts into the light of the moon,

1324

The sad light of the moon, so lovely fair
That all the birds dream in the leafy shade
And the slim fountains sob into the air
Among the marble statues in the glade.

Fêtes galantes (1869)
Translated by Arthur Symons

As purely decorative writing, however, the FÊTES GALANTES *are in their way unique. What could be better, of its sort?*

HAROLD NICOLSON
Paul Verlaine (1921)

PAUL VERLAINE

1 8 4 4 — 1 8 9 6

PARSIFAL

Parsifal a vaincu les Filles, leur gentil
Babil et la luxure amusante—et sa pente
Vers la Chair de garçon vierge que cela tente
D'aimer les seins légers et ce gentil babil;

Il a vaincu la Femme belle, au cœur subtil,
Étalant ses bras frais et sa gorge excitante;
Il a vaincu l'Enfer et rentre sous sa tente
Avec un lourd trophée à son bras puéril,

Avec la lance qui perça le Flanc suprême!
Il a guéri le roi, le voici roi lui-même,
Et prêtre du très saint Trésor essentiel.

En robe d'or il adore, gloire et symbole,
Le vase pur où resplendit le Sang réel,
—Et, ô ces voix d'enfants chantant dans la coupole!

Parsifal has overcome the Lemans,
Their pretty babbling and amusing lusts,
And his own virginal boyhood's fleshly leanings
Teased by their pretty babbling and light breasts;

Overcome the Woman, beautiful, subtle-hearted,
Spreading her breast and fresh arms,
Overcome Hell; he strides into the tent
A heavy trophy on his boyish arm;

The lance that pierced the side of the Most High;
He cured the king and now is king himself,
Priest of the Essence, that Most Holy Treasure;

In gold robe, he adores the glory, the sign,
The chalice in which glows the Real Blood,
—Oh, all that children's singing from the Minster!

Amour (1888)
Translated by Denis Devlin

I know of no more perfect thing than this sonnet. The hiatus in the last line was at first a little trying, but I have learned to love it; not in Baudelaire nor even in Poe is there more beautiful poetry to be found.

GEORGE MOORE
Confessions of a Young Man (1888)

ANATOLE FRANCE

1 8 4 4 — 1 9 2 4

GOOD NIGHT, SWEET PRINCE

Vous êtes de tous les temps et de tous les pays. Vous n'avez pas vieilli d'une heure en trois siècles. Votre âme a l'âge de chacune de nos âmes. Nous vivons ensemble, prince Hamlet, et vous êtes ce que nous sommes, un homme au milieu du mal universel. On vous a chicané sur vos paroles et sur vos actions. On a montré que vous n'étiez pas d'accord avec vous-même. Comment saisir cet insaisissable personnage? a-t-on dit. Il pense tour à tour comme un moine du moyen âge et comme un savant de la Renaissance; il a la tête philosophique et pourtant pleine de diableries. Il a horreur du mensonge et sa vie n'est qu'un long mensonge. Il est irrésolu, c'est visible, et pourtant certains critiques l'ont jugé plein de décision, sans qu'on puisse leur donner tout à fait tort. Enfin, on a pré-tendu, mon prince, que vous étiez un magasin de pensées, un amas de contradictions et non pas un être humain. Mais c'est là, au contraire, le signe de votre profonde humanité. Vous êtes prompt et lent, audacieux et timide, bienveillant et cruel, vous croyez et vous doutez, vous êtes sage et par-dessus tout vous êtes fou. En un mot, vous vivez. Qui de nous ne vous ressemble en quelque chose? Qui de nous pense sans contradiction et agit sans incohérence? Qui de nous n'est fou? Qui de nous ne vous dit avec un mélange de pitié, de sympathie, d'admiration et d'horreur: "Bonne nuit, aimable prince!"

You belong to all times and all countries. You have not aged an hour in three centuries. Your soul is as old as each of our souls. You live with us, Prince Hamlet, and you are what we are, a man in the midst of universal evil. They have cavilled at your words and your actions. They have shown you are inconsistent. How are we to comprehend this incomprehensible character, they said. He thinks alternately like a monk of the Middle Ages and like a scholar of the Renaissance. He has the mind of a philosopher, and yet is full of deviltries. He has a horror of lies but his life is one long lie. He is plainly irresolute, and yet certain critics have judged him full of resolution, without being entirely wrong. Finally, my Prince, they have represented you as a storehouse of thought, a mass of contradictions, and not a human being. But that, on the contrary, is the token of your profound humanity. You are prompt and slow, bold and timid, kind and cruel; you believe and you doubt, you are wise, and above all you are mad. In a word, you live. Who of us does not resemble you in some way? Who of us thinks without contradiction, acts without inconsistency? Who of us is not mad? Who of us may not say to you with a mixture of pity, sympathy, admiration and horror; "Good night, sweet Prince!"

La Vie littéraire (1888–92)

It is just this mystery, emanating maybe from a man long since dust, which sets Hamlet in the timeless and universal theatre of our imagination, which so liberates him from his Elizabethan shell that we forget it altogether and count him a king of infinity. One does not usually look to the Gallic muse for songs in honour of Shakespeare. But I know no better tribute to the eternal Hamlet than a prose apostrophe by Anatole France after an evening at the Comédie-Française.

JOHN DOVER WILSON
Hamlet (1934)

FRIEDRICH NIETZSCHE

1 8 4 4 — 1 9 0 0

DIE SIEBEN SIEGEL

(Oder: das Ja- und Amen-Lied.)

1

Wenn ich ein Wahrsager bin und voll jenes wahrsagerischen Geistes, der auf hohem Joche zwischen
zwei Meeren wandelt,—

zwischen Vergangenem und Zukünftigem als schwere
Wolke wandelt,—schwülen Niederungen feind und Allem,
was müde ist und nicht sterben noch leben kann:

zum Blitze bereit im dunklen Busen und zum erlösenden
Lichtstrahle, schwanger von Blitzen, die Ja! sagen, Ja! lachen,
zu wahrsagerischen Blitzstrahlen:—

—selig aber ist der also Schwangere! Und wahrlich,
lange muss als schweres Wetter am Berge hängen, wer einst
das Licht der Zukunft zünden soll!—

Oh wie sollte ich nicht nach der Ewigkeit brünstig sein
und nach dem hochzeitlichen Ring der Ringe,—dem Ring
der Wiederkunft!

Nie noch fand ich das Weib, von dem ich Kinder mochte,
es sei denn dieses Weib, das ich liebe: denn ich liebe dich,
oh Ewigkeit!

Denn ich liebe dich, oh Ewigkeit!

2

Wenn mein Zorn je Gräber brach, Grenzsteine rückte
und alte Tafeln zerbrochen in steile Tiefen rollte:

Wenn mein Hohn je vermoderte Worte zerblies, und ich
wie ein Besen kam den Kreuzspinnen und als Fegewind
alten verdumpften Grabkammern:

Wenn ich je frohlockend sass, wo alte Götter begraben
liegen, weltsegnend, weltliebend neben den Denkmalen alter
Welt-Verleumder:—

—denn selbst Kirchen und Gottes-Gräber liebe ich, wenn
der Himmel erst reinen Auges durch ihre zerbrochenen
Decken blickt; gern sitze ich gleich Gras und rothem Mohne
auf zerbrochnen Kirchen—

Oh wie sollte ich nicht nach der Ewigkeit brünstig sein
und nach dem hochzeitlichen Ring der Ringe,—dem Ring
der Wiederkunft?

Nie noch fand ich das Weib, von dem ich Kinder mochte,
es sei denn dieses Weib, das ich liebe: denn ich liebe dich,
oh Ewigkeit!

Denn ich liebe dich, oh Ewigkeit!

3

Wenn je ein Hauch zu mir kam vom schöpferischen
Hauche und von jener himmlischen Noth, die noch
Zufälle zwingt, Sternen-Reigen zu tanzen:

Wenn ich je mit dem Lachen des schöpferischen Blitzes
lachte, dem der lange Donner der That grollend, aber ge-
horsam nachfolgt:

Wenn ich je am Göttertisch der Erde mit Göttern Würfel
spielte, dass die Erde bebte und brach und Feuerflüsse her-
aufschnob:—

—denn ein Göttertisch ist die Erde, und zitternd von
schöpferischen neuen Worten und Götter-Würfen:—

Oh wie sollte ich nicht nach der Ewigkeit brünstig sein
und nach dem hochzeitlichen Ring der Ringe,—dem Ring
der Wiederkunft?

Nie noch fand ich das Weib, von dem ich Kinder mochte,
es sei denn dieses Weib, das ich liebe: denn ich liebe dich,
oh Ewigkeit!

Denn ich liebe dich, oh Ewigkeit!

4

Wenn ich je vollen Zuges trank aus jenem schäumen-
den Würz- und Mischkruge, in dem alle Dinge gut
gemischt sind:

Wenn meine Hand je Fernstes zum Nächsten goss, und
Feuer zu Geist und Lust zu Leid und Schlimmstes zum
Gütigsten:

Wenn ich selber ein Korn bin von jenem erlösenden
Salze, welches macht, dass alle Dinge im Mischkruge gut sich
mischen:—

—denn es giebt ein Salz, das Gutes mit Bösem bindet;
und auch das Böseste ist zum Würzen würdig und zum
letzten Ueberschäumen:—

Oh wie sollte ich nicht nach der Ewigkeit brünstig sein
und nach dem hochzeitlichen Ring der Ringe,—dem Ring
der Wiederkunft?

Nie noch fand ich das Weib, von dem ich Kinder mochte,
es sei denn dieses Weib, das ich liebe: denn ich liebe dich,
oh Ewigkeit!

Denn ich liebe dich, oh Ewigkeit!

5

Wenn ich dem Meere hold bin und Allem, was Meeres-
Art ist, und am holdesten noch, wenn es mir zornig
widerspricht:

Wenn jene suchende Lust in mir ist, die nach Unent-
decktem die Segel treibt, wenn eine Seefahrer-Lust in meiner
Lust ist:

Wenn je mein Frohlocken rief: „die Küste schwand—
nun fiel mir die letzte Kette ab—

—das Grenzenlose braust um mich, weit hinaus glänzt
mir Raum und Zeit, wohlan! wohlauf! altes Herz!"—

Oh wie sollte ich nicht nach der Ewigkeit brünstig sein
und nach dem hochzeitlichen Ring der Ringe,—dem Ring
der Wiederkunft?

Nie noch fand ich das Weib, von dem ich Kinder mochte,
es sei denn dieses Weib, das ich liebe: denn ich liebe dich,
oh Ewigkeit!

Denn ich liebe dich, oh Ewigkeit!

6

Wenn meine Tugend eines Tänzers Tugend ist, und
ich oft mit beiden Füssen in gold-smaragdenes Ent-
zücken sprang:

Wenn meine Bosheit eine lachende Bosheit ist, heimisch
unter Rosenhängen und Lilien-Hecken:

—im Lachen nämlich ist alles Böse bei einander, aber
heilig- und losgesprochen durch seine eigne Seligkeit:—

Und wenn Das mein A und O ist, dass alles Schwere
leicht, aller Leib Tänzer, aller Geist Vogel werde: und
wahrlich, Das ist mein A und O!—

Oh wie sollte ich nicht nach der Ewigkeit brünstig sein
und nach dem hochzeitlichen Ring der Ringe,—dem Ring
der Wiederkunft?

Nie noch fand ich das Weib, von dem ich Kinder mochte,
es sei denn dieses Weib, das ich liebe: denn ich liebe dich,
oh Ewigkeit!

Denn ich liebe dich, oh Ewigkeit!

Wenn ich je stille Himmel über mir ausspannte und mit eignen Flügeln in eigne Himmel flog:

Wenn ich spielend in tiefen Licht-Fernen schwamm und meiner Freiheit Vogel-Weisheit kam:—

—so aber spricht Vogel-Weisheit: „Siehe, es giebt kein Oben, kein Unten! Wirf dich umher, hinaus, zurück, du Leichter! Singe! sprich nicht mehr!

—sind alle Worte nicht für die Schweren gemacht? Lügen dem Leichten nicht alle Worte! Singe! sprich nicht mehr!"—

Oh wie sollte ich nicht nach der Ewigkeit brünstig sein und nach dem hochzeitlichen Ring der Ringe,—dem Ring der Wiederkunft?

Nie noch fand ich das Weib, von dem ich Kinder mochte, es sei denn dieses Weib, das ich liebe: denn ich liebe dich, oh Ewigkeit!

Denn ich liebe dich, oh Ewigkeit!

THE SEVEN SEALS

(*Or the Yea and Amen Lay.*)

1

If I be a diviner and full of the divining spirit which wandereth on high mountain-ridges, 'twixt two seas,—

Wandereth 'twixt the past and the future as a heavy cloud—hostile to sultry plains, and to all that is weary and can neither die nor live:

Ready for lightning in its dark bosom, and for the redeeming flash of light, charged with lightnings which say Yea! which laugh Yea! ready for divining flashes of lightning:—

—Blessed, however, is he who is thus charged! And verily, long must he hang like a heavy tempest on the mountain, who shall one day kindle the light of the future!—

Oh, how could I not be ardent for Eternity and for the marriage-ring of rings—the ring of the return?

Never yet have I found the woman by whom I should like to have children, unless it be this woman whom I love: for I love thee, O Eternity!

For I love thee, O Eternity!

2

If ever my wrath hath burst graves, shifted landmarks, or rolled old shattered tables into precipitous depths:

If ever my scorn hath scattered mouldered words to the winds, and if I have come like a besom to cross-spiders, and as a cleansing wind to old charnel-houses:

If ever I have sat rejoicing where old Gods lie buried, world-blessing, world-loving, beside the monuments of old world-maligners:—

—For even churches and Gods'-graves do I love, if only heaven looketh through their ruined roofs with pure eyes; gladly do I sit like grass and red poppies on ruined churches—

Oh, how could I not be ardent for Eternity, and for the marriage-ring of rings—the ring of the return?

Never yet have I found the woman by whom I should like to have children, unless it be this woman whom I love: for I love thee, O Eternity!

For I love thee, O Eternity!

3

If ever a breath hath come to me of the creative breath, and of the heavenly necessity which compelleth even chances to dance star-dances:

If ever I have laughed with the laughter of the creative lightning, to which the long thunder of the deed followeth, grumblingly, but obediently:

If ever I have played dice with the Gods at the divine table of the earth, so that the earth quaked and ruptured, and snorted forth fire-streams:—

—For a divine table is the earth, and trembling with new creative dictums and dice-casts of the Gods:

Oh, how could I not be ardent for Eternity, and for the marriage-ring of rings—the ring of the return?

Never yet have I found the woman by whom I should like to have children, unless it be this woman whom I love: for I love thee, O Eternity!

For I love thee, O Eternity!

4

If ever I have drunk a full draught of the foaming spice- and confection-bowl in which all things are well mixed:

If ever my hand hath mingled the furthest with the nearest, fire with spirit, joy with sorrow, and the harshest with the kindest:

If I myself am a grain of the saving salt which maketh everything in the confection-bowl mix well:—

—For there is a salt which uniteth good with evil; and even the evilest is worthy, as spicing and as final overfoaming:—

Oh, how could I not be ardent for Eternity, and for the marriage-ring of rings—the ring of the return?

Never yet have I found the woman by whom I should like to have children, unless it be this woman whom I love: for I love thee, O Eternity!

For I love thee, O Eternity!

5

If I be fond of the sea, and all that is sealike, and fondest of it when it angrily contradicteth me:

If the exploring delight be in me, which impelleth sails to the undiscovered, if the seafarer's delight be in my delight:

If ever my rejoicing hath called out: "The shore hath vanished,— now hath fallen from me the last chain—

The boundless roareth around me, far away sparkle for me space and time,—well! cheer up! old heart!"—

Oh, how could I not be ardent for Eternity, and for the marriage-ring of rings—the ring of the return?

Never yet have I found the woman by whom I should like to have children, unless it be this woman whom I love: for I love thee, O Eternity!

For I love thee, O Eternity!

6

If my virtue be a dancer's virtue, and if I have often sprung with both feet into golden-emerald rapture:

If my wickedness be a laughing wickedness, at home among rose-banks and hedges of lilies:

—For in laughter is all evil present, but it is sanctified and absolved by its own bliss:—

And if it be my Alpha and Omega that everything heavy shall become light, every body a dancer, and every spirit a bird: and verily, that is my Alpha and Omega!—

Oh, how could I not be ardent for Eternity, and for the marriage-ring of rings—the ring of the return?

Never yet have I found the woman by whom I should like to have children, unless it be this woman whom I love: for I love thee, O Eternity!

For I love thee, O Eternity!

7

If ever I have spread out a tranquil heaven above me, and have flown into mine own heaven with mine own pinions:

If I have swum playfully in profound luminous distances, and if my freedom's avian wisdom hath come to me:—

—Thus however speaketh avian wisdom:—"Lo, there is no above and no below! Throw thyself about,—outward, backward, thou light one! Sing! speak no more!

—Are not all words made for the heavy? Do not all words lie to the light ones? Sing! speak no more!"—

Oh, how could I not be ardent for Eternity, and for the marriage-ring of rings—the ring of the return?

Never yet have I found the woman by whom I should like to have children, unless it be this woman whom I love: for I love thee, O Eternity!

For I love thee, O Eternity!

Also Sprach Zarathustra (1883–85)
Translated by Thomas Common

To communicate a state, an inner tension of pathos by means of signs, including the tempo of these signs,—that is the meaning of every style; and in view of the fact that the multiplicity of inner states in me is enormous, I am capable of many kinds of style—in short, the most multifarious art of style that any man has ever had at his disposal. Any style is GOOD *which genuinely communicates an inner condition, which does not blunder over the signs, over the tempo of the signs, or over* MOODS— *all the laws of phrasing are the outcome of representing moods artistically. Good style, in itself, is a piece of sheer foolery, mere idealism, like "beauty in itself," for instance, or "goodness in itself," or "the thing-in-itself." All this takes for granted, of course, that there exist ears that can hear, and such men as are capable and worthy of a like pathos, that those are not wanting unto whom one may communicate one's self. . . . No one has ever existed who has had more novel, more strange, and purposely created art forms to fling to the winds. The fact that such things were possible in the German language still awaited proof; formerly, I myself would have denied most emphatically that it was possible. Before my time people did not know what could be done with the German language—what could be done with language in general. The art of grand rhythm, of grand style in periods, for expressing the tremendous fluctuations of sublime and superhuman passion, was first discovered by me: with the dithyramb entitled "The Seven Seals," which constitutes the last discourse of the third part of Zarathustra, I soared miles above all that which heretofore has been called poetry.*

FRIEDRICH NIETZSCHE
Ecce Homo (1888)
Translated by Anthony M. Ludovici

THE LEADEN ECHO
AND THE GOLDEN ECHO

(Maidens' song from St. Winefred's Well)

THE LEADEN ECHO

How to kéep—is there ány any, is there none such, nowhere
    known some, bow or brooch or braid or brace, láce, latch
    or catch or key to keep
Back beauty, keep it, beauty, beauty, beauty, . . . from vanishing
    away?
Ó is there no frowning of these wrinkles, rankèd wrinkles deep,
Dówn? no waving off of these most mournful messengers, still
    messengers, sad and stealing messengers of grey?
No there's none, there's none, O no there's none,
Nor can you long be, what you now are, called fair,
Do what you may do, what, do what you may,
And wisdom is early to despair:
Be beginning; since, no, nothing can be done
To keep at bay
Age and age's evils, hoar hair,
Ruck and wrinkle, drooping, dying, death's worst, winding
    sheets, tombs and worms and tumbling to decay;
So be beginning, be beginning to despair.
O there's none; no no no there's none:
Be beginning to despair, to despair,
Despair, despair, despair, despair.

THE GOLDEN ECHO

      Spare!
There ís one, yes I have one (Hush there!);
Only not within seeing of the sun,
Not within the singeing of the strong sun,
Tall sun's tingeing, or treacherous the tainting of the earth's air,
Somewhere elsewhere there is ah well where! one,
Oñe. Yes I can tell such a key, I do know such a place,
Where whatever's prized and passes of us, everything that's
    fresh and fast flying of us, seems to us sweet of us and
    swiftly away with, done away with, undone,

Undone, done with, soon done with, and yet dearly and
   dangerously sweet
Of us, the wimpled-water-dimpled, not-by-morning-matchèd face,
The flower of beauty, fleece of beauty, too too apt to, ah! to fleet,
Never fleets móre, fastened with the tenderest truth
To its own best being and its loveliness of youth: it is an ever-
   lastingness of, O it is an all youth!
Come then, your ways and airs and looks, locks, maiden gear,
   gallantry and gaiety and grace,
Winning ways, airs innocent, maiden manners, sweet looks,
   loose locks, long locks, lovelocks, gaygear, going gallant,
   girlgrace—
Resign them, sign them, seal them, send them, motion them
   with breath,
And with sighs soaring, soaring síghs deliver
Them; beauty-in-the-ghost, deliver it, early now, long before
   death
Give beauty back, beauty, beauty, beauty, back to God, beauty's
   self and beauty's giver.
See; not a hair is, not an eyelash, not the least lash lost; every hair
Is, hair of the head, numbered.
Nay, what we had lighthanded left in surly the mere mould
Will have waked and have waxed and have walked with the wind
   what while we slept,
This side, that side hurling a heavyheaded hundredfold
What while we, while we slumbered.
O then, weary then whý should we tread? O why are we so
   haggard at the heart, so care-coiled, care-killed, so fagged,
   so fashed, so cogged, so cumbered,
When the thing we freely fórfeit is kept with fonder a care,
Fonder a care kept than we could have kept it, kept
Far with fonder a care (and we, we should have lost it) finer, fonder
A care kept.—Where kept? Do but tell us where kept, where.—
Yonder.—What high as that! We follow, now we follow.—
   Yonder, yes yonder, yonder,
Yonder.

(1882)

The most remarkable technical achievement of Victorian poetry.

CECIL DAY LEWIS
A Hope for Poetry (1934)

1 8 4 4 — 1 8 8 9

SONNET

Justus quidem tu es, Domine, si disputem tecum: verumtamen justa
loquar ad te: Quare via impiorum prosperatur? &c.

Thou art indeed just, Lord, if I contend
With thee; but, sir, so what I plead is just.
Why do sinners' ways prosper? and why must
Disappointment all I endeavour end?

Wert thou my enemy, O thou my friend,
How wouldst thou worse, I wonder, than thou dost
Defeat, thwart me? Oh, the sots and thralls of lust
Do in spare hours more thrive than I that spend,
Sir, life upon thy cause. See, banks and brakes
Now, leavèd how thick! lacèd they are again
With fretty chervil, look, and fresh wind shakes
Them; birds build—but not I build; no, but strain,
Time's eunuch, and not breed one work that wakes.
Mine, O thou lord of life, send my roots rain.

(1889)

Never, I think, has the just man's complaint against the universe been
put more forcibly, worded more tersely and fiercely than in Hopkins's
sonnet.

ALDOUS HUXLEY
Texts & Pretexts (1933)

GUY DE MAUPASSANT

1 8 5 0 — 1 8 9 3

A WINTER LANDSCAPE
IN THE EARLY MORNING

Un rideau de flocons blancs ininterrompu miroitait sans cesse en
descendant vers la terre; il effaçait les formes, poudrait les choses d'une
mousse de glace; et l'on n'entendait plus, dans le grand silence de la

ville calme et ensevelie sous l'hiver, que ce froissement vague, innommable et flottant, de la neige qui tombe, plutôt sensation que bruit, entremêlement d'atomes légers qui semblaient emplir l'espace, couvrir le monde.

A curtain of glistening snow-flakes descended towards the earth, veiling every human form and covering inanimate objects with an icy fleece. In the intense stillness of the town, plunged in the deep repose of winter, no sound was audible save that vague, indefinable, fluttering whisper of the falling snow, felt rather than heard, the mingling of airy atoms, which seemed to fill all space and envelop the whole world.

Boule de Suif (1880)
Translated by Marjorie Laurie

This sentence . . . seems to me one of the most perfect ever written.

MAURICE BARING
Have You Anything to Declare? (1936)

ARTHUR RIMBAUD

1 8 5 4 — 1 8 9 1

BATEAU IVRE

Comme je descendais des Fleuves impassibles,
Je ne me sentis plus guidé par les haleurs:
Des Peaux-Rouges criards les avaient pris pour cibles,
Les ayant cloués nus aux poteaux de couleurs.

J'étais insoucieux de tous les équipages,
Porteur de blés flamands ou de cotons anglais.
Quand avec mes haleurs ont fini ces tapages,
Les fleuves m'ont laissé descendre où je voulais.

Dans les clapotements furieux des marées,
Moi, l'autre hiver, plus sourd que les cerveaux d'enfants,
Je courus! et les Péninsules démarrées
N'ont pas subi tohu-bohus plus triomphants.

La tempête a béni mes éveils maritimes.
Plus léger qu'un bouchon j'ai dansé sur les flots
Qu'on appelle rouleurs éternels de victimes,
Dix nuits, sans regretter l'œil niais des falots.

Plus douce qu'aux enfants la chair des pommes sures
L'eau verte pénétra ma coque de sapin
Et des taches de vins bleus et des vomissures
Me lava, dispersant gouvernail et grappin.

Et, dès lors, je me suis baigné dans le poème
De la mer infusé d'astres et lactescent,
Dévorant les azurs verts où, flottaison blême
Et ravie, un noyé pensif, parfois, descend;

Où, teignant tout à coup les bleuités, délires
Et rhythmes lents sous les rutilements du jour,
Plus fortes que l'alcool, plus vastes que vos lyres,
Fermentent les rousseurs amères de l'amour!

Je sais les cieux crevant en éclairs, et les trombes
Et les ressacs et les courants; je sais le soir,
L'aube exaltée ainsi qu'un peuple de colombes,
Et j'ai vu quelquefois ce que l'homme a cru voir.

J'ai vu le soleil bas taché d'horreurs mystiques
Illuminant de longs figements violets,
Pareils à des acteurs de drames très antiques,
Les flots roulant au loin leurs frissons de volets.

J'ai rêvé la nuit verte aux neiges éblouies,
Baisers montant aux yeux des mers avec lenteur,
La circulation des sèves inouïes
Et l'éveil jaune et bleu des phosphores chanteurs.

J'ai suivi, des mois pleins, pareille aux vacheries
Hystériques, la houle à l'assaut des récifs,
Sans songer que les pieds lumineux des Maries
Pussent forcer le mufle aux Océans poussifs.

J'ai heurté, savez-vous? d'incroyables Florides
Mêlant aux fleurs des yeux de panthères aux peaux
D'hommes, des arcs-en-ciel tendus comme des brides,
Sous l'horizon des mers, à de glauques troupeaux.

J'ai vu fermenter les marais, énormes nasses
Où pourrit dans les joncs tout un Léviathan,
Des écroulements d'eaux au milieu des bonaces
Et les lointains vers les gouffres cataractant!

Glaciers, soleils d'argent, flots nacreux, cieux de braises,
Échouages hideux au fond des golfes bruns
Où les serpents géants dévorés des punaises
Choient des arbres tordus avec de noirs parfums!

J'aurais voulu montrer aux enfants ces dorades
Du flot bleu, ces poissons d'or, ces poissons chantants.
Des écumes de fleurs ont béni mes dérades,
Et d'ineffables vents m'ont ailé par instants.

Parfois, martyr lassé des pôles et des zones,
La mer, dont le sanglot faisait mon roulis doux,
Montait vers moi ses fleurs d'ombre aux ventouses jaunes
Et je restais ainsi qu'une femme à genoux,

Presqu'île ballottant sur mes bords les querelles
Et les fientes d'oiseaux clabaudeurs aux yeux blonds,
Et je voguais lorsqu'à travers mes liens frêles
Des noyés descendaient dormir à reculons . . .

Or, moi, bateau perdu sous les cheveux des anses,
Jeté par l'ouragan dans l'éther sans oiseau,
Moi dont les Monitors et les voiliers des Hanses
N'auraient pas repêché la carcasse ivre d'eau,

Libre, fumant, monté de brumes violettes,
Moi qui trouais le ciel rougeoyant comme un mur
Qui porte, confiture exquise aux bons poètes,
Des lichens de soleil et des morves d'azur,

Qui courais taché de lunules électriques,
Planche folle, escorté des hippocampes noirs,
Quand les Juillets faisaient crouler à coups de triques
Les cieux ultramarins aux ardents entonnoirs,

Moi qui tremblais, sentant geindre à cinquante lieues
Le rut des Béhémots et des Maelstroms épais,
Fileur éternel des immobilités bleues,
Je regrette l'Europe aux anciens parapets.

J'ai vu des archipels sidéraux! et des îles
Dont les cieux délirants sont ouverts au vogueur:
Est-ce en ces nuits sans fond que tu dors et t'exiles,
Million d'oiseaux d'or, ô future Vigueur?

Mais, vrai, j'ai trop pleuré. Les aubes sont navrantes,
Toute lune est atroce et tout soleil amer.
L'âcre amour m'a gonflé de torpeurs enivrantes.
Oh! que ma quille éclate! Oh! que j'aille à la mer!

Si je désire une eau d'Europe, c'est la flache
Noire et froide où vers le crépuscule embaumé
Un enfant accroupi, plein de tristesse, lâche
Un bateau frêle comme un papillon de mai.

Je ne puis plus, baigné de vos langueurs, ô lames,
Enlever leur sillage aux porteurs de cotons,
Ni traverser l'orgueil des drapeaux et des flammes,
Ni nager sous les yeux horribles des pontons!

THE DRUNKEN BOAT

As I proceeded down along impassive rivers,
I lost my crew of haulers; they'd been seized by hosts
Of whooping Redskins, who had emptied out their quivers
Against these naked targets, nailed to coloured posts.

Little I cared for any crew I bore, a rover
With Flemish wheat or English cottons in my hold.
When once the tribulations of my crew were over,
The rivers let me go where my own fancy told.

Amid the fury of the loudly chopping tide,
I, just last winter, with a child's insensate brain,
Ah, how I raced! And no Peninsulas untied
Were ever tossed in more triumphant hurricane.

The blessing of the storm on my sea-watch was shed.
More buoyant than a cork I darted for ten nights
Over the waves, those famed old trundlers of the dead,
Nor missed the foolish blink of homely warning lights.

The wash of the green water on my shell of pine,
Sweeter than apples to a child its pungent edge;
It cleansed me of the stains of vomits and blue wine
And carried off with it the rudder and the kedge.

And afterwards down through the poem of the sea,
A milky foam infused with stars, frantic I dive
Down through green heavens where, descending pensively,
Sometimes the pallid remnants of the drowned arrive;

Where suddenly the bluish tracts dissolve, desires
And rhythmic languors stir beneath the day's full glow.
Stronger than alcohol and vaster than your lyres,
The bitter humours of fermenting passion flow!

I know how lightning splits the skies, the current roves;
I know the surf and waterspouts and evening's fall;
I've seen the dawn arisen like a flock of doves;
Sometimes I've seen what men believe they can recall.

I've seen the low sun blotched with blasphemies sublime,
Projecting vividly long, violet formations
Which, like tragedians in very ancient mime
Bestride the latticed waves, that speed remote vibrations.

My dreams were of green night and its bedazzled snow,
Of kisses slowly mounting up to the sea's eyes,
Of winding courses where unheard-of fluids go,
Flares blue and yellow that from singing phosphors rise.

For whole months at a time I've ridden with the surge
That like mad byres a-toss keeps battering the reefs,
Nor thought that the bright touch of Mary's feet could urge
A muzzle on the seas, muting their wheezy griefs.

And, yes, on Florida's beyond belief I've fetched,
Where flowers and eyes of panthers mingle in confusion,
Panthers with human skin, rainbows like bridles stretched
Controlling glaucous herds beneath the sea's horizon.

I've seen fermenting marshes like huge lobster-traps
Where in the rushes rots a whole Leviathan,
Or in the midst of calm the water's face collapse
And cataracts pour in from all the distant span.

Glaciers, silver suns, pearl waves and skies afire,
Brown gulfs with loathsome strands in whose profundities
Huge serpents, vermin-plagued, drop down into the mire
With black effluvium from the contorted trees!

I longed to show the children how the dolphins sport
In the blue waves, these fish of gold, these fish that sing.
Flowers of foam have blessed my puttings-out from port,
Winds from I know not where at times have lent me wing.

And often, weary martyr of the poles and zones,
Dark blooms with yellow mouths reached towards me from the seas
On which I gently rocked, in time to their soft moans;
And I was left there like a woman on her knees.

Trembling peninsula, upon my decks I tossed
The dung of pale-eyed birds and clacking, angry sound;
And on I sailed while down through my frail cordage crossed
The sleeping, backwards falling bodies of the drowned.

I, lost boat in the hair of estuaries caught,
Hurled by the cyclone to a birdless apogee,
I, whom the Monitors and Hansamen had thought
Nor worth the fishing up—a carcase drunk with sea;

Free, smoking, touched with mists of violet above,
I, who the lurid heavens breached like some rare wall
Which boasts—confection that the goodly poets love—
Lichens of sunlight on a mucoid azure pall;

Who, with electric moons bedaubed, sped on my way,
A plank gone wild, black hippocamps my retinue,
When in July, beneath the cudgels of the day
Down fell the heavens and the craters of the blue;

I, trembling at the mutter, fifty leagues from me,
Of rutting Behemoths, the turbid Maelstrom's threats,
Spinning a motionless and blue eternity
I long for Europe, land of ancient parapets.

Such starry archipelagoes! Many an isle
With heavens fiercely to the wanderer wide-thrown;
Is it these depthless nights that your lone sleep beguile,
A million golden birds, O Vigour not yet known?

And yet, I've wept too much. The dawns are sharp distress,
All moons are baleful and all sunlight harsh to me
Swollen by acrid love, sagging with drunkenness—
Oh, that my keel might rend and give me to the sea!

If there's a water in all Europe that I crave,
It is the cold, black pond where 'neath the scented sky
Of eve a crouching infant, sorrowfully grave,
Launches a boat as frail as a May butterfly.

Soaked in your languors, waves, I can no more go hunting
The cotton-clippers' wake, no more can enterprise
Amid the proud displays of lofty flags and bunting,
Nor swim beneath the convict-hulks' appalling eyes!

(1871)

Translated by Norman Cameron

One of the most remarkable poems in the whole of literature, a completely original poem.

MARY M. COLUM
From These Roots (1938)

ARTHUR RIMBAUD

1854 — 1891

FROM A SEASON IN HELL

Je suis esclave de l'Époux infernal, celui qui a perdu les vierges folles. . . .

Je suis veuve . . .—J'étais veuve.—mais oui, j'ai été bien sérieuse jadis, et je ne suis pas née pour devenir squelette! . . .—Lui était presque un enfant . . . Ses délicatesses mystérieuses m'avaient séduite. J'ai oublié tout mon devoir humain pour le suivre. Quelle vie! La vraie vie est absente. Nous ne sommes pas au monde. Je vais où il va, il le faut. Et souvent il s'emporte contre moi, *moi, la pauvre âme*. Le Démon! —C'est un démon, vous savez, *ce n'est pas un homme*. . . .

Je l'écoute faisant de l'infamie une gloire, de la cruauté un charme. . . .

Il avait la pitié d'une mère méchante pour les petits enfants. . . .

A côté de son cher corps endormi, que d'heures des nuits j'ai veillé, cherchant pourquoi il voulait tant s'évader de la réalité. . . . Je reconnaissais,—sans craindre pour lui,—qu'il pouvait être un sérieux danger dans la société.—Il a peut-être des secrets pour *changer la vie?* . . . Hélas! je dépendais bien de lui. Mais que voulait-il avec mon existence terne et lâche? . . .

J'avais de plus en plus faim de sa bonté. . . .

Par instants, j'oublie la pitié où je suis tombée: lui me rendra forte, nous voyagerons, nous chasserons dans les déserts, nous dormirons sur les pavés des villes inconnues, sans soins, sans peines. Ou je me réveillerai, et les lois et les mœurs auront changé,—grâce à son pouvoir magique. . . .

Il m'attaque, il passe des heures à me faire honte de tout ce qui m'a pu toucher au monde, et s'indigne si je pleure. . . .

Hélas! il y avait des jours où tous les hommes agissant lui paraissaient les jouets de délires grotesques; il riait affreusement, longtemps.— Puis, il reprenait ses manières de jeune mère, de sœur aînée. S'il était moins sauvage, nous serions sauvés! Mais sa douceur aussi est mortelle. Je lui suis soumise.—Ah! je suis folle! . . .

Drôle de ménage!

I am the slave of the infernal Spouse, he who ruined the foolish virgins. . . .

I am a widow. . . . I was a widow. . . . Why yes, formerly I was very serious, and not born to become a skeleton! . . . He was almost a child! . . . His mysterious tendernesses seduced me. To follow him I forgot the whole of my human duty. What a life! The true life was absent. We were not in the world. Where he went I followed, for it had

to be so. And often he declaimed against me—*I, the poor soul.* Demon!—
He is a Demon, you know; *he is not a man.* . . .

I listened to him as he converted infamy into a glory and cruelty
into a charm. . . .

For little children he showed the pity of an ill-natured mother. . . .

At the side of his dear, slumbering body, how many nocturnal hours
have I not kept awake, seeking for the reason why he wished so
earnestly to escape from reality. . . . I recognized—but without fearing for him—that he might be a serious danger in society.—Perhaps he
has secret reasons for *changing his life?* . . . Alas! I was indeed subject to him. But what did he want with my dull and cowardly existence? . . .

I hungered more and more for his kindness. . . .

At moments I forget the pitiful state into which I have fallen. He will
restore me to strength; we shall travel and hunt in the deserts; we
shall sleep on the stones of unknown cities, unheeded, without vexations.
Or I shall awaken, and laws and morals will have changed,—thanks to
his magic power. . . .

He attacks me; he spends hours making me ashamed of everything
in the world which has had the power to touch me; and he becomes
indignant if I weep. . . .

Alas! he had days when all men of action appeared to him to be
the playthings of grotesque frenzies: he laughed both terribly and long.
—Then he resumed his manners as of a young mother, or beloved sister.
If he were less savage we should be saved. But his gentleness also is
deadly. I am under his power.—Ah! I am insane! . . .

Strange household!

Une Saison en enfer (1873)
Translated by George Frederic Lees

*In all literature it would be difficult to find a more cruel or a more
revelatory piece of writing.*

HAROLD NICOLSON
Paul Verlaine (1921)

ARTHUR RIMBAUD

1 8 5 4 — 1 8 9 1

MEMOIRE

I

L'eau claire; comme le sel des larmes d'enfance;
L'assaut au soleil des blancheurs des corps de femmes;
La soie, en foule et de lys pur, des oriflammes
Sous les murs dont quelque pucelle eut la défense;

L'ébat des anges,—non . . . le courant d'or en marche,
Meut ses bras, noirs et lourds et frais surtout, d'herbe. Elle,
Sombre, ayant le ciel bleu pour ciel de lit, appelle
Pour rideaux l'ombre de la colline et de l'arche.

II

Et l'humide carreau tend ses bouillons limpides!
L'eau meuble d'or pâle et sans fond les couches prêtes.
Les robes vertes et déteintes des fillettes
Font les saules, d'où sautent les oiseaux sans brides.

Plus jaune qu'un louis, pure et chaude paupière,
Le souci d'eau—ta foi conjugale, ô l'Épouse!—
Au midi prompt, de son terne miroir, jalouse
Au ciel gris de chaleur la sphère rose et chère.

III

Madame se tient trop debout dans la prairie
Prochaine où neigent les fils du travail; l'ombrelle
Aux doigts; foulant l'ombrelle; trop fière pour elle
Des enfants lisant dans la verdure fleurie

Leur livre de maroquin rouge. Hélas, Lui, comme
Mille anges blancs qui se séparent sur la route,
S'éloigne par delà la montagne; Elle, toute
Froide et noire, court! après le départ de l'homme!

IV

Regrets des bras épais et jeunes d'herbe pure!
Or des lunes d'avril au cœur du saint lit! joie
Des chantiers riverains à l'abandon, en proie
Aux soirs d'août qui faisaient germer ces pourritures!

Qu'elle pleure à présent sous les remparts; l'haleine
Des peupliers d'en haut est pour la seule brise.
Puis, c'est la nappe, sans reflets, source grise;
Un vieux dragueur, dans sa barque immobile, peine.

V

Jouet de cet œil d'eau morne, je n'y puis prendre,
O canot immobile! ô bras trop courts! ni l'une
Ni l'autre fleur; ni la jaune qui m'importune,
Là; ni la bleue, amis, à l'eau couleur de cendre.

Ah, la poudre des saules qu'une aile secoue!
Les roses des roses dès longtemps dévorées! . .
Mon canot toujours fixe; et sa chaîne tirée
Au fond de cet œil d'eau sans bords—à quelle boue?

MEMORY

I

Clear water; like the salt of childhood tears;
The assault in the sunlight of the whiteness of women's bodies;
The silk of banners, in masses and of pure lily,
Under the walls whose defense a maid held;

The play of angels,—no . . . the golden current in progress,
Moves its arms, black, heavy, and above all cool, of grass. The water,
Dark, having the blue sky for the sky's bed, calls up
For curtains the shadow of the hill and the arch.

II

And the wet stones extend their clear moisture!
The water furnishes the prepared beds with bottomless pale gold.
The green faded dresses of the girls
Are willow trees, out of which hop reinless birds.

More golden than a louis, pure and warm eyelid,
The care of the water—your conjugal faith, O Spouse!—
At prompt noon, from its tarnished mirror, jealous
In the sky grey with heat the rose and precious sphere.

III

The mother stands too upright in the field
Nearby where the sons of work appear white; the parasol
In her fingers; crushing the flowers too proud for her,
Children reading in the flowered grass

Their book of morocco leather. Alas, he, like
A thousand white angels separating on the road,
Goes off beyond the mountain; she, all
Cold and dark, runs off! after the man's departure!

IV

Regrets of arms thick and young with pure grass!
Gold of April moons in the heart of the holy bed; joy
Of abandoned river lumber yards, a prey
To August nights which caused the rotting to germinate!

Let her weep now under the walls: the breath
Of the poplars above is for the wind alone.
Then, here is the surface, with no reflection, grey water,
An old dredger, in his motionless boat, labors.

V

Toy of this eye of sad water, I can seize,
O motionless boat, O too short arms, neither this
Nor the other flower; neither the yellow one which troubles me,
There; nor the blue one, friends, in the ash colored water.

Ah, the powder of the willows which one wing shakes!
The roses of the reeds devoured long ago!
My boat still fixed; and its chain pulled
In the depths of that rimless watery eye—from what mud?

Translated by Wallace Fowlie

The purest expression in the French language of poetic fervor and beauty.

WALLACE FOWLIE
Rimbaud (1946)

OSCAR WILDE

1 8 5 6 — 1 9 0 0

PARABLE

Christ came from a white plain to a purple city, and as He passed through the first street, He heard voices overhead, and saw a young man lying drunk upon a window-sill, "Why do you waste your soul in drunkenness?" He said. "Lord, I was a leper and You healed me, what else can I do?" A little further through the town He saw a young man following a harlot, and said, "Why do you dissolve your soul in debauchery?" and the young man answered, "Lord, I was blind, and You healed me, what else can I do?" At last in the middle of the city He saw an old man crouching, weeping upon the ground, and when He asked why he wept, the old man answered, "Lord, I was dead, and You raised me into life, what else can I do but weep?"

He has written what he calls the best short story in the world, and will have it that he repeats it to himself on getting out of bed and before every meal. . . . Wilde published that story a little later, but spoiled it with the verbal decoration of his epoch, and I have to repeat it to myself as I first heard it, before I can see its terrible beauty. I no more doubt its sincerity than I doubt that his parade of gloom, all that late rising, and sleeping away his life, that elaborate playing with tragedy, was an attempt to escape from an emotion by its exaggeration.

WILLIAM BUTLER YEATS
Autobiographies (1926)

SIR WILLIAM WATSON

1 8 5 8 — 1 9 3 5

HYMN TO THE SEA

I

Grant, O regal in bounty, a subtle and delicate largess;
  Grant an ethereal alms, out of the wealth of thy soul:
Suffer a tarrying minstrel, who finds, not fashions his numbers—
  Who, from the commune of air, cages the volatile song—

Lightly to capture and prison some fugitive breath of thy descant,
  Thine and his own as thy roar lisped on the lips of a shell,
Now while the vernal impulsion makes lyrical all that hath language,
  While, through the veins of the Earth, riots the ichor of spring,
While, amid throes, amid raptures, with loosing of bonds, with
    unsealings—
  Arrowy pangs of delight, piercing the core of the world—
Tremors and coy unfoldings, reluctances, sweet agitations—
  Youth, irrepressibly fair, wakes like a wondering rose.

II

Lover whose vehement kisses on lips irresponsive are squandered,
  Lover that wooest in vain Earth's imperturbable heart;
Athlete mightily frustrate, who pittest thy thews against legions,
  Locked with fantastical hosts, bodiless arms of the sky;
Sea that breakest for ever, that breakest and never art broken,
  Like unto thine, from of old, springeth the spirit of man—
Nature's wooer and fighter, whose years are a suit and a wrestling,
  All their hours, from his birth, hot with desire and with fray;
Amorist agonist man, that, immortally pining and striving,
  Snatches the glory of life only from love and from war;
Man that, rejoicing in conflict, like thee when precipitate tempest,
  Charge after thundering charge, clangs on thy resonant mail,
Seemeth so easy to shatter, and proveth so hard to be cloven;
  Man whom the gods, in his pain, curse with a soul that endures;
Man whose deeds, to the doer, come back as thine own exhalations
  Into thy bosom return, weepings of mountain and vale;
Man with the cosmic fortunes and starry vicissitudes tangled,
  Chained to the wheel of the world, blind with the dust of its speed,
Even as thou, O giant, whom trailed in the wake of her conquests
  Night's sweet despot draws, bound to her ivory car;
Man with inviolate caverns, impregnable holds in his nature,
  Depths no storm can pierce, pierced with a shaft of the sun:
Man that is galled with his confines, and burdened yet more with his
    vastness,
  Born too great for his ends, never at peace with his goal;
Man whom Fate, his victor, magnanimous, clement in triumph,
  Holds as a captive king, mewed in a palace divine:
Many its leagues of pleasance, and ample of purview its windows;
  Airily falls, in its courts, laughter of fountains at play;
Nought, when the harpers are harping, untimely reminds him of
    durance;
  None, as he sits at the feast, utters Captivity's name;

But, would he parley with Silence, withdraw for a while unattended,
    Forth to the beckoning world 'scape for an hour and be free,
Lo, his adventurous fancy coercing at once and provoking,
    Rise the unscalable walls, built with a word at the prime;
Lo, in unslumbering watch, and with pitiless faces of iron,
    Armed at each obstinate gate, stand the impassable guards.

III

Miser whose coffered recesses the spoils of the ages cumber,
    Spendthrift foaming thy soul wildly in fury away—
We, self-amorous mortals, our own multitudinous image
    Seeking in all we behold, seek it and find it in thee:
Seek it and find it when o'er us the exquisite fabric of Silence
    Perilous-turreted hangs, trembles and dulcetly falls;
When the aërial armies engage amid orgies of music,
    Braying of arrogant brass, whimper of querulous reeds;
When, at his banquet, the Summer is languid and drowsed with
      repletion;
    When, to his anchorite board, taciturn Winter repairs;
When by the tempest are scattered magnificent ashes of Autumn;
    When, upon orchard and lane, breaks the white foam of the Spring:
When, in extravagant revel, the Dawn, a bacchante up-leaping,
    Spills, on the tresses of Night, vintages golden and red;
When, as a token at parting, munificent Day, for remembrance,
    Gives, unto men that forget, Ophirs of fabulous ore;
When irresistibly rushing, in luminous palpitant deluge,
    Hot from the summits of Life, poured is the lava of noon;
When, as up yonder, thy mistress, at height of her mutable glories,
    Wise from the magical East, comes like a sorceress pale.
Ah, she comes, she arises—impassive, emotionless, bloodless,
    Wasted and ashen of cheek, zoning her ruins with pearl.
Once she was warm, she was joyous, desire in her pulses abounding:
    Surely thou lovedst her well, then, in her conquering youth!
Surely not all unimpassioned, at sound of thy rough serenading,
    She, from the balconied night, unto her melodist leaned—
Leaned unto thee, her bondsman, who keepest to-day her
      commandments,
    All for the sake of old love, dead at thy heart though it lie.

IV

Yea, it is we, light perverts, that waver, and shift our allegiance;
    We, whom insurgence of blood dooms to be barren and waste.
Thou, with punctual service, fulfillest thy task, being constant;
    Thine but to ponder the Law, labour and greatly obey:

Wherefore, with leapings of spirit, thou chantest the chant of the
     faithful;
   Led by the chime of the worlds, linked with the league of the stars;
Thou thyself but a billow, a ripple, a drop of that Ocean,
    Which, labyrinthine of arm, folding us meshed in its coil,
Shall, as to-night, with elations, august exultations and ardours,
    Pour, in unfaltering tide, all its unanimous waves,
When, from this threshold of being, these steps of the Presence, this
     precinct,
   Into the matrix of Life darkly divinely resumed,
Man and his littleness perish, erased like an error and cancelled,
   Man and his greatness survive, lost in the greatness of God.

(1895)

Probably the best hexameters which have been composed in English.
JOHN CHURTON COLLINS
Ephemera Critica (1901)

JOHN ANDREW HAMILTON, LORD SUMNER OF IBSTONE

1 8 5 9 — 1 9 3 4

THE LIMITS OF RELIGIOUS TOLERATION

The words, as well as the acts, which tend to endanger society differ from time to time in proportion as society is stable or insecure in fact, or is believed by its reasonable members to be open to assault. In the present day meetings or processions are held lawful which a hundred and fifty years ago would have been deemed seditious, and this is not because the law is weaker or has changed, but because, the times having changed, society is stronger than before. In the present day reasonable men do not apprehend the dissolution or the downfall of society because religion is publicly assailed by methods not scandalous. Whether it is possible that in the future irreligious attacks, designed to undermine fundamental institutions of our society, may come to be criminal in themselves, as constituting a public danger, is a matter that does not arise. The fact that opinion grounded on experience has moved one way does not in law preclude the possibility of its moving on fresh experience in the other; nor does it bind succeeding generations, when conditions have again changed. After all, the question whether a given opinion is a danger to society is a question of the times and is a question of fact. I desire to say nothing that would limit the right of society to protect itself by process of law from the dangers of the moment, whatever that right may be, but only to say that, experience having proved dangers once thought real to be now negligible, and dangers once very possibly imminent to have now passed away, there is nothing in the general rules as to blasphemy and irreligion, as known to the law, which prevents us from varying their application to the particular circumstances of our time in accordance with that experience. If these considerations are right, and the attitude of the law both civil and criminal towards all religions depends fundamentally on the safety of the State and not on the doctrines or metaphysics of those who profess them, it is not necessary to consider whether or why any given body was relieved by the law at one time or frowned on at another, or to analyse creeds and tenets, Christian and other.

Bowman v. Secular Society, Ltd. (1917) A.C. 406

One of the finest pieces of prose to be found in the law reports.

SIR WILLIAM S. HOLDSWORTH
Essays in Law and History (1946)

FRANCIS THOMPSON

1 8 5 9 — 1 9 0 7

THE HOUND OF HEAVEN

I fled Him, down the nights and down the days;
   I fled Him, down the arches of the years;
I fled Him, down the labyrinthine ways
   Of my own mind; and in the mist of tears
I hid from Him, and under running laughter.
      Up vistaed hopes I sped;
      And shot, precipitated,
Adown Titanic glooms of chasmèd fears,
  From those strong Feet that followed, followed after.
     But with unhurrying chase,
     And unperturbèd pace,
Deliberate speed, majestic instancy,
    They beat—and a Voice beat
    More instant than the Feet—
'All things betray thee, who betrayest Me.'

I pleaded, outlaw-wise,
By many a hearted casement, curtained red,
  Trellised with intertwining charities;
(For, though I knew His love Who followèd,
        Yet was I sore adread
Lest, having Him, I must have naught beside.)
But, if one little casement parted wide,
  The gust of His approach would clash it to:
    Fear wist not to evade, as Love wist to pursue.
Across the margent of the world I fled,
  And troubled the gold gateways of the stars,
    Smiting for shelter on their clangèd bars;
        Fretted to dulcet jars
And silvern chatter the pale ports o' the moon.
I said to Dawn: Be sudden—to Eve: Be soon;
  With thy young skiey blossoms heap me over
        From this tremendous Lover—
Float thy vague veil about me, lest He see!
  I tempted all His servitors, but to find
My own betrayal in their constancy,
In faith to Him their fickleness to me,
  Their traitorous trueness, and their loyal deceit.
To all swift things for swiftness did I sue;
  Clung to the whistling mane of every wind.
      But whether they swept, smoothly fleet,
    The long savannahs of the blue;
        Or whether, Thunder-driven,
        They clanged his chariot 'thwart a heaven,
Plashy with flying lightnings round the spurn o' their feet:—
  Fear wist not to evade as Love wist to pursue.
        Still with unhurrying chase,
        And unperturbèd pace,
  Deliberate speed, majestic instancy,
        Came on the following Feet,
        And a Voice above their beat—
    'Naught shelters thee, who wilt not shelter Me.'

I sought no more that after which I strayed
        In face of man or maid;
But still within the little children's eyes
        Seems something, something that replies,
They at least are for me, surely for me!
I turned me to them very wistfully;
But just as their young eyes grew sudden fair
        With dawning answers there.

Their angel plucked them from me by the hair.
'Come then, ye other children, Nature's—share
With me' (said I) 'your delicate fellowship;
   Let me greet you lip to lip,
   Let me twine with you caresses,
    Wantoning
   With our Lady-Mother's vagrant tresses,
    Banqueting
   With her in her wind-walled palace,
   Underneath her azured daïs,
   Quaffing, as your taintless way is,
    From a chalice
Lucent-weeping out of the dayspring.'
    So it was done:
I in their delicate fellowship was one—
Drew the bolt of Nature's secrecies.
    I knew all the swift importings
   On the wilful face of skies;
   I knew how the clouds arise
   Spumèd of the wild sea-snortings;
    All that's born or dies
   Rose and drooped with; made them shapers
Of mine own moods, or wailful or divine;
   With them joyed and was bereaven.
   I was heavy with the even,
   When she lit her glimmering tapers
   Round the day's dead sanctities.
   I laughed in the morning's eyes.
I triumphed and I saddened with all weather,
   Heaven and I wept together,
And its sweet tears were salt with mortal mine:
Against the red throb of its sunset-heart
   I laid my own to beat,
   And share commingling heat;
But not by that, by that, was eased my human smart.
In vain my tears were wet on Heaven's grey cheek.
For ah! we know not what each other says,
   These things and I; in sound *I* speak—
Their sound is but their stir, they speak by silences.
Nature, poor stepdame, cannot slake my drouth;
   Let her, if she would owe me,
Drop yon blue bosom-veil of sky, and show me
   The breasts o' her tenderness:
Never did any milk of hers once bless
   My thirsting mouth.

Nigh and nigh draws the chase,
With unperturbèd pace,
Deliberate speed, majestic instancy;
And past those noisèd Feet
A voice comes yet more fleet—
'Lo! naught contents thee, who content'st not Me.

Naked I wait Thy love's uplifted stroke!
My harness piece by piece Thou hast hewn from me,
And smitten me to my knee;
I am defenceless utterly.
I slept, methinks, and woke,
And, slowly gazing, find me stripped in sleep.
In the rash lustihead of my young powers,
I shook the pillaring hours
And pulled my life upon me; grimed with smears,
I stand amid the dust o' the mounded years—
My mangled youth lies dead beneath the heap.
My days have crackled and gone up in smoke,
Have puffed and burst as sun-starts on a stream.
Yea, faileth now even dream
The dreamer, and the lute the lutanist;
Even the linked fantasies, in whose blossomy twist
I swung the earth a trinket at my wrist,
Are yielding; cords of all too weak account
For earth with heavy griefs so overplussed.
Ah! is Thy love indeed
A weed, albeit an amaranthine weed,
Suffering no flowers except its own to mount?
Ah! must—
Designer infinite!—
Ah! must Thou char the wood ere Thou canst limn with it?
My freshness spent its wavering shower i' the dust;
And now my heart is as a broken fount,
Wherein tear-drippings stagnate, spilt down ever
From the dank thoughts that shiver
Upon the sighful branches of my mind.
Such is; what is to be?
The pulp so bitter, how shall taste the rind?
I dimly guess what Time in mists confounds;
Yet ever and anon a trumpet sounds
From the hid battlements of Eternity;
These shaken mists a space unsettle, then
Round the half-glimpsèd turrets slowly wash again.

But not ere him who summoneth
    I first have seen, enwound
With glooming robes purpureal, cypress-crowned;
His name I know, and what his trumpet saith.
Whether man's heart or life it be which yields
    Thee harvest, must Thy harvest-fields
    Be dunged with rotten death?

    Now of that long pursuit
    Comes on at hand the bruit;
That Voice is round me like a bursting sea:
    'And is thy earth so marred,
    Shattered in shard on shard?
Lo, all things fly thee, for thou fliest Me!
    Strange, piteous, futile thing!
Wherefore should any set thee love apart?
Seeing none but I makes much of naught' (He said),
'And human love needs human meriting:
    How hast thou merited—
Of all man's clotted clay the dingiest clot?
    Alack, thou knowest not
How little worthy of any love thou art!
Whom wilt thou find to love ignoble thee,
    Save Me, save only Me?
All which I took from thee I did but take,
    Not for thy harms,
But just that thou might'st seek it in My arms.
    All which thy child's mistake
Fancies as lost, I have stored for thee at home:
    Rise, clasp My hand, and come!'
    Halts by me that footfall:
    Is my gloom, after all,
Shade of His hand, outstretched caressingly?
    'Ah, fondest, blindest, weakest,
    I am He Whom thou seekest!
Thou dravest love from thee, who dravest Me.'

Poems (1893)

The 'Hound of Heaven' has so great and passionate and such a metre-creating motive, that we are carried over all obstructions of the rhythmical current, and are compelled to pronounce it, at the end, one of the very few 'great' odes of which the language can boast.

COVENTRY PATMORE

Francis Thompson, A New Poet (Fortnightly Review, 1894)

LE VASE

Mon marteau lourd sonnait dans l'air léger,
Je voyais la rivière et le verger,
La prairie et jusques au bois
Sous le ciel plus bleu d'heure en heure,
Puis rose et mauve au crépuscule;
Alors je me levais tout droit
Et m'étirais heureux de la tâche des heures,
Gourd de m'être accroupi de l'aube au crépuscule
Devant le bloc de marbre où je taillais les pans
Du vase fruste encor que mon marteau pesant,
Rythmant le matin clair et la bonne journée,
Heurtait, joyeux d'être sonore en l'air léger!

Le vase naissait dans la pierre façonnée.
Svelte et pur il avait grandi
Informe encor en sa sveltesse,
Et j'attendis,
Les mains oisives et inquiètes,
Pendant des jours, tournant la tête
A gauche, à droite, au moindre bruit,
Sans plus polir la panse ou lever le marteau.
L'eau
Coulait de la fontaine comme haletante.
Dans le silence
J'entendais, un à un, aux arbres du verger,
Les fruits tomber de branche en branche,
Je respirais un parfum messager
De fleurs lointaines sur le vent;
Souvent,
Je croyais qu'on avait parlé bas,
Et, un jour que je rêvais—ne dormant pas—
J'entendis par delà les prés et la rivière
Chanter des flûtes . . .

Un jour, encor,
Entre les feuilles d'ocre et d'or
Du bois, je vis, avec ses jambes de poil jaune,
Danser un faune;
Je l'aperçus aussi, une autre fois,
Sortir du bois

Le long de la route et s'asseoir sur une borne
Pour prendre un papillon à l'une de ses cornes.

Une autre fois,
Un centaure passa la rivière à la nage;
L'eau ruisselait sur sa peau d'homme et son pelage;
Il s'avança de quelques pas dans les roseaux,
Flaira le vent, hennit, repassa l'eau;
Le lendemain, j'ai vu l'ongle de ses sabots
Marqué dans l'herbe . . .

Des femmes nues
Passèrent en portant des paniers et des gerbes,
Très loin, tout au bout de la plaine.
Un matin, j'en trouvai trois à la fontaine
Dont l'une me parla. Elle était nue.
Elle me dit: Sculpte la pierre
Selon la forme de mon corps en tes pensées,
Et fais sourire au bloc ma face claire;
Écoute autour de toi les heures dansées
Par mes sœurs dont la ronde se renoue,
Entrelacée,
Et tourne et chante et se dénoue.

Et je sentis sa bouche tiède sur ma joue.

Alors le verger vaste et le bois et la plaine
Tressaillirent d'un bruit étrange, et la fontaine
Coula plus vive avec un rie dans ses eaux;
Les trois Nymphes debout auprès des trois roseaux
Se prirent par la main et dansèrent; du bois
Les faunes roux sortaient par troupes, et des voix
Chantèrent par delà les arbres du verger
Avec des flûtes en éveil dans l'air léger.
La terre retentit du galop des centaures;
Il en venait du fond de l'horizon sonore,
Et l'on voyait, assis sur la croupe qui rue,
Tenant des thyrses tors et des outres ventrues,
Des satyres boiteux piqués par des abeilles,
Et les bouches de crin et les lèvres vermeilles
Se baisaient, et la ronde immense et frénétique,
Sabots lourds, pieds légers, toisons, croupes, tuniques,
Tournait éperdument autour de moi qui, grave,
Au passage, sculptais aux flancs gonflés du vase
Le tourbillonnement des forces de la vie.

Du parfum exhalé de la terre mûrie
Une ivresse montait à travers mes pensées,
Et dans l'odeur des fruits et des grappes pressées,
Dans le choc des sabots et le heurt des talons,
En de fauves odeurs de boucs et d'étalons,
Sous le vent de la ronde et la grêle des rires,
Au marbre je taillais ce que j'entendais bruire;
Et parmi la chair chaude et les effluves tièdes,
Hennissement du mufle ou murmure des lèvres,
Je sentais sur mes mains, amoureux ou farouches,
Des souffles de naseaux ou des baisers de bouches.

Le crépuscule vint et je tournai la tête.

Mon ivresse était morte avec la tâche faite;
Et sur son socle enfin, du pied jusques aux anses,
Le grand Vase se dressait nu dans le silence,
Et, sculptée en spirale à son marbre vivant,
La ronde dispersée et dont un faible vent
Apportait dans l'écho la rumeur disparue,
Tournait avec ses boucs, ses dieux, ses femmes nues,
Ses centaures cabrés et ses faunes adroits,
Silencieusement autour de la paroi,
Tandis que, seul, parmi, à jamais, la nuit sombre,
Je maudissais l'aurore et je pleurais vers l'ombre.

THE VASE

My heavy hammer rang in the light air; I saw the river and the
orchard, the field, and as far as the woods, growing bluer beneath the
sky hour by hour, then rose and mauve in the twilight; then I stood up
straight and stretched myself, happy in the task of the hours, numb with
having crouched from dawn till twilight before the block of marble upon
which I cut out the sides of the vase, still in its shell, that my ponderous
hammer struck, stressing the clear morning and the good day, happy at
being resonant in the light air.

The vase took shape in the worked stone. Slender and pure, it had
grown larger, still unformed in its slenderness, and I waited, with idle
and unquiet hands, for days, turning my head to the left, to the right,
at the slightest sound, without polishing the belly or lifting the hammer.
The water ran from the spring as though breathless. In the silence, I
heard the fruits of the orchard trees falling, one by one, from branch to
branch; I breathed a heralding perfume of distant flowers on the wind;
often I thought that someone spoke low, and one day that I dreamed—

not sleeping—I heard, beyond the fields and the river, the playing of flutes.

Still another day, between the ochre and gold leaves of the woods, I saw a faun with shaggy yellow legs dancing; I caught sight of him also, another time, coming out of the wood, along the road, and sitting down upon a stump to take a butterfly from one of his horns.

Another time, a centaur crossed the river swimming, the water streamed from his man's skin and his horse's coat; he advanced a few steps into the reeds, snuffed the wind, whinneyed, and crossed back over the water; the next day I saw the prints of his hoofs stamped in the grass.

Naked women passed carrying baskets and sheaves, very far off, quite at the other end of the plain. One morning I found three at the spring, and one of them spoke to me. She was naked. She said to me: "Carve the stone after the form of my body in your thoughts, and make my bright face smile in the marble block; listen all round you to the hours danced by my sisters, whose circle winds itself, interlaced, and revolves and sings and unwinds."

And I felt her warm mouth upon my cheek.

Then the vast orchard, and the woods, and the plain, shivered to a strange noise, and the spring ran faster with a laugh in its waters; the three Nymphs standing near the three reeds took one another by the hand and danced; red-haired fauns came out of the wood in troupes, and voices sang beyond the trees of the orchard with flutes awake in the light air. The ground echoed to the galop of centaurs; they came from the depths of the resonant horizon, and one saw lame satyrs, stung by bees, sitting on the rushing cruppers, holding twisted staves and big-bellied leather bottles; hairy mouths and vermillion lips kissed each other, and the immense and frenzied circle—heavy hoofs, light feet, fleeces, cruppers, tunics—turned wildly about me, who, grave while it went on, carved on the rounded side of the vase the whirl of the forces of life.

From the perfume sent out by the ripe earth, an intoxication mounted through my thoughts, and in the smell of fruits and crushed grapes, in the shock of hoofs and the stamping of heels, in the fallow odour of goats and stallions, under the breeze of the circle and the hail of laughter, I carved upon the marble what I heard humming, and amidst the hot flesh and the warm exhalations, neighings of muzzles or murmurings of lips, I felt, loving or savage, upon my hands, the breath of nostrils or the kisses of mouths.

Twilight came and I turned my head.

My intoxication was dead with the accomplished task; and upon its
pedestal, at last, from foot to handles, the great vase stood up naked in
the silence, and carved in a spiral about its living marble, the dispersed
circle, of which a feeble wind brought the echo of the vanished noise,
turned, with its goats, its gods, its naked women, its rearing centaurs,
and its nimble fauns, silently round the side, while I, alone for ever in
the gloomy night, I cursed the dawn and wept toward the darkness.

Translated by Amy Lowell

*The most perfect presentation of the creative faculty at work that I
know of in any literature.*

A M Y   L O W E L L
Six French Poets (1915)

R U D Y A R D   K I P L I N G

1 8 6 5 — 1 9 3 6

DANNY DEEVER

'What are the bugles blowin' for?' said Files-on-Parade.
'To turn you out, to turn you out,' the Colour-Sergeant said.
'What makes you look so white, so white?' said Files-on-Parade.
'I'm dreadin' what I've got to watch,' the Colour-Sergeant said.
   For they're hangin' Danny Deever, you can hear the Dead March play,
   The Regiment's in 'ollow square—they're hangin' him to-day;
   They've taken of his buttons off an' cut his stripes away,
   An' they're hangin' Danny Deever in the mornin'.

'What makes the rear-rank breathe so 'ard?' said Files-on-Parade.
'It's bitter cold, it's bitter cold,' the Colour-Sergeant said.
'What makes that front-rank man fall down?' said Files-on-Parade.
'A touch o' sun, a touch o' sun,' the Colour-Sergeant said.
   They are hangin' Danny Deever, they are marchin' of 'im round,
   They 'ave 'alted Danny Deever by 'is coffin on the ground;
   An' 'e'll swing in 'arf a minute for a sneakin' shootin' hound—
   O they're hangin' Danny Deever in the mornin'.

' 'Is cot was right-'and cot to mine,' said Files-on-Parade.
' 'E's sleepin' out an' far to-night,' the Colour-Sergeant said.
'I've drunk 'is beer a score o' times,' said Files-on-Parade.
' 'E's drinkin' bitter beer alone,' the Colour-Sergeant said.

They are hangin' Danny Deever, you must mark 'im to 'is place,
For 'e shot a comrade sleepin'—you must look 'im in the face;
Nine 'undred of 'is county an' the Regiment's disgrace,
While they're hangin' Danny Deever in the mornin'.

'What's that so black agin the sun?' said Files-on-Parade.
'It's Danny fightin' 'ard for life,' the Colour-Sergeant said.
'What's that that whimpers over'ead?' said Files-on-Parade.
'It's Danny's soul that's passin' now,' the Colour-Sergeant said.
    For they're done with Danny Deever, you can 'ear the quickstep play,
    The Regiment's in column, an' they're marchin' us away;
    Ho! the young recruits are shakin', an' they'll want their beer to-day,
    After hangin' Danny Deever in the mornin'!

RECESSIONAL

God of our fathers, known of old,
    Lord of our far-flung battle-line,
Beneath whose awful Hand we hold
    Dominion over palm and pine—
Lord God of Hosts, be with us yet,
Lest we forget—lest we forget!

The tumult and the shouting dies;
    The Captains and the Kings depart:
Still stands Thine ancient sacrifice,
    An humble and a contrite heart.
Lord God of Hosts, be with us yet,
Lest we forget—lest we forget!

Far-called, our navies melt away;
    On dune and headland sinks the fire:
Lo, all our pomp of yesterday
    Is one with Nineveh and Tyre!
Judge of the Nations, spare us yet,
Lest we forget—lest we forget!

If, drunk with sight of power, we loose
    Wild tongues that have not Thee in awe,
Such boastings as the Gentiles use,
    Or lesser breeds without the Law—
Lord God of Hosts, be with us yet,
Lest we forget—lest we forget!

For heathen heart that puts her trust
    In reeking tube and iron shard,
All valiant dust that builds on dust,

And guarding, calls not Thee to guard,
For frantic boast and foolish word—
Thy mercy on Thy People, Lord!

(1897)

EPITAPHS OF THE WAR, 1914-18

AN ONLY SON

I have slain none except my Mother. She
(Blessing her slayer) died of grief for me.

THE COWARD

I could not look on Death, which being known,
Men led me to him, blindfold and alone.

THE BEGINNER

On the first hour of my first day
In the front trench I fell.
(Children in boxes at a play
Stand up to watch it well.)

COMMON FORM

If any question why we died,
Tell them, because our fathers lied.

A DEAD STATESMAN

I could not dig: I dared not rob:
Therefore I lied to please the mob.
Now all my lies are proved untrue
And I must face the men I slew.
What tale shall serve me here among
Mine angry and defrauded young?

SALONIKAN GRAVE

I have watched a thousand days
Push out and crawl into night
Slowly as tortoises.
Now I, too, follow these.
It is fever, and not the fight—
Time, not battle,—that slays.

I make no apology for having used the terms 'verse' and 'poetry' in a loose way: so that while I speak of Kipling's work as verse and not as poetry, I am still able to speak of individual compositions as poems, and also to maintain that there is 'poetry' in the 'verse'. Where terminology is loose, where we have not the vocabulary for distinctions which we feel, our only precision is found in being aware of the imperfection of our tools, and of the different senses in which we are using the same words. It should be clear that when I contrast 'verse' with 'poetry' I am not, IN THIS CONTEXT, implying a value judgement. I do not mean, here, by verse, the work of a man who would write poetry if he could: I mean by it something which does what 'poetry' could not do. The difference which would turn Kipling's verse into poetry, does not represent a failure or deficiency: he knew perfectly well what he was doing; and from his point of view more 'poetry' would interfere with his purpose. And I make the claim, that in speaking of Kipling we are entitled to say 'GREAT verse'. What other famous poets should be put into the category of great verse writers is a question which I do not here attempt to answer. That question is complicated by the fact that we should be dealing with matters as imprecise as the shape and size of a cloud or the beginning and end of a wave. But the writer whose work is ALWAYS clearly verse, is not a great verse writer: if a writer is to be that, there must be some of his work of which we cannot say whether it is verse or poetry. And the poet who could not write 'verse' when verse was needed, would be without that sense of structure which is required to make a poem of any length readable. I would suggest also that we too easily assume that what is most valuable is also most rare, and vice versa. I can think of a number of poets who have written great poetry, only of a very few whom I should call great verse writers. And unless I am mistaken, Kipling's position in this class is not only high, but unique.

T. S. ELIOT
Rudyard Kipling (1941)

W. B. YEATS

1 8 6 5 — 1 9 3 9

DARK UNDER FROTH

Maybe a twelvemonth since
Suddenly I began,
In scorn of this audience,
Imagining a man,

And his sun-freckled face,
And grey Connemara cloth,
Climbing up to a place
Where stone is dark under froth,
And the down-turn of his twist
When the flies drop in the stream;
A man who does not exist,
A man who is but a dream;
And cried, 'Before I am old
I shall have written him one
Poem maybe as cold
And passionate as the dawn.'

The Fisherman (1919)

SALT SEA WIND

I call to the eye of the mind
A well long choked up and dry
And boughs long stripped by the wind,
And I call to the mind's eye
Pallor of an ivory face,
Its lofty dissolute air,
A man climbing up to a place
The salt sea wind has swept bare.

At the Hawk's Well (1921)

FOR MY OWN

To write for my own race
And the reality.

The Fisherman (1919)

DAYS OF MY YOUTH

Through all the lying days of my youth
I swayed my leaves and flowers in the sun;
Now I may wither into the truth.

The Coming of Wisdom with Time (1910)

WATERS OF THE BOYNE

Merchant and scholar who have left me blood
That has not passed through any huckster's loin,
Soldiers that gave, whatever die was cast:
A Butler or an Armstrong that withstood
Beside the brackish waters of the Boyne
James and his Irish when the Dutchman crossed.

Responsibilities (1914)

COURAGE EQUAL TO DESIRE

Why should I blame her that she filled my days
With misery, or that she would of late
Have taught to ignorant men most violent ways,
Or hurled the little streets upon the great,
Had they but courage equal to desire?

No Second Troy (1910)

SO GREAT A SWEETNESS

And what of her that took
All till my youth was gone
With scarce a pitying look?
How could I praise that one?
When day begins to break
I count my good and bad,
Being wakeful for her sake,
Remembering what she had,
What eagle look still shows,
While up from my heart's root
So great a sweetness flows
I shake from head to foot.

Friends (1914)

With the development of this maturer style, it became impossible any
longer to regard Yeats merely as one of the best of the English lyric
poets of the nineties. The author of "The Lake of Innisfree," which had
so delighted Robert Louis Stevenson, had grown, in an interval of ten
years during which nobody outside of Ireland had apparently paid

much attention to him, to the unmistakable stature of a master. *No other poet writing English in our time has been able to deal with supreme artistic success with such interesting and such varied experience. No other writer has been able to sustain the traditional grand manner of the poet with so little effect of self-consciousness.*

EDMUND WILSON
Axel's Castle (1931)

STEPHEN PHILLIPS

1 8 6 8 — 1 9 1 5

THE DEAD

I did not know the dead could have such hair.

Paolo and Francesca, Act iv (1902)

There is little in tragedy more beautiful.

GEORGE GORDON
Airy Nothings Or What You Will (1917)

MARCEL PROUST

1 8 7 1 — 1 9 2 2

MY GRANDMOTHER'S ILLNESS

Cottard, whom we had called in to see my grandmother, and who had infuriated us by asking with a dry smile, the moment we told him that she was ill: "Ill? You're sure it's not what they call a diplomatic illness?" He tried to soothe his patient's restlessness by a milk diet. But incessant bowls of milk soup gave her no relief, because my grandmother sprinkled them liberally with salt (the toxic effects of which were as yet, Widal not having made his discoveries, unknown). For, medicine being a compendium of the successive and contradictory mistakes of medical practitioners, when we summon the wisest of them to our aid, the chances are that we may be relying on a scientific truth the error of which will be recognised in a few years' time. So that to believe in medicine would be the height of folly, if not to believe in it were not greater folly still, for from this mass of errors there have emerged in the course of time many truths. Cottard had told us to take her temperature. A thermometer was fetched. Throughout almost all its length it was clear of mercury. Scarcely could one make out, crouching at the foot of the tube, in its little cell, the silver salamander. It seemed dead. The glass reed was slipped into my grandmother's mouth. We had no need to leave it there for long; the little sorceress had not been slow in casting her horoscope. We found her motionless, perched half-way up her tower, and declining to move, shewing us with precision the figure that we had asked of her, a figure with which all the most careful examination that my grandmother's mind could have devoted to herself would have been incapable of furnishing her: 101 degrees. For the first time we felt some anxiety. We shook the thermometer well, to erase the ominous line, as though we were able thus to reduce the patient's fever simultaneously with the figure shewn on the scale. Alas, it was only too clear that the little sibyl, unreasoning as she was, had not pronounced judgment arbitrarily, for the next day, scarcely had the thermometer been inserted between my grandmother's lips when almost at once, as though with a single bound, exulting in her certainty and in her intuition of a fact that to us was imperceptible, the little prophetess had come to a halt at the same point, in an implacable immobility, and pointed once again to that figure 101 with the tip of her gleaming wand. Nothing more did she tell us; in vain might we long, seek, pray, she was deaf to our entreaties; it seemed as though this were her final utterance, a warning and a menace. Then, in an attempt to constrain her to modify her response, we had recourse to another creature of the same kingdom, but more potent, which is not content with questioning the body but can command it, a febrifuge of the same order as the modern aspirin, which had not then come into use. We had not shaken the thermometer down below 99.5, and hoped that it would not have to rise from there. We made my grandmother swallow this drug and then replaced the thermometer in her mouth. Like an implacable warder to whom one presents a permit signed by a higher authority whose protecting influence one has sought, and who, finding it to be in order, replies: "Very well; I have nothing to say; if it's like that you may pass," this time the watcher in the tower did not move. But sullenly she seemed to be saying: "What use will that be to you? Since you are friends with quinine, she may give me the order not to go up, once, ten times, twenty times. And then she will grow tired of telling me, I know her; get along with you. This won't last for ever. And then you'll be a lot better off." Thereupon my grandmother felt the presence within her of a creature which knew the human body better than herself, the presence of a contemporary of the races that have vanished from the earth, the presence of earth's first inhabitant—long anterior to the creation of thinking man—she felt that aeonial ally who was sounding her, a little roughly even, in the head, the heart, the elbow; he found out the weak places, organised everything for the prehistoric combat which began at once to be fought. In a moment a trampled Python, the fever, was vanquished by the potent chemical substance to which my grandmother, across the series of kingdoms, reaching out beyond all animal and vegetable life, would fain have been able to give thanks. And she remained moved by this glimpse which she had caught, through the mists of so many centuries, of a climate anterior to the creation even of plants.

Le Côté de Guermantes (1920)
Translated by C. K. Scott Moncrieff

The picture of the grandmother at death, when the animal and the mineral forces get hold of her, is unequalled in literature.

D E N I S   S A U R A T
Modern French Literature 1870–1940 (1946)

PAUL VALÉRY

1 8 7 1 — 1 9 4 5

LA SOIRÉE AVEC MONSIEUR TESTE

Vita Cartesii res est simplicissima.
M. de Raey à M. Van Limborch.

La bêtise n'est pas mon fort. J'ai vu beaucoup d'individus, j'ai visité quelques nations, j'ai pris ma part d'entreprises diverses sans les aimer, j'ai mangé presque tous les jours, j'ai touché à des femmes. Je revois maintenant quelques centaines de visages, deux ou trois grands spectacles, et peut-être la substance de vingt livres. Je n'ai pas retenu le meilleur ni le pire de ces choses: est resté ce qui l'a pu.

Cette arithmétique m'épargne de m'étonner de vieillir. Je pourrais aussi faire le compte des moments victorieux de mon esprit, et les imaginer unis et soudés, composant une vie *heureuse* . . . Mais je crois m'être toujours bien jugé. Je me suis rarement perdu de vue; je me suis détesté, je me suis adoré,—puis nous avons vieilli ensemble.

Souvent, j'ai supposé que tout était fini pour moi, et je me terminais de toutes mes forces, anxieux d'épuiser, d'éclairer quelque situation douloureuse. Cela m'a fait connaître que nous apprécions notre propre pensée beaucoup trop d'après l'*expression* de celle des autres! Dès lors, les milliards de mots qui ont bourdonné à mes oreilles, m'ont rarement ébranlé par ce qu'on voulait leur faire dire; et tous ceux que j'ai moi-même prononcés à autrui, je les ai senti se distinguer toujours de ma pensée,—car ils devenaient *invariables*.

Si j'avais décidé comme la plupart des hommes, non seulement je me serais cru leur supérieur, mais je l'aurais paru. Je me suis préféré. Ce qu'ils nomment un être supérieur est un être qui s'est trompé. Pour s'étonner de lui, il faut le voir,—et pour être vu il faut qu'il se montre. Et il me montre que la niaise manie de son nom le possède. Ainsi, chaque grand homme est taché d'une erreur. Chaque esprit qu'on trouve puissant, commence par la faute qui le fait connaître. En échange du pourboire public, il donne le temps qu'il faut pour se rendre perceptible, l'énergie dissipée à se transmettre et à préparer la satisfaction étrangère. Il va jusqu'à comparer les jeux informes de la gloire, à la joie de se sentir unique—grande volupté particulière.

J'ai rêvé alors que les têtes les plus fortes, les inventeurs les plus sagaces, les connaisseurs le plus exactement de la pensée devaient être des inconnus, des avares, des hommes qui meurent sans avouer. Leur existence m'était révélée par celle même des individus éclatants, un peu moins *solides*.

L'induction était si facile que j'en voyais la formation à chaque instant. Il suffisait d'imaginer les grands hommes ordinaires, purs de leur première erreur, ou de s'appuyer sur cette erreur même pour concevoir un degré de conscience plus élevé, un sentiment de la liberté d'esprit moins grossier. Une opération aussi simple me livrait des étendues curieuses, comme si j'étais descendu dans la mer. Perdus dans l'éclat des découvertes publiées, mais à côté des inventions méconnues que le commerce, la peur, l'ennui, la misère commettent chaque jour, je croyais distinguer des chefs-d'œuvre intérieurs. Je m'amusais à éteindre l'histoire connue sous les annales de l'anonymat.

C'étaient, invisibles dans leurs vies limpides, des solitaires qui savaient avant tout le monde. Ils me semblaient doubler, tripler, multiplier dans l'obscurité chaque personne célèbre,—eux, avec le dédain de livrer leurs chances et leurs résultats particuliers. Ils auraient refusé, à mon sentiment, de se considérer comme autre chose que des choses . . .

Ces idées me venaient pendant l'octobre de 93, dans les instants de loisir où la pensée se joue seulement à exister.

Je commençais de n'y plus songer, quand je fis la connaissance de M. Teste. (Je pense maintenant aux traces qu'un homme laisse dans le petit espace où il se meut chaque jour.) Avant de me lier avec M. Teste, j'étais attiré par ses allures particulières. J'ai étudié ses yeux, ses vêtements, ses moindres paroles sourdes au garçon du café où je le voyais. Je me demandais s'il se sentait observé. Je détournais vivement mon regard du sien, pour surprendre le sien me suivre. Je prenais les journaux qu'il venait de lire, je recommençais mentalement les sobres gestes qui lui échappaient; je notais que personne ne faisait attention à lui.

Je n'avais plus rien de ce genre à apprendre, lorsque nous entrâmes en relation. Je ne l'ai jamais vu que la nuit. Une fois dans une sorte de b . . . ; souvent au théâtre. On m'a dit qu'il vivait de médiocres opérations hebdomadaires à la Bourse. Il prenait ses repas dans un petit restaurant de la rue Vivienne. Là, il mangeait comme on se purge, avec le même entrain. Parfois, il s'accordait ailleurs un repas lent et fin.

M. Teste avait peut-être quarante ans. Sa parole était extraordinairement rapide, et sa voix sourde. Tout s'effaçait en lui, les yeux, les mains. Il avait pourtant les épaules militaires, et le pas d'une régularité qui étonnait. Quand il parlait, il ne levait jamais un bras ni un doigt: il avait *tué la marionnette*. Il ne souriait pas, ne disait ni bonjour ni bonsoir; il semblait ne pas entendre le «Comment allez-vous?»

Sa mémoire me donna beaucoup à penser. Les traits par lesquels j'en pouvais juger, me firent imaginer une gymnastique intellectuelle sans exemple. Ce n'était pas chez lui une faculté excessive,—c'était une faculté éduquée ou transformée. Voici ses propres paroles: «Il y a vingt ans que je n'ai plus de livres. J'ai brûlé mes papiers aussi. Je rature le vif . . . Je retiens ce que je veux. Mais le difficile n'est pas là. *Il est de retenir ce dont je voudrai demain!* . . . J'ai cherché un crible machinal . . . »

A force d'y penser, j'ai fini par croire que M. Teste était arrivé à découvrir des lois de l'esprit que nous ignorons. Sûrement, il avait dû consacrer des années à cette recherche: plus sûrement, des années encore, et beaucoup d'autres années avaient été disposées pour mûrir ses inventions et pour en faire ses instincts. Trouver n'est rien. Le difficile est de s'ajouter ce qu'on trouve.

L'art délicat de la durée, le temps, sa distribution et son régime,—sa dépense à des choses bien choisies, pour les nourrir spécialement,— était une des grandes recherches de M. Teste. Il veillait à la répétition de certaines idées; il les arrosait de nombre. Ceci lui servait à rendre finalement machinale l'application de ses études conscientes. Il cherchait même à résumer ce travail. Il disait souvent: «*Maturare!* . . .»

Certainement sa mémoire singulière devait presque uniquement lui retenir cette partie de nos impressions que notre imagination toute seule est impuissante à construire. Si nous imaginons un voyage en ballon, nous pouvons avec sagacité, avec puissance, *produire* beaucoup de sensations probables d'un aéronaute; mais il restera toujours quelque chose d'individuel à l'ascension réelle, dont la différence avec notre rêverie exprime la valeur des méthodes d'un Edmond Teste.

Cet homme avait connu de bonne heure l'importance de ce qu'on pourrait nommer la *plasticité* humaine. Il en avait cherché les limites et le mécanisme. Combien il avait dû rêver à sa propre malléabilité!

J'entrevoyais des sentiments qui me faisaient frémir, une terrible obstination dans des expériences enivrantes. Il était l'être absorbé dans sa variation, celui qui devient son système, celui qui se livre tout entier à la discipline effrayante de l'esprit libre, et qui fait tuer ses joies par ses joies, la plus faible par la plus forte,—la plus douce, la temporelle, celle de l'instant et de l'heure commencée, par la fondamentale—par l'espoir de la fondamentale.

Et je sentais qu'il était le maître de sa pensée: j'écris là cette absurdité. L'expression d'un sentiment est toujours absurde.

M. Teste n'avait pas d'opinions. Je crois qu'il se passionnait à son gré, et pour atteindre un but défini. Qu'avait-il fait de sa personnalité? Comment se voyait-il? . . . Jamais il ne riait, jamais un air de malheur sur son visage. Il haïssait la mélancolie.

Il parlait, et on se sentait dans son idée, confondu avec les choses: on se sentait reculé, mêlé aux maisons, aux grandeurs de l'espace, au coloris remué de la rue, aux coins . . . Et les paroles le plus adroitement touchantes,—celles même qui font leur auteur plus près de nous qu'aucun autre homme, celles qui font croire que le mur éternel entre les esprits tombe,—pouvaient venir à lui . . . Il savait admirablement qu'elles auraient ému *tout autre*. Il parlait, et sans pouvoir préciser les motifs ni l'étendue de la proscription, on constatait qu'un grand nombre de mots étaient bannis de son discours. Ceux dont il se servait, étaient parfois si curieusement tenus par sa voix ou éclairés par sa phrase que leur poids était altéré, leur valeur nouvelle. Parfois, ils perdaient tout leur sens, ils paraissaient remplir uniquement une place vide dont le terme destinataire était douteux encore ou imprévu par la langue. Je l'ai entendu désigner un objet matériel par un groupe de mots abstraits et de noms propres.

A ce qu'il disait, il n'y avait rien à répondre. Il tuait l'assentiment poli. On prolongeait les conversations par des bonds qui ne l'étonnaient pas.

Si cet homme avait changé l'objet de ses méditations fermées, s'il eût tourné contre le monde la puissance régulière de son esprit, rien ne lui eût résisté. Je regrette d'en parler comme on parle de ceux dont on fait les statues. Je sens bien qu'entre le «génie» et lui, il y a une quantité de faiblesse. Lui, si véritable! si neuf! si pur de toute duperie et de toutes merveilles, si dur! Mon propre enthousiasme me le gâte . . .

Comment ne pas en ressentir pour celui qui ne disait jamais rien de *vague?* pour celui qui déclarait avec calme: «Je n'apprécie en toute chose que la *facilité* ou la *difficulté* de les connaître, de les accomplir. Je mets un soin extrême à mesurer ces degrés, et à ne pas m'attacher . . . Et que n'importe ce que je sais fort bien?»

Comment ne pas s'abandonner à un être dont l'esprit paraissait transformer pour soi seul tout ce qui est, et qui *opérait* tout ce qui lui était proposé? Je devinais cet esprit maniant et mêlant, faisant varier, mettant en communication, et dans l'étendue du champ de sa connaissance, pouvant couper et dévier, éclairer, glacer ceci, chauffer cela, noyer, exhausser, nommer ce qui manque de nom, oublier ce qu'il voulait, endormir ou colorer ceci et cela . . .

Je simplifie grossièrement des propriétés impénétrables. Je n'ose pas dire tout ce que mon objet me dit. La logique m'arrête. Mais, en moi-même, toutes les fois que se pose le problème de Teste, apparaissent de curieuses formations.

Il y a des jours où je le retrouve très nettement. Il se représente à mon souvenir, à côté de moi. Je respire la fumée de nos cigares, je l'entends, je me *méfie*. Parfois, la lecture d'un journal me fait me heurter à sa pensée, quand un événement maintenant la justifie. Et je tente encore quelques-unes de ces expériences illusoires qui me délectaient à l'époque de nos soirées. C'est-à-dire que je me le figure faisant ce que je ne lui ai pas vu faire. Que devient M. Teste souffrant?—Amoureux, comment raisonne-t-il?—Peut-il être triste?—De quoi aurait-il peur?—Qu'est-ce qui le ferait trembler?—. . . Je cherchais. Je maintenais entière l'image de l'homme rigoureux, je tâchais de la faire répondre à mes questions . . . Elle s'altérait.

Il aime, il souffre, il s'ennuie. Tout le monde s'imite. Mais, au soupir, au gémissement élémentaire, je veux qu'il mêle les règles et les figures de tout son esprit.

Ce soir, il y a précisément deux ans et trois mois que j'étais avec lui au théâtre, dans une loge prêtée. J'y ai songé tout aujourd'hui.

Je le revois debout avec la colonne d'or de l'Opéra, ensemble.

Il ne regardait que la salle. Il aspirait la grande bouffée brûlante, au bord du trou. Il était rouge.

Une immense fille de cuivre nous séparait d'un groupe murmurant au delà de l'éblouissement. Au fond de la vapeur, brillait un morceau nu de femme, doux comme un caillou. Beaucoup d'éventails indépendants vivaient sur le monde sombre et clair, écumant jusqu'aux feux du haut. Mon regard épelait mille petites figures, tombait sur une tête triste, courait sur des bras, sur les gens, et enfin se brûlait.

Chacun était à sa place, libre d'un petit mouvement. Je goûtais le système de classification, la simplicité presque théorique de l'assemblée, l'ordre social. J'avais la sensation délicieuse que tout ce qui respirait dans ce cube, allait suivre ses lois, flamber de rires par grands cercles, s'émouvoir par plaques, ressentir par *masses* des choses *intimes,—uniques,*—des remuements secrets, s'élever à l'inavouable! J'errais sur ces étages d'hommes, de ligne en ligne, par orbites, avec la fantaisie de joindre idéalement entre eux, tous ceux ayant la même maladie, ou la même théorie, ou le même vice . . . Une musique nous touchait tous, abondait, puis devenait toute petite.

Elle disparut. M. Teste murmurait: «On n'est *beau*, on n'est extraordinaire que pour les autres! *Ils* sont mangés par les autres!»

Le dernier mot sortit du silence que faisait l'orchestre. Teste respira.

Sa face enflammée où soufflaient la chaleur et la couleur, ses larges épaules, son être noir mordoré par les lumières, la forme de tout son bloc vêtu, étayé par la grosse colonne, me reprirent. Il ne perdait pas un atome de tout ce qui devenait sensible, à chaque instant, dans cette grandeur rouge et or.

Je regardai ce crâne qui faisait connaissance avec les angles du chapiteau, cette main droite qui se rafraîchissait aux dorures; et, dans l'ombre de pourpre, les grands pieds. Des lointains de la salle, ses yeux vinrent vers moi; sa bouche dit: «La discipline n'est pas mauvaise . . . C'est un petit commencement . . .»

Je ne savais répondre. Il dit de sa voix basse et vite: «Qu'ils jouissent et obéissent!»

Il fixa longuement un jeune homme placé en face de nous, puis une dame, puis tout un groupe dans les galeries supérieures,—qui débordait du balcon par cinq ou six visages brûlants,—et puis tout le monde, tout le théâtre, plein comme les cieux, ardent, fasciné par la scène que nous ne voyions pas. La stupidité de tous les autres nous révélait qu'il se passait n'importe quoi de sublime. Nous regardions se mourir le jour que faisaient toutes les figures dans la salle. Et quand il fut très bas, quand la lumière ne rayonna plus, il ne resta que la vaste phosphorescence de ces mille figures. J'éprouvais que ce crépuscule faisait tous ces êtres passifs. Leur attention et l'obscurité croissantes formaient un équilibre continu. J'étais moi-même attentif *forcément*,—à toute cette attention.

M. Teste dit: «Le suprême *les* simplifie. Je parie qu'ils pensent tous, de plus en plus, *vers* la même chose. Ils seront égaux devant la crise ou limite commune. Du reste, la loi n'est pas si simple . . . puisqu'elle me néglige,—et—je suis ici.»

Il ajouta: «L'éclairage les tient.»

Je dis en riant: «Vous aussi?»

Il répondit: «Vous, aussi.»

—«Quel dramaturge vous feriez! lui dis-je, vous semblez surveiller quelque expérience créée aux confins de toutes les sciences! Je voudrais voir un théâtre inspiré de vos méditations . . .»

Il dit: «Personne ne médite.»

L'applaudissement et la lumière complète nous chassèrent. Nous circulâmes, nous descendîmes. Les passants semblaient en liberté. M. Teste se plaignit légèrement de la fraîcheur de minuit. Il fit allusion à d'anciennes douleurs.

Nous marchions, et il lui échappait des phrases presque incohérentes. Malgré mes efforts, je ne suivais ses paroles qu'à grand'peine, me bornant enfin à les retenir. L'incohérence d'un discours dépend de celui qui l'écoute. L'esprit me paraît ainsi fait qu'il ne peut être incohérent pour soi-même. Aussi me suis-je gardé de classer Teste parmi les fous. D'ailleurs, j'apercevais vaguement le lien de ses idées, je n'y remarquais aucune contradiction;—et puis, j'aurais redouté une solution trop simple.

Nous allions dans les rues adoucies par la nuit, nous tournions à des angles, dans le vide, trouvant d'instinct notre voie,—plus large, plus étroite, plus large. Son pas militaire se soumettait le mien ...

—«Pourtant, *répondis-je*, comment se soustraire à une musique si puissante! Et pourquoi? J'y trouve une ivresse particulière, dois-je la dédaigner? J'y trouve l'illusion d'un travail immense, qui, tout à coup me deviendrait possible ... Elle me donne des *sensations abstraites*, des figures délicieuses de tout ce que j'aime,—du changement, du mouvement, du mélange, du flux, de la transformation ... Nierez-vous qu'il y ait des choses anesthésiques? Des arbres qui saoulent, des hommes qui donnent de la force, des filles qui paralysent, des ciels qui coupent la parole?

M. Teste reprit assez haut:

—«Eh! Monsieur! que m'importe le «talent» de vos arbres—et des autres! ... Je suis chez MOI, je parle ma langue, je hais les choses extraordinaires. C'est le besoin des esprits faibles. Croyez-moi à la lettre: le génie est *facile*, la fortune est *facile*, la *divinité* est *facile* ... Je veux dire simplement—que je sais comment cela se conçoit. C'est *facile*.

«Autrefois,—il y a bien vingt ans,—toute chose au-dessus de l'ordinaire accomplie par un autre homme, m'était une défaite personnelle. Dans le passé, je ne voyais qu'idées volées à moi! Quelle bêtise! ... Dire que notre propre image ne nous est pas indifférente! Dans les combats imaginaires, nous la traitons *trop bien* ou *trop mal!* ...»

Il toussa. Il se dit: «Que peut un homme? ... Que peut un homme! ...» Il me dit: «Vous connaissez un homme sachant qu'il ne sait ce qu'il dit!»

Nous étions à sa porte. Il me pria de venir fumer un cigare chez lui.

Au haut de la maison, nous entrâmes dans un très petit appartement «garni». Je ne vis pas un livre. Rien n'indiquait le travail traditionnel devant une table, sous une lampe, au milieu de papiers et de plumes. Dans la chambre verdâtre qui sentait la menthe, il n'y avait autour de la bougie que le morne mobilier abstrait,—le lit, la pendule, l'armoire à glace, deux fauteuils—comme des êtres de raison. Sur la cheminée, quelques journaux, une douzaine de cartes de visite couvertes de chiffres, et un flacon pharmaceutique. Je n'ai jamais eu plus fortement l'impression du *quelconque*. C'était le logis quelconque, analogue au point quelconque des théorèmes,—et peut-être aussi utile. Mon hôte existait dans l'intérieur le plus général. Je songeai aux heures qu'il faisait dans ce fauteuil. J'eus peur de l'infinie tristesse possible dans ce lieu pur et banal. J'ai vécu dans de telles chambres, je n'ai jamais pu les croire définitives, sans horreur.

M. Teste parla de l'argent. Je ne sais pas reproduire son éloquence spéciale: elle me semblait moins précise que d'ordinaire. La fatigue, le silence qui se fortifiait avec l'heure, les cigares amers, l'abandon nocturne semblaient l'atteindre. J'entends sa voix baissée et ralentie qui faisait danser la flamme de l'unique bougie brûlant entre nous, à mesure qu'il citait de très grands nombres avec lassitude. Huit cent dix millions soixante quinze mille cinq cent cinquante . . . J'écoutais cette musique inouïe sans suivre le calcul. Il me communiquait le tremblement de la Bourse, et les longues suites de noms de nombres me prenaient comme une poésie. Il rapprochait les événements, les phénomènes industriels, le goût public et les passions, les chiffres encore, les uns des autres. Il disait: «L'or est comme l'esprit de la société.»

Tout à coup, il se tut. Il souffrit.

J'examinai de nouveau la chambre froide, la nullité du meuble, pour ne pas le regarder. Il prit sa fiole et but. Je me levai pour partir.

—«Restez encore, dit-il, vous ne vous ennuyez pas. Je vais me mettre au lit. Dans peu d'instants, je dormirai. Vous prendrez la bougie pour descendre.»

Il se dévêtit tranquillement. Son corps sec se baigna dans les draps et fit le mort. Ensuite il se tourna, et s'enfonça davantage dans le lit trop court.

Il me dit en souriant: «Je fais la planche. Je flotte! . . . Je sens un roulis imperceptible dessous,—un mouvement immense? Je dors une heure ou deux tout au plus, moi qui adore la navigation de la nuit. Souvent je ne distingue plus ma pensée d'avant le sommeil. Je ne sais pas si j'ai dormi. Autrefois, en m'assoupissant, je pensais à tous ceux qui m'avaient fait plaisir, figures, choses, minutes. Je les faisais venir pour que la pensée fût aussi douce que possible, facile comme le lit . . . Je suis vieux. Je puis vous montrer que je me sens vieux . . . Rappelez-vous!—Quand on est enfant on se *découvre,* on découvre lentement l'espace de son corps, on exprime la particularité de son corps par une série d'efforts, je suppose? On se tord et on se trouve ou on se retrouve, et on s'étonne! on touche son talon, on saisit son pied droit avec sa main gauche, on obtient le pied froid dans la paume chaude! . . . Maintenant, je me sais par cœur. Le cœur aussi. Bah! toute la terre est marquée, tous les pavillons couvrent tous les territoires . . . Reste mon lit. J'aime ce courant de sommeil et de linge: ce linge qui se tend et se plisse, ou se froisse,—qui descend sur moi comme du sable, quand je fais le mort,—qui se caille autour de moi dans le sommeil . . . C'est de la mécanique bien complexe. Dans le sens de la trame ou de la chaîne, une déformation très petite . . . Ah!»

Il souffrit.

« Mais qu'avez-vous? lui dis-je, je puis . . . »

«J'ai, dit-il, . . . pas grand'chose. J'ai . . . un dixième de seconde qui se montre . . . Attendez . . . Il y a des instants où mon corps s'illumine . . . C'est très curieux. J'y vois tout à coup en moi . . . je distingue les profondeurs des couches de ma chair; et je sens des zones de douleur, des anneaux, des pôles, des aigrettes de douleur. Voyez-vous ces figures vives? cette géométrie de ma souffrance? Il y a de ces éclairs qui ressemblent tout à fait à des idées. Ils font comprendre,—d'ici, jusque-là . . . Et pourtant ils me laissent *incertain*. Incertain n'est pas le mot . . . Quand *cela* va venir, je trouve en moi quelque chose de confus ou de diffus. Il se fait dans mon être des endroits . . . brumeux, il y a des étendues qui font leur apparition. Alors, je prends dans ma mémoire une question, un problème quelconque . . . Je m'y enfonce. Je compte des grains de sable . . . et, tant que je les vois . . .—Ma douleur grossissante me force à l'observer. J'y pense!—Je n'attends que mon cri, . . . et dès que je l'ai entendu—*l'objet*, le terrible *objet*, devenant plus petit, et encore plus petit, se dérobe à ma vue intérieure . . .

«Que peut un homme? Je combats tout,—hors la souffrance de mon corps, au delà d'une certaine grandeur. C'est là, pourtant, que je devrais commencer. Car, souffrir, c'est donner à quelque chose une attention suprême, et je suis un peu l'homme de l'attention . . . Sachez que j'avais prévu la maladie future. J'avais songé avec précision à ce dont tout le monde est sûr. Je crois que cette vue sur une portion évidente de l'avenir, devrait faire partie de l'éducation. Oui, j'avais prévu ce qui commence maintenant. C'était, alors, une idée comme les autres. Ainsi, j'ai pu la suivre.»

Il devint calme.

Il se plia sur le côté, baissa les yeux; et, au bout d'une minute, parlait de nouveau. Il commençait à se perdre. Sa voix n'était qu'un murmure dans l'oreiller. Sa main rougissante dormait déjà.

Il disait encore: «Je pense, et cela ne gêne rien. Je suis seul. Que la solitude est confortable! Rien de doux ne me pèse . . . La même rêverie ici, que dans la cabine du navire, la même au café Lambert . . . Les bras d'une Berthe, s'ils prennent de l'importance, je suis volé,—comme par la douleur . . . Celui qui me parle, s'il ne prouve pas,—c'est un ennemi. J'aime mieux l'éclat du moindre fait qui se produit. Je suis étant, et me voyant; me voyant me voir, et ainsi de suite . . . Pensons de tout près. Bah! on s'endort sur n'importe quel sujet . . . Le sommeil continue n'importe quelle idée . . .»

Il ronflait doucement. Un peu plus doucement, je pris la bougie, je sortis à pas de loup.

AN EVENING WITH M. TESTE [*]

Stupidity is not my strong point. I have seen many persons; I have visited several nations; I have taken part in divers enterprises without liking them; I have eaten nearly every day; I have touched women. I now recall several hundred faces, two or three great events, and perhaps the substance of twenty books. I have not retained the best nor the worst of these things. What could stick, did.

This bit of arithmetic spares me surprise at getting old. I could also add up the victorious moments of my mind, and imagine them joined and soldered, composing a *happy* life. . . . But I think I have always been a good judge of myself. I have rarely lost sight of myself; I have detested, and adored myself—and so, we have grown old together.

Often I have supposed that all was over for me, and I would begin ending with all my strength, anxious to exhaust and clear up some painful situation. This has made me realize that we interpret our own thought too much according to the *expression* of other people's! Since then, the thousands of words that have buzzed in my ears have rarely shaken me with what they were meant to mean. And all those I have myself spoken to others, I could always feel them become distinct from my thought—for they were becoming *invariable*.

If I had gone on as most men do, not only would I have believed myself their superior, but would have seemed so. I have preferred myself. What they call a superior being is one who has deceived himself. To wonder at him, we have to see him—and to be seen, he has to show himself. And he shows me that he has a silly obsession with his own name. Every great man is thus flawed with an error. Every mind considered powerful begins with the fault that makes it known. In exchange for a public fee, it gives the time necessary to make itself knowable, the energy spent in transmitting itself in preparing the alien satisfaction. It even goes so far as to compare the formless games of glory to the joy of feeling unique—the great private pleasure.

And so I have surmised that the strongest heads, the most sagacious inventors, the most exacting connoisseurs of thought, must be unknown men, misers, who die without giving up their secret. Their existence was revealed to me by just those showy, somewhat less *solid* individuals.

This induction was so easy that I could see it taking shape from one moment to the next. It was only necessary to imagine ordinary great men pure of their first error, or to take this error itself as a basis for conceiving a higher degree of consciousness, a fuller sense of the freed mind. Such a simple process opened curious vistas before me, as if I had gone

[*] Reprinted from *Monsieur Teste* by Paul Valéry, by permission of and special arrangement with Alfred A. Knopf, Inc. Translated from the original French by Jackson Mathews. Copyright 1947 by Alfred A. Knopf, Inc.

down into the sea. I thought that I perceived there, dimmed by the brilliance of published discoveries, but side by side with the unsung inventions recorded every day by business, fear, boredom, and poverty, *many inner masterpieces*. I amused myself with smothering known history beneath the annals of anonymity.

Here they were, solitary figures, invisible in their limpid lives, but knowing beyond anyone in the world. They seemed in their obscurity twice, three times, many times greater than any celebrated person— they, in their disdain for making known their lucky finds and private achievements. I believe they would have refused to consider themselves as anything but things. . . .

These ideas came to me during October of 93, at those moments of leisure when thought practices simply existing.

I was beginning to think no more about them when I made the acquaintance of M. Teste. (I am now thinking of the traces a man leaves in the little space through which he moves each day.) Before I knew M. Teste, I was attracted by his rather special manner. I studied his eyes, his clothes, his slightest low word to the waiter at the café where I used to see him. I wondered whether he felt observed. I would turn my eyes quickly away from his, only to catch my own following me. I would pick up the newspapers he had just been reading, and go over in my mind the sober gestures that rose from him; I noticed that no one paid any attention to him.

I had nothing more of this kind to learn when our relations began. I never saw him except at night. Once in a kind of b—; often at the theater. I heard that he lived on modest weekly speculations at the Bourse. He used to take his meals at a small restaurant on the rue Vivienne. Here, he would eat as if he were taking a purgative, with the same rush. From time to time he would go elsewhere and allow himself a fine, leisurely meal.

M. Teste was perhaps forty years old. His speech was extraordinarily rapid, and his voice quiet. Everything about him was fading, his eyes, his hands. His shoulders, however, were military, and his step had a regularity that was amazing. When he spoke he never raised an arm or a finger: he had *killed his puppet*. He did not smile, and said neither hello nor good-by. He seemed not to hear a "How do you do?"

His memory gave me much to think about. Signs that I could judge by led me to imagine in him unequaled intellectual gymnastics. It was not that this faculty in him was excessive—it was rather trained or transformed. These are his own words: "I have not had a book for twenty years. I have burned my papers also. I scribble in the flesh. . . . I can retain what I wish. That is not the difficulty. *It is rather to retain what I shall want tomorrow!* I have tried to invent a mechanical sieve. . . ."

Thinking about it convinced me that M. Teste had managed to discover laws of the mind we know nothing of. Surely he must have devoted years to this research; even more surely, other years, and many more years, had been given to maturing his findings, making them into instincts. Discovery is nothing. The difficulty is to acquire what we discover.

The delicate art of duration: time, its distribution and regulation—expending it upon well chosen objects, to give them special nourishment —was one of M. Teste's main preoccupations. He watched for the repetition of certain ideas; he watered them with number. This served to make the application of his conscious studies in the end mechanical. He even sought to sum up this whole effort. He often said: *"Maturare!"* . . .

Certainly his singular memory must have retained for him exclusively those impressions which the imagination by itself is powerless to construct. If we imagine an ascent in a balloon, we can, with sagacity and vigor, *produce* many of the probable sensations of an aeronaut; but there will always remain something peculiar to a real ascent, which by contrast with our imagined one shows the value of the methods of an Edmond Teste.

This man had early known the importance of what might be called human *plasticity*. He had tried to find out its limits and its laws. How deeply he must have thought about his own malleability!

In him I sensed feelings that made me shudder, a terrible obstinacy in delirious experience. He was a being absorbed in his own variation, one who becomes his own system, who gives himself up wholly to the frightful discipline of the free mind, and who sets his joys to killing one another, the stronger killing the weaker—the milder, the temporal, the joy of a moment, of an hour just begun, killed by the fundamental— by hope for the fundamental.

And I felt that he was master of his thought: I write down this absurdity here. The expression of a feeling is always absurd.

M. Teste had no opinions. I believe he could become impassioned at will, and to attain a definite end. What had he done with his personality? How did he regard himself? . . . He never laughed, never a look of unhappiness on his face. He hated melancholy.

He spoke, and one felt oneself confounded with *things* in his mind: one felt withdrawn, mingled with houses, with the grandeurs of space, with the shuffled colors of the street, with street corners. . . . And the most cleverly touching words—the very ones that bring their author closer to us than any other man, those that make us believe the eternal wall between minds is falling—could come to him. He knew wonderfully that they would have moved *anyone else.* He spoke, and without being able to tell precisely the motives or the extent of the proscription, one knew that a large number of words had been banished from his discourse. The ones he used were sometimes so curiously held by his voice or lighted by his phrase that their weight was altered, their value new. Sometimes they would lose all sense, they seemed to serve only to fill an empty place for which the proper term was still in doubt or not provided by the language. I have heard him designate a simple object by a group of abstract words and proper names.

To what he said, there was nothing to reply. He killed polite assent. Conversation was kept going in leaps that were no surprise to him.

If this man had reversed the direction of his inward meditations, if he had turned against the world the regular power of his mind, nothing could have resisted him. I am sorry to speak of him as we speak of those we make statues of. I am well aware that between "genius" and him, there is a quantity of weakness. He, so genuine! So new! So free of all trickery and magic, so hard! My own enthusiasm spoils him for me. . . .

How is it possible not to feel enthusiasm for a man who never said anything *vague*? for a man who calmly declared: "In all things I am interested only in the *facility* or *difficulty* of knowing them, of doing them. I give extreme care to measuring the degree of each quality, and to not getting attached to the problem. . . . What do I care for what I know quite well already?"

How is it possible not to be won over to a being whose mind seemed to transform to its own use all that is, a mind that *performed* everything suggested to it. I imagined this mind managing, mixing, making variations, connections, and throughout the whole field of its knowledge able to intercept and shunt, to guide, to freeze this and warm that, to drown, to raise, to name what has no name, to forget what it wished, to put to sleep or to color this and that. . . .

I am grossly simplifying his impenetrable powers. I do not dare say all my object tells me. Logic stops me. But, within me, every time the problem of Teste arises, curious formations appear.

On certain days I can recover him quite clearly. He reappears in my memory, beside me. I breathe the smoke of our cigars, I listen to him, I am wary. Sometimes, in reading a newspaper I encounter his thought, which some event has just justified. And I try again some of those illusory experiments that used to delight me during our evenings together. That is, I imagine him doing what I have not seen him do. What is M. Teste like when he is sick? How does he reason when he is in love! Is it possible for him to be sad? What would he be afraid of? What could make him tremble? . . . I wondered. I kept before me the complete image of this rigorous man, trying to make it answer my questions. . . . But it kept changing.

He loves, he suffers, he is bored. People all imitate themselves. But he must combine in his sigh, in his elemental moan, the rules and forms of his whole mind.

Exactly two years and three months ago this evening, I was at the theater with him, in a box someone had offered us. I have thought about this all day today.

I can still see him standing with the golden column of the Opera; together.

He looked only at the audience. He was *breathing in* the great blast of brilliance, on the edge of the pit. He was red.

An immense copper girl stood between us and a group murmuring beyond the dazzlement. Deep in the haze shone a naked bit of woman, smooth as a pebble. A number of independent fans were breathing over the crowd, dim and clear, that foamed up to the level of the top lights. My eyes spelled a thousand little faces, settled on a sad head, ran along arms, over people, and finally flickered out.

Each one was in his place, freed by a slight movement. I tasted the system of classification, the almost theoretical simplicity of the audience, the social order. I had the delicious sensation that everything breathing in this cube was going to follow its laws, flare up with laughter in great circles, be moved in rows, feel as a mass *intimate*, even *unique* things, secret urges, be lifted to the unavowable! I strayed over these layers of men, from level to level, in orbits, fancying that I could join ideally together all those with the same illness, or the same theory, or the same vice. . . . One music moved us all, swelled, and then became quite small.

It disappeared. M. Teste was murmuring: "We are *beautiful*, extraordinary, only to others! *We* are eaten by others!"

The last word stood out in the silence created by the orchestra. Teste drew a deep breath.

His fiery face, glowing with heat and color, his broad shoulders, his dark figure bronzed by the lights, the form of the whole clothed mass of him propped by the heavy column, took hold of me again. He lost not an atom of all that at each moment became perceptible in that grandeur of red and gold.

I watched his skull making acquaintance with the angles of the capital, his right hand refreshing itself among the gilt ornaments; and, in the purple shadow, his large feet. From a distant part of the theater his eyes came back to me; his mouth said: "Discipline is not bad. . . . It is at least a beginning. . . ."

I did not know what to answer. He said in his low quick voice: "Let them enjoy and obey!"

He fixed his eyes for a long time on a young man opposite us, then on a lady, then on a whole group in the higher galleries—overflowing the balcony in five or six burning faces—and then on everybody, the whole theater full as the heavens, ardent, held by the stage which we could not see. The stupor they were all in showed us that something or other sublime was going on. We watched the light dying from all the faces in the audience. And when it was quite low, when the light no longer shone, there remained only the vast phosphorescence of those thousand faces. I saw that this twilight made these beings passive. Their attention and the darkness mounting together formed a continuous equilibrium. I was myself attentive, *necessarily*, to all this attention.

M. Teste said: "The supreme simplifies *them*. I bet they are all thinking, more and more, *toward* the same thing. They will be equal at the crisis, the common limit. Besides, the law is not so simple . . . since it does not include me—and—I am here."

He added: "The lighting is what holds them."

I said, laughing: "You too?"

He replied: "You too."

"What a dramatist you would make," I said to him. "You seem to be watching some experiment going on beyond the limits of all the sciences! I would like to see a theater inspired by your meditations."

He said: "No one meditates."

The applause and the house lights drove us out. We circled, and went down. The passers-by seemed set free. M. Teste complained slightly of the midnight coolness. He alluded to old pains.

As we walked along, almost incoherent phrases sprang from him. Despite my efforts, I could follow his words only with great difficulty, finally deciding merely to remember them. The incoherence of speech depends on the one listening to it. The mind seems to me so made that it cannot be incoherent to itself. For that reason I refused to consider Teste as mad. Anyway, I could vaguely make out the thread of his ideas, and I saw no contradiction in them; also, I would have been wary of too simple a solution.

We went through streets quieted by the night, we turned corners, in the void, by instinct finding our way—wider, narrower, wider. His military step subdued mine. . . .

"Yet, *I replied*, how can we escape a music so powerful! And why should we? I find in it a peculiar excitement. Must I reject this? I find in it the illusion of an immense effort, which suddenly might become possible. . . . It gives me *abstract sensations*, delightful images of everything I love—change, movement, mixture, flux, transformation. . . . Will you deny that certain things are anaesthetic? That there are trees that intoxicate us, men that give us strength, girls that paralyze us, skies that stop our speech?"

M. Teste put in, in a rather loud voice:

". . . But, sir, what is the 'talent' of your trees—or of anyone! . . . to me! I am at home in MYSELF, I speak my language, I hate extraordinary things. Only weak minds need them. Believe me literally: *genius* is *easy, divinity* is *easy*. . . . I mean simply—that I know how it is conceived. It is *easy*.

1384

"Long ago—at least twenty years—the least thing out of the ordinary that some other man accomplished was for me a personal defeat. I used to see only ideas stolen from me! What nonsense! . . . Imagine thinking our own image is not indifferent to us! In our imaginary struggles, we treat ourselves *too well* or *too ill!* . . ."

He coughed. He said to himself: "What can a man do? . . . What can a man do? . . ." He said to me: "You know a man who knows that he does not know what he is saying!"

We were at his door. He asked me to come in and smoke a cigar with him.

On the top floor of the house we went into a very small "furnished" apartment. I did not see a book. Nothing indicated the traditional manner of work, at a table, under a lamp, in the midst of papers and pens.

In the greenish bedroom, smelling of mint, there was only a candle and, sitting around it, the dull abstract furniture—the bed, the clock, the wardrobe with a mirror, two armchairs—like rational beings. On the mantel, a few newspapers, a dozen visiting cards covered with figures, and a medicine bottle. I have never had a stronger impression of the *ordinary*. It was *any lodging*, like geometry's *any point*—and perhaps as useful. My host existed in the most general interior. I thought of the hours he had spent in that armchair. I was frightened at the infinite drabness possible in this pure and banal room. I have lived in such rooms. I have never been able to believe them final, without horror.

M. Teste talked of money. I do not know how to reproduce his special eloquence: it seemed less precise than usual. Fatigue, the silence becoming deeper with the late hour, the bitter cigars, the abandon of night seemed to overtake him. I can still hear his voice, lowered and slow, making the flame dance above the single candle that burned between us, as he recited very large numbers, wearily. Eight hundred ten million seventy-five thousand five hundred fifty. . . . I listened to this unheard-of music without following the calculation. He conveyed to me the fever of the Bourse, and these long series of names of numbers gripped me like poetry. He correlated news events, industrial phenomena, public taste and the passions, and still more figures, one with another. He was saying: "Gold is, as it were, the mind of society."

Suddenly he stopped. He was in pain.

I again scanned the cold room, the nullity of the furnishings, to keep from looking at him. He took out his little bottle and drank. I got up to go.

"Stay awhile longer," he said. "You don't mind. I am going to get in bed. In a few moments I'll be asleep. You can take the candle to go down."

He undressed quietly. His gaunt body bathed in the covers, and lay still. Then he turned over and plunged farther down in the bed, too short for him.

He smiled and said to me: "I am like a plank. I am floating! . . . I feel an imperceptible rolling under me—an immense movement? I sleep an hour or two at the very most; I adore navigating the night. Often I can not distinguish thought before from sleep. I do not know whether I have slept. It used to be, when I dozed, I thought of all those who had afforded me pleasure; faces, things, minutes. I would summon them so that my thought might be as sweet as possible, easy as the bed. . . . I am old. I can show you that I feel old. . . . You remember! When we are children we *discover* ourselves, we slowly discover the extent of our bodies, we express the particularity of our bodies by a series of efforts, I suppose? We squirm and discover or recover ourselves, and are surprised! We touch a heel, grasp the right foot with the left hand, take a cold foot in a warm palm! . . . Now I know myself by heart. Even my heart. Bah! the world is all marked off, all the flags are flying over all territories. . . . My bed remains. I love this stream of sleep and linen: this linen that stretches and folds, or crumples—runs over me like sand, when I lie still—curdles around me in sleep. . . . It is a very complex bit of mechanics. In the direction of the woof or the warp, a very slight deviation. . . . Ah!"

He was in pain.

"What is it?" I said. "I can . . ."

"Nothing . . . much," he said. "Nothing but . . . a tenth of a second appearing. . . . Wait. . . . At certain moments my body is illuminated. . . . It is very curious. Suddenly I see into myself . . . I can make out the depth of the layers of my flesh; and I feel zones of pain, rings, poles, plumes of pain. Do you see these living figures, this geometry of my suffering? Some of these flashes are exactly like ideas. They make me understand—from here, to there. . . . And yet they leave me *uncertain.* Uncertain is not the word. . . . When *it* is about to appear, I find in myself something confused or diffused. Areas that are . . . hazy, occur in my being, wide spaces suddenly make their appearance. Then I choose a question from my memory, any problem at all . . . and I plunge into it. I count grains of sand . . . and so long as I can see them . . . My increasing pain forces me to observe it. I think about it! I only await my cry, and as soon as I have heard it—the *object,* the terrible *object,* getting smaller, and still smaller, escapes from my inner sight. . . .

"What is possible, what can a man do? I can withstand anything—except the suffering of my body, beyond a certain intensity. Yet, that is where I ought to begin. For, to suffer is to give supreme attention to something, and I am somewhat a man of attention. You know, I had foreseen my future illness. I had visualized precisely what everybody now knows. I believe the vision of a manifest portion of the future should be part of our education. Yes, I foresaw what is now beginning. At that time, it was just an idea like any other. So, I was able to follow it."

He grew calm.

He turned over on his side, lowered his eyes; and after a moment, was talking again. He was beginning to lose himself. His voice was only a murmur in the pillow. His reddening hand was already asleep.

He was still saying: "I think, and it doesn't bother at all. I am alone. How comfortable solitude is! Not the slightest thing weighs on me. . . . The same reverie here as in the ship's cabin, the same at the Café Lambert. . . . If some Bertha's arms take on importance, I am robbed— as by pain. . . . If anyone says something and doesn't prove it—he's an enemy. I prefer the sound of the least fact, happening. I am being and seeing myself, seeing me see myself, and so forth. . . . Let's think very closely. Bah! you can fall asleep on any subject. . . . Sleep can continue any idea. . . ."

He was snoring softly. A little more softly still, I took the candle, and went out on tiptoe.

(1895)
Translated by Jackson Mathews

Before retreating into silence, Valéry consented to publish two works, one immediately after the other, in two different reviews—'La Méthode de Léonard de Vinci' (1894) in Madame Adam's Nouvelle Revue and, in Le Centaure, at that time edited by Pierre Louys, the astounding 'Soirée avec M. Teste' (1895). To that extraordinary creation, unparalleled in any other tongue, to that accomplished and perfect work, each one of us was compelled to do homage. As he had just disclosed his method to us through the medium of Leonardo, Valéry, thanks to this semi-mythical alibi, here revealed his ethic, his attitude towards things, beings, ideas, life. This he maintained and to the end remained faithful—constant to himself, so that a little while before his death he was able to say (I quote his very words), 'The principal themes round which I have grouped my thoughts are still in my mind UNSHAKEABLE.' He spoke this last word strongly, accentuating each syllable.

ANDRÉ GIDE
Paul Valéry (1945)
Translated by Dorothy Bussy

PAUL VALÉRY

1 8 7 1 — 1 9 4 5

FROM *LA JEUNE PARQUE*

J'ai de mes bras épais environné mes tempes,
Et longtemps de mon âme attendu les éclairs?
Toute? . . . dans mes doux liens, à mon sang suspendue,
Je me voyais me voir, sinueuse, et dorais
De regards en regards, mes profondes forêts.

J'y suivais un serpent qui venait de me mordre.

. . . . Adieu, pensai-je, MOI, mortelle sœur, mensonge.

I buried my head in my thick arms, and for a long time awaited illumination from my soul. . . . In harmonious oscillation with my blood, in my own soft bonds, I, sinuous, beheld myself contemplating myself, and gilding my own deep inward forests in a succession of glances. I was tracking a snake which had just bitten me. . . . Goodbye, I thought, oh me, oh mortal sister, delusion!

(1917)

Valéry is not only the successful expression of Mallarmé, though that would be enough to make him great; he is, besides, the poetical, orderly, and concise expression of those 'modern' ideas, which Proust was attempting at the same time to put into prose. . . . Here is at last perfect poetry.

DENIS SAURAT
Modern French Literature 1870–1940 (1946)

JAMES JOYCE

1 8 8 2 — 1 9 4 1

DUBLIN WASHERWOMEN SCRUB BESIDE THE RIVER, AND THEIR VOICES FADE INTO THE DUSK

. . . Lord save us! And ho! Hey? What all men. Hot? His tittering daughters of. Whawk?
Can't hear with the waters of. The chittering waters of. Flittering bats, fieldmice bawk talk. Ho! Are you not gone ahome? What Thom

Malone? Can't hear with bawk of bats, all thim liffeying waters of. Ho, talk save us! My foos won't moos. I feel as old as yonder elm. A tale told of Shaun or Shem? All Livia's daughtersons. Dark hawks hear us. Night! Night! My ho head halls. I feel as heavy as yonder stone. Tell me of John or Shaun? Who were Shem and Shaun the living sons or daughters of? Night now! Tell me, tell me, tell me, elm! Night night! Telmetale of stem or stone. Beside the rivering waters of, hitherandthithering waters of. Night!

Finnegans Wake (1939)

The writer who has taken experimentation farthest of all is, of course, Mr. James Joyce.

BONAMY DOBRÉE
Modern Prose Style (1934)

SAMUEL JOHNSON

1 7 0 9 — 1 7 8 4

TRIFLES

The greater part of readers, instead of blaming us for passing trifles, will wonder that on mere trifles so much labour is expended, with such importance of debate, and such solemnity of diction. To these I answer with confidence, that they are judging of an art which they do not understand; yet cannot much reproach them with their ignorance, nor promise that they would become in general, by learning criticism, more useful, happier or wiser.

Preface to Shakespeare (1765)

The last word.

R. W. CHAPMAN
The Portrait of a Scholar (1922)

APPENDIX

TOUCHSTONES OF GREAT POETRY

HOMER

D A T E S   U N K N O W N

Ὡς φάτο· τοὺς δ' ἤδη κατέχεν φυσίζοος αἶα
ἐν Λακεδαίμονι αὖθι, φίλῃ ἐν πατρίδι γαίῃ.

So said she;—long since they in Earth's soft Arms were reposing,
There, in their own dear Land, their Father-Land, Lakedaimon.

Iliad, iii, 243–4
Translated by E. C. Hawtrey

Ἆ δειλώ, τί σφῶϊ δόμεν Πηλῆϊ ἄνακτι
θνητῷ, ὑμεῖς δ' ἐστὸν ἀγήρω τ' ἀθανάτω τε!
ἦ ἵνα δυστήνοισι μετ' ἀνδράσιν ἄλγε' ἔχητον;

Ah, unhappy pair, why gave we you to King Peleus, to a mortal? but
ye are without old age, and immortal. Was it that with men born to
misery ye might have sorrow?

Iliad, xvii, 443–5
Translated by Matthew Arnold

Καὶ σὲ γέρον τὸ πρὶν μὲν ἀκούομεν ὄλβιον εἶναι.

Nay, and thou too, old man, in former days wast, as we hear, happy.

Iliad, xxiv, 543
Translated by Matthew Arnold

DANTE ALIGHIERI

1 2 6 5 — 1 3 2 1

Io non piangeva, sí dentro impietrai;
    piangevan elli.

I wailed not, so of stone grew I within:—*they* wailed.

Inferno, xxxiii, 49
Translated by Matthew Arnold

Io son fatta da Dio, sua mercè, tale,
che la vostra miseria non mi tange,
nè fiamma d' esto incendio non m' assale.

Of such sort hath God, thanked be His mercy, made me, that your
misery toucheth me not, neither doth the flame of this fire strike me.

Inferno, ii, 91–3
Translated by Matthew Arnold

E la sua volontade è nostra pace.

In His will is our peace.

Paradiso, iii, 85
Translated by Matthew Arnold

WILLIAM SHAKESPEARE

1 5 6 4 — 1 6 1 6

Wilt thou vpon the high and giddy Mast,
Seale vp the ship-boies eies, and rocke his braines,
In cradle of the rude imperious surge.

King Henry the Fourth, Part Two, Act iii, Scene i (1600)

If thou did'st euer hold me in thy hart,
Absent thee from felicity a while,
And in this harsh world drawe thy breath in paine
To tell my storie.

Hamlet, Act v, Scene ii (1604)

JOHN MILTON

1 6 0 8 — 1 6 7 4

Dark'n'd so, yet shon
Above them all th' Arch Angel: but his face
Deep scars of Thunder had intrencht, and care
Sat on his faded cheek.

Paradise Lost, i (1667)

And courage never to submit or yield:
And what is else not to be overcome.

Paradise Lost, i (1667)

Which cost *Ceres* all that pain
To seek her through the world.

Paradise Lost, iv (1667)

There can be no more useful help for discovering what poetry belongs
to the class of the truly excellent, and can therefore do us most good,
than to have always in one's mind lines and expressions of the great
masters, and to apply them as a touchstone to other poetry. Of course
we are not to require this other poetry to resemble them; it may be
very dissimilar. But if we have any tact we shall find them, when we
have lodged them well in our minds, an infallible touchstone for detect-
ing the presence or absence of high poetic quality, and also the degree
of this quality, in all other poetry which we may place beside them.

MATTHEW ARNOLD
Essays in Criticism, Second Series (1888)

THOMAS WYATT

1 5 0 3 ? — 1 5 4 2

And then may chaunce the to repent
  The tyme that thou hast lost and spent
To cause thy lovers sigh and swone;
  Then shalt thou knowe beaultie but lent,
    And wisshe and want as I have done.

                            Poems (1528–36)

WILLIAM SHAKESPEARE

1 5 6 4 — 1 6 1 6

That time of yeare thou maist in me behold,
When yellow leaues, or none, or few doe hange
Vpon those boughes which shake against the could,
Bare ruin'd quiers, where late the sweet birds sang.

                         Sonnets (1609), lxxiii

WILLIAM SHAKESPEARE

1 5 6 4 — 1 6 1 6

And my poore Foole is hang'd: no, no, no life?
Why should a Dog, a Horse, a Rat haue life,
And thou no breath at all? Thou'lt come no more,
Neuer, neuer, neuer, neuer, neuer.
Pray you vndo this Button. Thanke you Sir,
Do you see this? Looke on her? Looke, her lips!
Looke there, looke there.

                King Lear, Act v, Scene iii (1623)

THOMAS NASHE

1 5 6 7 — 1 6 0 1

Beauty is but a flowre,
Which wrinckles will deuoure,
Brightnesse falls from the ayre,
Queenes haue died yong and faire,
Dust hath closde *Helens* eye.
I am sick, I must dye:
　　Lord, haue mercy on vs.
　　　　Summers Last Will and Testament (1600)

JOHN WEBSTER

1 5 8 0 ? — ? 1 6 2 5

Cover her face: Mine eyes dazell: she di'd yong.
　　　The Dutchesse of Malfy, Act iv, Scene ii (c.1614)

THOMAS CAREW

1 5 9 5 ? — ? 1 6 4 5

Ask me no more whither doth hast
The Nightingale when May is past:
For in your sweet dividing throat
She winters, and keeps warm her note.
　　　　　　A Song (1640)

ANDREW MARVELL

1 6 2 1 — 1 6 7 8

'Tis Madness to resist or blame
The force of angry Heavens flame:
　　And, if we would speak true,
　　Much to the Man is due.

1397

Who, from his private Gardens, where
He liv'd reserved and austere,
    As if his highest plot
    To plant the Bergamot,
Could by industrious Valour climbe
To ruine the great Work of Time,
    And cast the Kingdome old
    Into another Mold.
An Horatian Ode upon Cromwell's
Return from Ireland (1650)

W. B. YEATS

1 8 6 5 — 1 9 3 9

'I am of Ireland
And the Holy Land of Ireland
And time runs on' cried she
'Come out of charity
And dance with me in Ireland'
Words for Music Perhaps
And Other Poems (1932)

T. S. ELIOT

1 8 8 8 —

We have lingered in the chambers of the sea
By sea-girls wreathed with seaweed red and brown
Till human voices wake us, and we drown.
The Love Song of J. Alfred Prufrock (1917)

HART CRANE

1 8 9 9 — 1 9 3 2

O Thou steeled Cognizance whose leap commits
The agile precincts of the lark's return.
The Bridge (1930)

I wish now to introduce other kinds of instance, and to let them stand for us as a sort of Arnoldish touchstones to the perfection that poetic statement has occasionally reached.

ALLEN TATE

Reason in Madness (1941)

GLOSSARY

abrayde, started up
achaat, buying
achátours, buyers
after oon, of uniform quality
alderbest, best of all
alenge, miserable
Algezir, Algeciras
Alisaundre, Alexandria
aller cok, rooster's crow for all
anlaas, dagger
apikèd, trimmed
appele, accuse
arewe, in a row
asterte, escape
astronomye, astrology
áventure, chance

bachelor, young knight
baite, resting-place
baundoun, power
bawdryk, belt
Belmarye, Benmarin
bemès, trumpets
bismótered, stained
bitore, bittern
biwreyè, betray
boote, remedy
bord bigonne, seat of honor
bote, unless
bourde, jest
bracér, arm-guard
briddès, birds
broukè, have the use of
buen, be
bulte it to the bren, sift it to the bran
burdoun, base accompaniment

carl, man
catel, property
ceint, girdle
chapèd, mounted

chaunterie, a job singing daily masses
ches, chose
chevyssaunce, dishonest deals
chyvachie, cavalry raid
cleped, called
clerk, student
coillons, testicles
colpons, bunches
complecciouns, temperaments
conscïence, feelings
contekes, fights
cope, top
coráges, hearts
cote, cottage
coude, knew
countour, auditor
covyne, tricks
coy, modest
croys of latoun, cross of copper and zinc
    alloy
crulle, curled

daunger, control
daungerous, arrogant
dawngerouse, haughty
dees, dice
delyvere, agile
depeint, soiled
despitous, scornful
deye, dairy woman
dissaite, deceit
drecchèd, troubled
drede, doubt
dreynt, drowned

eek, also
embrouded, embroidered
engyned, racked
envynèd, stocked with wine
estatlich, dignified
evene, average
ey, egg

1401

faldyng, coarse wool
faren in londe, gone to the country
farsed, stuffed
fee symple, absolute possession
fen, chapter
fernè, distant
ferrer twynne, go farther
ferthyng, speck
fetisly, precisely
fetys, handsome
feye, stricken
floytynge, fluting
flytt, fled
foo, foe
foond, provided for
for-dronke, very drunk
forneys of a leed, furnace under
    a caldron
forpynèd, wasted by suffering
fors, attention
forslewthen, waste
forthi, for this
forwake, tired out
forward, agreement
fother, load
fredom, generosity
fynch eek koude he pulle, have his own
    concubine
fyne, cease

galle, sore spot
galyngale, a spice
gamed, prospered
gargat, throat
gat-tothèd, teeth widely spaced
gauded, gauds or large beads
Gernade, Grenada
geynest, fairest
gipser, purse
girlès, both sexes
gise, manner
goliardeys, teller of dirty stories
gore, garment
Gretè See, Mediterranean
grope, test
ground, texture
grys, costly gray fur
gypon, tunic

habergeon, coat of mail
halwès, shrines
hap, lot
harre, hinges
haunt, skill
he, she; the knight
hele, conceal
hendy, happy
hente, obtain; took
herberwe, inn
here, their
hett, promised
heu, color
hierde, herdsman
hightè, named
holt, farm
hyre, her

iantilnesse, waywardness
ichabbe, I have
icham, I am
ichot, I wot
in feere, together

janglere, noisy talker
jet, fashion

knarre, stout fellow
kowthe, known

lele, loyal
lemes, flames
lent, turned away
lesynges, lies
lette, prevented
Lettow, Lithuania
letuaries, medicines
levedi, lady
libbe, live
licóur, sap
lith, limb
lode-menage, piloting
loh, laughed
Looth, Lot
losengeour, flatterer
lossom, lovable
love-dayes, arbitration days
lud, voice

Lyeys, Ayas
lyht, has lighted
lymytour, licensed to beg in a limited
    area
lyven, live

make, mate
makeles, matchless
male, bag
mareys, marsh
mede, reward
mekyl, much
mene, pity
mette, dreamed
meynee, followers
middel, waist
moot I thee, may I thrive
moote sterven wood, may die mad
mort, dead
mortreux, stew
morwenynges, mornings
Myda, Midas
myster, craft

narette, blame
narre, nearer
ne, not
nis, is not
nones, occasion
normal, a sore
not-heed, closely cut hair
nyghtertale, nighttime

on, in
ounces, strands
overeste courtepy, upper short coat

paas, walking pace
pace, go; surpass
Palatye, Balat
Parvys, lawyers' meeting place
pers, blue-gray
philosophre, alchemist
pilėd, scanty
pilwė-beer, pillowcase
pistel, word
pocok, peacock

poraille, poor people
poudrė-marchant, a sour seasoning
preevė, experience
prikasour, hunter on horseback
proprė, own
prow, profit
Pruce, Prussia
purchas, money from begging
purtreye, draw
pyned, tortured

rage, play around
rakė-stele, rake handle
raughte, reached
recche, interpret
reed, advice; adviser
remes, realms
rethor, author
reve me, rob me of
reysėd, raided
roun, song
rouncy, a nag
rownėd, whispered
Ruce, Russia

Satalye, Attalia
sautrie, psaltery
sawcėfleem, pimply
scathe, a pity
scoleye, attend school
see, protect
seeke, sick
semlokest, loveliest
senténce, meaning
sette hir aller cappe, fooled them all
sewed, pursued
seynd, broiled
sheeldės, French coins
shentė, harmed
shoope, planned
Significavit, writ of arrest
    for excommunication
siker, certain
sikerly, certainly
sithes, times
so, as
soond, sand
soote, refreshing

1403

sownynge, emphasizing
spicèd, overscrupulous
stape, advanced
stent, stopped
stepe, protruding
sterve, die
stevene, voice
stoor, stock
strondes, shores
stuwe, fishpond
swelte, swooned
swevene, dream
swithe, quickly
swych, such
swynk, work
swynkere, worker
swyre, neck

taille, credit
talen, tell tales
tappestere, barmaid
Tapycer, tapestry weaver
targe, shield
temple, law school
theech, may I thrive
tho, those
tholien whyle sore, to endure for a time
tollen, take toll for grinding
tombesteres, dancing girls
toon, toes
toune, season
toverbyde, outlive
Tramyssene, Tremessen
tretys, neat

undermelès, afternoons
undren, forenoon
unkyndèly, unnaturally

vavasour, squire
vernycle, copy of St. Veronica's handkerchief bearing the face of Christ
verray, true
vertú, power
vigiliès, religious services

warice, cure
wastel, fine white
Webbe, weaver
wende, turn
wight, person
wlatsom, loathsome
wonges, cheeks
wonyng, dwelling
wonynge, living
wood, crazy
wore, weir
wowyng, wooing
wyter, wise

yeddynges, singing contests
yede, went
yën, eyes
yerne, eagerly
yhent, won
y-lad, drawn
y-lymèd, caught
yore, long
y-purfiled, trimmed
y-yerned, yearned

INDEXES

INDEX OF AUTHORS AND CRITICS

The names of critics are printed in italics

Hamilton, John Andrew
    Holdsworth, Sir William S. 1353

Hardy, Thomas
    Cecil, David 1306

Harpe, Jean François de La. *See* La Harpe

Harris, Frank
    Emerson, Ralph Waldo 1184
    Goethe, Johann Wolfgang von 964
    Meredith, George 1278
    Pater, Walter 1306
    Wordsworth, William 1019

Hawthorne, Nathaniel
    James, Henry 1187

Hawtrey, Edward Craven
    Arnold, Matthew 1090

Hazlitt, William
    Campbell, Thomas 1075
    Coleridge, Samuel Taylor 1054

Heine, Heinrich
    Brandes, Georg 1152
    Monahan, Michael 1153

Heredia José-Maria de
    Heredia on Chénier, André 1007
    Legge, J. G. 1318

Hölderlin, Friedrich
    Montgomery, Marshall 1029
    Stansfield, Agnes 1028

Holdsworth, Sir William S.
    Hamilton, John Andrew 1353

Homer
    Arnold, Matthew 1395

Hood, Thomas
    Poe, Edgar Allan 1164
    Symons, Arthur 1165

Hopkins, Gerard Manley
    Huxley, Aldous 1337
    Lewis, Cecil Day 1336

Housman, A. E.
    Blake, William 974

Lisle, Leconte de. *See* Leconte de Lisle

INDEX OF TITLES

INDEX OF FIRST LINES
OF POEMS AND PLAYS